Brazilian Science Fiction Film

SUNY series in Latin American Cinema

Ignacio M. Sánchez Prado and Leslie L. Marsh, editors

# Brazilian Science Fiction Film
## A Critical History

ALFREDO SUPPIA

Cover credit: *À Margem do Universo*, dir. Tiago Carneiro Rolim Esmeraldo (2016). Used with permission.

Published by State University of New York Press, Albany

© 2024 State University of New York

All rights reserved

Printed in the United States of America

No part of this book may be used or reproduced in any manner whatsoever without written permission. No part of this book may be stored in a retrieval system or transmitted in any form or by any means including electronic, electrostatic, magnetic tape, mechanical, photocopying, recording, or otherwise without the prior permission in writing of the publisher.

Links to third-party websites are provided as a convenience and for informational purposes only. They do not constitute an endorsement or an approval of any of the products, services, or opinions of the organization, companies, or individuals. SUNY Press bears no responsibility for the accuracy, legality, or content of a URL, the external website, or for that of subsequent websites.

For information, contact State University of New York Press, Albany, NY
www.sunypress.edu

### Library of Congress Cataloging-in-Publication Data

Name: Suppia, Alfredo, author.
Title: Brazilian science fiction film : a critical history / Alfredo Suppia.
Description: Albany : State University of New York Press, [2024]. | Series: SUNY series in Latin American cinema | Includes bibliographical references and index.
Identifiers: LCCN 2024019354 | ISBN 9798855800487 (hardcover : alk. paper) | ISBN 9798855800494 (ebook) | ISBN 9798855800470 (pbk. : alk. paper)
Subjects: LCSH: Science fiction films—History and criticism. | Motion pictures—Brazil—History and criticism.
Classification: LCC PN1995.9.S26 S83 2024 | DDC 791.43/615—dc23/eng/20240522
LC record available at https://lccn.loc.gov/2024019354

*To Dolores and Francisco.*
*Love and gratitude.*

Whomever is not seriously concerned and
perplexed
is not well informed.

(Quem não estiver seriamente preocupado e
perplexo
não está bem informado.)

—Francisco Alvim, "Disseram na Câmara,"
English translation by Alfredo Suppia and Felipe de Souza Mello

# Contents

List of Illustrations — ix

Acknowledgments — xi

Introduction or Unidentified Filmic Objects: Understanding Science Fiction in Brazil — 1

1. Laughing at the Future: On the Origins of Brazilian SF Cinema in Comedy and Satire — 13

2. Subliminal Waves: Brazilian SF Cinema in the Early 1960s — 27

3. Brazil, Love it or Leave it—for the Stars: SF Film during the Era of the Military Hardliners (1969–1973) — 45

4. Coming Up for Air: The Brazilian Ecodystopian Film — 63

5. Proxy Futures and Other Simulacra: The Brazilian SF Comedy Endures, along with the Adventure Movie and the Musical — 85

6. The Ghost in the Machine: Brazilian SF and the Revival of Spiritist Films — 115

7. Southern Short Circuits: Contemporary Brazilian SF Film as Political Film — 145

8. Find your Escape Pod: Afrofuturism, Amazofuturism, and Queer Sci-Fi — 187

9. A Strange Object South of the Equator: Hypotheses and Investigations about Restraints against SF Literature and Films in Brazil                                241

10. Do Brazilians Dream of Edenic (or Industrial) Futures?     273

Final Remarks, or, Hurry Up! We Are Dreaming!                  285

Notes                                                          297

References                                                     327

Interviews                                                     347

Index                                                          349

# Illustrations

| | | |
|---|---|---|
| Figure 1.1 | Silveira Sampaio. *Uma Aventura aos 40* (1947). | 19 |
| Figure 1.2 | Carlos Manga. *O Homem do Sputnik* (1959). | 24 |
| Figure 4.1 | Roberto Pires. *Abrigo Nuclear* (1981). | 72 |
| Figure 4.2 | Roberto Pires. *Abrigo Nuclear* (1981). | 73 |
| Figure 5.1 | Arturo Uranga. Sketch for Francisco de Paula's *Areias Escaldantes* (1985). | 105 |
| Figure 5.2 | Francisco de Paula. *Areias Escaldantes* (1985). | 107 |
| Figure 7.1 | Adirley Queirós. *Branco Sai, Preto Fica* (2014). | 151 |
| Figure 7.2 | Gabriel Mascaro. *Divino Amor* (2019). | 164 |
| Figure 7.3 | Juliano Dornelles and Kléber Mendonça Filho. *Bacurau* (2019). | 179 |
| Figure 7.4 | Thiago Foresti. *Algoritmo* (2020). | 181 |
| Figure 8.1 | Kléber Mendonça Filho. *Recife Frio* (2009). | 190 |
| Figure 8.2 | Tiago Esmeraldo. *À Margem do Universo* (2017). | 216 |
| Figure 8.3 | Henrique Arruda. *Os Últimos Românticos do Mundo* (2020). | 227 |
| Figure 8.4 | Joel Caetano. *Missão Berço Esplêndido* (2021). | 229 |
| Figure 9.1 | The development of science brings problems to society (%). | 261 |

Figure 9.2  Do you believe there is science and technology in
           the country?                                              262

Figure 9.3  In your opinion, to what extent do you feel that the
           state finances scientific research?                       263

Figure 9.4  Why is there no more development in science and
           technology?                                               264

Figure 9.5  What do you think of the results that scientists
           obtain?                                                   264

Figure 9.6  Brazil: scientific articles published in international
           journals indexed by the Institute for Scientific
           Information (ISI), 1981–2004.                             265

# Acknowledgments

I cannot express enough thanks to Prof. Leslie Marsh and Dr. Rebecca Colesworthy for inviting me to submit the manuscript of this book to SUNY Press. Many thanks for your faith in this project and all of your patience and kind support.

This project could not have been accomplished without the support of Fapesp (Fundação de Amparo à Pesquisa do Estado de São Paulo) and the Capes-Fulbright Visiting Fellowship and Award 2019/2020. Both grants made possible a period of thorough research and exchange with students and colleagues at the University of Florida from October 2019 through February 2021. The completion of this book also benefited from a research scholarship granted by CNPq (Conselho Nacional de Desenvolvimento Científico e Tecnológico, bolsa PQ).

My deepest gratitude to Prof. Mary Elizabeth "Libby" Ginway, whose work has always been fundamental to my research. Prof. Ginway and her husband, Prof. David Pharies, were extremely kind, generous, and patient during my stay in Gainesville. I am very fond of our friendship. Thanks, Libby and David, for all your help.

I must also thank my friend Dr. Roberto de Sousa Causo, Brazilian SF scholar, writer, critic, and editor, for generously sharing his vast knowledge on Brazilian science fiction, always with invaluable pieces of advice regarding resources and the history of the genre. My deepest gratitude also to my dear fellow academics and friends Dr. Mariano Paz and Dr. Miguel Ángel Fernández Delgado for our constant, fruitful, and long-lasting collaboration. All my thanks to André Carneiro (*in memoriam*), Brazilian writer, poet, one of the great masters of Brazilian science fiction literature and author of the pioneering work *Introdução ao Estudo da "Science Fiction"* (1967). This book tries to follow in your footsteps.

xii | Acknowledgments

Special thanks to Augusto Cesar Areal for introducing me to the universe of Fritz Lang's *Metropolis* many years ago, during my MA studies. Thank you, Marcos Bertoni, visual artist, Super-8 filmmaker, dear friend, and longtime partner in cinematic adventures and source of inspiration!

Many thanks to all my students and fellow academics who attended or took part in any of my graduate courses on science fiction studies at the Federal University of Juiz de Fora (Universidade Federal de Juiz de Fora) from January 2009 through March 2014, and at the State University of Campinas (Universidade Estadual de Campinas) from April 2014 up until present times. In particular, many thanks to all the graduate students and postdoc researchers who took part in my science fiction courses in the second semester of 2021: Dr. Edson Costa, Juliane Cristina Helanski, Hellen da Fonseca, Anelise de Brito Ferrão, Jeynne do Amaral Carrillo, Victor Guimarães Loturco, Leonardo José Porto Passos, Matheus Maltempi, Ester Marçal Fér, and Monica Regina Miranda. These individuals read several chapters of the original manuscript throughout our journey into the history of Brazilian SF cinema and engaged in extremely valuable discussions that helped improve this work. Also, many thanks to Prof. Suely Kofes, Prof. Maria Dora Mourão, Prof. Francisco Foot Hardman, Prof. Antonio Carlos Amâncio, and Prof. Luiz Antônio Mousinho for their insightful comments on the original manuscript. Our conversations were fundamental to the betterment of this book project and further thoughts on this chimeric object: the Brazilian SF cinema.

Many thanks to my dear friends in the US: Keith and Sharon Ponitz, Cody Case (you rock—and samba!), and all my dear Fulbrighter friends. Thank you, Mat Guzzo, for the excellent companionship in the US, "movin' right along in search of good times and good news, with good friends you can't lose, this could become a habit!" I must also thank Rodolfo Marini Teixeira for all his kind support at Unicamp while doing my research at the University of Florida.

My gratitude to artists Eryk Souza, João Queiroz, and Vitor Wiedegrün for sharing their unique SF illustrations. Many thanks to the Brazilian filmmakers Paulo Bastos Martins, Adirley Queirós, Edgar Franco, Francisco de Paula, Gabriel Mascaro, Grace Passô, Henrique Arruda, Joel Caetano, Kléber Mendonça Filho, Marco Antônio Pereira, Maurílio Martins, Petrus Pires, Susan Kalik, Thiago Foresti, and Tiago Esmeraldo. Thanks for sharing your films and stills, without which this work would have never been possible. Also, thanks to my friends Lea Monteiro and Eduardo Santana, curators of the film festivals Antropokaos and Cinefantasy, respectively.

Special thanks to Dr. Valquíria Magrini and Dr. Nilton Domingos Jr. (you kept me steadfast), Rupert Lyons, Paul Dixon, Felipe de Souza Mello, Bruna Ricardi, her parents and family. Natalie Diesel, thank you so much for your help with revisions! My gratitude to my dear friends Bráulio Tavares and Luiz Brás, who kindly shared their poems and edited collections with me. I'm also grateful for the kind support from Prof. Pedro Maciel Guimarães and the Graduate Program in Multimeios at the University of Campinas (Unicamp). Thanks to Prof. Diego Vicentim from the Social Sciences Graduate Program at Unicamp for this institutional support as well. Special thanks to my "academic" parents: Prof. Lúcia Nagib and Prof. José Mário Ortiz Ramos (*in memoriam*). There is much from you here. Thanks to Nuno César Abreu (*in memoriam*) for the joyful conversations and his lessons on Nelson Pereira dos Santos. Also thanks to Paulo Martins for his generosity and our fruitful conversations when I was a PhD student. My loving gratitude to my dear friends and academic fellows Fernando Almeida Diniz and Ewa Mazierska—two sources of inspiration.

Many thanks to Cinemateca Brasileira in São Paulo and Cinemateca do Museu de Arte Moderna in Rio de Janeiro, namely Hernani Heffner, Fábio Vellozo, José Quental, Renato Noviello, Guilherme Albani, and Elisa Ximenes. Thanks to Diane Ganeles, Michael Sandlin, Aimee Harrison, Julia Cosacchi, and all the SUNY Press team that guided my steps while making this book real. Thanks to my friends and colleagues who put me in contact with film directors: Dr. Natália Christofoletti Barrenha, Prof. Ângela Prysthon, Dr. Jamer Guterres de Mello, Prof. Wilson Antônio Lazaretti, and Prof. Luciana Corrêa de Araújo. Thank you, Prof. Chantal Medaets and Prof. Wilmar D'Angelis, for the help with native Brazilian languages—especially the "soul-word" (*nheẽ*).

Last but not least, my heartfelt thanks to my mother, Dolores, and my loving son, Francisco. This book is for you.

# Introduction
# or On Unidentified Filmic Objects
## Understanding Science Fiction in Brazil

Love,
I'm sad because
I'm the only Brazilian alive
Who has never seen a flying saucer. (. . .)[1]

—Carlos Drummond de Andrade, "Falta Um Disco"

Considered a "barometer" of social, political, economic, and cultural tensions and contradictions in the country, Brazilian science fiction (SF) provides, according to M. Elizabeth Ginway (2004, 221), an intriguing and eloquent showcase for investigating national memory and identity, as well as social contradictions and Brazilian expectations about the future, with its multiple cultural crossroads and mixed feelings toward modernity and Western values.

Nevertheless, few spectators and fewer film scholars have been able to identify SF in Brazilian cinema. Why is Brazilian SF cinema so "invisible" to broader audiences? This is just one of the questions that drives the present investigation.

This book provides a critical history of SF in the Brazilian film industry, scrutinizing the main trends, traits, and peculiarities that have shaped the genre in an allegedly "exotic" national environment and vice versa. Covering a genre that is often disregarded by film scholars, this is the first comprehensive study of Brazilian SF cinema in English. Part of a global rejuvenation wave of SF spurred by innovative contributions of the southern hemisphere or non-Western film culture, Brazilian SF cinema is growing rapidly, gaining broader visibility, and introducing alternative approaches to international SF film as a whole.

At first glance, Brazil lacks a tradition of research and critique on SF: the few short-lived Brazilian film studios invested much more in comedies or melodramas than in monster movies or space operas. However, this scene has been gradually changing. Articles, theses, and dissertations on Brazilian genre films, notably Brazilian SF, fantasy, and horror (SF&F&H)—or speculative fiction (Spec-F) in audiovisual media—have proliferated over the last twenty years (e.g., Piedade 2002; Suppia 2007; Suppia 2008; Cánepa 2008; Causo 2003). Not only has Brazilian academia given more attention to SF, but Brazilian authors and artists have also been gaining international recognition. In this regard, we deem it necessary to mention some scholars whose works have enhanced the understanding of SF in the southern hemisphere, such as Rachel Haywood Ferreira (2011), Ginway (2004), Roberto Causo (2003), and Yolanda Molina-Gavilán et al. (2007).

In addition, contemporary film studies by Ítala Schmelz (2006) and Mariano Paz (2008), among others, have prompted a turnaround toward a more comprehensive and global approach to SF cinema. The metaphor of "waves" invoked by Dudley Andrew—that is, national filmographies or film movements whose reverberations reorient other national filmographies and film movements (2006, 21–22)—might be useful in this context, since Latin American SF film is particularly influenced by both North American and European SF cinema: this influence has been increasingly reciprocated.

Therefore, another curious aspect revealed by this study concerns the flows and interchanges between the different national SF filmographies. Geographic proximity does not mean aesthetic affinity or thematic similarity in terms of SF cinema. Mexico borders the US, but its SF film production has more in common with SF cinema from Brazil or Argentina. By the same token, Argentina borders Brazil, but its SF films seem to blend in well with the European film industry. As to Eastern European countries and their SF, including the former Czechoslovakia, for example, there is also a suggestion of more elements in common with the Brazilian or Latin American film industry—more than we would suspect at first glance.

Conceived as another step in the work in progress that is the study of cinema history and theory, such as the idea of an "atlas of world cinemas" (Andrew 2006, 19–29) and a "positive definition of world cinema" (Nagib 2006, 30–37),[2] this book attempts to provide the reader a comprehensive critical history of Brazilian SF cinema. From Andrew's (2006) and Nagib's

(2006) perspectives, more concerned with a cinema in movement—that is, in its global interconnections and transcultural contributions—the SF film genre is given a more universal character, which invites us to wider and more in-depth discussions, as free as possible from elitist and restrictive economic, political, and cultural paradigms.

For much of the twentieth century, Brazilian SF, and notably Brazilian SF cinema, was considered invisible, if not entirely nonexistent. Such an understanding evolved from the notion that SF would be an "alien" object in the Brazilian cultural landscapes or mediascapes (Appadurai 1996), a "misplaced" idea, so that it could only appear as an eccentricity in sparse, sporadic cultural phenomena and devoid of any true artistic quality. This idea somehow reverberates in the metaphor of Brazilian SF as a scarcely inhabited planet, a semideserted landscape populated by just a few chimeric, queer specimens. The scarcity of Brazilian SF sets the tone for a pioneering essay written by Brazilian writer and literary critic Fausto Cunha: "SF in Brazil: a sparsely inhabited planet" ("Ficção Científica no Brasil: um planeta quase desabitado," in Allen 1976, 5–20). Cunha's metaphor for Brazilian SF literature as a semideserted planet seems to be also applicable to the study of SF in Brazilian cinema. However, insofar as cinematic SF appears in multiple subtle ways in numerous Brazilian films and audiovisual media, the situation is more complex than it seems.

John Rieder (2008, 2010, 2017) is a key author in our approach to analyzing Brazilian SF film. Drawing on both Altman (1999) and John Frow (2014), Rieder recognized two genre systems in constant tension or friction (mass production genre system vs. preexisting classical and academic genre system)—a movement that can be regarded as a productive force. According to Rieder, "The way generic terms and choices signify in relation to other terms and choices is constantly in flux" (2010, 199). Such an idea is fundamental to our theoretical approach here. To assert the straightforwardness of his argument, Rieder cites Fowler: "It is neither possible nor even desirable to arrive at a very high degree of precision in using generic terms. The overlapping and mutability of genres mean that an 'imprecise' terminology is more efficient" (Fowler qtd. in Rieder 2010, 199). Such a degree of flexibility is instrumental to any closer look into world SF cinemas, mostly Latin American SF cinemas.

However, as theoretical models focused on North American film industry proposed by North American or other Western scholars are not equally effective and applicable to world cinemas or non-Western cinemas, we shall resort to several different perspectives. Likewise, the ideas and definitions offered by Darko Suvin in *Metamorphoses of Science Fiction* (1979)—the starting point of our understanding of SF—need to be adapted, transposed, and redesigned in favor of a more updated, encompassing, and thorough approach to Brazilian SF cinema. According to Suvin, "*SF is, then, a literary genre whose necessary and sufficient conditions are the presence and interaction of estrangement and cognition, and whose main formal device is an imaginative framework alternative to the author's empirical environment.* Estrangement differentiates SF from the "realistic" literary mainstream extending from the eighteenth century into the twentieth. Cognition differentiates it not only from myth, but also from the folk (fairy) tale and the fantasy" (Suvin 1979, 7–8; emphasis in the original). Suvin's concept of novum (1979, 64) is crucial to the author's theory on SF as the literature of "cognitive estrangement": "*SF is distinguished by the narrative dominance and hegemony of a fictional 'novum' (novelty, innovation) validated by cognitive logic*" (1979, 63; emphasis in the original). Internationally recognized as a pioneering contribution to studies on SF, Suvin's original ideas, mostly dating from 1972 and 1979, were repeatedly revised, contradicted, and/or updated both by the author himself and by many other scholars. Halfway between literary criticism and film studies, the understanding of SF as an "anamorphic estrangement" proposed by Matthew Beaumont (2009)—a thought both inspired and illustrated by visual arts, namely Hans Holbein the Younger's painting *The Ambassadors* (1533)—seems to be one among several other contributions to Suvin's original definition of SF. As much as Altman's proposals on film genre and Rieder's on SF, the ideas developed by Suvin are fundamental to our investigation of Brazilian SF cinema, *mutatis mutandis*. Obviously, the original treatment of literary SF by Suvin and Brazilian SF exposes a huge gap, if not an abyss to be transposed, thus requiring the design of an applicable theoretical model.

Perhaps the "invisibility" or "oddity" of Brazilian SF cinema has something to do with queerness. For the sake of a more encompassing perspective, we will momentarily call speculative fiction (or Spec-F, for short) all Brazilian fiction that might be categorized as horror, fantasy and/or SF, or any sort of chimeric fiction inhabiting the transitional zones of any of these terms and territories. Having said that, we dare say that all Brazilian SF, notably Brazilian SF film, might be queer in essence, insofar as it constantly defies the norm of SF as to the Western tradition. As pointed by Arlene Stein and Kenneth Plummer (qtd. in Subero 2016, 45), queer is an organizing principle of the social order that basically encompasses four traits, most of them related to sexual power, the problematization of sexual and gender categories (also, identities), and a willingness to interrogate areas which normally would not be seen as the terrain of sexuality. The third trait of queer identified by Sten and Plummer is perhaps the most useful to me here, as it consists of "a rejection of civil rights strategies in favor of a politics of carnival, transgression, and parody which leads to deconstruction, decentering revisionist readings and an anti-assimilationist politics (. . .)" (Stein and Plummer qtd. in Subero 2016, 134).

With that, one might wonder whether Brazilian SF, notably Brazilian SF cinema, has been invisible by virtue of its very queerness and its inherent unwillingness to fit in well-set profiles and canonic norms regarding genre and narrativity. My proposal, here, is to embrace the chimeric quality and the queerness of Brazilian SF cinema. Although a universal genre, SF is not monolithic—it is "liquid," to quote Zygmunt Bauman's conceptualization of (post)modernity (Bauman 1997, 2000) and life (Bauman 2005)—and adapts itself to any given national recipient.

The very background and mediascapes (Appadurai 1996) related to the "discovery" of Brazil and the creation of its foundational myths sustain intriguing links to utopian and even futuristic thinking. Among many examples, in one of his books, Austrian writer Stefan Zweig deemed Brazil as "the land of the future," while British director Terry Gilliam titled one of his films—a futurist dystopia—*Brazil*. Brasília, the country's modernist capital, as well as São Paulo and Rio de Janeiro, the two largest Brazilian cities, have continually fueled the imagination of SF writers and filmmakers, as much as the "lost civilizations" of the Amazon and other exotic, exuberant Latin American regions: from Arthur Conan Doyle's *The Lost World* (1912, along with its 1925 film adaptation, directed by Harry O. Hoyt), to Ian McDonald's *Brasyl* (2007). Throughout the centuries and across different media, the Amazon has inspired a whole history of the imagination in itself. The intersection of Brazil (or an ideal of Brazil) and SF is not infrequent in mediascapes from other countries—both Western and non-Western, as in Václav Vorlíček's Czech comedy film *Who Wants to Kill Jessie?* (*Kdo chce zabít Jesii?*, 1966), in which a Brazilian scientist lectures in unintelligible Portuguese.

The number of Brazilian SF films has only expanded over the last thirty years or so. And the impact of Brazilian speculative cinema on both audiences and academia has been increasingly significant along with the growing number of national horror films. Nearly fifty years after the publication of Cunha's essay, the metaphor of a "scarcely-inhabited planet" to refer to Brazilian SF is no longer accurate, since the presence of such a genre in literature and audiovisual media has thrived in the new millennium.

Whereas the United States saw a boom in SF cinema in the early 1950s, SF tropes first appeared in Brazilian cinema most likely in the late 1940s, within the *chanchadas*—a very popular kind of musical comedy that became a national film genre from the mid-1930s onward. In the early 1960s, Brazilian SF cinema underwent a diversification process: some comedies and parodies with SF motifs shared the market with "serious" films about high-tech cloak-and-dagger narratives and otherworldly encounters. By the late 1960s, SF became instrumental to some film directors who aimed to criticize the country's social, political, and economic situation, dodging the fierce censorship imposed on all arts and artists under the military rule (1964–1985). It was during this time modern Brazilian cinema (Cinema Novo and Cinema Marginal) also expanded into SF tropes, and SF parables continued appearing throughout the 1970s and 1980s. At this point, SF iconography could be found in a variety of films. However, most research addressing Brazilian film of that period completely overlooked genre film, especially SF, rather focusing on complex and consolidated topics such as the Cinema Novo movement, modernist literature and film adaptations, Tropicalism, national cinemas, the "Cinema da Retomada,"[3] and the newest Brazilian cinema. Other works focused on specific Brazilian films, such as Glauber Rocha's *Black God, White Devil* (*Deus e o Diabo na Terra do Sol*, 1964), Joaquim Pedro de Andrade's *Macunaíma* (1969), and Kátia Lund and Fernando Meirelles's *City of God* (*Cidade de Deus*, 2002). These works adopted methodologies that predominantly include cultural studies, social/economic analyses, literary criticism, Bakhtinian literary criticism adapted to film studies, classical historiography of Brazilian cinema, auteur theory, gender and feminist studies, postcolonialist critique, soft power, and Deleuzian approaches (e.g., Foster 1999; Johnson 1989; Johnson and Stam 1995; Marsh 2012; Nagib 2003; Sadlier 2008; Shaw 2007; Dennison and Shaw 2004; Shaw and Dennison 2007; Stam and Johnson 1979; Vieira 1995; Xavier 1997). Notwithstanding their value, none of the aforementioned works have focused on film genre nor considered the genre film, let alone Brazilian SF film, as a cultural phenomenon that deserves further studies in Brazilian cinema history. This book aims to fill this gap, offering a complementary approach to Brazilian film history.

In addition to this gradual shift in terms of scholarly perception, this book is also underpinned in major changes in most of the audiovisual industry in the country. SF film survived both during and after the latest significant crisis in Brazilian cinema, between approximately 1989 and 1994. With the rise of the newest Brazilian cinema, in the wake of the "Retomada," SF films have gained momentum amid a new generation of young directors debuting in short films. In the first decennia of the twenty-first century, Brazilian SF cinema no longer appears to be a stranger in a strange land. The relatively stable Brazilian film industry, the arrival of a new generation of filmmakers, and the wider access to digital technologies have set the ground for Brazilian SF film to thrive in international SF cinema from the southern hemisphere or non-Western world (e.g., Latin America, Africa, southern Asia).

Yet, as "empires" often strike back, contemporary Brazilian SF cinema recently suffered from the perils of an authoritarian, far-right government that did its best to terminate Brazilian art and culture; it did its best to destroy not only our film industry but also our national literature and poetry, our theater, free press, and free speech, along with the savage deforestation of the country and the murder of hundreds of thousands of Brazilians due to historical and science negationism, fake news, and a disastrous policy in favor—yes, in favor, not against—of spreading the virus that causes the coronavirus disease (Covid-19). Today, Brazilian SF cinema is once again well equipped to address the chaos and absurdity of early 2020s Brazil.

Thus, this book's primary purpose is to tell a different history of Brazilian cinema, briefly summarized as a history of Brazilian SF film in the context of world cinemas. The book will focus on the major themes that have shaped SF film production in Brazil, such as the original combination of SF with satire and parody, the anthropophagic[4] and carnivalesque drives, ecodystopias and the global environmental agenda, military dictatorship and the critique of the regime, spiritualist utopias/dystopias (see Cánepa 2013; Cánepa and Suppia 2017), a more contemporary critique of neoliberalism through SF&F&H parables, and dystopian speculations on the return of far-right parties. Structured around these themes or topics, this book will outline a novel history of the Brazilian cinema based on SF film. Considering Brazil's multiculturalism and the tripartite origins of its nationhood (Native Brazilians, Europeans, and Africans), this book will also address issues such as Afrofuturism and Indigenous Futurism, late modernization, and enduring social inequality.

The first chapter, "Laughing at the Future: On the Origins of Brazilian SF Cinema in Comedy and Satire," focuses on the emergence of SF in

Brazilian cinema as a more stable and recognizable genre, often combined with comedy. With the rise of the Brazilian *chanchada*—a rather pantagruelian, anthropophagic genre—SF provided fictional "fuel" for great box office and a charismatic Brazilian star system. Initially combined with musical comedy (*chanchada*) or simply comedy, Brazilian SF films elicited both entertaining and thought-provoking comments on the Cold War and the 1950s world geopolitical situation.

Modernization dreams in the "land of the future," counterbalanced by fears of the Cold War and political instability, provided the framework for these eventful years, as we try to demonstrate in the second chapter, "Subliminal Waves: Brazilian SF Cinema in the Early 1960s." This chapter offers an in-depth analysis of two Brazilian SF films released between 1962 and 1963, here considered eloquent representatives of two trends in Brazilian SF cinema. Virtually unknown by film historians and often overlooked and underrated by film scholars: Alberto Pieralisi's *The 5th Power (O 5o Poder)* and Victor Lima's *The Cosmonauts (Os Cosmonautas)*. These films provide interesting clues regarding the often awkward, love-and-hate relationship between Brazilian cinema and SF, as well as notes on the rather tense contemporary political situation in the country.

The 1964 coup d'état and the establishment of a military dictatorship set the tone for the cultural arena. Considering that, the following chapter, "Brazil, Love it or Leave it—for the Stars: SF Film during the Era of the Military Hardliners (1969–1973)," is named after a parody of a widespread slogan during the Brazilian dictatorship: "Brazil: Love it or leave it!" (*"Brasil: Ame-o ou deixe-o"*), used by people in sporting events or as stickers affixed to car bumpers or windows. It could also be associated with an even older popular saying, well-known by any Brazilian: "The bothered ones should be the ones to move out" (*"Os incomodados que se mudem"*), in other words: "If you can't stand the heat, get out of the kitchen." Slogans such as these are particularly illustrative of the long-lasting history of authoritarianism and the blurred lines that separate Brazil's private and public spheres (see DaMatta 2004, 18). This division between "patriots" and "traitors" (in this case, synonymous with "communists") gained momentum toward the end of the 1960s—and, believe it or not, are back at stake in early 2020, the age of social networks, fake news, and techno-feudalism.

In "Coming Up for Air: The Brazilian Ecodystopian Film," we further explain how SF remains instrumental in Brazilian cinema throughout the 1970s, with the criticism of the military rule encrypted in dystopian parables. The films discussed in this chapter reveal that ecological issues became an effective "checkpoint" for criticizing the regime, since the Brazilian military government followed a course of reckless industrial development that has not distributed equal wealth among the citizens nor provided gains in social welfare. However, such a regime did leave a legacy: an enormous footprint of deforestation and the mass murder of Native Brazilian peoples.

The next chapter, "Proxy Futures and Other Simulacra: the Brazilian SF Comedy Endures, along with the Adventure Movie and the Musical," focuses on the late 1970s and early 1980s, when the country set into motion a gradual return to democracy. While environmentalism remained as a central issue in some Brazilian SF films, major box-office success was attained by means of both parodies and the pastiche of North American SF blockbusters—Steven Spielberg's *Jaws* (1975), for instance, became Adriano Stuart's *Codfish* (*Bacs*, 1976) in Brazil. Likewise, George Lucas's *Star Wars* (1977) was downsized into Adriano Stuart's *The Goofs in the War of the Planets* (*Os Trapalhões na Guerra dos Planetas*, 1978). Brazilian comedy film, notably the kind of juvenile film aimed at young audiences, took advantage of the ironic imitation or overtly sloppy simulacra of major Hollywood films, a commercial strategy well-known since the rise of the *chanchadas* in the 1930s and further scrutinized and criticized by authors such as João Luiz Vieira (1995). Despite this, some serious introspective attempts at a more genuine kind of Brazilian SF cinema, free from sophisticated special effects, also occurred in the 1980s, as in Walter Hugo Khouri's *Voracious Love* (*Amor Voraz*, 1984). The 1980s also set the stage for films inspired by the Brazilian pop music scene, starring pop singers and/or a new generation of TV actors, as in Francisco de Paula's *Scalding Sands* (*Areias Escaldantes*, 1985). The welcomed rebirth of democracy seemed to infuse Brazilian cinema with some general hope, yet the political criticism remained in the guise of both SF comedy and parables.

In "The Ghost in the Machine: Brazilian SF and the Revival of Spiritist Films" I will discuss the impact of Kardecism/Spiritism in Brazilian culture and how a new wave of spiritist films emerged in the early twenty-first century, rendering curious encounters between religion and SF in often conservative or reactionary popular films. Here I am going to delve further into the alleged "resurrection" of the Brazilian spiritist film, insofar as Spiritism in general, and notably Kardecism, may be a key cultural factor in the "domestication," "familiarization," or even "nationalization" of SF in Brazilian cinema.

The chapter titled "Southern Short Circuits: Contemporary Brazilian SF Film as Political Film," investigates a rather diverse and heterogeneous film production, focused on politically engaged SF allegories of the "land of the future" and the miseries of late capitalism. This chapter also seeks to provide a thorough account of approximately ten years of SF cinema under the government of the Workers' Party (PT), an allegedly left-wing party. A crucial hypothesis in this chapter is that the fall of the left and the rise of the far right have triggered new SF allegories, thus fostering new cinematic comments on the country's reality and its history of inequality, oppression, and exclusion. As in the early 1960s, when Brazilian SF cinema seemed to have foreseen events (e.g., Alberto Pieralisi's film *O 5o*, 1962), utopias/dystopias in the recent film landscape in Brazil, such as Adirley Queirós's *White Out, Black In (Branco Sai, Preto Fica*, 2014), seems to likewise foresee the detour to the right after more than ten years of social democracy and leftist politics altogether. To outline further developments in the genre, this chapter also addresses the national SF film production from the late 2010s onward.

The next chapter, "Find your Escape Pod: Afrofuturism, Amazofuturism, and Queer Sci-Fi" advances the hypothesis delineated in the previous chapter—on how Brazilian SF cinema has been responding to the latest shift to the far-right and how social-environmentalism has reappeared on Brazilian film screens.

The following chapter, "A Strange Object South of the Equator: Hypotheses and Investigations about Restraints against SF Literature and Films in Brazil," aims to further investigate the possible cultural, economic, sociological, and political obstacles to SF in Brazilian cinema. In an attempt to provide a better understanding of the history of SF in this context, I will revisit the history of Brazil, as well as some theories or concepts such as Roberto Schwarz's (1992) "misplaced ideas," Ginway's (2004) comments on the supposed prevalence of nineteenth-century realism-naturalism in Brazilian culture, the Brazilian scientific/technological imaginary, the public perception of science in Brazil (Vogt and Polito 2003), and some other crucial issues or "blind spots."

Anticipating some conclusions or final remarks, the chapter "Do Brazilians Dream of Edenic (or Industrial) Futures?" makes reference to the well-known novel by Philip K. Dick to address some fundamental issues in the formation of Brazil as a nation. Darcy Ribeiro's thoughts are quoted and brought into a discussion against the backdrop of the Brazilian

SF cinema and the country's contemporary political agenda. What has changed and how much, if at all?

Finally, the last chapter, "Wake Up! We Are Dreaming!," defends the universality of SF, thus recognizing the vernacular SF that may thrive in any given film culture. For the sake of final remarks, we will acknowledge the heterogeneity of world SF cinema as manifest in vernacular SF films and queer Brazilian SF cinema.

The chapters and their specific order are intended to conciliate chronological and critical approaches, diachronic and synchronic perspectives. However, some back and forth will be inevitable, and certain films might be repeated in more than one chapter: but under different circumstances and perspectives. Thus, these two approaches (history-based/diachronic and theme-based/synchronic) will be susceptible to occasional overlapping, helping to keep readers oriented in terms of time and space. The chapters, in turn, are autonomous and can be read independently, as critical surveys on themes or motifs such as environmentalism or Afrofuturism in Brazil. Either directly or indirectly, this work focuses on the positions and presuppositions presented by a wide range of authors and works from various intellectual traditions, epistemologies, and different regions of the world. This means to say that this book is chimerical in itself. It seeks to approach Brazilian SF cinema through transversal and kaleidoscopic readings, contrasting film, historical context, and meanings produced from the clash between art and discourse. In commenting on several short and feature-length films, we will also be commenting on the history of Brazil and vice versa.

Two additional concepts emerge as instrumental to this book, which will be clear toward the last chapters, when I will outline a response to the usual approach to SF focusing on contemporary Brazilian SF cinema, namely: *mediascapes*, proposed by Arjun Appadurai (1996), and *amphitextuality* (*amphitextualité*), by Nathalie Denizot (2010). By and large, my argumentation draws on Appadurai's mediascapes as global networks in which national imaginaries are constantly remapped. As remarked by Appadurai, "the US is no longer the puppeteer of a world system of images but is only one node of a complex transnational construction of imaginary landscapes" (Appadurai 1996, 31). Still according to Appadurai, "The image, the imagined, the imaginary—these are all terms that direct us to something critical and new in global cultural processes: *the imagination as a social practice*" (Appadurai 1996, 31; emphasis in the original).

Imagination is immaterial. Undoubtedly, imagination can have an impact on reality; to some extent, it can shape reality and vice versa; likewise, it can spread by traveling rapidly, regardless of geopolitical frontiers and, sometimes, economic power. Brazilian SF cinema is part of a mediascape or a mediascape in itself among other world SF mediascapes. Just as sands can travel airborne, forming dunes in different landscapes depending on the winds, films can drift overseas and have their impacts on different mediascapes, thus reshaping film landscapes. For a long time, North American SF cinema was a vast, influential mediascape; however, the scenario is no longer that simple.

Another key concept in our approach to Brazilian SF is *amphitextuality*. According to Denizot (2010), the concept of amphitextuality (from ancient Greek amphi: around, on both sides) aims to describe the textual solidarities in which texts and genres are taken into account by scholars, students, and broader audiences. The author describes these textual solidarities—which may link a given text to one or more texts beside which it is placed, a relation that is not purely paratextual (since each of the texts can also be accompanied by a paratext)—as another possible mode of relationship alongside the five types of transtextual relations defined by Gérard Genette (1992, 11–12): metatextuality, hypertextuality, paratextuality, intertextuality, and architextuality. For texts and genres are rarely perceived in isolation, being constantly caught in networks that can modify the vantage point of their readership, amphitextuality seems to be of particular interest in the study of textual genres, that is, both in film and literature (Denizot 2010, 222). Still, according to Denizot, "to name, define and delimit a genre, it is first of all to look at a text in a certain way. In a way, genres are about the point of view. A certain text can belong to one genre depending on the point of view one adopts, whereas another text, according to the point of view then adopted, can be associated to another genre" (2010, 226).[5] Accordingly, the Brazilian films mentioned in this book are, to a large extent, "amphibious" objects: they are SF, but not only SF. Likewise, our analyses of such SF+ films are also reminiscent of both Rieder's (2010) approach to SF and Denizot's (2010) amphitextuality: the film genre is, herein, an interface; a lens through which, at a certain point in space and time, SF may provide insightful "probes" and "decryption machines" to extract further meanings of a given film, or vernacular film culture.

In the following pages, I intend to introduce you to the chimeric, queer, and amphibious film creatures that populate Brazilian SF mediascape.

1

# Laughing at the Future

## On the Origins of Brazilian SF Cinema in Comedy and Satire

To pinpoint the earliest appearances of SF in Brazilian cinema is an extremely difficult (if not impossible) task. In other words, talking about SF or proto-SF (see Stableford 1993) in the Brazilian silent film era is perhaps as complicated as proving the existence of flying saucers.

Throughout the first thirteen years of Brazilian cinema, a national scientific film production did gain momentum. But what about a proto-SF film production? Whereas in France there were filmmakers like Georges Méliès, Ferdinand Zecca, and Segundo de Chomón, with a remarkable filmography in terms of fantasy films or proto-SF cinema, in Brazil there was no name identified with the so-called comic-fantastic (*cômico-phantástico*) (i.e., speculative fiction). However, some Brazilian fantasy films did appear in the silent era.

The pioneering filmmaker Antonio Campos produced, directed, and starred in one of the rare Brazilian fantasy films in the silent era: *The Devil* (*O Diabo*, 1908). According to Francisco Campos's interview with Maria Rita Galvão, it was "a little movie made in the fashion of Méliès's magical films. The story of a man who dreamed of the devil, or met the devil, or something like that" (Galvão et al. 1984, 26–27; our translation). This description reminds us of Segundo de Chomón's influential short *The Red Spectre* (*Le Spectre Rouge*, 1907). Antonio Campos's film may well have been a remake of Chomón's original *Red Spectre*, or a work more loosely inspired on the fantasy films of Méliès, Chomón, or Zecca.

The Photo-Cinematographia Co., and producers Labanca, Leal & Co. also made some "comic-fantastic" films such as *Chef's Duel* (*Duello de Cozinheiros*, 1908), *The Elixir of Youth* (*Elixir da Juventude*, or *Elixir da Juventude Carioca*, 1908), and *The Electoral Matchstick* (*O Fósforo Eleitoral* or *O Caso do Rio*, 1909). Managed by the Italian businessman Giuseppe Labanca, with the Portuguese filmmaker Antônio Leal as the main executive producer, Photo-Cinematographia Co. was inaugurated in 1907 as the first production company in Rio de Janeiro to undertake a more ambitious project, with studios in which both fiction and documentary films were made.

On October 10, 1908, the newspaper *Jornal do Brasil* announced the premiere of *Duello de Cozinheiros* at the Grande Cinematógrafo Parisiense in Rio, referring to the film as a "graceful, fantastic comic tape in which, after a fight, when legs, arms, etc. move out from the trunks of the fighting cooks, the limbs return to their original bodies with the apparition of the Cupid." A day later, on October 11, 1908, *Jornal do Brasil* kept the reference to the screening of the film at the Grande Cinematographo Parisiense as a "fantastic comic tape." In another film theater ad, the film had a different title, *Duello de Marmitões*: "An original duel between cooks. Irresistible comic scenes. The sad disappointment of the duelists."

*The Electoral Matchstick* or *The Rio Case* (*O Fósforo Eleitoral* ou *O Caso do Rio*, 1909), directed by Antonio Serra, was released at Cinema Palace in Rio de Janeiro on February 11, 1909,[1] and announced by the *Jornal do Brasil* on February 9, 1909, as a "comic-fantastic story, a severe and playful criticism on the making of elections in Rio de Janeiro" (see Noronha 1997, 205–6). Once again, the Brazilian press used the label "*comico-phantastico*" to refer to a "different," unconventional trick film. Although these films are completely lost in the present day[2] and thereby impossible to analyze with precision, we could assume, based on documents, synopses, and newspapers that the Brazilian *comico-phantastico* films explored wonder and fascination with science and technology under the guise of comedy, not so differently from films such as the Lumière Brothers' *The Mechanical Butcher* (*La Charcuterie Méchanique*, 1895), or Edison Co.'s *Dog Factory* (1904).

In addition to the aforementioned titles, a number of other fantasy films, mostly American and European productions, were screened in Brazilian film theaters, thus proving the familiarity of Brazilian film audiences with fantasy or proto-SF cinema. The *Jornal do Brasil* on October 8, 1908, referred to the exhibition of *It Glues Everything . . . Even Iron!*

(*Colla Tudo, Mesmo . . . Ferro!*) at Cinema-Pathé in Rio as follows: "An infernal substance whose properties are felt even at a distance! The comic absurdity led to excess! Unspeakable situations! Endless joy!" The *Jornal do Brasil* of February 9, 1909, announced the film *Transfiguration* (*Transfiguração*) as an attraction at Cinematographo Paris (Tiradentes Square, 50), with "amusing comic scenes. A prodigious machine that transfigures everything. Constant hilarity." Still according to *Jornal do Brasil*, on that same date the film *In the Country of the Dreams* (*No Paiz dos Sonhos*) was screened at Cinematographo Paraíso do Rio (Central Av., 105): "a very rich colored fantastic composition. A graceful girl who falls asleep in bed while reading Jules Verne, she dreams of taking a balloon trip to a wonderful country, where the most pleasant surprises take place." On February 25, 1909, the same *Jornal do Brasil* announced the exhibition of *Wonderful Eggs* (*Ovos Maravilhosos*) at the Cinema-Palace (Rua do Ouvidor, 185, Rio de Janeiro), a "colorful, fantastic comic tape," whereas the Grande Cinematographo Parisiense featured *A Great Discovery by Dr. Right* (*Uma Grande Descoberta do Dr. Right*), an "extra-comic scene that shows us an ingenious device." This same film was mentioned again in *Jornal do Brasil* on February 27, 1909, with another title, *The Invention of Dr. Right* (*O Invento do Dr. Right*), on screen at Cinematographo Paris: "There is no more paraplegics thanks to science! (*sic*) Hilarious scenes!." Probably a foreign film, *The Invention of Dr. Right* was also screened at Cinematographo Rio Branco (Visconde do Rio Branco St., 40), referred to as a "comic film, about a medicine against paralysis."[3] If we enlarge the framework of early proto-SF cinema in Brazil, considering dramatized scientific or pseudoscientific films and any kind of documentary remotely inspired by scientific motifs or events, the number of titles deserving attention increases. This is the case, for instance, for films like *The Comet* (*O Cometa*), produced by Empresa F. Serrador & Cia. and cinematography by Julio Ferrez, or *606*, a.k.a. *606 Against the Pale Spirochete* (*606 Contra o Espiroqueta Pálido*), both released in 1910. *The Comet* was a *cantante*,[4] referred to as a *revista*[5] that commented on the appearance of Halley's Comet in 1910: an astronomical event that, according to popular superstition, announced the end of the world. Structured around three acts and a prologue, the film featured a chronicle of urban life in Rio de Janeiro while the comet quickly approached the planet (Noronha 2008, 148). Another *cantante*, *606 Against the Pale Spirochete* was referred to as a humorous *revista* that addressed several truths of the time. The film's title alluded to the serum invented and manufactured by the German scientist Paul Ehrlich to treat syphilis, the disease caused by the *Spirochaeta pallida*. The serum began being sold in Brazil in 1910 and the injections soon had the fame of a miraculous medicine (Galvão et al. 1984, 72). Despite the possible parallel, oblique relationship one might see between such films and a proto-SF cinema, it is extremely difficult to come to any uncontroversial conclusion, given the absence of any surviving copy of the aforementioned films. Moreover, the remaining documents or film reviews are very succinct, so several films that could be early proto-SF or fantasy films do not provide us with any evidence beyond their suggestive, ambiguous titles.

In the 1930s, however, fantasy and science fiction left clearer footprints in the Brazilian cinematic landscape, with the appearance of one of its first time-travel tales. *The Young Great-Grandfather* (*O Jovem Tataravô*), a 1936 film by Luiz de Barros (and still available), features a man of the nineteenth century who is brought back to life by his great-great-grandson in the twentieth century. However, the mechanism that provides this time travel or resurrection has no science fiction-related feature: it consists of a magical ritual of "White Table" ("Mesa Branca"),[6] a supernatural conjuring oriented by a manuscript, about the use of a magical powder capable of reincarnating spirits. There is no (pseudo)scientific or technological motif, even though the ability to bring people back to life is assigned to "secrets acquired in Egypt" or an "occult science learned by an Egyptologist."[7] However, we should not underestimate this kind of narrative as a possible attempt at proto-scientific fiction or early SF in Brazil. In nineteenth-century literature generally associated with SF, interplanetary or time-travel adventures were often ascribed to supernatural or spiritualist beliefs. For instance, in *Pages from the History of Brazil Written in the Year 2000* (*Páginas da História do Brasil Escripta no Anno de 2000*, 1957 [1868–72]), by the Brazilian writer Joaquim Felício dos Santos, a text is brought from the future by a medium. In her article "The First Wave: Latin American Science Fiction Discovers Its Roots" (2007), Rachel Haywood Ferreira analyzes three of the earliest works in Latin American SF (or proto-SF) literature: Fósforo-Cerillos's (pseudonym) "Mexico in the Year 1970" ("México en el año 1970," first published in 1844), Joaquim Felicio dos Santos's *Pages from the History of Brazil Written in the Year 2000*, and Eduardo Ladislao Holmberg's *The Marvelous Journey of Mr. Nic-Nac to the Planet Mars* (*Viaje maravilloso del Señor Nic-Nac en el que se refieren las prodijiosas aventuras de este señor y se dan á conocer las instituciones, costumbres y preocupaciones de um mundo desconocido: Fantasia espiritista,*

2006 [1875]), respectively from Mexico, Brazil, and Argentina. Analyzing these three pioneering Latin American proto-SF narratives, Rachel Haywood Ferreira notes that Felicio dos Santos's choice of spiritism as a method of time travel in the context of typical SF methods of travel through time and space prior to Wells's *Time Machine* (2007, 446).

Haywood Ferreira (2007) further refers to the influence of spiritism in Brazil, a doctrine originating in the writings of Allan Kardec (pseudonym of Hippolyte Léon Denizard Rivail) in France in the early 1850s, which found widespread acceptance among the Brazilian middle-class and elite toward the 1870s. In her analysis of Holmberg's *The Marvelous Journey of Mr. Nic-Nac to the Planet Mars*, Haywood Ferreira also identifies the appearance of spiritist ideas to make interplanetary travel ("transplanetation") possible with the help of a medium—similar to Felicio dos Santos's Pedro II in *Pages from the History of Brazil Written in the Year 2000*. Haywood Ferreira highlights that: "(. . .) as with *Brasil 2000*, this method of transportation in *Nic-Nac* should not be read as an avoidance of technology in Latin American SF. Rocketships were not yet de rigueur for space travel in early science fiction, and Holmberg undoubtedly modeled Nic-Nac's voyage after the ideas of the French scientist, popularizer of science, and spiritist Camille Flammarion (1842–1925) (2007, 451). Therefore, the amalgamation of religious, spiritist, and supernatural motifs in some of the first interplanetary travel stories or space adventures were common across a number of national literatures and cinemas, be they European or not.[8]

By considering that the world's SF cinema from the 1910s through the 1940s is often regarded as "proto-SF"—previous experimental ventures into cinematic SF, prior to the American 1950s SF film boom—it is reasonable to assume that only with the coming of the talkies were there clearer manifestations of SF in Brazilian cinema. This void in Brazilian SF cinema throughout the first thirty years or so of the twentieth century could also be ascribed to the invasion of Hollywood films and the consequent dilution of a tentative national film industry in the first half of the century. In the silent era, the Brazilian fiction film production declined considerably in favor of foreign films, notably Hollywood cinema, also due to the lack of proper infrastructure in Brazil—such as the scarcity of electricity, generally available only in big urban areas like São Paulo and Rio de Janeiro, and lackluster still. Paulo Emílio Salles Gomes explains the extremely slow pace with which the film trade developed from 1896 to 1906 in Brazil as follows: "If cinema did not become a Brazilian habit for approximately a decade, it was due to our underdevelopment in electricity. Once energy was industrialized in Rio de Janeiro, exhibition proliferated like mushrooms" (Salles Gomes qtd. in Martin 1997, 264).[9] An agrarian country in the turn of the nineteenth to the twentieth century and all along the First Republic ("Primeira República," also known as "Old Republic"/"República Velha," from 1889 through 1930), with its economy totally based on plantations and the export of commodities, it is worth noting that the first wave of modernization/industrialization in Brazil took place no sooner than toward the end of the 1930s.[10]

Therefore, we shall commence our journey through Brazilian SF cinema in the late 1940s after WWII, acknowledging how SF has seemingly set its roots in a number of national cinemas, both Western and non-Western, by means of an overt complicity with comedy—an older, well-established genre.

Silveira Sampaio's *An Adventure at 40* (*Uma Aventura aos 40*, 1947) is one of the first films in which an SF element clearly stands out in the guise of a futuristic, fully interactive television. A comedy framed by SF, this film was released in 1947, but its story begins in 1975, when Prof. Carlos de Miranda's (Sampaio himself) seventieth birthday is celebrated by a television channel. The TV presenter begins with Miranda's biography but is soon interrupted by the professor himself, who wants to clear up some facts. In this future, the spectator can interact directly with the TV set. According to Paulo Emílio Salles Gomes, *An Adventure at 40* "suggested the possibility of a more sophisticated and lighter film comedy. However, this film remained as an isolated experience, with no further consequences" (1996, 75–76). The SF dimension in Sampaio's film was apparently overlooked by film critics and scholars at the time of its premiere and afterward. The film also aptly represented Brazilian independent cinema since it was made with a shoestring budget in a sort of friendly, domestic enterprise and with no state funding. Silveira Sampaio was a doctor who had a passion for theater. As a playwright, he convinced friends and spent his own money to make *An Adventure at 40*, as explained by the opening credits. In retrospect, *An Adventure at 40* can be seen as a pioneering step toward a future trend in Brazilian cinema: the fruitful combination of SF and comedy, made possible by low-budget productions (see fig. 1.1).

The 1940s were also marked by the ascension of this typical Brazilian genre, the *chanchada*, a combination of musical and comedy sometimes revolving around a parody of an American classic or blockbuster, such as

Figure 1.1. Silveira Sampaio playing the role of Prof. Carlos de Miranda in *An Adventure at 40* (*Uma Aventura aos 40*, 1947). According to this SF comedy, in the future, interactive TV shows celebrate VIPs' birthdays. *Source*: *An Adventure at 40* (*Uma Aventura aos 40*). Dir. Silveira Sampaio. Prod. Co.: Centauro do Brasil Cinematográfica Ltda.Brasil, 1947, 35mm, B&W, 77min. Courtesy: Cinemateca Brasileira.

Cecil B. DeMille's *Samson and Delilah* (1949) or Fred Zinnemann's *High Noon* (1952). These productions inspired two of the best examples of the Brazilian *chanchada* in the mid-1950s: *Neither Samson nor Delilah* (*Nem Sansão nem Dalila*, 1954) and *To Kill or to Run* (*Matar ou Correr*, 1954), both directed by Carlos Manga.

João Luiz Vieira defines the *chanchada* as the widely popular film genre that best synthesizes and defines Brazilian cinema in the 1930s, 1940s, and mainly the 1950s, produced mostly in Rio de Janeiro (2004, 117).[11] Lisa Shaw and Stephanie Dennison comment that "although initially a pejorative term, often used by journalists to refer with contempt to the low-budget musical comedy films produced in Brazil in the 1930s, the label *chanchada* gradually lost its implications of poor quality and worthlessness, and came to be the accepted way of referring to this emerging tradition"

(2007, 71). The pinnacle of the *chanchada* was definitively reached by the massive productivity of Atlântida Cinematográfica when Luís Severiano Ribeiro, owner of the largest national chain of film theaters, became its main shareholder and executive mastermind, from 1947 onward. Founded on September 18, 1941, by Moacir Fenelon, Alinor Azevedo, and José Carlos Burle, Atlântida had as its main goal a patriotic set of tenets for the creation of a strong national film industry.

According to Lisa Shaw and Stephanie Dennison, "Atlântida set out to establish a national cinema industry [. . .]. It also aimed to represent real life on screen, and to introduce an element of social commentary into its films" (2004, 62). Shaw and Dennison further remark that "the chanchadas of the 1940s overturned established hierarchies of social norms or aesthetic standards in a spirit of carnivalesque irreverence, giving status to popular culture, particularly music, and ridiculing examples of elite culture, usually in the form of parody or pastiche. As the chanchada gradually lost close associations with carnival music in the late 1940 and early 1950s, the inversions so intrinsic to carnival became central to this cinematic genre" (2004, 66). From the 1950s onward, SF has come to stay on the planet of Brazilian *chanchadas*. This combination of SF and comedy is well illustrated by films such as Alberto Cavalcanti's *Simon, the One-Eyed* (*Simão, o Caolho*, 1952), in which an artificial eye gives its owner the gift of invisibility. Another good example of a *chanchada* combined with SF motifs is Watson Macedo's *Carnival on Mars* (*Carnaval em Marte*, 1954), about a woman who dreams of being the Martian queen, thus leading a Martian female expedition to Earth and deciding to take the Brazilian Carnival back to the Red Planet.

*Carnival on Mars* provides an interesting showcase not only of the Brazilian SF comedy but also the state of Brazilian film industry in the mid-1950s. In this film, rumors about the arrival of flying saucers inspire Aunt Petrolina (Violeta Ferraz) who, after a little accident, faints and dreams of being the "Queen of Mars." Due to an epidemic on the Red Planet, Martian men were utterly extinct. For the sake of reproduction, male humans had to be abducted during expeditions to Earth. This time, however, the Martian female expeditionaries, led by their Queen (Violeta Ferraz in a double role), arrive in Rio de Janeiro in the middle of Carnival and, enchanted by the party, decide to take it to Mars. The script of *Carnival on Mars* was written by Alinor Azevedo and Watson Macedo, with the collaboration of Leon Eliachar, who was mostly responsible for the gags. The film was likely inspired by the "alien invasion" American

B-movies in the 1950s SF film genre, and by comedies such as Charles Lamont's *Abbott and Costello Go to Mars* (1953), which was released one year before Macedo's film entered production phase.

*Carnival on Mars* was given both sympathetic and harsh reviews. Among the most negative is a review by Van Jafa (1955), to whom *Carnival on Mars* was a "cinematographic hoax," an utter failure, a film full of bad taste with no decent script. The Brazilian film critic Francisco Amazonense (1955) highlighted the grotesque in a particular scene and criticized the overall precariousness of the film's production.[12] Still, according to Amazonense, *Carnival on Mars* was produced in near-record time (just over thirty days), in a joint effort by Watson Macedo, Anselmo Duarte, and Roberto Acácio working together as co-producers.

*Carnival on Mars* triggered discussions on the Brazilian film market/industry again in the newspaper *Diário da Noite* from February 12, 1955: "It is thus a film that adds nothing to the genre, being at the level of a commercial comedy, which, we repeat, stands for national cinema as one of its only possibilities, since its difficulties in all sectors of production, distribution and exhibition persist, while no protective legislation comes to its rescue."[13] It is worth noting how different the assessments regarding high standards of cinematic quality are even more evident when the SF film genre is at stake. Among the most tolerant critics was A. Gomes Prata,[14] to whom "*Carnaval em Marte*, a satire on flying saucer hysteria, is a movie that amuses."[15] The critic further observes that "to a certain extent, [*Carnival on Mars*] escapes the old clichés, [it] brings up interesting things to the joy of carnival on the screen, linked to the life of our people."[16] Prata underlines the peaceful message as part of the film's heyday: "This is when the reporter, on the brink of an 'invasion' from Mars, proclaims that 'in our world not everyone wants war, destruction, and my people [from Brazil] send a message of brotherhood, friendship, peace and music.'"[17] Prata also highlighted a scene with more controversial political overtones, the one in which President Getúlio Vargas's Special Police (Polícia Especial) breaks into a party with its usual violence (see Prata 1955).

Since there is no surviving copy of *Carnival on Mars*: all we know about this film is based on reviews or newspapers articles. It is therefore impossible to accurately gauge the political discourse possibly embedded in this film written by Alinor Azevedo (1913–1974), one of the most prolific scriptwriters in the Brazilian cinema of the 1940s and 1950s. However, Alinor Azevedo's biography and his previous works may well suggest that this SF comedy could have been remotely inspired by Yakov Protazanov's *Aelita, Queen of Mars* (1924), given some similarities in terms of plot and characters. Indeed, in *Aelita* the Russian Revolution is exported to Mars, whereas in *Carnival on Mars* it is the Brazilian carnival that is imported by the Martians. Yet, both films resort to characters dreaming as a narrative artifice, and both films feature "Martian Queens" of utopian societies. Moreover, Alinor Azevedo was also involved in the production of one of the first Communist Brazilian films: the short documentary *Rally: São Paulo to Luiz Carlos Prestes* (*Comício: São Paulo a Luiz Carlos Prestes*, 1945), directed by Ruy Santos.[18]

However, by reviewing Watson Macedo's *Carnival on Mars*, several critics tackled issues related to the Brazilian film market and industry, such as the need for state intervention against the American cultural imperialism. Thereby, *Carnival on Mars* may well have reverberated a counter-hegemonic discourse, though unintentionally, by triggering further discussions about the grip of the American film industry in Brazil. Furthermore, as a satire of flying saucer movies, it may have featured a counterpoint to the widely popular American B-movies on alien invasion, often seen as parables warning about the Red Peril, such as William Cameron Menzies's *Invaders from Mars* (1953). In Macedo's *Carnival on Mars*, the Martian invaders are no less than gorgeous women eager to imitate our lifestyle, with absolutely no interest in eating the Earthlings' brains or possessing their souls. Following *Carnival on Mars*, the Cold War agenda and its space race became more and more intertwined with the space opera in Brazilian comedy films with SF tropes.

Still in 1954, another *chanchada* produced by Atlântida Cinematográfica appears to have employed futuristic motifs: *Rascals in the Fourth Dimension* (*Malandros na Quarta Dimensão*). Written by Gita de Barros and Luiz de Barros, and directed by Luiz de Barros, *Rascals . . .* featured an eccentric main character, Prof. Gia Not, a millionaire and inventor of the "four-dimensional cinema." Like *Carnival on Mars*, there is no surviving copy of this comedy.

In the late 1950s, José Cajado Filho's script of *The Sputnik Man* (*O Homem do Sputnik*), produced by Atlântida Cinematográfica, capitalized on the beginnings of the space race. Directed by Carlos Manga and released in 1959, *The Sputnik Man* is about the adventure of a couple of country folk, from the moment when the Sputnik supposedly falls into their chicken coop. The artificial satellite is of great strategic value and becomes the focus of a "treasure hunt" involving the American, French, and Soviet governments.

According to critics at the time of its release, the techniques behind the opening credits were purportedly copied from those created by Saul Bass for Otto Preminger's *The Man with the Golden Arm* (1955).[19]

This brilliant parody of the Cold War is undoubtedly one of the best films ever released by Atlântida Cinematográfica. *The Sputnik Man* preserves the "carnivalesque realm of the *chanchada*," whereby "the motif of inversion or *troca* (exchange) constantly resurfaces, whether in the form of irreverent overturning of social hierarchies, dramatic changes of identity or the simple exchange of one object for another, characteristically via a dishonest ruse" (Shaw and Dennison 2007, 72). Shaw and Dennison add that "while some chanchadas were content to occasionally mimic a stock element of Hollywood movies or even a well-known star, Atlântida's relationship with the North American film industry evolved in the 1950s, giving rise to sophisticated film parodies" (2004, 103). Unlike *To Kill or to Run* or *Neither Samson nor Delilah*, *The Sputnik Man* does not address any specific original film as its preferential target. In this case, the parodic "machine-gun" keeps shifting the target of its intertextual "victims." The European auteur cinema and its celebrities (Brigitte Bardot), Hollywood films (*Kiss Me Deadly*), classical texts (Dostoyevsky's *The Brothers Karamazov*), popular culture (rock'n'roll, Coca-Cola, chewing gum), the American foreign affairs and the "Big Stick" politics, as well as national and international authorities and institutions are all parodied in a *chanchada* that, overall, targets the Cold War era and its political agenda, from the viewpoint of an everyman inhabiting a peripheral land in a peripheral nation, and to whom the *malandragem*[20] (DaMatta 2004, 51) provides the only available "survival kit."

In the 1960s, under constant fire from the Brazilian *intelligentsia*, eclipsed by Cinema Novo and threatened by the onset of television industry in the country, Atlântida's *chanchadas* declined. Nevertheless, smaller studios like Herbert Richers still produced the genre.

Furthermore, it is worth considering that both SF and the *chanchada* are essentially "symbiotic" genres in which "friendliness" (or "unfriendliness") hinge on extraneous iconography or imagery but also cannibalize orbiting motifs. This quality can often complicate the analysis. All in all, since we are not looking for "pure specimens," any Brazilian film that nods to science fiction imagery may be of interest. Whereas *The Cosmonauts* appears to be a typical Brazilian SF comedy in the *chanchada* style, *The Sputnik Man* is also noteworthy for its circumstantial adherence to the SF film genre, with all of its mixed feelings toward American culture and

Figure 1.2. Film poster of Carlos Manga's 1959 film *The Sputnik Man* (*O Homem do Sputnik*), one of the most memorable Brazilian chanchadas with a touch of SF. *Source*: *The Sputnik Man* (*O Homem do Sputnik*). Dir. Carlos Manga. Prod. Co.: Atlântida Empresa Cinematográfica do Brasil S.A., Brasil, 1959, 35mm, BP, 97min Courtesy: Cinemateca Brasileira.

imperialism (see fig. 1.2).

As one can see in examples such as *An Adventure at 40* and *Carnival on Mars*, Brazilian audiences likely made their acquaintance with SF through comedy and parodic films in the late 1940s and mid-1950s, which is not an exclusively Brazilian phenomenon. On the contrary, the same could be said about French, British, and/or American early SF cinema. However, it seems that the initial overlap between SF and comedy in Latin American cinemas took a little longer, but perhaps had a more evident, straightforward impact on broader audiences, often resulting in commercial success. Despite the fact that other national cinemas such as the Mexican and the Argentinean film industry would later (or concomitantly) make a number of "serious" SF and fantasy films,[21] the initial combination of SF with the swashbuckler or the comedy film appears to have prevailed as the most appealing product for broader audiences in Latin America. Examples of these productions include the Argentinean film *The Beast Man, or The Adventures of Captain Richard* (*El Hombre Bestia, o Las Aventuras del Capitan Richard*, 1934), directed by C. Z. Soprani, *The Superwiseman* (*El Supersabio*, 1948), by Miguel M. Delgado and starring the famous Mexican comedian Cantinflas, and the *lucha libre* genre—notably the films starring the Mexican wrestler Santo. Thenceforth, films like *El Supersabio*, or Alfredo B. Crevenna's *Santo vs. the Martian Invasion* (*El Santo contra la Invasión de los Marcianos*, 1967) became "paradigms" for Latin American SF film for years to come.

Regardless of any revision of the *chanchada*'s role in the history of Brazilian cinema, it is notorious that it somehow opened the doors to the production of SF films in Brazil, insofar as an SF comedy can still be an SF film. My purpose here was to demonstrate this legacy of the Brazilian comedy, mostly the *chanchada*, as the cannibalizing genre that could be held accountable for the first acquaintances of Brazilian audiences with SF iconography. The legacy and imprints of such an achievement can be seen up to the present day in TV shows, TV soap operas, and some of the most popular Brazilian SF comedy films, as in Cláudio Torres's *The Man from the Future* (*O Homem do Futuro*, 2011). As a matter of fact, Brazilian cinema has often laughed in the face of the future.

2

# Subliminal Waves

## Brazilian SF Cinema in the Early 1960s

Indeed, the early 1960s saw major achievements for Brazilian cinema, with 1962 being especially noteworthy. It had no less than a dozen remarkable titles being released, with one film winning the Palme d'Or at Cannes that year. That film was Anselmo Duarte's *The Given Word* (*O Pagador de Promessas*), adapted from the play of the same name by Alfredo Dias Gomes; its victory at Cannes made it one of the most prestigious Brazilian films of all time. But several other outstanding Brazilian movies were released in 1962. By that time, Glauber Rocha made his debut in feature films with *Barravento*, and other titles representative of a new wave in Brazilian cinema (Cinema Novo) gained momentum in film festivals around the world.

The birth of the Brazilian Cinema Novo captured the attention of the film world, and that was just the beginning. In the wake of the aforementioned 1962 Brazilian film achievements, Nelson Pereira dos Santos's *Barren Lives* (*Vidas Secas*, 1963) and Glauber Rocha's *Black God, White Devil*, among other evocative titles, left an indelible mark in the history of modern world cinema.

But 1962 also set the stage for genre films that should not be neglected, and appraising their legacy tells an entirely different story of Brazilian cinema. I refer to films like Eurides Ramos's crime story *Murder in Copacabana* (*Assassinato em Copacabana*) and Carlos Manga's *The Seven Eves* (*As Sete Evas*) but first and foremost two Brazilian SF films produced in the same year: Victor Lima's *The Cosmonauts* and Alberto

Pieralisi's *The 5th Power*. These two films may well have been eclipsed by Anselmo Duarte's Palme d'Or win and the Cinema Novo's critical acclaim, and yet they represent, respectively, two competing paradigms for Brazilian SF cinema.

## The Day When Laughter Stood Free

*The Cosmonauts* (*Os Cosmonautas*, 1962) is an SF comedy in which the scientist Inacius Isidorius (Álvaro Aquiar) attempts to outpace both the Americans and the Soviets by trying to send the first manned mission to the moon. Victor Lima, the film's director, was hired as translator by the American government in 1945 and stayed in the United States for three years. He studied set design and scriptwriting at Northwestern University and also spent some time in Hollywood learning under the supervision of cinematographer Gregg Toland (from Orson Welles's 1941 film *Citizen Kane*, among other titles). Lima also worked at Metro-Goldwyn-Mayer (MGM) in Culver City and Walt Disney studios. In 1947 he returned to Brazil and started working in the film industry (Ramos and Miranda 2004, 327). According to Sérgio Augusto, Victor Lima was a tireless promoter of comedy as the most vibrant means of expression for Brazilian cinema (Ramos and Miranda 2004, 327). *The Cosmonauts* was produced by Herbert Richers, the Brazilian film producer who founded his own production company, Produções Cinematográficas Herbert Richers, after working for almost five years (1948–1952) at Atlântida Cinematográfica in Rio. Richers's productions were more modest than those of Atlântida and, in the early 1960s, he had already incorporated television aesthetics in his comedies (Ramos and Miranda 2004, 461).

*The Cosmonauts* is representative of a later phase of the *chanchada* that was influenced by the rise of television industry. Shaw and Dennison point out that "the decline in the popularity of the *chanchada* went hand in hand with the expansion of television, which became increasingly accessible as the 1950s drew to a close" (2004, 118). Television's rise promoted some consolidation and strategic ties among *chanchada* producers and TV studios, such as Herbert Richers's association with TV Rio in Rio de Janeiro or Maristella's partnering with TV Record in São Paulo. João Luiz Vieira remarks that the increase of television's popularity made it a "naturally" attractive medium for the *chanchada* style, themes, and stars. According to him, *chanchadas* are a hybrid drawing from several aspects of popular comedy, with origins in radio programs, the circus, and the *teatro de revista*. All of these elements were perfected in *chanchadas* and responsible for their popular appeal even as they gradually moved over to television in that period (Vieira in Ramos and Miranda 2004, 119).

In *The Cosmonauts*, the space program as a national project born from the massive scientific and financial achievements of wealthy nations is replaced by the more economical resource of an individual genius. For comedic effect, he is a distracted, forgetful scientist who makes frequent malapropisms. This plot has clear parallels with the beginnings of aviation in the work of individual entrepreneurs, and one could also mention what we would call the "Santos Dumont effect"[1] in Brazilian scientific-technological contexts: it refers to the impact of talented, pioneering individuals who innovate regardless of the lack of proper infrastructure, economic stimulus, and national policies in science and technology.

*The Cosmonauts'* initial credits explore some typical SF motifs using cartoons that depict deep space, flying saucers, and the actors Grande Otelo and Ronald Golias wearing space suits; the animations were drawn by the famous Brazilian writer and cartoonist Ziraldo. At the end of the initial credits, there is a warning: "This film shows Brazilian locations, characters acting like Brazilians, and some facts about Brazil. However, it must be stated at the very beginning that all this is nothing more than mere coincidence."[2] The ironic admonition suggests the impossibility of combining Brazilian characters and locales with science, advanced technology, and even SF, as if the presence of Brazilianness in such a genre could only be an accident. By the same token, any essential SF qualities in a Brazilian film would have to be nothing more than circumstantial, a "misplaced" apparition. Moreover, the initial admonishment somehow echoes Paulo Emílio Salles Gomes's well-known comment on the Brazilian "creative incapacity for copying" ("incompetência criativa em copiar," as put by Salles Gomes in Martin 1997, 263). The initial warning also suggests how *The Cosmonauts* stands out not only as a model in terms of Brazilian SF comedy film, but also (unwittingly, perhaps) nods at the half-hearted or uneasy relationship between Brazilian cinema and the genre film, notably SF.

*The Cosmonauts'* plot begins at "Cape Carnival," the Brazilian Space Research Center, which is made plausible by photomontage and American archival footage of NASA's Cape Canaveral in Florida. This documentary footage of NASA's rocket launch belonged to Herbert Richers's studio; using it aided the film's verisimilitude and saved money for the production company. Although there is no musical number in the film, the reference to carnivalesque imagery is made at the very beginning, literally in the name of the irreverent Brazilian space station: "Cape Carnival" ("Cabo Carnaval"). Fragments of newsreels about the American space program are interspersed with fictional footage in these initial scenes. The appropriation of American footage (in the rocket launch or the rescue of a space capsule, among others) occurs subversively throughout the film, which constantly alternates between documentary and fictional mode, intercalating not only the aforementioned documentary footage from the American space program but also images of Brazilian events and celebrations, mostly exterior shots. In its opening scenes, the film shifts from documentary footage of the launching of a space rocket to the interior of a control room (clearly in Herbert Richers's studios), where an enthusiastic reporter announces: "The space rocket Nationalist I has just been successfully launched at Cape Carnival, an event that makes Brazil the third national power in the space race."

By this point in the film, the premise of SF has already been established. Frederico, the ape cosmonaut that travels on Nationalist I, safely returns to Earth, making room for the release of Nationalist II, a two-passenger space rocket bound for the moon. A year after Yuri Gagarin became the first person to travel in outer space, and about seven years before American astronauts set foot on the moon, Brazilian cinema dreamed of planting its green and yellow flag on the gray surface of our natural satellite, leaving the superpowers behind. The film imagines other ways for Brazil to rival the superpowers: in addition to founding the Brazilian space program, Prof. Isidorius also secretly invents a "400-megaton cobalt bomb, the first of its kind, capable of destroying Rio, São Paulo and Belo Horizonte at the same time." In the words of a politician who befriends the professor, "Nothing better than a very powerful bomb to ensure an international reputation. Brazil will be feared, at last!"

In search of two cosmonauts, Prof. Isidorius turns to Zenóbio da Silva (Grande Otelo), chief of the "FBI" (Fiscalização Brasileira de Investigações—in English it translates awkwardly as "Brazilian Surveillance of Investigations"). Isidorius asks Zenóbio to find two "useless" individuals, the kind of people that nobody would miss if they did not return from the space mission. After some misadventures on the streets, Zenóbio presents two "candidates" to the professor: Zeca (Átila Iório), a gangster who runs an illegal gambling joint, and Gagarino (Ronald Golias), a clumsy vacuum cleaner salesman. Before starting his training program to become a cosmonaut, Gagarino is kept in isolation in the space center and visited by a beautiful alien (Neyde Aparecida) capable of passing through walls, turning invisible, teleporting, etc. She comes from "Korson," a planet far outside the solar system but very similar to Earth. The society inhabiting this planet is much more advanced than Earth civilizations and, therefore, peaceful. The alien asks Gagarino to persuade humans to cease expenditures on weapons, wars, bombs, and space exploration. Instead, the alien implores that nations should start investing more money in the welfare of people. The similarities of this plot to Robert Wise's *The Day the Earth Stood Still* (1951) are obvious.

However, shortly before the rocket launch, the wily Zeca manages to put Zenóbio into his place in the rocket. The mission fails, and the cosmonauts do not reach the moon. They remain in orbit around the Earth and are eventually saved by the alien. Thanks to her superpowers, and unbeknownst to the Brazilian authorities, the alien from Korson had placed the bomb in the space capsule. Following her instructions, the cosmonauts warn Prof. Isidorius that they will drop the "cobalt bomb" on one of the Earth's biggest cities if humankind does not stop its warfare and instead work to eradicate poverty, disease, hunger, and other ills.

*The Cosmonauts* makes great use of ellipsis and metonymy, as in the scene where a variety of hats floating in the air suggests a summit meeting of the UN disarmament committee. Moreover, the skillful use of archival footage stands out and gives greater versatility and verisimilitude to the narrative, regardless of its comic or ironic overtones. The documentary footage creates a sharper and more interesting contrast with the movie's fictiveness—and its imagining of utopian events based on real events (e.g., space programs) that were already in progress. Such creative alternatives were warranted by the modest budget that was typical of Brazilian film comedies in the 1940s, 1950s, and 1960s.

At the end of Victor Lima's film, the cosmonauts return triumphant as the superpowers sign a treaty to destroy their weapons and end wars while the politicians in the capital Brasília decide to make use of eight hundred billion cruzeiros to improve the lives of Brazilians instead of funding Prof. Isidorius's bombs and spaceships. When the Brazilian state decides to attend to more humane matters, abandoning "misplaced ideas" such as investments in science and technology, Prof. Isidorius is finally framed as a mere mad scientist.

Back on Earth, the cosmonauts are welcomed as heroes responsible for a new era of peace and prosperity. But the happiness is short lived, and soon the press is again reporting on rearmament and tension among the superpowers, much to the dismay of the well-meaning alien from Korson. The film ends pessimistically during a beach scene in which the alien played by Neyde Aparecida throws into the sea the radio that announces the resumption of the Cold War.

*The Cosmonauts* diegetically incorporates radio and television in a rather postmodern process of the utilitarian use of other media, such as in the comments made by the reporter who covers the events at Cape Carnival. After the release of Nationalist II, crewed by Gagarino and Zenóbio, the image of this reporter appears doubled on two TV monitors next to each other; it is an unusual metaphor for corporate media merged with merchandising since the trademark logo of Philco, a TV manufacturer, then appears on the screen. This reporter acts as an intra-diegetic narrator who always appears in time to comment on the whole space adventure, offering a continuous gloss on the situation of the heroes and the geopolitical context.

It is also worth noting the film settings in *The Cosmonauts*. In the scenes that take place in the Research Center of Cape Carnival, gadgets and other SF icons abound, like test tubes and beakers full of colored, bubbling liquids. The film uses these stereotypical images of SF whenever possible: rockets, chemical labs, computers and automatic doors seem to be in every shot even when it is absurd for them to be there. Cryogenics also appears in the film during a scene when Gagarino and Zeca are frozen to prevent them from leaving the base before the rocket launch. Once they are in space, zero gravity is also depicted, a requisite in any space adventure film, and it is conveniently abolished by the use of a "magnetic field." Regardless of the excesses in the set designs, these stereotypical props and settings and costumes are not exclusive to Latin American SF film productions. The same tropes appear in a vast number of American SF films from the 1950s.

Here, too, the film shares the zeitgeist that guided Brazilian SF in literature. David Lincoln Dunbar further studied the humor in the SF of the period (Dunbar 1976, 113), and writers such as Leon Eliachar, Guido Wilmar Sassi, Levy Menezes, Domingos Carvalho da Silva, and Nilson D. Martello also resorted to humour and irony in their SF stories to a large extent (Sassi even seems to have sought to write fiction inspired by Hollywood B movies). The treatment of technology in *The Cosmonauts* is consistent with the Brazilian tendency at the time, of distrusting what Peter Nicholls (1984, 6–7) called "extrapolative science" (such as large-scale space travel) and "imaginary science" (time travel or traveling faster than light), in favor of "new technologies" assimilated by everyday life: the vacuum cleaner, the portable radio and cars "made in Brazil." *The Cosmonauts*' uncomplicated and sometimes moralizing pacifism also finds a parallel in its contemporary works by Jerônymo Monteiro (1908–1970).

As in Carlos Manga's *The Sputnik Man* (*O Homem do Sputnik*, 1959), social and political critique provides a great deal of the fuel for comedy and parody in *The Cosmonauts*. Such criticism is embedded not only in the parody of Robert Wise's *The Day the Earth Stood Still* but also in myriad references to the Cold War or the Brazilian internal affairs and politics. The social and political critical vein, while very good-natured (as expected in any good *chanchada*), can be clearly seen in scenes such as the one in which Prof. Isidorius's political friend says: "Don't worry, professor, 'cause your funds will come. We are considering reducing the budgets of the Ministries of Health, Education, and Agriculture in order to raise money for your bombs and rockets." The film sees a direct connection between scientific/technological development and warfare. Another example is when Gagarino warns the world that he will drop Isidorius's cobalt bomb on an unspecified major city on Earth if national governments do not stop making war, and Zenóbio, who wants to redistribute money set aside for war and scientific research, eventually adds: "That's it! Let's get over with the shantytowns, the diseases, the wars, the money for the wars and space rockets, OK?" Even the Brazilian *malandragem* is criticized to some extent, as in the sequence when Zéca is caught stealing money from Isidorius's vault but manages to escape by scattering some of the cash so that his captors are distracted trying to pick up the money. But the scene that best synthesizes the bitter political criticism, recalling *The Sputnik Man*, is also one of the funniest parts in the film, when Brasilia contacts Washington, which in turn contacts Moscow, which in turn contacts Havana, resulting in an agreement to stop the Cold War. The call to Havana interrupts a "paredón" (an execution), in a scene that nods to the film's disapproval of Castro's regime. A film review from 1962 in *O Estado de São Paulo*[3] highlighted "the manner in which three global political figures are dealt with (Kennedy, Khrushchev, and Castro) alongside the simplistic or naïve message related to the need for a world without wars." Commenting on *The Cosmonauts* against the backdrop of the recent Cuban missile crisis, the same critic remarks that "a fortunate coincidence has transformed a mediocre feature into the most relevant work of film concerning a problem which has frightened the entire world this past week" (Arquivo Cinemateca Brasileira 1962).

Notwithstanding, the critic concludes by grouping *The Cosmonauts* with the bulk of well-known *chanchadas* in that "the film does not escape the lowest kind of humor adopted for this genre by the Brazilian cinema: it has a good technical execution, reasonably fluid directing, wasted acting talent and, essentially, a lack of ambition" (Arquivo Cinemateca Brasileira 1962). Something similar was written by the Brazilian film critic Pedro Lima, who begins by pointing out a certain intention on Herbert Richers's part to rehabilitate the *chanchada*. Nevertheless, Lima finishes by severely criticizing *The Cosmonauts*, notably because of alleged flaws in editing, direction, and acting, among other aspects (Lima, 1962). In a nutshell, the film garnered mixed reviews, but today it is a subject of renewed interest: a document of its era.

Making a parallel overview with literature, Roberto de Sousa Causo once commented that *The Cosmonauts* has something of the spirit of the First Wave of Brazilian SF, especially in its preoccupation with the Cold War and in its ambivalence about the modernization of the country. Causo also claims that, like American sci-fi comedies (e.g., *Abbott and Costello Meet Frankenstein,* 1948, or *The Three Stooges in Orbit,* 1962), *The Cosmonauts* is a satire of science fiction B movies that cleverly uses the visual language of those genre films—as opposed to what *The Goofs* (Os Trapalhões),[4] for instance, would do fifteen or twenty years later. *The Cosmonauts* appears during a time when the appealing modernization of President Juscelino Kubitscheck's era was about to be replaced by the more threatening model of reactionary modernization espoused by the military dictatorship. Along with the laboratory, rockets, and space capsules, other technologies presented in the film are more personal and domestic in nature: TVs, battery-operated radios, vacuum cleaners, and the Gordini car in which Gagarino and his girlfriend leave for the beach are depicted in ambivalent tones. *The Cosmonauts* is thus a rare example of comedy in which SF has a truly creative role, or at least competes on an equal level with comedy. In fact, *The Cosmonauts* demonstrates fluent ease and expressive capacity for the conventions of SF that would not be seen very often, either before or after its release, in any other Brazilian comedy of its kind. Victor Lima's film might have yielded more fruit in terms of a fortuitous pairing of SF with comedy in Brazilian cinema, but no other films rose to inherit its mantle. Both *The Cosmonauts* and *The 5th Power,* which we will discuss next, mapped out two very different possible routes for the blossoming of SF in Brazilian cinema.

## A Country Under Siege

Alberto Pieralisi's *The 5th Power* (*O 5o Poder*, 1963), produced and written by Carlos Pedregal, is one of the most original Brazilian SF films ever made. Produced in 1962, the film premiered in Brazil on June 29, 1963. Its plot focuses on an international intrigue revolving around the threat of subliminal technology. Famous for his comedies and one of the most successful directors in Brazil in the 1970s, Italian filmmaker Alberto Pieralisi had worked in the European studios of Cines and Cinecittà before coming to Brazil in the 1950s to work at Vera Cruz Studios (Cia. Cinematográfica Vera Cruz). Before focusing on *The 5th Power*, however, it is worth remembering its context, and part of the history of his mastermind, the writer and producer Carlos Pedregal.

*The 5th Power* capitalizes on discussions about subliminal technology, a subject already theorized about for centuries. The issue gained new momentum in the late 1950s with the popularization of television and the advertising industry's increasing social and political influence. The famous experiment with Joshua Logan's film *Picnic* (1955) in 1957 spurred debates over subliminal technology and also led to hoaxes and conspiracy theories. In this allegedly scientific experiment, which was held in a movie theater over six weeks in Fort Lee, New Jersey, American "motivation researcher" James M. Vicary tested subliminal messaging on over forty-five thousand moviegoers. Using a special device he called "tachistoscope" to project text on the film screen, Vicary claimed to have inserted the following two sentences throughout the projection of Logan's *Picnic*: "Drink Coke" and "Eat Popcorn." The messages were flashed on the screen (often on the faces of *Picnic*'s actors, William Holden and Kim Novak) for three thousandths of a second and displayed once every 5 seconds, or 12 times per minute. The spectators did not perceive any of the sentences hidden in the film but, according to Vicary, sales of Coke and popcorn increased 57.5 percent and 18.1 percent, respectively. Vicary's experiment was covered in *The Billboard* on September 16, 1957. On its front page, the magazine then announced the possibilities of "the new invisible commercial ad," also reporting that a major ad agency, J. Walter Thompson, was circulating a memo discussing the applications of subliminal propaganda in TV campaigns. In the same article, Vicary's experiment is compared to "something out of Orwell's *1984*. Without even being aware of it, viewers begin to be dimly aware of a thirst—and a buy-impulse—for Coca-Cola" (1957, 1).

Eventually, Vicary applied for patents related to his gadget and founded a firm: Subliminal Projection Company, Inc. The article also mentions that the technique was long known to psychologists but, with the advent of television, major companies had an entirely new interest in using the technology: "One TV test of the process has already been made, using the BBC TV in England. No commercials were involved, however, and the test was a purely psychological experiment" (1957, 13).

Reports like this had an influence on many articles and books on the subject for years afterward (e.g., in Brazil, see Calazans 1992). Nevertheless, the circumstances surrounding the experiment have always been murky. The dates of its performance were never confirmed, and accounts of the event varied. Summoned by the Federal Communications Commission to hold a public demonstration, Vicary obtained no conclusive results (see Roque 2018). But by then it was too late and the experiment was already influential: the theory of subliminal messaging was by far more seductive than the factual data that could not confirm it.

According to Daniel Roque (2018), the first rumors about the insertion of hidden messages in movie screenings appeared in Brazil already on June 11, 1956. An AFP (Agence France-Presse) note reproduced by the Rio de Janeiro's newspaper *Tribuna da Imprensa* announced the "birth of invisible advertising" in the United States. According to the article, the technique of subliminal messaging had given an unidentified ice cream brand a 60 percent increase in sales of its products. The possibilities and implications of the technique were discussed at a round table organized by the Brazilian Advertising Association (ABP, Associação Brasileira de Propaganda) at its headquarters in Rio de Janeiro on April 11, 1958 (Roque 2018). The public debate over the phenomenon spread quickly and had been addressed by a number of newspapers already by 1958.

Around the same time, the celebrated British author Aldous Huxley was visiting Brazil and, in August 1958, at a large public gathering hosted by the Itamaraty Palace in Rio, the writer expressed his fear that subliminal messages could serve a dark agenda: "The enslavement of humanity can be done through the brainwashing him into loving slavery. The state will rule man until it dominates his subconscious. Subliminal advertising is just the first step" (Huxley qtd. in Roque 2018). Huxley exposed his concerns more than twenty years after the publication of *Brave New World* at a time when he was about to publish a collection of essays on democracy, totalitarianism, political propaganda, and mind control. Under the title of *Brave New World Revisited*, this book's essays offer a panorama of the most discussed conflict of the time: psychological warfare, in which the implementation of ideologies would equal territorial disputes and conventional warfare. Huxley's *Brave New World Revisited*, which had just been translated into Portuguese in 1959, looked prophetic in Brazil at the time.

Today, however, subliminal technology does not seem as incredible or frightening as it once did to the public. Recent research indicates that subliminal images can be formed in the visual cortex, but they end up dissipating in the brain shortly after, thus having no actual efficacy. Vicary's experiment was never replicated with the same alleged findings, whereas several experiments with results published in respectable journals either contradicted or relativized Vicary's alleged findings and overall assumptions (see Karremans et al. 2006; Smith and Rogers 1994; Vokey and Read 1985).

Nevertheless, Jim Vicary's late 1950s experiment had a strong influence on Carlos Pedregal, writer and producer of *The 5th Power*, who was a unique personality in the Brazilian media landscape. The man who eventually introduced subliminal advertising to Brazil, Pedregal was twenty-one years old when he first arrived in the country, coming from Argentina. As told by Roque (2018), Pedregal carried a temporary visa issued in July 1947 by the Consulate General of Brazil in Buenos Aires. His papers claimed he was a single Spaniard traveling as a journalist. This description of him would substantially change over the next decade, when Pedregal went by the name of Professor Baskarán, "world-renowned hypnotist and psychologist." Dressed in clothing that suggested a Hindu guru, he practiced palmistry in Copacabana nightclubs, sitting at the guests' tables while performing "psychological tests" on them. In interviews, Baskarán claimed to have been born in the Chinese city of Nanjing and to have led an adventurous life around the world. His experiments, he said, had already been carried out in every country "except the US and part of Australia" (Roque 2018).

In April 1951, Pedregal premiered his own radio show on Rádio Globo: *Revelations of the Subconscious* (*Revelações do Subsciente*) was broadcast Monday through Friday at 9:30 a.m. On and off the show, Prof. Baskarán lectured on graphology and body language, counseled his listeners, and wrote advice columns in different publications where he answered letters from people in all kinds of trouble. He also detailed psychological profiles of famous people: artists, socialites, athletes, famous criminals, and especially politicians. At a certain point Pedregal/Baskarán met the famous Brazilian politician Adhemar de Barros and became his political advisor.

Having conquered radio and newspapers, soon Baskarán carved out a space in television. His first television experiments took place in October 1951 on *Experimental Psychology* (*Psicologia Experimental*), which aired on Tuesdays on TV Tupi. The show, which consisted of brief video sessions of hypnotism, was claimed to have caused deep sleep in hundreds of spectators.

In June 1958, when controversies about subliminal messages reached their peak, Carlos Pedregal dropped the name Professor Baskarán and returned to TV Tupi to present a new show that aired on Friday nights: *The Boldest Experiment of the Century* (*A Mais Arrojada Experiência do Século*). Over the next three months, he conducted a series of experiments on the unconscious reception of visual and sound stimuli in TV Tupi's studios. But what Pedregal truly intended with *The Boldest Experiment* was to re-create Vicary's experiment with his TV audience, perhaps in the spirit of Orson Welles and the Mercury Theater's famous 1938 radio show *War of the Worlds*. According to Pedregal, his TV show featured the first subliminal experiment broadcast to a large audience and potentially affected a huge number of spectators in Rio de Janeiro, a city with approximately 3 million people at the time.

In December 1961, Pedregal announced that he was working on the script for a movie called *Subliminal, Secret Weapon* (*Subliminar, Arma Secreta*). Originally conceived as a documentary, the film ended up funded by the National Bank of Minas Gerais (Banco Nacional de Minas Gerais) and turned out to be a fiction film starring well-known actors. The film's title was changed to *The 5th Power*. Alberto Pieralisi was invited to direct the film, and actors Eva Wilma, Oswaldo Loureiro, Sebastião Vasconcelos, Augusto César Vannucci, and Orlando Villar headed the cast. It was a tumultuous production that was drawn out by numerous problems: "What could be done in five months dragged on for almost a year and a half," vented Pedregal to *Intervalo*, the extinct gossip magazine published by Editora Abril (Roque 2018). Pedregal and Pieralisi reportedly quarreled during the shooting of *The 5th Power*. As remarked by Roque (2018), the Italian-born director set the film at a slow pace, with an emphasis on acting and dialogue, but Pedregal wanted a faster pace with gunfights, car chases, and body combat. Pieralisi considered leaving the film, but Eva Wilma refused to be directed by anyone else. The team came to an agreement: Pieralisi would be in charge of the scenes starring the actress while Pedregal would work as an uncredited director on everything else.

According to Roque (2018), the constant delays and re-shootings made *The 5th Power* the most expensive film ever produced in Brazil. On the eve of its commercial debut, the film's negatives and most of its copies were accidentally destroyed in a fire at Herbert Richers's studios in Rio. Four people died in the incident, including an employee of Herbert Richers, the film's distribution company.

*The 5th Power*'s opening title sequence projects a documentary approach, as if the film were an announcement about the threat of subliminal control. It is a fitting beginning for a film that was originally envisioned as a documentary by Pedregal. The plot, however, unfolds as follows: undercover foreign agents scheme to control the Brazilian people through subliminal messages transmitted by planting devices that hijack radio and TV signals. Their mission is part of an international plot to seize Brazilian natural resources. These agents begin broadcasting the subliminal signals and chaos ensues, with street riots multiplying all over Rio de Janeiro. Brazilians start clamoring for a revolution. Seen today, *The 5th Power* seems uncannily prescient of Brazil's infamous military coup d'état in 1964.

In a remarkable scene, the aerial tram on Sugar Loaf (Pão de Açúcar) is the scene for a thrilling fight involving the hero and one of the villains. It forecasts the best action sequences in later James Bond films. Possibly inspired by Alfred Hitchcock's, Orson Welles's, and Fritz Lang's works, the film's dénouement is set on Corcovado, with magnificent shots of Rio's statue of Christ the Redeemer, one of the most famous Brazilian landmarks. To some extent, especially in the use of local landmarks as background for an SF story, *The 5th Power* also recalls films such as René Clair's *Paris Qui Dort* (1923), which features the Eiffel Tower in key scenes, or Merian Cooper and Ernest Schoedsack's *King Kong* (1933), whose final scenes are set in Manhattan. In addition, *The 5th Power* inhabits a genre skillfully explored by Austrian director Fritz Lang: the techno spy film. A review published in the newspaper *O Estado de S. Paulo* praised Pieralisi's film, and underscored: "The suspenseful, thrilling atmosphere [that] recalls science fiction works by William Cameron Menzies and Edgar G. Ulmer. Rio de Janeiro has never been featured so beautifully in the cinema."[5]

It is improbable that Pedregal devised *The 5th Power* as an SF film from the very beginning of the project. At least there are no available documents that suggest this to be true. And, as explained above, his original intention was to make a documentary film on subliminal messaging.

But, as noted, critics at the time did see similarities between *The 5th Power* and its contemporary SF cinema. Furthermore, Pedregal himself had already made a live performance and TV career by capitalizing on the ideas of popular science. His alias, Prof. Baskarán, created mass entertainment using popular science, no matter how thin or controversial the research behind it was, and it is also in this vein that *The 5th Power* should be seen as an SF film. As put by Oliver Gaycken in his study of common features in both popular science films and crime melodramas in the 1910s (e.g., Louis Feuillade's *Fantômas* and *Les Vampires*), "popular science dramatizes technical progress, providing a space for imagining its dark side, the dystopian imaginary, modern life's haunting double, the "terrors of technology" (Gaycken 2015, 188). Also according to Gaycken, "*Fantômas* and *Les Vampires* contain marked similarities to popular science films, both stylistically and in terms of their obsession with registering the impact of science and technology on modern life" (2015, 188). Years later, Pieralisi's *The 5th Power* could also be seen as a film that draws on similar fears about modernity and technology while sharing some of the educational characteristics of popular science films, such as those studied by Gaycken. As a huge popular science figure in radio, TV, and newspapers, Pedregal likely conceived his feature film along the same lines, as a work that spread scientific ideas. This background has been virtually ignored and overlooked by film scholars and historians and only partly noticed by film critics during Pieralisi's time. Likely, this is why *The 5th Power* has never been recognized as a relevant Brazilian SF film. According to more recent film scholarship, in *The 5th Power* Alberto Pieralisi brought to this "Hitchcock-style spy movie" his straightforward approach and fast-paced découpage (Ramos and Miranda 2004, 428). This typical interpretation ignores both the history of the production of *The 5th Power* and genre film studies, as contemporary scholars tend to haphazardly reproduce secondhand glosses of the film and interpret it only as a minor Hitchcock imitation.

*The 5th Power* was an ideologically ambiguous film that invites multiple interpretations. For example, the nationalities of the international conspirators are never revealed. This ambiguity divided the critics, some of whom saw either anticommunist propaganda or anti-imperialist nuances in the film. Were the villains in line with the American or the Soviet bloc? Would the popular revolution be a leftist or right-wing project? The film plot does not answer these questions with any certainty. As an example of the anticommunist reading, Benedito Junqueira Duarte's review on the newspaper *Folha de S. Paulo* claimed that the film's warnings about the communist (*sic*) menace had come at a timely moment, just when Brazil was poised "on the brink of the deepest leftist abyss (. . .)."⁶

However, it makes much more sense to interpret the film as a speculative fiction about American imperialism. The foreign invaders speak mostly English, Portuguese, and some German. In a quite intriguing scene, during a meeting in their clandestine headquarters, the apparent leader instructs the group to speak only Portuguese from that point forward. He adds that German may be used as second language but never, under any circumstances, should they speak their native language (English?). The leader insists that their true "nationality must absolutely remain top secret." So, since all their names, or codenames, sound Anglo-Saxon (e.g., Frank, Peter, etc.), and the leader instructs them to speak only Portuguese and, occasionally, German, in order to keep their native tongue a secret, it might be reasonable to assume that the whole group consists of English native speakers. To see those agents as Soviet spies, or simply as representatives of a "red peril" demands some credulity and a rather clumsy rationale. It is a clearer cut to see the spies as Anglo-Saxon invaders or as representatives of some Western imperialist power.

Political differences aside, the criticism contemporary with the film was unanimous in pointing out *The 5th Power* as a strange body in the Brazilian cultural scene. The film was not in tune with the *chanchadas* nor with the intellectual engagement and aesthetic ambitions of the then-ascendant Cinema Novo. Along with Joaquim Pedro de Andrade's documentary film Garrincha, Joy of the People (*Garrincha, Alegria do Povo*), *The 5th Power* was selected to represent Brazil in the noncompetitive exhibition of the Berlin Festival in 1963. Poor distribution, however, made the movie a box-office failure. Despite its poor earnings, *The 5th Power* won some prizes in Brazil: the "Saci" for Best Edit given to Ismar Porto (SP, 1964), the "Governor of the State of São Paulo" for Best Screenplay to Carlos Pedregal (SP, 1964), and the 5th Prize of Cinema Prizes from the Fourth Centenary (RJ, 1965) (Silva Neto 2002, 685). Less than a year after the release of *The 5th Power*, the Brazilian army carried out the *coup* that established the military rule in the country.

*The 5th Power*'s anticipation of national events does not end there. On May 1, 1964, a month after the fall of João Goulart, Petrobras officials and technicians were accused by the DOPS (Department of Political and Social Order) to have turned the state-owned oil company into a communist cell and its official house organ into a "subversive advertising vehicle through subliminal messaging." About fifty years later, in 2016, Petrobras would once be again under the spotlight, accused by the media and conservatives of having been raided and ruled by "reds," "corrupt socialists." Marx was maybe partially right when he said that history repeats itself, first as tragedy, then as farce (2006). Sometimes it keeps repeating itself, endlessly, as a degrading form of miserable, tragicomic pastiche.

Restored, *The 5th Power* was given a special session at the Brasilia Film Festival (Festival de Cinema de Brasília) in 2006. To the moviegoers who attended the event, Pedregal explained that during the Cold War he had been harassed by spies interested in buying the rights to the film in order to screen it for the intelligence services of their respective countries (Oricchio 2006). It was the last public appearance of "the wizard" before his death due to lung cancer. The Brazilian film critic Luiz Zanin Oricchio attended the session in Brasília and published a report on his blog, in which he highlights some of the same features and virtues of *The 5th Power* already spotted by film critics in the early 1960s.

*The 5th Power* does seem premonitory of the 1964 military coup d'état in Brazil, but the film remains relevant today for a couple of other reasons. First, there is the undeniably brilliant way it handles the trope of a foreign, "alien" invasion, which constitutes a whole subgenre in SF: the city-under-siege story. Following *The 5th Power*, Hugo Santiago's *Invasión* (1969), a film prophetic of the military coup in Argentina, featured a similar plot. Based on a story by Jorge Luis Borges, with a script written by Borges, Adolfo Bioy-Casares, and Hugo Santiago, *Invasión* features a group of resistance fighters in the fictional city of Aquilea, which has been gradually invaded by mysterious foreign agents. More recently, in 2019, Juliano Dornelles and Kléber Mendonça Filhos's *Bacurau* (2019) revisits a similar kind of speculation on foreign invaders attacking a remote inland Brazilian town. It is worth comparing similar scenes, in both *Bacurau* and *The 5th Power*, in which the foreign invaders sit around a table in order to discuss their respective strategies. And the series of coincidences or premonitory insights in *The 5th Power* only become more interesting because Pedregal himself was often a significant behind-the-scenes player in Brazilian politics from the 1950s onward. See, for instance, Jânio de Freitas's article on the onset of the coup in 1964 (2004), published fifty years after the incident, in which Pedregal is mentioned.

The second reason for *The 5th Power*'s relevance lies in its very approach to media technology and the manipulation of popular mobilization. Even if subliminal technology did not stir up a revolution in

Brazil, it is a perfect stand-in for newer trends and technologies. It is undeniable that the proliferation of fake news and the presence of bots on social networks and communication platforms such as Facebook and WhatsApp played a significant role in the 2018 presidential run in Brazil. The national media discourse was warped by a variety of techniques based on constant replication and exponential multiplication of fake news that revived fascist sentiments and fears of a "communist threat."[7]

An allegory of the recurrent sociopolitical instability in Brazilian history, *The 5th Power* deserves to be remembered and further studied as one of the most memorable achievements in Brazilian SF cinema.

3

# Brazil, Love It or Leave It — for the Stars

## SF Film during the Era of the Military Hardliners (1969–1973)

The cinematic/audiovisual memory of the Brazilian military dictatorship (1964–1985) has been the subject of a variety of recent research, such as José (2007); Gutfreind, Stigger and Carmona (2011); Simis (2015); Leme (2012, 2016); and Morettin and Napolitano (2018). For instance, Caroline Gomes Leme (2012) investigated the dramatization of torture and references to the military coup in Brazilian fiction films produced in the wake of Brazil's redemocratization. The films analyzed by Leme are mostly realistic-naturalistic fiction films, with characters either totally or partially mirroring real people who did live under the military regime, suffered torture, and/or were murdered by the state. Along the following lines, I will offer a somewhat similar survey but with a focus on Brazilian SF cinema. Is it possible to confront the 1964 coup and the military dictatorship at the fictional "extremes" of Brazilian cinema—that is, SF and fantasy films? If so, how did Brazilian speculative fiction films engender such discourses of criticism and confrontation? To proceed with this investigation, I initially suggest "time travel" back to the 1960s, a remarkable period in the history of Brazil, the world, and the SF film genre. According to Phil Hardy (1995, 196), the 1960s were the decade in which SF cinema not only became a respectable film genre but, perhaps most importantly, also went global. This attracted the interest of film directors worldwide, who often used SF as a "test tube" for both cinematic experimentation and political criticism (Hardy 1995, 196).

In October 1962, the international incident known as the Cuban missile crisis occurred, one of the most nail-biting episodes in the Cold War era. The crisis began when the Soviets set up nuclear missile bases in Cuba, in retaliation for the American invasion of that country in 1961 and for the installation of American nuclear missiles in Turkey in the same year. On October 28, 1962, thirteen days after it started, the crisis came to an end, with Nikita Khrushchev agreeing to remove the Soviet missiles from Cuba, after the withdrawal of the American warheads from Turkey. As seen in our last chapter, in that same year SF appeared in Brazilian cinema in two isolated and sensibly different experiences that, unfortunately, did not yield much offspring: Alberto Pieralisi's *The 5th Power*, and Victor Lima's *The Cosmonauts*. Released at a time that coincides with the pinnacle of the Cold War, these two film productions represent, respectively, two basic trends or models in the Brazilian SF cinema: the "serious" film based on the conventional plot structure and performances of the action-adventure movie (thriller or drama) and the SF comedy, often revolving around parody and a carnivalesque approach to both Brazilian and world cinemas, in a contagious laugh at the future and the peculiarities of SF film as a well-established genre.[1] The *5th Power* and *The Cosmonauts* both premiered about two years prior to the 1964 military coup. Each of these films, in its own way, appears to elaborate on the symptoms of a Brazilian society on the verge of radical transformation for the worse. Toward the end of the 1960s, some Brazilian film directors did venture into SF cinema in order to take advantage of this genre's symbolism and potential to convey "encrypted messages" at times of widespread, brutal repression, and censorship (notably from 1968 onward).

On April 1, 1964, a civil-military coup ended the government of democratically elected president João Goulart. About four years later, a "coup within the coup" was engendered and put forth by the military hardliners. It was based on a series of political measures, the most notable one being the Institutional Act No. 5 (Ato Institucional n. 5), or simply AI-5, for short. This was an act issued on December 13, 1968, under the presidency of General Costa e Silva. The AI-5 was in effect until December 1978. In the meantime (about ten years, from 1968 through 1978), the AI-5 favored a tsunami of authoritarianism and crimes committed by the state against human rights and Brazilian democracy.

Written by Zelito Viana, Luís Carlos Maciel, and Eduardo Coutinho, *The Man Who Bought the World* (*O Homem que Comprou o Mundo*, 1968), directed by Eduardo Coutinho, begins with opening credits situating the drama in a country named "Reserva 17." After leaving his fiancée Rosinha (Marília Pêra) at home, the ordinary man called José Guerra (Flávio Migliaccio) witnesses a couple of motorcyclists attacking an apparently exotic man who wears a turban. Speaking in an unintelligible language, this "Hindu" gives José Guerra a check of "100,000 strikmas" just before he dies. The hero tries to cash the check, but a bank's "supercomputer" crashes when trying to convert the amount into Brazilian currency. An alarm is triggered, and José Guerra receives an arrest warrant for national security reasons. Professor Bagdá Pompéia (Abel Pêra), the author of a monograph on the strikmas, is then summoned to explain the value of such a strange currency. According to the professor: "The Strikmas are coins minted by Pharaoh Ramses II in Ancient Egypt, in the year 1219 BC, by the laparotomy process." After having to listen to a tedious lecture on the subject, the authorities finally find out the value of a strikma, which would be made of "raw gold," a metal so rare that it would only be found in the strikmas themselves. Each strikma would be worth a hundred million dollars and would be "the size of a Fenemê [car] tire." Therefore, a hundred thousand strikmas would be worth a hundred trillion dollars.

Coveting José Guerra's fortune, Reserva 17's authorities decide to overprotect the now trillionaire ordinary man by holding him captive in a fortress. After all, as a citizen of Reserva 17, José Guerra has made his country the richest nation in the world. The authorities celebrate the new economic power of Reserva 17. They are planning to put an end to "illiteracy, malaria, hunger, the flu, and dishonesty" but also to rule out "the class struggle, the tropical weather, the Cinema Novo, and the cordel literature."[2] Reserva 17 is an allegory of Brazil, while the "Anterior Power" or "Former Power" (P.A.) is equivalent to the United States, and the "Posterior Power" or "Next Power" (P.P.) to the Soviet Union. Other denominations, such as "Neutral Country" ("País Neutro"), or "The Union of the Neutral Banks" ("União dos Bancos Neutros"), also contribute to the caricature of a Cartesian, positivistic atmosphere of dystopian SF. The Kafkaesque features of *The Man Who Bought the World* are suggested not only by the names of the countries but also by the way the authorities treat José Guerra and keep him under constant surveillance. The intellectual characters in the film, its eccentricities including peculiar jargon and elaborate lines bordering complete nonsense, seem to beckon with a critique of the Brazilian academia or *intelligentsia*.

Still in 1968, Rogério Sganzerla's *The Red Light Bandit* (*O Bandido da Luz Vermelha*) also drags SF iconography into its experimental whirlwind of genres. This film is emblematic of the Brazilian film movement known as Cinema Marginal. It was loosely inspired by the biography of a murderer named João Acácio Pereira da Costa, known as the "Red Light Bandit." This man was set free in 1997, after thirty years in jail, ending up murdered just a few months after his release. In Sganzerla's film, the Red Light Bandit is Jorge (Paulo Villaça), a skilled robber who carries a red lantern during his crimes and has sex with his victims, mostly attractive rich women. The bandit lives by escaping from the police, but his romance with his criminal partner, Janete Jane (Helena Ignez), his involvement with the populist politician J. B. (Pagano Sobrinho), and his problems with the criminal organization "Dark Hand" ("Mão Negra") eventually push him to death.

All the way through Jorge's fictional journey, the possibility of alien contact or even invasion hangs in the air, regularly reported by the press that, in addition to comments on the actions of the Red Light Bandit (often referred to simply as "Light" by other characters), also accompanies the appearances of the feared flying saucer. As Ismail Xavier observes, "To make things even more bizarre, the fragmentation of diegetic actions is juxtaposed with strange images of flying saucers and planetary battles borrowed from a TV science fiction serial. The images of flying saucers often flash as the supposed chase pursues its 'normal' course" (1997, 98). The flying saucer "character" produces a twofold meaning throughout the whole film, both when it appears onscreen—a clear reference to 1950s American B-movies—and is referred to offscreen by voice-over narrators. It is a disruptive factor (Xavier 1993, 98) that interferes in the order of the representation/narration, thus imposing an increasingly central relevance as the epitome of the external menace that constantly permeates the film. The UFO also clearly symbolizes American imperialism and the subjugation of so-called Third World countries, insofar as it literally blows out the fictional world inhabited by the Red Light Bandit.

Sganzerla's film parodically references, among other works and genres, the famous broadcast of H. G. Wells's *The War of the Worlds* by Orson Welles and the Mercury Theater in 1938. The flying saucer as a sign of dreary politics or out-of-order social reality appears in Brazilian literary utopias and dystopias between 1972 and 1982, books that further explored SF elements, such as Dolabela Chagas's *Miss Ferrovia 1999* (1982), a novella that denounces the spurious relationship between the government and greedy contractors, and Márcio Souza's *A Ordem do Dia* (1982), a novel that satirizes the authoritarianism of the military regime.

In *The Red Light Bandit*, the rupture of the established order symbolized by the UFO may suggest the structural weaknesses of the regime and the possibility of its ending. This interpretation extrapolates the idea of the flying saucer as a simple metaphor for the diverting, alienating powers of the mass media. Moreover, Sganzerla's film is perhaps the quintessence of the Brazilian cinema's parodic attitude toward SF and other allegedly foreign genres, something summarized in lines such as this one from the Red Light Bandit himself: "When you can't do anything, you mock."[3] This irreverent stance, which had already appeared in some previous Brazilian films with SF motifs, will find fertile ground in several later films.

While dystopian geopolitics and supercomputers appeared in Coutinho's *The Man Who Bought the World* and a UFO was added to the thrills in Sganzerla's *The Red Light Bandit*, one of the first robots in Brazilian SF cinema can be found in Olney São Paulo's *Grayish Morning* (*Manhã Cinzenta*), an iconic 1969 short film sometimes identified with both the Brazilian Cinema Novo and the Cinema Marginal. *Grayish Morning* somehow anticipates Peter Watkins's feature film *Punishment Park* (1971) in its dramatic account of young rebels captured and tortured by an authoritarian government's police force. Made between 1968 and 1969, and based on the homonymous short story by Olney São Paulo written in 1966, *Grayish Morning* is about the misfortune of a couple of university students who go on a march in which the young man, a political activist, leads the rally. The peripatetic narrative employs temporal leaps and incorporates archival footage in the *cinéma-vérité* style, thus prompting a general effect of discursive overlap of several topics related to the military dictatorship, intolerance, repression, and widespread censorship. The "narrative allegorically and directly reflects the post-war geopolitics being updated symbolically for the local situation" (Novaes 2011, 68). The political activism of the university's youth stands out as a sign of hope, despite their martyrdom (e.g., the character Alda, who is executed toward the end of the film), and the female nudity can also be seen as a symbol of freedom. The clash between different discourses and vantage points in the film stresses the opposition between the dissidents' ideals and the establishment's moral rhetoric about family values and children representing the future of the nation.

In *Grayish Morning*, the aforementioned couple is detained during the march and tortured in prison. They are sent to court and submitted to an absurd trial presided by a robot and an "electronic brain." This scene serves to illustrate the frequent affiliation of SF iconography in Brazilian film and literature to dictatorship and totalitarianism in the period (the 1960s and 1970s)—as if there was a chain reaction connecting the highly industrialized modernity and foreignness of SF to authoritarian governments. The electronic brain in *Grayish Morning* demands the censoring of the image of a woman with her breasts exposed, an order that echoes a number of other Brazilian SF texts in which almighty computers manage human sexuality (and reproduction), such as in André Carneiro's short story "The Perfect Marriage" ("O Casamento Perfeito," 1966), and his novels *Free Swimming Pool* (*Piscina Livre*, 1980) and *Amorquia* (1991), Floro Freitas Andrade's novel *Terminal Game* (*Jogo Terminal*, 1988), Paulo de Sousa Ramos's *The Other Side of the Protocol* (*O Outro Lado do Protocolo*, 1985), and Walmir Ayala's *The New Terra* (*A Nova Terra*, 2012, a posthumous publication).

*Grayish Morning* was shot in 16mm by Fernando Coni Campos and Olney São Paulo himself. The film also incorporates archival footage about street demonstrations, cinematographed by José Carlos Avellar. In an attempt to better circulate the film, Olney made several copies of *Grayish Morning* and sent them to various cinematheques and film festivals overseas.

On October 8, 1969, the first hijacking of a Brazilian airplane took place, carried out by members of the MR-8 organization, a rebel group that fought the military dictatorship. At that moment, Olney São Paulo's cinema and life took an unexpected turn. While the plane was diverted to Cuba, one of the hijackers, a member of the board of the Federation of Rio de Janeiro's Film Clubs (Federação Carioca de Cineclubistas), screened a copy of *Grayish Morning* on board. Olney was then somehow linked to the hijacking by the authorities, for the mere fact his movie would have been screened on board the aircraft. He was arrested and sent to an unknown location where he was tortured, remaining incommunicado for twelve days. Finally released, both mentally and physically exhausted, the filmmaker would later be saluted as a martyr for the Brazilian arts during the military rule.

The negatives and copies of *Grayish Morning* were confiscated by the military government, but one of the copies was saved by Cosme Alves Neto, then director of the Cinematheque of the Museum of Modern Art in Rio de Janeiro (Cinemateca do MAM). This salvaged copy stayed in the film archives of MAM for more than twenty-five years (Santos 2011). Olney's original project for *Grayish Morning* was to use it as part of a feature film containing three stories. Two episodes would be added: a comedy, and a segment in the cinéma-vérité genre. "However, with the apprehension of *Manhã Cinzenta* and the censorship, the project was abandoned by Olney, leaving only an independent film which had never been officially released in Brazil, but had a lot of repercussions in other countries" (Santos 2013, 36).[4] Another paradox concerning Olney's film is the uncensored reception of the short story/screenplay, written in 1966 and published in the same year as the film (1969). This event served as a response to the censorship of the film, with the short story/screenplay being published with no restrictions (Novaes and Reis 2011, 4).

Although banned in Brazil by federal censorship, the film was screened in Italy, at the Pesaro Film Festival, at the Viña del Mar International Film Festival, and at the Cannes Film Festival Fortnight in 1970. It also participated in the XIX International Week of Mannheim, winning the award for Best Medium-length Film. *Grayish Morning* also received an award at the Oberhausen Film Festival in Germany, 1972.

Films like *Grayish Morning* appear to have spearheaded a strategy for Brazilian SF cinema in the 1970s and 1980s: the genre as a useful "code" for artistic and political expression under the tight grip of military rule. According to Claudio C. Novaes, "The artists articulated several strategies to divert their works from the censor's cut, sometimes transforming them into a narrative of direct confrontation with the system and thus running the risk of total interdiction, other times with the strategy of criticism in the form of allegory, as is the case of [Brazilian] fantastic literature and post-Cinema Novo allegorical cinema from the late 1960s through the 1970s" (Novaes 2011, 59). Such a strategy—the subtle use of SF for sociopolitical comment—is to some extent analogous to developments in American cinema in the 1950s and 1960s. According to Thomas D. Clareson, during McCarthyism, SF was the only literary form that could criticize government policies, as politicians either were not aware of or interested in the genre or could not understand the deeper meaning of the stories (Clareson 1971, 22). Mutatis mutandis, a quite similar scenario could be applicable to Brazil under military rule. Olney São Paulo's short story "Grayish Morning," was published uncensored, whereas his homonymous film was censored and banished in 1969 (due to the fact it would have been screened by a rebel group): this might confirm Clareson's argument also in the Brazilian political scenario.

In addition to *Grayish Morning*, a 1969 Brazilian feature film directed by Walter Lima Jr. seems to resort to a similar strategy. *Brazil Year 2000* (*Brasil Ano 2000*) features a futuristic Brazil, still ruled by the military after the "Great Nuclear War of 1989" that devastated the northern hemisphere.

As Ismail Xavier suggests in his book *Allegories of Underdevelopment* (1997, first published in Brazil as *Alegorias do Subdesenvolvimento*, 1993),[5] it is worth comparing Lima Jr.'s *Brazil Year 2000* to Sganzerla's *The Red Light Bandit* insofar as, despite the differences between their respective narrative styles, both address a similar theme; and the story of the former appears to start where the latter's plot ends (that is, with the atomic explosion).[6] According to Ismail Xavier,

> *Brazil Year 2000* (*Brasil Ano 2000*, 1969), made by Walter Lima Jr., uses a postnuclear parable to discuss the relationship between national identity and modernization: The developed nations destroyed themselves and have left the planet to the underdeveloped, and the country's failure within this new stage of world affairs resurrects the idea of a congenital technological incompetence. Lima's film focuses on the attack on racial prejudice against Native Brazilians to allude to the official ideology of modernization. In its opposition to the country of the "economic miracle," cinema underlines the theme of the culture that was exterminated by foreign powers, emphasizing the destructive side of technical and economic advances. Such identification with the defeated Natives did not aim at assuming specific values of the indigenous culture; it basically took indigenous culture as a signifier of the predatory nature of capital expansion, a symbol of the difference of the oppressed. (Xavier 1997, 237–38)

The story in *Brazil Year 2000* begins with a woman and her siblings heading north, in search of better living conditions: yes, the future of *Brazil Year 2000* speculates on an inversion of the migratory flows and the country's geopolitics, with a wealthy Northern region in contrast to the poor South.[7] This middle-class family takes the plight of drought-stricken peasants. Unlike these, however, they drag down the road a curious glass cabinet (*cristaleira*), a piece of furniture that represents "all the tradition that the group insists on carrying, even if reduced to an uncomfortable, useless burden" (Xavier 1993, 121). The glass cabinet for silverware and crystals, a symbol of status and past values, contains the "relics of a stable time prior to the debacle" (Xavier 1993, 121). On their way, the three characters stop at "Me Esqueci" (literally "I Forgot"), a small town that enthusiastically prepares for a ceremony related to the launch of a rocket into space, with the presence of a general. The name of the city alludes to its peripheral, abandoned condition, as well as to the need to forget the past and roots for the nation to be pushed forward into true progress. In *Me Esqueci*, the mother and her two siblings are offered housing, food, and money from a government official, as long as they pretend to be native Brazilians before the population and the visiting general. According to Ismail Xavier, "In general lines, the film by Walter Lima Jr. speaks of a country that, in repressing its history, shuffles its modernization" (Xavier 1993, 120). *Brazil Year 2000* won the Silver Bear at the 1969 Berlin Film Festival (Silva Neto 2002, 129) and is quoted as "a muted political allegory" in *The Overlook Film Encyclopedia: Science Fiction* (Hardy 1995, 271). It is also the one and only Brazilian film cited in Hardy's encyclopedia. The Brazilian filmmaker, critic, and film historian Alex Viany had already associated *Brazil Year 2000* with the SF film genre while discussing the diversity of forms in the Brazilian Cinema Novo (Viany 1993, 147).

It is also worth mentioning the use of SF in *Brazil Year 2000* as an essentially discursive strategy, in theory less subjected to possible censorship and external interferences.[8] Thus, *Brazil Year 2000* clearly resorts to a quite familiar kind of SF satire that shifts the context to the future, but whose main purpose is to discuss or criticize the current reality. As Ismail Xavier explained, "Science fiction helps to circumvent censorship and creates the unified context for the simulation of a society that alludes to militarized Brazil of 1969/70 and its modernization projects" (Xavier 1993, 124–25). Thereby, the SF iconography in *Brazil Year 2000* is featured in a constantly ambiguous way, often bearing twofold meanings. As remarked by Xavier, the Brazilian rocket in the film epitomizes the "bound-to-failure" national conjuncture (Xavier 1993, 126).

Therefore, as a film especially focused on the critique of Brazil's present reality (that is, of the dictatorship and the long-lasting social, political, and economic inequalities), *Brazil Year 2000* is representative of the dystopian trend in SF cinema in tandem with an extremely allegorical final stage in the history of Cinema Novo.[9]

Furthermore, Glauber Rocha also recognizes in *Brazil Year 2000* not an "Eisensteinian lineage" but rather a "Tropicalist" trend, privileging the spectacle, the dramatic structure and staging, with an emphasis on each shot and the film frame itself (Rocha 2004, 202).[10]

In summary, *Brazil Year 2000* is a dystopian SF film that makes unrestricted use of allegory in its effort to scrutinize Brazilian reality, that of acute social inequalities and contradictions, as well as a pusillanimous dictatorial regime. In this film, the SF genre is notably instrumental. Moreover, the contrast between an inferred technology and the popular culture in *Brazil Year 2000* echoes what Ginway says about dystopia in Brazilian literature: "It is clear that these texts criticize modernization just as much, if not more, than they do the military regime itself. It is mainly technology that is seen to rob Brazilians of their identity, especially when placed in the hands of an authoritarian government. Pitted against the destructive powers of technology is the myth of identity, which, perceived as natural and unchanging, takes the form of nature, women, sexuality, and the land" (2004, 139).

Although applicable to the study of ecodystopias in Brazilian cinema, by and large Ginway's conclusions are debatable and raise an issue already noted by Ismail Xavier regarding *Brazil Year 2000*. According to Xavier, problems in *Brazil Year 2000*'s intertextual game (and in the film's narrative structure itself) sabotage its "conscience of underdevelopment, turning it into resenting underdevelopment" (Xavier 1993, 125). Ismail Xavier adds that "science fiction and the musical are the genres of mass culture in which Walter Lima Jr.'s film is inscribed programmatically, willing to explore the distances that separate it from the 'good accomplishment.'" In this sense, "neither as a science fiction nor as a musical, *Brazil Year 2000* sets itself as a show based on the intensity of effects. Its trademark is scarcity, the artisanal arrangement of settings and *mise-en-scène* in order to incorporate certain aspects of the genre film and, at the same time, indicate its national origin as economically underdeveloped" (Xavier 1993, 125). Such an observation addresses a central issue in this present work, regarding a certain way film critics and scholars view SF as a film genre inextricably dependent on "the intensity of effects." According to this viewpoint, SF cinema is synonymous with film spectacle rife with sophisticated special/visual effects. Still according to Xavier, "the parody of modernization slips into the diagnosis of general incompetence, as in *O Bandido*" (Xavier 1993, 130). Under Xavier's perspective (1993, 134), *Brazil Year 2000* could be regarded as "anti-SF," a film whose main discourse ends up pointing to a total incompatibility between modernity and nationalism—

thereby, between Brazilian cinema and SF cinema. In order to "move forward," it would be necessary "to forget," and this action ultimately constitutes an attempt at the most genuine national identity. In addition, an innate incompetence, awkwardness, and authoritarianism would be identity traits always ready to reemerge in the Brazilian society as a whole. However, by looking at the film in hindsight, Xavier's coherent reading of Walter Lima Jr.'s film could be revised, insofar as it makes total sense as long as the allegory is deciphered against its proper historical background, as presumably all cinematic allegories must be, in principle. Notwithstanding, in its clear exposure of the contradictions inherent to the mid-1960s Brazilian wave of reactionary modernization—one in which, paradoxically, it was necessary to "forget the past" in order to "embrace the future"—*Brazil Year 2000* may have been premonitory in some ways. For instance, by underlining the aforementioned opposition between native Brazilians and military rulers, but one in which Brazilian nativeness had a rather different status. Contemporary knowledge on Brazilian biomes and ecosystems, the Native Brazilian nations, and their respective systems of beliefs or axioms, in addition to cutting-edge biotech and science applied to or in relation to the environment in Brazil, all have granted a new status to native Brazilians and this alleged dichotomy during the military rule: the putative clash between "civilization" (the military) and "barbarism" (native Brazilians). Today, it makes far less sense to "forget the past" in order to "move forward into the future," and it does not represent any kind of criticism to Walter Lima Jr.'s whatsoever. On the contrary, this film may well have been prophetic in its exposure of such an elusive, false antinomy between "forgetting" and "progressing."

A further word should be said about the seminal work by Ismail Xavier, whose contribution to a deeper understanding of the discursive power in both Cinema Novo and Cinema Marginal is absolutely essential. We would just like to comment on an issue that might help us better understand how Brazilian film scholarship has traditionally addressed SF cinema, and how the rest of the world has received such works. In Xavier's 1993 book *Alegorias do Subdesenvolvimento*, more than once the author refers to SF all along his thorough analyses of films like Sganzerla's *The Red Light Bandit* and Lima Jr.'s *Brazil Year 2000*. The term "science fiction" ("ficção científica") and icons related to this genre appear at least on half a dozen different pages, likely more than that. However, in Xavier's 1997 *Allegories of Underdevelopment*, the term "science fiction" is practically nonexistent, diluted in analyses that do refer to SF icons, even if obliquely, such as "Martian invasion" and "postnuclear parable." Much of this discrepancy can be ascribed to the subtraction of Xavier's in-depth analysis of *Brazil Year 2000* from the 1997 book. In his original 1993 book, Xavier dedicates no less than eighteen pages to Walter Lima Jr.'s feature-length film. From all the films analyzed by Xavier in *Allegories of Underdevelopment*, there is no doubt that *Brazil Year 2000* is the most "magnetic" in terms of SF scholarship. Therefore, it seems natural that *Brazil Year 2000* deserved an entry in Phil Hardy's *The Overlook Film Encyclopedia—Science Fiction* (1995)—yet its sole presence as a Brazilian representative is quite intriguing. Our argument here is the following: whereas Ismail Xavier's 1993 Brazilian book *Alegorias do Subdesenvolvimento* does offer an important contribution to SF film scholarship, even though collaterally, in the 1997 American book *Allegories of Underdevelopment* (by the same author), the idea that Brazilian cinema—and, most importantly, Brazilian modern cinema—has ventured into SF is significantly eclipsed.

The year 1969, in which a third, more acutely allegorical phase of Cinema Novo produced at least two remarkable feature films (Joaquim Pedro de Andrade's *Macunaíma*, and Walter Lima Jr.'s *Brazil Year 2000*), was also a key year in terms of Brazilian SF for other reasons. It was in 1969 that the Brazilian film critic José Sanz and his supporters organized the SF Symposium (FC Simpósio, or Simpósio de Ficção Científica), one of the biggest and most relevant events concerning the genre in Brazil. This event was linked to the II International Film Festival (II Festival Internacional do Filme), which officially opened on March 17, 1969, with a gala session screening Carol Reed's *Oliver* at the Cine Metro-Copacabana, in Rio de Janeiro (*Correio da Manhã* 1969, 6). The II FIF was supported by the National Institute of Cinema (Instituto Nacional do Cinema), or INC for short, the state agency that would later become the Brazilian Film Company (Empresa Brasileira de Filmes) or Embrafilme.[11] José Sanz was one of the few Brazilian film critics who overtly valued SF cinema, and his SF Symposium had no equivalent in the history of Brazilian film festivals. According to an article published in the famous newspaper *Correio da Manhã*, on March 9, 1969 (6), the American visual artist Ed Emshwhiller presented some of his pictorial works, as well as some of his underground films, such as *Totem* (1963) and *Project Apolo* (1968), while his wife, the SF writer Carol Emshwiller, lectured at the American embassy. The opening of the SF Symposium also featured Otoniel Santos Pereira 16mm short film *The Pedestrian* (*O Pedestre*), a free adaptation of Ray Bradbury's short story (see Ferreira 2007).

The article in *Correio da Manhã* announces the screening of George Pal's *The Time Machine* (1960), with a new copy especially made for the SF Symposium in Brazil, and also comments on the arrival of international guests, such as French writer and paleontologist Francis Corsac, the American writers Kate Wilhelm, Karen Anderson, and Alfred Bester (*Correio da Manhã* 1969, 6). Over approximately ten days, SF writers and film directors lectured and took part in Q&A sessions, such as Arthur C. Clarke, Wolf Rilla, Poul Anderson, Robert Bloch, and Forrest J. Ackerman. In addition, Clarke was paid homage and received a miniature of the "black monolith" on March 27, as a tribute to his work as scriptwriter of Stanley Kubrick's *2001: A Space Odyssey* (1968).

The *Tenth Victim* (*La Decima Vittima*, 1965), starring Ursula Andress, was another film in the SF Symposium announced by this article in *Correio da Manhã*. According to José Sanz, cited in the same article, this major event taking place in Brazil and gathering some of the most renowned artists in the SF field will demonstrate that "many critics are mistaken by considering SF as a sub-literature." Still according to Sanz, such critics would not be in tune with their age, hence their contempt for a literature they simply cannot understand. Sanz ends his interview to *Correio da Manhã* by saying that, beyond the mere divulgation of the SF genre, the SF Symposium will call the attention of both international and Brazilian film producers, for the sake of the betterment of SF cinema, insofar as it is "the vivid literature of the 20$^{th}$ century" (*Correio da Manhã* 1969, 6).

The SF Symposium resulted in a bilingual publication, edited by José Sanz (1969), *SF Symposium/FC Simpósio*, featuring essays by Forrest J. Ackerman, Sam Moskowitz, Robert Bloch, A. E. Van Vogt, Brian W. Aldiss, Poul Anderson, Luis Gasca, John Brunner, Harry Harrison, Alfred Bester, Wolf Rilla, Frederik Pohl, J. G. Ballard, Jacques Sadoul, Harlan Ellison, and Arthur C. Clarke. It was the first time such a "dream team" of SF writers and filmmakers had their nonfiction texts translated into Portuguese. This book also listed the members or participants in the organizing committee of the symposium: José Sanz as its overall coordinator, assisted by Fred Madersbacher, Wilson Cunha, and Monica Leib. The international team of consultants and members of the organizing committee included André Carneiro, Clóvis Garcia, Ruy Jungmann, Álvaro Malheiros, Walter Martins and Jerônymo Monteiro representing Brazil, Forrest J. Ackerman, Karen Anderson, Poul Anderson, Alfred Bester, Robert Bloch, Leigh Chapman, Roger Corman, Ed Emshwiller, Carol Emshwiller, Harlan Ellison, Philip José Farmer, Harry Harrison, Robert A. Heinlein, Damon Knight, Sam Moskowitz, George Pal, Frederik Pohl, Robert Scheckley, A. E. Van Vogt, and Kate Wilhelm representing the United States, Luis Gasca representing Spain, Jacques Baratier, Robert Benayoun, Michel Caen, and Jacques Sadoul representing France, Brian W. Aldiss, J. G. Ballard, John Brunner, Val Guest, and Wolf Rilla representing the United Kingdom, and Marcial Souto representing Uruguay. Alongside André Carneiro's *Introduction to* the Study of Science Fiction (*Introdução ao Estudo da "Science Fiction,"* 1967), José Sanz's *SF Symposium* (1969) stands out as a pioneering work in the Brazilian SF scholarship.

As seen above, with José Sanz's SF Symposium in Rio and films like Olney São Paulo's *Grayish Morning* and Walter Lima Jr.'s *Brazil Year 2000*, 1969 seems to be another key year in terms of SF in Brazil, representative of a period in the history of Brazilian cinema in which a number of filmmakers ventured into high levels of experimentalism, parody, and allegory, with fruitful experiences for years to come.

Filmed in Cataguases-MG,[12] Paulo Bastos Martins's *The Announcer: The Man of the Storms* (*O Anunciador: O Homem das Tormentas*, 1970) appears to confirm and push the boundaries of Brazilian SF film experimentalism. Filmed in Cataguases, in the state of Minas Gerais, this film is about the odd events that follow the arrival of an unknown young man in a small town in the state of Minas Gerais. This film has at least five SF elements in its plot: (1) the "Modern Multiplier Factory," an industry of clones; (2) the allusion to a "General Confederation of Space"; (3) a public questionnaire with the following first question: "Who will be the first creature born in space?"; (4) "the woman who walks, runs and dies pursued by invisible men," and finally (5) the very origin of the unknown visitor, who can be an extraterrestrial. As the visitor remains in town, the city dwellers mysteriously die, one by one. Those few who still survive try to flee from the city. It is worth noting a certain similarity between the plot of Paulo Martins's film and João Guimarães Rosa's short story "A Very White Man" ("Um Moço Muito Branco," 2001), an ambiguous narrative, possibly SF, in which a man of mysterious origin causes strange events in a small town.

*The Announcer* satirizes a number of topics, Brazilian characters and institutions, such as capitalism, television, the Brazilian intelligentsia, Cinema Novo, and the advertising industry. Luiz F. A. Miranda (1990, 240) refers to *The Announcer* as an "attempt at science fiction under a countryside perspective."

Paulo Bastos Martins dedicated *The Announcer* to the celebrated pioneering filmmaker Humberto Mauro, who was born in Volta Grande (state of Minas Gerais), but whose *début* as a film director took place in Cataguases in the mid-1920s. Mauro was present at the film's release in May 1970 in the city—as reported by the Brazilian critic and historian Paulo Emílio Salles Gomes, who had traveled for twelve hours with the flu to attend the premiere. In a review published in *Jornal da Tarde* on April

19, 1973, titled "The film which nobody saw. And nobody liked it" ("O filme que o público não viu. E não gostou"), in reference to the screening of *The Announcer* in São Paulo. at the Cosmos 70 movie theater, Salles Gomes observed: "Reviewed today, *The Announcer* seems to have come from far away. The production must have been complicated, prolonged and, when the film was ready in 1970, it was too late" (in Calil and Machado 1986, 278). Still, according to Salles Gomes, Paulo Bastos Martins's film was intended to announce an evolution in the Brazilian Cinema Novo. The attempts at modern sound montage and the dramatic use of graphic signs and intertitles in *The Announcer*, emphasized Salles Gomes, would be welcome experiments in the Brazilian film scene.

Salles Gomes further notes that "*The Announcer* announces too much, and the director Paulo Bastos Martins better expresses his talent precisely when he interrupts the speech of the young prophet" (in Calil and Machado 1986, 278). The character that lends the film its title, according to Salles Gomes, would suffer from an excessive eloquence (in Calil and Machado 1986, 279). Salles Gomes further criticizes the excessive eloquence in the film as a whole: even the welcome interruptions in the announcer's lines would often be unnecessarily prolonged—and a certain contradiction between image and discourse in *The Announcer* is also noted by the film critic (in Calil and Machado 1986, 278).

After narrating his picturesque experience as one of the only three film spectators who were present at the film screening at the Cosmos 70 movie theater in São Paulo—and the only one to watch the entire film—Salles Gomes provokes Brazilian cinema and its audience by asking something that "has long defied the experts' acumen": "I knew that the audience would not like *The Announcer: The Man of the Storms*, but how come did it also know it beforehand, to the point of not even going to see it?" (in Calil and Machado 1986, 280).

*The Announcer*, along with José Agrippino's *Hitler 3rd World* (*Hitler 3o Mundo*, 1968), are both good examples of the Brazilian late 1960s or 1970s experimental cinema that "uses and abuses" SF. Also released in 1970 and often identified with Brazilian experimental cinema and Cinema Marginal, Elyseu Visconti's *The Monsters of Babaloo* (*Os Monstros de Babaloo*) remotely evokes SF iconography in its approach to the family of a rich womanizer industrialist who leads a fictional insulated community called Babaloo. But just like André Luiz Oliveira's *Meteorango Kid: Intergalactic Hero* (*Meteorango Kid, Hero Intergaláctico*, 1969) and other Brazilian films identified with Cinema Marginal, the affinity with SF does not go beyond the film's title. Visconti himself, quoted by Luiz F. A. Miranda, explains that *The Monsters of Babaloo* is a "fun horror-musical film, narrating demonstratively and realistically the adventures of an industrialist's family on the fictional island of Babaloo" (Miranda 1990, 356). According to João Carlos Rodrigues (2004, 67), Visconti's film is a "metaphor for the avid and uneducated middle class that prevailed at the time of the so-called 'Brazilian miracle.'" As usual at the time, *The Monsters of Babaloo* was censored by the military regime in 1970.

In March 1974, at the beginning of his administration, General Ernesto Geisel acquiesced in proposals for a "gradual, but secure, democratic improvement." The so-called Abertura ("Opening") period begins, "when it became possible for [Brazilian] cinema to make more direct considerations, and with some distance, about the dictatorship that was running out" (Leme 2012, 273). On October 13, 1978, the AI-5 was finally revoked, and on August 28, 1979, "The Amnesty Law" ("Lei da Anistia") was issued.

In her study of Brazilian SF literature, Ginway argues that a critical study of "Brazilian myths of national identity in science fiction make it clear that the genre provides a barometer to measure attitudes toward technology, while at the same time reflecting the social implications of modernization in Brazilian society" (2004, 212).[13] Focusing particularly on the literary production of the 1960s, covering the period of the Brazilian military dictatorship (1964–1985) and the restoration of democracy in Brazil (from 1985), Ginway traces, in the works by Brazilian authors, a reasonable amount of social and political criticism, directly or indirectly addressing issues such as sex, racism, imperialism, globalization, the role of Brazil in the global context, national myths, and so on. According to Ginway, "While Christopher Dunn affirms that the postmodern and cannibalistic aesthetic was most "successfully consummated in the realism of popular music" in the form of the short-lived yet fruitful Tropicalia vanguard movement, it could be argued that Brazilian science fiction also combines symbols of "underdevelopment and ultramodernity" and effectively captures Brazilian historical and economic predicament" (Ginway 2004, 142). What Ginway observes in regard to Brazilian literature could also be applied to Brazilian cinema. As a matter of fact, sometimes SF provided Brazilian cinema with the proper atmosphere and instruments for social and political criticism, especially under the military rule. Regarding literature of the dictatorial period, Ginway states that "in general, Brazilian dystopian texts portray a rebellion against a technocratic regime as an allegory of the Brazilian people's protest of the military dictatorship" (Ginway 2004, 33).[14] At dangerous times, when art was forced to make use of allegories and parables, SF was instrumental in films with more acid criticism.

In most of the films commented on in this chapter, SF was instrumental in connoting the contrast between inferred science and technology and Brazilian popular culture. This echoes Ginway on dystopia in Brazilian literature: "The vehemence of dystopian fiction in Brazil demonstrates one literary response to an increasingly technological world. The dystopian tendency to exaggerate nightmarish aspect of the future allows for a clean delineation of the conflicts between private experience and state authority, simplifying a complex struggle into the opposition between the forces of good and evil. For this reason, Brazilian dystopias will probably remain among the clearest indictments of the military's policies and its use of technology" (2004, 134).

An apparently emblematic film, which best synthesizes Ginway's diagnosis of Brazilian SF literature (and at the crossroads between film and literature, given the fact this film was based on a short story written by the director) is undoubtedly *Grayish Morning*, by Olney São Paulo. The allegory that ties technology to authoritarianism finds its culmination in the aforementioned scene of the trial led by the infamous robot. Since Alberto Pieralisi's *The 5th Power* and later, in films like Roberto Farias's *Roberto Carlos in Adventure Rhythm* (*Roberto Carlos em Ritmo de Aventura*, 1968), Brazilian cinema keeps linking computer sciences and technology to the threat of foreign invasion, the encroachment of our natural resources and talents, torture, and authoritarianism. Artificial intelligence seems to mirror the machinelike political system, functioning as a clear threat to human existence.

4

# Coming Up for Air

## The Brazilian Ecodystopian Film

In "Science Fiction and Ecology," Brian Stableford (in Seed 2007, 127–41) reminds us that the term "ecology" was coined by Ernst Haeckel in 1873, but it was not established as a formal discipline before the late 1920s, with Charles Elton's *Animal Ecology* (1927), the first notable work on environmental issues, with its concept of the "Eltonian pyramid."[1] Shortly after, ecological concern started sprouting in the SF field through works such as J. D. Beresford's "The Man Who Hated Flies" (1929), a kind of ecocatastrophe avant la lettre. Stableford analyzes the exchanges between the ecological conscience and SF literature, addressing issues such as the reenactment of Malthusian theories, James Lovelock's "Gaia hypothesis," the 1950s Population Council, Paul Ehrlich's "population bomb," and Greenpeace. This is done in parallel to literary approaches, interpretations, and extrapolations, such as the idea of "terraforming," the negative environmental impacts of space colonization, antitechnological or even mystical readings of modern civilization, genetic engineering, and posthumanism, all with a touch of bitter irony. From books to films, one may see a gradual increase both in terms of quantity, quality, and relevance of eco-sci-fi movies since the 1950s, but especially throughout the 1960s and 1970s, with the popularization of a new, more widespread and, to some extent, left-wing ecological conscience around the world.

Stableford's concerns lie in the Anglophone or Anglo-Saxon literary tradition. However, time has proved that ecology cannot be circumscribed to any nation in particular, with environmental issues being a global concern today. And what about "environmental fiction"? It is well known that Brazil, among other Latin American or non-Western countries, inspires in foreign observers the ideal of an exotic, wild, and even romantic land. This can be seen in movies such as Harry Hoyt's *The Lost World* (1925, based on A. Conan Doyle's namesake novel) or Jack Arnold's *Creature from the Black Lagoon* (1954), among numerous other titles whose stories are set in the Amazon, for instance. In spite of being frequently exaggerated, this mythological nature is partially nurtured by Brazilians' self-imagery. The conflict between modernity and nature has always had a role in Brazilian SF texts. Toward the end of the 1960s, and throughout the 1970s and 1980s, this conflict intensified in cinematic speculations about the future of Brazil and the world being forced to cope with environmental catastrophes. The ecological debate as manifested in Brazilian films, amid the controversial national policies concerning environmental issues, became an effective access point in terms of critique of the regime: a way of dodging censorship by taking advantage of a worldwide agenda in order to protest against an authoritarian military government.

The aim of this chapter is to introduce and discuss some examples of the first Brazilian cinematic ecodystopias, considering their historical and political background, as well as some aesthetic features. In addition, this work intends to "science-fictionally" consider these films—often regarded as everything but SF, especially in Brazil—to review them against the backdrop of Brazilian anxieties regarding modernization in the nuclear era.

It is worth mentioning beforehand that some of the films herein discussed were produced and released during the Brazilian military dictatorship (1964–1985). As mentioned in the previous chapter, in the early 1960s Brazil was about to set a social-democrat agenda, but it was thwarted by the military coup d'état in 1964. Guerrilla groups sprouted up around Brazil, being mostly isolated efforts with poor coordination and results. However, the armed resistance provided the perfect excuse for the military to unleash its savage repression. Claudinê Perina Camargo's *93º Tunnel* (*Túnel 93o*, 1972) and José de Anchieta's *Stop 88: Alert Limit* (*Parada 88: O Limite de Alerta*, 1978) belong to this framework, while Roberto Pires's *Nuclear Shelter* (*Abrigo Nuclear*, 1981) and Marcos Bertoni's *Armadillo Blood* (*Sangue de Tatu*, 1986) emerge in a period of gradual détente. It was not until the late 1970s (precisely 1979) that the military loosened some of the grip they exerted over Brazilian society and, eventually, in 1985, they acquiesced to the return of democracy. The first civilian president (José

Sarney) in twenty-one years was inaugurated in 1985, although not elected by the people. The first free presidential elections took place only in 1989.

## Ecodystopian Films during the Military Rule

The first example of Brazilian ecodystopian film to be discussed here is Claudinê Perina's *93º Tunnel*, a short made by undergraduate students of the Catholic University of Campinas (PUC-Campinas). This film alternates between a postapocalyptic, claustrophobic future and the memories of a life on the surface. Archival footage describes the twentieth century and its increase in air pollution. After a serious environmental crisis, the Earth's atmosphere becomes deadly to humankind, which is then forced to find refuge in fallout shelters. In this subterranean village, people "recover" chlorophyll and oxygen in order to survive. Mankind becomes a mutant species, as scientists create noseless human beings. The main character's lifespan ends. He must now leave the shelter and go to the surface in order to face death in the hazardous atmosphere. Shot in Super-8, a format frequently chosen by both experimental and amateur directors from the 1960s to the 1980s, *93º Tunnel* is reminiscent of something from a late modernist, even avant-garde approach, in a kind of audiovisual poem on the themes of nostalgia and environmental degradation. *93° Tunnel* seems to be a sequel to Perina's previous short Super-8 experimental film *Once upon a time . . . (Era uma vez . . .)*, which speculated on a dying planet, with images of trees being cut and burnt, one after another, until only one couple managed to survive amid the wasteland. Other films by Perina, like *End of the Line (Fim da Linha)*, on the dismantling of the Brazilian railroad network, suggest a long-lasting concern with the environment in the work of this director who was most active in the 1970s.

The first feature-length, 35mm ecodystopian film made in Brazil is likely José de Anchieta's *Stop 88: Alert Limit*. The film's plot is set in the fictional city of Parada 88 in December 1999, six years after the explosion of a cosmetics factory named Night Valley (Vale da Noite) that has poisoned the air with tons of toxic waste. On the night of April 21, 1994, the reactor's safety valve in the factory eventually fails, causing an explosion that scatters hundreds of pounds of dioxin into the air, forming a reddish color toxic cloud, highly poisonous and corrosive. The survivors—less than half of the city's population before the accident—live quarantined in the city, paying for breathable air and circulating through plastic tunnels that connect the buildings. The prolonged quarantine is the result of state bureaucracy and negligence. A group from the gas control department is finally deployed to locate the persistent leak in the city's collapsed reactor. Meanwhile, Joaquim Porfírio (Joel Barcellos) struggles to make his living along with his wife (Yara Amaral) and blind young daughter (Regina Duarte). The family has to pay for overdue air bills, and a weird kind of "lottery," promoted by the quarantined community, seems to be a salvation. Joaquim is drawn and thereby chosen in an auditorium (more precisely, some sort of small circus arena) and accepts the challenge of leaving the protection zone to explore the ruins of the Valley of the Night. He is supposed to bring news about what is going on outside the town. If he gets back alive, the prize would be three months' paid air and food supplies.

Joaquim goes on his mission but succumbs to poisonous gases in the area of the old chemical factory. The team from the gas control department that was working there rescues him, and he ends up undergoing surgery in which his lungs, dried and burned by the poisonous air, are replaced by artificial lungs.[2] Here is one of the rare cyborgs in Brazilian cinema, perhaps the only one with no clearly comic intentions.

While Joaquim is staying in a hospital outside the city, sinister air collectors traveling on motorcycles, wearing black leather and gas masks pay a visit to his wife and daughter. The air tax collectors resemble (or foresee) characters from George Miller's *Mad Max* (1979), a film that was to be released the following year. They threaten to cut the family's air supply and eventually vandalize Joaquim's house. One of them rapes his daughter. The group leaves, but promises to return soon to collect the debt.

Now recovered, Joaquim returns to the city of Parada 88 on December 31, 1999. He claims his prize and goes home, where his wife tells him about the incident with the collectors. Joaquim plans revenge: to kill the collectors when they return and leave the city with his family. Under the New Year's Eve fireworks, the inhabitants of Parada 88 break the protective plastic tunnels that keep the city under quarantine. The movie ends with Joaquim and family traveling on a wasteland landscape on January 1, 2000.

Dark and depressing, *Stop 88* recalls the overall atmosphere in films such as Stanley Kubrick's A *Clockwork Orange* (1971), Miller's *Mad Max* (1979), or even Ridley Scott's *Blade Runner* (1982). Shot by the Brazilian cinematographer and director Chico Botelho, *Stop 88* is almost totally immersed in the darkness and closeness of tunnels and decaying buildings.

Anchieta's deeply pessimistic film seems to forecast something from 1980s cyberpunk—or Tupinipunk (Causo 1996; 2015).[3]

Shot in Paranapiacaba, in the state of São Paulo, Brazil, a town particularly known for its fog and old railroads, the sets for *Stop 88* were designed by architect Alcino Izzo, who was responsible for the complex plastic tunnel network. The fog in *Stop 88* has a central narrative role, it is constitutive of the set designs. Much of the film set in *Stop 88* was made out of large plastic tubes. According to José de Anchieta, kilometers of plastic pipes were built, with a kind of valve between them to keep the air inside: "A circus company owned by a man called Marugan was responsible for the work. Since my first shorts I have used plastic materials."[4] With a previous career in theater, José de Anchieta explains that he gave special attention to the sets and lighting in *Stop 88* in order to emphasize a theatrical mood. Still, according to the filmmaker, sets and lighting are mutually dependent in the most diverse circumstances. Anchieta also underscores the important work of architect Alcino Izzo as set designer. Sharing the authorship of set design with the director, Izzo created the plastic tunnel complexes, thus granting a fundamental contribution to the film. The set design of *Stop 88* won the 1978 APCA Award.[5]

*Stop 88* is certainly one of the first Brazilian feature films truly representative of the tradition of ecodystopias. According to Brian Stableford, ecodystopias or ecocatastrophes in literature have given rise to a new awareness of the environment and ecology in SF (qtd. in Ginway 2004, 121). Ginway (2004, 121) comments that, in Brazil, the first ecological movements started around 1971. Previously, in 1968, the Biosphere Conference was held in Paris, which was a predominantly scientific event. The Club of Rome and the document "The Limits to Growth" (Meadows et al., 1972), written by experts, were quite influential with the thesis that a reduction in industrialization and economic growth would be the only way to avoid a global environmental catastrophe. This thesis, however, went against the interests of the developing countries, among them Brazil, and it was later criticized for putting the most developed countries in a very special position—as in the metaphor later made by Ha-Joon Chang (2002), another way to "kick away the ladder" out of developing countries' reach. The military government depended heavily on the success of economic growth and industrialization, achievements that were used to legitimize the regime. In this scenario, Brazil contested the Northerners' postulations, stating that the concept of absolute sovereignty should take precedence over analyses by the international community. As other Third World countries, Brazil's government defended the idea that the country should first develop, then "pay the bill" for the damage to the world, as rich countries might have done (Duarte 2003, 17).

In 1972, the United Nations World Conference on the Environment, held in Stockholm, set new guidelines for environmental research. At the Conference of Stockholm, the Brazilian delegation played a combative role, contested the rich countries, and won the sympathy of other developing countries, such as China and India. Duarte summarizes the Brazilian theses taken to the Conference of Stockholm as follows: pollution is not an absolute concept (like sovereignty), but relative. If human interference with the environment was taken in absolute terms, it would be necessary to eliminate humankind. Countries do not pollute: they have areas of pollution. In underdeveloped countries, a great deal of environmental degradation stems from poverty, which causes phenomena such as soil erosion, shantytowns, and deforestation. With economic growth the pollution caused by poverty might be diminished, and part of the wealth might be allocated to fight against pollution, as is the pollution resulting from overconsumption in developed countries (Duarte 2003, 18–19).

To better understand the role of Brazil as a major player in the global environmental scenario it is worth talking about the Legal Amazon (Amazônia Legal), an administrative area created in 1966 (by the Law n. 5173 from October 27, which extinguished the SPVEA and created SUDAM), but whose original concept was born with the Law 1.806 from January 6, 1953. The Legal Amazon contains the Amazon Basin, the largest hydrographic basin in the world, with about one fifth of the total volume of fresh water on the planet (Cf. Abramovay 2019, 26; ((o))eco 2014). As remarked by Darlene Sadlier, "Covering approximately 60 percent of the country, the Amazon River Basin historically has held a special place in the way Brazil has been imagined. Once described as 'the Sweet Sea' and 'Empress and Queen of all Floods,' the river itself has been the subject of wonder and fantasy since the arrival of the Europeans in 1500" (Sadlier 2008, 275). In the late 1970s, only a handful of filmmakers had the environmental issue so clear in mind. The inspiration for *Stop 88*'s screenplay, Anchieta explains, came from his eldest son, who during childhood suffered from a serious breathing disorder caused by São Paulo's polluted air.

> The issue of air and its pollutants has always been discussed in my films, because my first son Daniel, today 36 years old,

at birth had the bronchi compromised by air pollution in São Paulo. When I saw him breathing inside an oxygen tent I decided that I had to open a discussion about it. At that time (1974/1975) we still breathed the air of dictatorship and, being a leftist, I was not persecuted by the military, but by my own party peers who claimed my concerns to be "escapist," far from reality. For the party [the Communist Party], a functioning chimney was more important than a destroyed one, because where there was a chimney there was work . . . A concept of the 19th century. Anyway, after the film was made, I was very persecuted for reversing the socialist pamphlet. However, the elements brought up by fiction, like robotics, are now ruthlessly installed in all world industry, including Brazil. The global warming disaster is also a reality that had already been addressed by 1975. And all, or virtually all chimneys were eventually demolished.[6]

The script of *Stop 88* was written by Anchieta himself, in collaboration with Brazilian filmmaker Roberto Santos, and eventually subjected to scrutiny by the writer and science fiction scholar André Carneiro. According to Carneiro, however, his suggestions were not implemented.[7]

José de Anchieta recalls that since the beginning of the project, *Stop 88* was made to be an ecological warning. Still, according to the director, the film is the sum of three of his previous short films: *The Flute of Vertebrae* (*A Flauta das Vértebras*), *Ellipsis* (*Reticências*), and *Full Stop* (*Ponto Final*), all of which served to test his ideas. Anchieta says he participated with *Reticências* in an ecological film festival in Montreal, Canada, in 1978, where he witnessed a heated debate about the environment. *Reticências* won a special award "maybe because the jury was concerned about the absence of a discussion on these issues in Brazil. There was already at that time a great concern with the future of the Amazon."[8]

*Stop 88*'s music score was composed by Egberto Gismonti, who along with Geraldo Carneiro created the song "Happy New Year" ("Feliz Ano Novo"). The soundtrack was performed by Brazilian artists such as Joyce, the Symphonic Orchestra of the city of Campinas, and the University of Campinas's Choir, conducted by Benito Juarez (Silva Neto 2002, 620). The film demonstrates an unusual awareness of the role of the soundtrack in an SF narrative, for Brazilian standards. And more than thirty years after its release, *Stop 88* remains prescient, as seen in the UN's IPCC report and in films such as the documentary *An Inconvenient Truth* (2006), directed by Davis Guggenheim and starring former US Vice President Al Gore. The rise of an extreme-right president of Brazil in 2018 only makes *Stop 88* once again a consequential piece of criticism, insofar as it demonstrates that history can repeat itself, and twice as tragedy.

*Stop 88* was produced by Embrafilme, the Brazilian state production company then headed by director Roberto Farias, who regarded Anchieta's project as "a new language, different from the most fashionable aesthetics of the time, 'the aesthetics of hunger.'"[9] Although Anchieta intended to differentiate *Stop 88* from the Cinema Novo aesthetics, the film does present some characteristics that end up also being a form of "aesthetics of hunger" in comparison to American SF film standards. This can be seen in the film settings and cinematography, which according to the director himself were very well accomplished, despite budgetary constraints. As the funding from the state production company Embrafilme was not enough to complete the film, Egberto Gismonti and actress Regina Duarte spent their own money to finish making the movie.

José de Anchieta's *Stop 88* went beyond *93º Tunnel* in terms of addressing environmental issues by means of a partially experimentalist film aesthetic: a somewhat hybridized cinematic/theatrical narrative with echoes of the Brazilian *chanchada* and the circus, as well as some influence of Tropicalism and Brazilian Popular Music (MPB). The classical narrative framework is sometimes fractured in Anchieta's film, punctuated by modernist "attractions" coming from theater, Brazilian architecture, and reminiscences of Brazilian *antropofagia*.[10] Just a few years later, in 1981, with Brazil still under military rule but after the repeal of the Institutional Act n. 5 (AI-5), another 35mm feature film with environmentalist concerns was released: Roberto Pires's *Nuclear Shelter*, a dystopian, postapocalyptic film with a focus on the perils of atomic energy and its ecological implications. The plot was inspired by some ideas from the Brazilian physicist César Lattes.[11] Pires, the director of *Nuclear Shelter*, also plays the leading role in the film. Contemporary with Glauber Rocha's film generation, Pires represented the Cinema Novo in the Brazilian state of Bahia, with films like *Tocaia no Asfalto* (1962). Environmentalism and atomic energy seemed to be major concerns in Pires's career in the 1980s and 90s.

The plot in *Nuclear Shelter* unfolds as follows: Lat (Roberto Pires) is in charge of checking and handling radioactive disposal on a desert surface. During his last routine inspection, he discovers serious problems with the nuclear waste container. A possible explosion could put the subterranean citadel at risk. However, his report is underestimated by Avo (Conceição Senna), the commander who keeps people under strict control and unaware that, in the past, mankind had once lived on the surface. So, Lat joins a rebel group that aims to disable nuclear power plants, develop clean energy methods, and return to the surface once again.

Based on its plot and set design, as well as on its main character, Pires's film vaguely recalls George Lucas's *THX 1138* (1971), another dystopia inspired by the classic situation of an individual who refuses to follow techno-futuristic laws or conventions, and something already seen in SF novels such as Aldous Huxley's *Brave New World* (1932), Yevgeny Zamyatin's *We* (1924), and George Orwell's *1984* (1948). Designed by Roberto Pires himself, *Nuclear Shelter*'s costumes and settings also recall some American and even British SF films of the time.

*Nuclear Shelter* was shot in the sandy landscapes of Arembepe, in the state of Bahia. Roberto Pires was the mastermind and main creator of the film's settings and props, such as the futuristic hover car, built on the platform of a Volkswagen Beetle. In Petrus Pires's (one of Roberto Pires's sons) thirty-five-minute documentary *Bahia Sci-Fi* (2015),[12] the cast and crew of *Nuclear Shelter* give their testimony on how this Brazilian ecodystopia represented a tour de force, resulting from Pires's craftsmanship, ingenuity, and determination. Interviewees such as the co-writer Orlando Senna, the actress Conceição Senna, Pires's son César Pires (who played a role as a young rebel in the underground city), and Laura Carneiro, all of them emphasize the cooperative and somewhat "domestic" mood in the production of *Nuclear Shelter*, set forth with the participation of Roberto Pires's family, friends, and neighbors, both professional and nonprofessional actors (see fig. 4.1). The film also benefitted from the "circuit-bending" or "remix" of ordinary objects, such as pipes, home appliances, and kitchen items redesigned to appear as futuristic props in the settings. In his creative endeavor to circumvent budgetary constraints, Pires also foresaw today's technologies such as the flash drive, and Skype calls in scenes shot with multiple cameras and including Super-8 projections.

Produced during the dictatorship and released in the same year as Ignácio de Loyola Brandão's famous dystopian novel *And Still the Earth* (*Não Verás País Nenhum*, 1981), *Nuclear Shelter* was contemporary with the "atomic euphoria" of the Brazilian government, which had high expectations for its nuclear power plants in the coastal city of Angra dos Reis, in the state of Rio de Janeiro. This "atomic euphoria" had roots in the democratic era, when President Juscelino Kubitsheck created the National

Figure 4.1. Citizens of the underground city in Roberto Pires's *Nuclear Shelter* (*Abrigo Nuclear*, 1981). Source: *Nuclear Shelter* (*Abrigo Nuclear*). Dir. Roberto Pires. Prod. Co.: Bahia Filmes; Iglu Filmes Produções Ltda., Brasil, 1981, 35mm, COR, 88min. Courtesy: Petrus Pires (private collection).

Commission for Nuclear Energy (CNEN), in 1956. In 1967, under military rule, President General Costa e Silva started the Nuclear Program. Brazil signed an agreement with Germany in 1975 and started building the nuclear power plant Angra 1 in 1976. It started providing electrical power in 1982 and, in 1987, it was officially announced that Brazil had control over the process of uranium enrichment by ultracentrifugation, a technology that was essential for the development of an atomic bomb. In 1988, the new constitution forbade nuclear weaponry, and the Autonomous Nuclear Program, the Brazilian parallel nuclear program created in 1978 by the Navy merged with the official program.[13] Needless to say, the military nuclear program had less to do with energy policy than with military dreams of supremacy in the hemisphere. After all, Brazilian hydrographic resources and waterpower productivity contradicted any need for risky and expensive nuclear energy. In 2021, 66 percent of the energy produced in Brazil came from hydroelectric power plants, whereas only about 2 percent of the country's energy was nuclear (see Empresa de

Pesquisa Energética—Brazilian Energy Balance 2021; EIA 2021).[14] Following *Nuclear Shelter*, Roberto Pires wrote and directed only one more 35mm feature-film, *Cesium 137: Goiânia's Nightmare (Césio 137: O Pesadelo de Goiânia*, 1990), a dramatization of real events about radioactive contamination. The film reenacts the tragic events in the city of Goiânia, state of Goiás, in 1987, when civilians were exposed to hazardous radioactive medical waste. The contamination began on September 13, 1987, when a device used for radiotherapy was found inside an abandoned clinic in downtown Goiânia. It was classified as level 5 (accidents with far-reaching consequences) in the International Nuclear Accident Scale, which ranges from zero to seven. The piece of equipment was found by a junkyard collector who thought it to be scrap. It was disassembled and passed on to other hands, including children, generating a contamination trail that gravely affected the health of hundreds of people. The cesium-137 incident was the largest radioactive accident in Brazil and the largest ever reported to have happened outside a nuclear power plant anywhere in the world. In 2001, Pires died of cancer, which might have been caused by his exposure to contaminated areas while working on his last film (see fig. 4.2).

Figure 4.2. An explorer from the underground city, wearing radiation protective outfit, meets the unprotected Lat (Roberto Pires) on the surface by the beach. *Source*: *Abrigo Nuclear*, 1981. Courtesy: Petrus Pires (private collection).

## Come Hell or High Water:
## Ecodystopian Films in the Redemocratization

Anyhow, the Stockholm Conference in 1972 set the stage for heated debate, spotlighting the clash of opinion essentially between the industrialized north and the south in development. It also generated a series of expectations and measures, including the creation of UNEP (United Nations Environment Program). Also, as a consequence of the 1972 Stockholm Conference, in October 1973 the Brazilian government created the Special Bureau for the Environment (SEMA, or Secretaria Especial do Meio Ambiente). In 1983, the UN formed a commission chaired by the Norwegian diplomat Gro Harlem Brundtland, who in 1987 presented the document titled "Our Common Future," also known as the Brundtland Report, in which the state of the planet's environment was discussed, and new directions were recommended for its proper management. This document consolidated the term "sustainable development." Following this report, in 1988 the UN General Assembly adopted a resolution determining the organization of a new international conference to assess the progress since Stockholm. Brazil offered to host the conference and the proposal was accepted. Duarte notes that, in the second half of the 1980s, when José Sarney assumed the presidency, "international spotlights focused on Brazil as the worst environmental villain in action" (Duarte 2003, 31). Such a bad reputation before the eyes of international public opinion was the result of military development with little or no concern for environmental degradation, worsened by the exponential growth of deforestation in the Amazon area.

Just about a year after the end of the military dictatorship (1985), Marcos Bertoni's Super-8 short film *Armadillo Blood* (*Sangue de Tatu*) featured an ecodystopia based on "what if" a serious accident at the nuclear power plants of Angra dos Reis had actually happened. Released the same year the Chernobyl disaster occurred (1986) and nearly a year before the incident with Cesium 137 in Goiânia, *Armadillo Blood* tells the story of a nuclear power plant employee who escapes to the mountains after a radioactive leakage.

Bertoni's film is imbued with the ecological conscience that grew in the 1970s and 1980s, wrapped up in his characteristically dark humor and irony as a Super-8 filmmaker. The first part of *Armadillo Blood* features documentary footage, images of a real demonstration against nuclear energy, followed by unauthorized footage of the Brazilian nuclear power plants in Angra dos Reis. These unauthorized images, taken from a certain distance, appear repeatedly throughout the whole film. A shot of authentic newspaper headlines announces the imminent catastrophe in the film. Not even the Brazilian faith suggested by picturesque religious icons inside the power plant can prevent the terrible accident. Starting in the very room where the Brazilian atomic bomb is kept in secret, the radioactive leakage spreads chaos across the city.

Despite being an independent film, *Armadillo Blood*'s rhythm and plot recall feature films like James Bridges's *The China Syndrome* (1979), among others. Images of computer monitors, the soundtrack and the use of Gurgel[15] cars help to establish an effective SF "atmosphere" or "mood." The appropriate balance between documentary and fiction lends verisimilitude and cohesion to the narrative, perhaps the high point of this modest and yet eloquent short film. Armadillo Blood won the Best Short Fiction Screenplay award in the well-known Gramado Film Festival in 1989.

*Armadillo Blood* was made in 1986, after the end of military rule. However, the film itself suggests that it might actually be too soon to breathe some "fresh air." In other words, Brazilian society could not yet enjoy a radically different atmosphere, just a year after the military delivered the presidency back to civilians. On the contrary, many things remained the same, as one could see in the continuity of the Brazilian nuclear program. It is worth noting that, at the time, nuclear energy was highly criticized by environmentalists, and most of the initiatives related to the Brazilian nuclear power plants in Angra remained murky and classified because of national security and alleged economic interests. In addition, it is worth remembering that the political transition from a military to a civilian administration was not completely transparent, and actually happened behind closed doors to a large extent, with informal political agreements and the coincidental sudden death from cancer of Tancredo Neves, the first civilian president in approximately twenty years. José Sarney, the first civilian president after twenty-one years of military dictatorship, was in fact the vice-president of Tancredo Neves, and a politician known for his close ties to the military.

Both allusions and overt references to the military rule and American imperialism are rather intense all throughout Bertoni's short film, mostly around the character of the foreign scientist who directs the nuclear power plant. Played by Louis Chilson, the character is depicted as a "gringo" (American? German?) who diligently serves the military generals and American interests while despising Brazilian people and the environment. His counterpart in the film is the old countryman or *caboclo*[16] (Olavo Ribeiro Fernandes), a real character found by Bertoni during the film's production. Whereas the foreign scientist stands for the high-tech-no-heart imperialist menace, the caboclo is some sort of shaman (in Brazilian culture, *pajé* would be a more appropriate term), the guardian of ancient popular wisdom based on a peaceful coexistence with other beings and nature. The main character, the nuclear power plant's employee played by Henrique Zanetta, moves between these two "archetypes" (the mad scientist and the shaman), and finally finds refuge under the auspices of the *caboclo*, after he is forced to look for shelter in the hills following the catastrophe in the nuclear power plant located by the sea. The *caboclo* teaches the man from the city that by bathing in armadillo's blood he could become invulnerable to the effects of radiation. The idea of becoming invulnerable, or with a *corpo fechado* ("closed body" or "unbreakable"), by virtue of a deity or divine nature is quite popular in Brazilian culture, as in other cultures around the world. Thus, Bertoni's film reaffirms the opposition between science and nature (or ancient wisdom), while also affiliating science and technology with some kind of alien, foreign menace, as in Alberto Pieralisi's *The 5th Power*. In one of the most striking scenes in *Armadillo Blood* is when the nuclear power plant is collapsing and the foreign scientist is trapped in his office. He apparently does not die of radiation or any explosion, as one might expect. As the building shakes, a kitsch iron miniature of the Statue of Liberty, apparently heavy, falls down from a shelf and onto the scientist's chest, in an eloquent and comic nod at the perils of scientific development in tandem with imperialist interests.

*Armadillo Blood* is a radical independent short film made by Bertoni and friends in a period where the Brazilian audiovisual industry had already shown signs of economic decay, foreshadowing the economic neoliberal wave that would soon hold sway over the country's economy and society. In March 1990, the extinction of Embrafilme put an end to an era in terms of state film production and distribution in Brazil (for academic works on the rise and fall of Embrafilme, see Stam and Johnson 1979; Ortiz Ramos 1997; and Melo Souza 1993, among others). At the beginning of the 1990s, with Fernando Collor as president, a series of economic neoliberal policies put the culture industry in danger and the Brazilian production of commercial feature films dropped to almost zero. But among the few Brazilian 35mm feature films made in the period, there was an ambitious venture into SF based on environmental speculation.

About seven years after *Armadillo*, in the Rio-92 or ECO-92, held in Rio de Janeiro in 1992 and a sequel to the 1972 United Nations World Environment Conference, gaining momentum was the notion that the highly industrialized countries (e.g., the United States, the EU, Japan) are actually responsible for the bulk of emissions of pollutants into the atmosphere and other damage to the environment. ECO-92 published documents and introduced measures such as Agenda 21 and the Kyoto Protocol, and helped Brazil to ameliorate its image of being the "environment's public enemy number one," provoking intense debates that extrapolated the official milieux. By that time, environmentalism—or at least a growing ecological awareness—had already been fairly well established around the world, even in some poor countries. Meanwhile, the United States was beginning to look at the new environmental proposals as obstacles to maintaining its economy, the largest and most polluting on the planet. "Ironically, protest posters no longer identified Brazil as the villain, but the United States" (Duarte 2003, 43).

Shot between 1989 and 1993, *Atlantis Ocean* (*Oceano Atlantis*), directed by Francisco de Paula, featured the city of Rio de Janeiro in a near future, when global warming had melted the planet's polar ice caps and elevated the surface of the oceans a few meters. In this ecodystopian future, a deluge left much of Rio underwater, and what were once called *favelas* became the only safe areas for the remaining city dwellers. The main character in this film is a diver and bounty hunter (Nuno Leal Maia) who had fled from a mental hospital and now dives regularly in search for food and a mysterious "lost treasure." On one of these dives he finds an underwater society, allegedly descended from the mythical Atlanteans. The film's plot is rather clumsy, however, and the true origin of the characters as well as their intentions are quite difficult to grasp. Several dialogues in foreign languages like Italian, Greek, and German, as well as Portuguese and English, make the whole story even more difficult to understand. It seems that the survivors on the surface feed on colored liquids but need solid food to maintain their health. All the solid food lies submerged and thus the need for divers to retrieve supplies. In fact, the movie refers to this food shortage in the following terms in its enigmatic opening credits: "In Rio de Janeiro, a flood leaves as survivors those who took refuge high in the mountains. With not enough food or land for harvesting, the government prohibits the sacrifice of animals, except some species of edible dogs."[17] In the apparently more advanced underwater society, people seem protected by some sort of ancient wisdom, a legacy from the Atlanteans.

The film's cast includes iconic actresses and actors. Besides Nuno Leal Maia, Arduíno Colasanti plays the role of a wise leader in the underwater civilization. Antonio Abujamra is a scientist in the same community, and Dercy Gonçalves, then eighty-four years old, plays a mute Atlantean lady who, like her fellows, communicates through telepathy. For this role Dercy Gonçalves won the Best Supporting Actress Award at the XXVI Brasília Film Festival. Never commercially released but screened in relevant festivals such as the Brasília Film Festival and Rio-Cine, *Oceano Atlantis* also won the 1993 Rio-Cine Festival Critics Award (Silva Neto 2002, 595).

Francisco de Paula's film combines disaster movie tropes with the tradition of utopian stories about Atlantis, the lost continent. Documentary images of trains, slums, and other *carioca*[18] landmarks are interspersed with the fictional narrative, which seems to progress regardless of some nonsensical scenes and questionable experimentalism. All in all, the film has some interesting ideas, such as the linguistic diversity and the social transformations imposed by the deluge, with the remapping of Rio de Janeiro's center and periphery. Several scenes are beautifully cinematographed by the renowned Brazilian cinematographers Dib Lufti and Pedro Farkas, although these same images sometimes seem displaced in the narrative flow. Some of these scenes were shot in Fernando de Noronha, the archipelago in the Atlantic Ocean, in the far Northeast of Brazil. Fernando de Noronha is a natural reserve and military area, a lush, trendy tourist destination. Francisco de Paula directed *Oceano Atlantis* when he was only twenty-two years old. It was his second feature film, and a genuine independent project of Brazilian SF cinema against all odds. His first feature, *Scalding Sands* (*Areias Escaldantes*, 1985) also had some circumstantial science fictionish iconography, especially in some futurist set designs drawn by Arturo Uranga, with its plot being remotely inspired by dystopian literature. More a musical than SF film, *Scalding Sands* is a remarkable document of the Brazilian pop music scene in the 1980s, a particularly rich and eventful period toward the end of the dictatorship, when a young generation of poets and musicians rediscussed the nation through their art. *Scalding Sands* was supposed to be a more somber SF film noir or technoir, perhaps one of the first quasi-cyberpunk Brazilian films. However, the production and budgetary constraints turned it into an SF musical comedy, in tune with the emerging Brazilian rock/pop music scene in the mid-1980s.

Shortly after the completion of *Atlantis Ocean*, between 1993 and 1994, a kind of renaissance in Brazilian cinema took place, the so-called

Cinema da Retomada. Fundamentally fueled by the industry's access to renewed sources of state funding, the Retomada was predominately brought about by fiscal exemptions allowed by the Audiovisual Law (Lei do Audiovisual n. 8.685, July 20, 1993), in tandem with grants and awards such as the Prêmio Resgate do Cinema Brasileiro. The Rouanet Law (Lei Rouanet n. 8.313, December 23, 1991) also widened and strengthened funding possibilities not only for films but also cultural projects and events in general. Likewise, municipal and state laws promoting fiscal exemption had a positive impact on the recovery of film production in the country. All these laws and state initiatives allowed the private sector to redirect funds from taxes to film production: for better or for worse, in the sense that private initiative thenceforth could decide which kind of film should or should not be produced.

*93º Tunnel, Stop 88, Nuclear Shelter, Armadillo Blood,* and *Atlantis Ocean* are clear Brazilian contributions to ecodystopian fabulation, a subgenre that according to Gary Wolfe, operates under the sign of the wasteland (Wolfe, 1979). The films commented on above mirror the first signs of this new sensibility concerning the environment in Brazil, following a literary tradition held by works such as Plínio Cabral's *Umbra* (1977), or Ignacio de Loyola Brandão's short story "The Man Who Spread the Desert" ("O Homem que Espalhou o Deserto," 2003 [originally published in 1979]) and his novel *And Still the Earth*, among several other authors and titles. Ginway points out that, in these literary works, "environmental degradation goes hand in hand with eroding personal freedom as Brazil faces the ecological and political consequences of military rule" (Molina-Gávilan et al. 2007, 382).

The films mentioned here are also imbued with a kind of antimodern or antitechnological discourse. In *Stop 88*, for instance, the main character and his family abandon the city. Likewise, in *Nuclear Shelter* Lat gives up on the subterranean city to embrace an idyllic life on the beach. *Armadillo Blood* also has a remarkable antimodern aspiration, obvious in the *caboclo*, the countryman who rescues the power-plant employee that had fled from a nuclear accident. The countryman is a "real" character representing popular wisdom, a sort of knowledge opposed to the scientists' and army's hubris. He obtains all the energy he needs from water power and represents a "clean" way of life. This way of life, nonetheless, is not free from superstition.

According to Brian Stableford (in Seed 2007, 131–34), mysticism is a recurring element in literary ecodystopias. It also often appears in tandem with the characters' memories of the past in some of the films analyzed here. Thus, nostalgia may stand out as a relevant value in all these films. In *Stop 88*, for instance, it is this feeling that pushes the characters forward. This same nostalgia can be felt in *Nuclear Shelter*, through the rebel desire for rediscovering the past, and in *93º Tunnel*, especially through the imagery and the voice-over poem related to the main character's memories. A romantic viewpoint or even a kind of Luddism can be recognized through the nostalgic treatment and worship of nature in the Brazilian cinematic ecodystopias, where modernity, attached to the armed forces and bureaucracy, also brings imprisonment and the loss of the original ties to nature: an imagery that can be translated, according to Ginway, into an attempt at national identity (Ginway 2004, 90–91).

However, the films herein discussed do not present an obviously mystical discourse. Being antimodern does not necessarily imply being mystical. Only *Armadillo Blood* presents a more evident archaic-mystical counterpart, perhaps represented by the *caboclo*. On the other hand, none of these movies conceal their left-wing tendencies. *93º Tunnel* is the only one in which the main character eventually dies due to the poisoned atmosphere. But in both *Nuclear Shelter* and *Stop 88*, the characters venture into the polluted air, challenging the status quo and opening new possibilities for social change.

Nostalgia is perhaps the most standout trait that Brazilian SF ecodystopian film shares with Western and even Eastern European filmography. For instance, American ecodystopias such as Richard Fleischer's *Soylent Green* (1973) and Ridley Scott's *Blade Runner* obviously refer to a "greener" past, but nostalgia is not treated in the same way as in Brazilian films such as *93o Tunnel*, or *Nuclear Shelter*. Pursuing an idyllic life on a wild beach (as in *Nuclear Shelter*) or retrieving one's original Native American origin is not exactly an option for most American or Anglophone SF film characters. If there is any nostalgia in a film such as Miller's *Mad Max*, it cannot be immediately translated as "memories of green" and does not refer directly to any myth of origin. It happens as though technological man has come to stay, there being no point of return any farther back in time before the Industrial Revolution. Curiously, Australia and Brazil, both former colonies, have some similarities that are not equally reflected in their respective SF cinemas. Reasons for this could lie, perhaps, in their different metropolitan backgrounds (the UK and Portugal, respectively). One could say that, in Anglo-Saxon SF ecodystopian cinema, archaism is not an essential narrative factor, and modernity (science and technology included) is not usually regarded as a threat per se, let alone as a foreign menace, regardless of the numerous English-spoken technophobic dystopias. On the contrary, technological armageddon often follows some kind of hubris or the breaking of an equilibrium: see, for instance, Andy and Larry Wachowski's *The Matrix* (1999), also an ecodystopian film. It is often a matter of "technology in the wrong hands," a widespread cliché in SF cinema in general. In the Brazilian ecodystopian film, or maybe in the whole of Brazilian SF, technology appears to be far less neutral. It may be a problem in itself as an intruder, an exotic agent that is often spoken of in foreign languages.

Furthermore, in a film such as Douglas Trumbull's *Silent Running* (1979), the "green" does depend on technology. Therefore, to what extent are nature and technology interwoven in American SF films? This question has no prompt answer. Conversely, Brazil's 7,367 km of shoreline, the Amazonian mythology and Indigenous myths of origin seem to have an important role in Brazilian SF ecodystopias, both in literature and film. The panorama may not be the same in the SF cinemas from other underdeveloped or developing countries, such as Eastern Europe's. This is just a preliminary hypothesis, but the socialist or communist agenda seems to have had an impact on this issue,[19] helping to efface surviving romantic myths of origin in favor of a more materialist, modern worldview.

Apart from being cinematic protests against reckless modernization, the films herein discussed cannot be dissociated from wider critical approaches to the Brazilian economic, social, and political contexts during the military dictatorship, its aftermath, and the more recent complicated scenario. In other words, all the aforementioned SF films can be seen as allegories representing a society under pressure, incapable of breathing fresh air and subjected to invisible, bureaucratic, authoritarian, and even Kafkaesque powers and threats. More examples could be added to the mediascapes of Brazilian cinematic dystopias, such as Walter Lima Jr.'s 35mm feature-length film *Brazil Year 2000* (*Brasil Ano 2000*), a highly allegorical film that represents a later stage in Brazilian Cinema Novo. As seen in a previous chapter in this book, Walter Lima Jr.'s *Brazil Year 2000* presents a postapocalyptic future in which World War III ruined the north of the planet, thus paving the way for Brazil to emerge as a new superpower.

Nelson Pereira dos Santos's postapocalyptic film *Who is Beta?* (*Quem é Beta?*, or *Pas de Violence entre Nous*, 1972), is a French-Brazilian co-production that can also be added to the galaxy of Brazilian ecodystopian films. In *Who is Beta?* the aftermath of a global war suspends civilizational constraints and plunges mankind into a lawless world, leaving human beings free to fulfill their most basic instincts while a zombie outbreak is set in motion. Shot in the city of Paraty, in the state of Rio de Janeiro, amid an exuberant landscape characteristic of the Mata Atlântica, Nelson Pereira dos Santo's *Who is Beta?* tells the story of a love triangle in its fight for survival in that postapocalyptic world. The trio live in between a premodern, idyllic lifestyle reminiscent of counterculture, evocative of hippie culture and the African-Brazilian religion called Candomblé,[20] and the scarcity of supplies amid the zombie apocalypse. Along with *A Very Crazy Asylum* (*Azyllo Muito Louco*, 1970), *How Tasty was my Frenchman* (*Como Era Gostoso o meu Francês*, 1971), and *Hunger for Love* (*Fome de Amor*, 1968), *Who is Beta?* represents the last work in Nelson Pereira dos Santos's filmography known as "the Paraty phase," when the director and his crew lived isolated in the small historic town in the state of Rio de Janeiro, far from big urban areas and the tense political atmosphere under the military regime. These films represent a more acutely psychedelic stage in Nelson Pereira dos Santos's career, resulting from his and his crew's own experience of isolation in a hippie community. Both *Azyllo Muito Louco* and *Quem é Beta?* can be related to SF iconography by and large. Some remarkable scenes in *Who is Beta?* anticipated international SF films like Wim Wenders's *Until the End of the World* (*Bis ans Ende der Welt*, 1991), when a holography is enacted. In *Who is Beta?*, the main characters can access their memories in some sort of "holodeck" made out of moving images screened on a smoke curtain.

The fact that all the main characters are eventually banished or exiled is also noteworthy in the Brazilian ecodystopian films discussed here, notably the ones released during or immediately after the military rule. As expressed in the title of the previous chapter in this book, "Brazil: Love It or Leave It" ("Brasil: ame-o ou deixe-o"), it was a popular motto during the military dictatorship. In the Brazilian cinematic ecodystopia, the main character is always forced to leave her/his town, something that expresses the pessimism behind fiction involving social change. The Brazilian ecodystopian hero is, above all, an exile.

In summary, the films discussed in this chapter demonstrate that the ecological issue became an effective interface for the critique of the regime since the Brazilian military government followed a course of reckless industrial development that has not equally distributed wealth among the citizens nor provided gains in social welfare—yet it did increase deforestation and the genocide of Indigenous peoples.

For instance, in José de Anchieta's *Stop 88*, a film directed by an ex-member of the Communist Party in Brazil, the state is a great absent but oppressive "ghost" whose power is felt through bans, checkpoints, rigid protocols, charges and fees. As noticed in the scene of the meeting at the department of gas control, the city is kept in such a long quarantine due to the mind-boggling bureaucracy and inefficiency of the government. It turns out to be contradictory that such a state, little concerned about the welfare of the survivors in Parada 88, ends up rescuing Joaquim Porfírio. José de Anchieta justifies this scene in the movie by commenting that, although it was not clear, Joaquim Porfírio is saved by political interest. According to Anchieta, *Stop 88* is essentially a metaphor about the dementia of power.[21] Likewise, the passion of Ana, Joaquim Porfírio's daughter, for Angel Face (Terence Tullgren), the air tax collector who violates her, could also be understood as a metaphor for an entranced people fascinated by its oppressor. Eventually, Ana reluctantly leaves the city, angry at her father as he had killed Angel Face in revenge. Toward the end of the film, Ana shouts "I hate you" against her father. On criticism of the state bureaucracy and the authoritarian regime, José de Anchieta comments: "I was taken by the spirit of the time and adopted the metaphor as language, a kind of wisdom that protected me from the harm of censorship. But I have never faced problems with censorship. I was massacred by the press, not the censorship."[22]

Like many other filmmakers and writers at the time, José de Anchieta adopted the strategy of SF metaphor as film language in *Stop 88* mostly for the sake of dodging the censorship. Nearly thirty years after the redemocratization of Brazil, the ecodystopian imaginary continues to fuel debates on the reckoning with a history of authoritarianism and the increase in the world's social inequality favored by economic neoliberal governments. This can be seen in Kléber Mendonça Filho's *Cold Tropics* (*Recife Frio*), a 2009 short film that criticizes the status quo represented by real estate speculation and financial capital, and in Luiz Bolognesi's *Rio 2096* (*Uma História de Amor e Fúria*, 2013), a feature-length animation with a focus on the enduring authoritarianism and the never-paid-off-debt concerning the majority of Brazilians, massacred people who were never properly redeemed by the official history.[23] After a brief period of social advancement in this regard, between the late-1990s and the 2000s, the return of the extreme right to power induces a review of all the aforementioned films, as their encoded warnings may remain valid at recent or present times. The ecodystopian film exists, therefore, as one of the most structured and everlasting manifestations of SF in Brazilian cinema, offering critical and speculative visions at the crossroads of social, political, and environmental issues.

5

# Proxy Futures and Other Simulacra

The Brazilian SF Comedy Endures,
along with the Adventure Movie and the Musical

As previously detailed in chapter 1, Brazilian film audiences likely made their first acquaintance with SF cinema through comedy and parodic films from the late 1940s through the mid-1950s. This was not an exclusively Brazilian phenomenon, as other national cinemas, such as Mexican or Argentinean cinema, may well have had similar histories. Around the world, SF film has always had close ties to the literary and dramatic tradition of satire. In Latin America, the combination between these two "molecules"—comedy and SF—seems to have always been explosively hilarious. Brazilian cinema was not so different from other countries in this regard, even though it consistently lacked the proper film industrialization that took place in Argentina and Mexico at various times (Cuarterolo 2007; Schmelz 2006; Barrios 2006; Paz 2008; Delgado 2001). All evidence suggests that the combination of SF and comedy endured as the dominant trend during the history of Brazilian SF cinema. Therefore, this chapter will concentrate on the Brazilian SF comedies that proliferated in the 1970s, 1980s, and 1990s, thus extending the legacy of *chanchada*.

Among numerous self-mocking parodies that took advantage of foreign blockbusters (such as R. L. Stevenson's oeuvre, Franklin J. Schaffner's *Planet of the Apes*, 1968; George Lucas's *Star Wars*, 1977; and Steven Spielberg's *Jaws*, 1975), there was a consistent and profitable spate of SF comedies throughout the 1970s and 1980s in Brazil. These films usually targeted children or juvenile audiences and were directed by experienced directors originating from the *chanchada*'s golden age and the biggest Brazilian studios, such as Atlântida Cinematográfica.[1] Prime examples from the 1970s and 1980s wave of SF comedies include J. B. Tanko's *The Goofs at the Ape's Plateau* (*Os Trapalhões no Planalto dos Macacos*, 1976), Adriano Stuart's *The Goofs in the War of the Planets* (*Os Trapalhões na Guerra dos Planetas*, 1978), *The Incredible Goof Monster* (*O Incrível Monstro Trapalhão*, 1981), and *Cuddly and the Lost Spaceship* (*Fofão e a Espaçonave Perdida*, 1989), among other titles. The Goofs (Os Trapalhões) were a very popular group of comedians that began with a successful television career, particularly after they were hired by the emerging Rede Globo (the largest TV channel in Brazil) in the mid-1960s, and expanded into film and comic strips, with parody being a recurrent motif in their films. Another example of this strong and long-lasting parodic trend is Roberto Farias's *Roberto Carlos in Adventure Rhythm* (*Roberto Carlos em Ritmo de Aventura*, 1968), a parody of James Bond films, starring the famous Brazilian singer. These films are among those that will be examined in the present chapter.

SF may well be regarded as a multimedia or intermedial genre, a macro-genre with extremely agile tentacles and skillful shapeshifting abilities that help it transit from one medium to another with ease. Nineteen-fifties American SF cinema cannot be comprehended differently, cut out from the space opera and pulp fiction tradition. The same applies to American SF television and its subsequent influence on video games. In the blink of an eye, SF teleported itself from one medium to another and soon extended its reach and influence across multiple media.

A number of Brazilian films from the 1970s and 1980s featured mind-boggling parodies of American blockbusters, attempting to re-create or "retrofit" popular American film genres with local colors. In this scenario, SF and fantasy stood out as genres of choice, as was often the case with Brazilian adventure films targeted at juvenile audiences. In addition to the aforementioned films, one can consider titles as varied as Ivan Cardoso's films *The Mummy's Secret* (*O Segredo da Múmia*, 1982) and *The Seven Vampires* (*As Sete Vampiras*, 1986), and Francisco de Paula's *Scalding Sands* (*Areias Escaldantes*, 1985). Some of these films are particularly interesting from an intermedial perspective, insofar as they are often musicals starring popular Brazilian singers or rock bands. By featuring popular showbiz artists and songs, these hybrid films lured generations of young viewers to the cinema until the shutdown of the state production company Embrafilme in 1990, the latest major crisis in the history of Brazilian cinema. It is worth mentioning that in addition to the enduring combination of SF and comedy, the redesign of such film production from the perspective of the juvenile film or teenpic played an important role in 1970s and 1980s Brazilian cinema.

Following the decline of the Brazilian *chanchada*, the 1970s and 1980s set the stage for a new generation of highly popular productions. The term "teenpic" may make one think of a very popular genre of American movie, made popular by directors such as John Hughes (*Weird Science*, 1985; *The Breakfast Club*, 1985; *Ferris Bueller's Day Off*, 1986), John Landis (*The Blues Brothers*, 1980; *An American Werewolf in London*, 1981) and Joe Dante (*Rock 'n' Roll High School*, 1979, with Allan Arkush; *Gremlins*, 1984). But Zuleika Bueno reminds us that the cultural revolution represented by the "power of youth" and the "juvenilization of social life" took place not only in America but also became a global trend in film production (Bueno 2005, 15). She also explains that Brazil has produced films targeted at juvenile audiences since the 1950s, but it was only in the 1980s that Brazilian teenpics gained momentum (2005, 15). Bueno further scrutinizes the rise of juvenile cinema in Brazil in her work titled *Read the Book, See the Film, Buy the Record: The Rise of Brazilian Juvenile Cinema* (*Leia o Livro, Veja o Filme, Compre o Disco: A Formação do Cinema Juvenil Brasileiro*, 2016).

The *chanchada*, as well as its cinematic offspring have been frequently accused of reaffirming a biased stereotypical, colonialist viewpoint. This critique relies on the assumption that often the carnivalesque aesthetics infused in the *chanchadas* only served to blur a rather conservative attitude. In "From *High Noon* to *Jaws*: Carnival and Parody in Brazilian Cinema," João Luiz Vieira (1995) analyzes "Brazilian cinema's love-hate relationship to its North American counterpart" in the light of dependency theory, Mikhail Bakhtin's notion of the carnivalesque, and Roberto Da Matta's (1997) work on present-day carnival in Rio. Despite the value of allegorical visions proposed by some *chanchadas*—for instance, Carlos Manga's *Neither Samson nor Delilah*—and Paulo Emilio Salles Gomes's thoughts on the remarkable popularity of the genre in the 1940s and 1950s (Salles Gomes 1996, 74), Vieira does not share the same enthusiasm regarding the Brazilian erotic comedy or juvenile films released in the 1970s, and ultimately concludes that most film parodies in the *pornochanchada* style ended up doing a disservice to Brazilian cinema. According to Vieira,

> Parody in Brazilian cinema arises as an indication of the relationship of power existent in the struggle for the cinematic market in Brazil, pointing toward the dominant force in that market: the foreign film, and predominantly the American film. The simple fact that parody in Brazilian cinema is directed primarily at the American film indicates its wide penetration in Brazilian cinematic culture. This penetration appears on an economic level in the form of domination of the market and is reflected culturally in the colonized attitudes of those who make and consume cinema in the country. The fact that parody in Brazilian cinema generally points toward a situation of cultural and economic dependency, does not mean, however, that it has consciously criticized and revealed this condition. What exists, rather, is a situation in which (as Paulo Emílio Salles Gomes has observed) Brazilian cinema itself is criticized for its creative incompetence in copying, within the standards dreamed of by filmmakers and the public, the powerful technological efficiency of such American films as *Jaws* or *King Kong*. (Vieira 1995, 259)

This conclusion perhaps does not exclude future revisions, as new readings of the *chanchadas*, the *pornochanchadas* (see Abreu 2006, 2012), and popular cinema as a whole have cast new light on the value of some underestimated cultural products (in addition to Salles Gomes 1996, 74, see Lyra and Santana 2006, 2008, and 2012). Despite being underrated by film critics and a new generation of young filmmakers in its time (e.g., Glauber Rocha), the *chanchada* did create a cinematic environment that took full advantage of generous communication with broader film audiences in Brazil. In the next section we will focus on specific films from the late 1960s to mid-1990s that followed in the footsteps of this *chanchada* tradition.

## No Machine Rivals the King

José Mário Ortiz Ramos refers to Roberto Carlos's films as a blend of action movie, detective film, and musical, all adapted to a Brazilian context (Ortiz Ramos 2004, 201). *Roberto Carlos in Adventure Rhythm* (1968, from now on referred to as *RCAR*), the first of a trilogy written and directed by Roberto Farias,[2] is a parody of the Bond films that takes advantage of metalinguistics, a touch of nonsense, and a local Brazilian take on of the American musical. As expected, in the cultural logic of this film, the hero stands for an archetype: Roberto Carlos is a master of all trades, arts, and crafts. However, despite his outstanding ability to pilot both race cars and helicopters, he does not entirely depend on technology: his natural gifts suffice. Popular SF elements in the film (cannibalized mostly from American B movies and the Bond series) can be ascribed mostly to the villains, who want to abduct Roberto Carlos and hold sway over his genius by "downloading" his musical talent into an "electronic brain," in order to ramp up the singer's musical production and, thus, make a fortune. The villains' computer that was featured in the film, lent by the Bank of the State of Guanabara,[3] worked with magnetic tapes and perforated cards: cutting-edge technology at that time. Brigitte (a foreign name), mentor of the villains, wears glossy futuristic outfits. Meanwhile, another SF icon is showcased when Roberto Carlos travels on a space rocket launched from Cape Kennedy in the United States to Brazil, in a sequence made up of documentary footage (Suppia 2013, 56). To shoot scenes at Cape Kennedy, the film crew achieved an unprecedented feat: they got NASA's permission to shoot in the rocket launch towers. As a result, Roberto Carlos "travels through space" with proper archival footage showing the Blue Planet from high above. The film included locations in some of Rio de Janeiro's most famous landmarks, such as the Corcovado, the Maracanã stadium, and Guanabara Bay, in addition to the scenes shot in São Paulo and New York. To defeat the foreign villains, Roberto Carlos is featured in risky stunt scenes, like getting inside a car hanging from a crane or crossing the Pasmado Tunnel in Rio while piloting a helicopter. The shooting featuring the helicopter scenes stopped traffic in Copacabana, while the scenes with airplanes were made using pilots of the Smoke Squadron (Esquadrilha da Fumaça, a famous team of acrobatic air pilots). In some of these scenes, director Roberto Farias himself was aboard the aircraft. *RCAR* had a total audience of over 2.5 million in cinemas. José Mário Ortiz Ramos remarks that *RCAR* is constantly punctuated by moments of narrative interruption, in which the characters speak about the film as a work in progress: "The parody of adventure and detective films appears, therefore, interlaced with the dismantling of narrative illusionism, or through the usage of metalanguage, as usual in the 70s" (2004, 199).[4] An example of this procedure is the sequence in which a character portraying a movie director, played by Reginaldo Faria

(Roberto Farias's brother), discusses his art and craft on the rooftop of a building, his face appearing alternately bearded and shaved in consecutive shots. In this scene in particular, Ortiz Ramos comments that *RCAR* "tried to dodge difficulties inherent in Brazilian film production by resorting to parody and following the footsteps of the *chanchada* (. . .). But the film also tried to escape from pure entertainment, resorting to deconstruction and doses of cinematic erudition" (Ortiz Ramos 2004, 199).

These "doses of erudition," however, were not able to shield Roberto Farias from critics who accused him of being a "mercantilist" director for having made a film with "the King" Roberto Carlos (Ortiz Ramos 2004, 200).[5] For instance, the Brazilian critic and filmmaker Alex Viany (1993, 144) disapproved of Farias's film by affirming that "in abandoning promising projects, again he [Roberto Farias] looks for easy commercial success, by means of a comedy starring the idol of the *iêiêiê*[6] youth, Roberto Carlos." Ortiz Ramos also recalls that *RCAR* took great advantage of media and publicity from the start of its production. An example of such media effort was a public TV and magazine contest aimed at selecting the female equivalent to the "Bond girls" to eventually cast them in the film starring Roberto Carlos. Needless to say, although cinema would be a "new frontier" for Roberto Carlos, the popular singer already had an extremely successful career on radio and TV. In addition to taking part in numerous TV-broadcasted music festivals, Roberto Carlos presented, along with his friends Erasmo Carlos and Wanderléa, the TV show titled *Jovem Guarda* (1965–1968).

Ortiz Ramos further observes that the more communicative, popular cinema intended by Roberto Farias "ended up catalyzing the contradictions of a broader cultural process" (2004, 200). Indeed, Farias's film suggests a "desire for modernity" revealed by means of costume design, sets, props, camera set-ups, and its adherence to science fiction-ish semantics and syntax. When production problems intervened and the so-called modernity was perhaps compromised, Farias seemed to resort to irony and meta-language. According to Ortiz Ramos, whereas "a certain precariousness emerges everywhere, revealing problems of film production," one could also identify an "obvious attraction for 'modern technology,' the desire to be in tune with the developed world" (Ortiz Ramos 2004, 200). Ultimately, one may wonder if the modern narrative in Farias's film stems from the precarious production apparatus rather than from something initially preplanned. This is supported by a number of scenes from the Roberto Carlos's trilogy, further analyzed by Ortiz Ramos. In films like *RCAR*, the appeal of international settings and a more transparent, classical narrative suggest that the rebellion and parody of 1968 gave way to an expansion of dialogue with the market, including the music industry (Ortiz Ramos 2004, 204).

### The Potion Is Ours: The Goofs' SF Film Parodies[7]

Another "heir" to the *chanchada* tradition can be found in the films starring Os Trapalhões,[8] a popular group of comedians who had an extremely successful career on TV, especially after they were hired by Rede Globo, hegemonic from the 1970s onward, and only now challenged by other media or platforms such as streaming services, YouTube, etc. With a successful TV show aired by Globo every Sunday at 7 p.m., the Goofs' prime audience was children and adolescents, in addition to a vast number of adult viewers. Initially consisting of a duo, Didi (Renato Aragão) and Dedé (Manfried Santana), the team quickly welcomed a third member, Mussum (Antônio Carlos Bernardes Gomes), and finally a fourth character, Zacarias (Mauro Faccio Gonçalves).[9] The show that would later become a great success on Globo began in embryonic form in *The Unsocial Ones* (*Os Insociáveis*), broadcast by RecordTV from 1972 to 1974. Directed by Wilton Franco, *Os Insociáveis* featured Renato Aragão (Didi), Manfried Santana (Dedé) and Antonio Carlos (Mussum) as the trio of troublemakers involved in comic sketches.

It is worth noting that the Goofs represent one of the first examples of consistently high ratings in tandem with the rise of television as the hegemonic media industry in the country. From the mid-1960s onward, the number of households with a TV set rose exponentially. Throughout the 1960s, only 4.6 percent of residences had a TV: the southeast, the most urbanized and industrialized region, accounted for 12.4 percent of the total number of TVs. Throughout the 1980s, the average number of TV sets in the country increased to 56.1 percent. In 1991, 71 percent of Brazilian homes had a TV set and, in 2006, this number was 93 percent (Cesário 2010, 139).

Between 1978 and 1990, the quartet's comics were the stars, in no less than twenty feature films (not to mention a documentary and an animated feature) that, together, brought more than 74 million viewers to cinemas. Not surprisingly, the film considered to be the first feature starring the Goofs takes advantage of the pop music scene, notably the Jovem Guarda movement: *Na onda do Iê-iê-iê* (*On the Wave of Iêiêiê*, 1966), directed by Aurélio Teixeira, starred the duo Didi (Renato Aragão) and Maloca (Manfried Santana). The relationship with the Jovem Guarda would continue through the work at RecordTV, when the group performed along with the singer Vanusa. After leaving the Jovem Guarda, fully "rebranded," Roberto Carlos performed in more than one episode of the Goofs.

Approximately fourteen of the thirty highest-grossing Brazilian films bear the Goofs brand. Five films starring the comedians, released between 1977 and 1981, achieved an audience of more than five million.[10] From Teixeira's *Na onda do iêiêiê* in 1966, until the dissolution of the quartet by the late 1990s, each of the films featuring the Goofs brand were among the most successful commercial enterprises of Brazilian cinema. In total, approximately 120 million people have watched films starring the Goofs. According to a list recently published by the National Cinema Agency (Ancine), between 1971 and 1991, the films starring the Goofs, whether featuring the whole quartet or starring only Renato Aragão, achieved no less than thirteen titles among the top-twenty box office hits in Brazil. Over these approximately twenty years, thirty-two feature films starring the group exceeded an audience of one million people (Moser 2014).

The films starring Didi, Dedé, Mussum, and Zacarias were released mostly between the 1970s and 1990s and during the time of the military rule and the heyday of its state production company, Embrafilme. Galvanized by their overwhelming success on TV, the Goofs stand out in the history of the Brazilian film industry due to the successful connection the group was able to establish with audiences of diverse ages. Experienced directors such as Carlos Manga, J. B. Tanko, Adriano Stuart, Daniel Filho, and Roberto Farias helped make the Goofs an unprecedented cinematic phenomenon in Brazil, with more than forty feature-length films.[11]

Unlike Roberto Carlos, whose cinematic career was rather short in comparison and came in the wake of his fame from radio, television, and music festivals, the Goofs appear to have had a career that spanned both TV and film. The group also spread its tentacles over the music industry, having released no fewer than twenty-three albums. José Mário Ortiz Ramos, one of the Brazilian film scholars who paid most attention to the media phenomenon of Os Trapalhões, divides the group's extensive filmography into three groups or "subserialities," which he called (1) Foreign Literary Themes, (2) Social / National Themes, and (3) Modernized Cinematic Themes (Ortiz Ramos 2004, 125–26). We are herein essentially interested in the third group, films inspired by contemporary international cinema, concerned with scripts, settings, and visual effects (Ortiz Ramos 2004, 126). It is also worth noting the recurrence of a model structure in the Goofs' films, as Ortiz Ramos details by drawing on Umberto Eco's "scheme / variation" popular mass culture (Ortiz Ramos 2004, 143; Eco 1989, 123–24). Therefore, repetition emerges as a central artifice in the films starring the Goofs and, still according to Ortiz Ramos, "The repetition arises, therefore, connected with a valorization of the lived moment" (2004, 151). Thus, in 1976, the Goofs swallow *The Planet of the Apes* (1968), by Franklin J. Schaffner, and regurgitate *The Goofs in the Apes' Plateau* (*Os Trapalhões no Planalto dos Macacos*), a 1978 film written, directed, and produced by J. B. Tanko. According to the director, this was his fifth film with the Goofs, and the most expensive up to that point, costing about three million cruzeiros, with masks and costumes imported from the States (Neves 1977). In this first film bearing the Goofs' brand, with the participation of Mussum (Antonio Carlos Gomes), Conde (Renato Aragão) is the clumsy inventor of a motorized surfboard. A parodic reference to Steven Spielberg's *Jaws* is staged when Conde tests his motorized board for the first time. Conde is swallowed by a giant shark but ends up being rescued unscathed from inside the predator, which was in fact a purposely crude replica of the animal, about seven meters long and seven hundred kilos in weight. Confused for thieves of a jewelry store, Conde and his partner Alex (Dedé Santana) are chased by the clumsy policeman Azevedo (Mussum). In the escape, the three end up on board a special balloon, built by a foreign scientist, Prof. Bicard (Carlos Kumstat, or Carlos Kurt), to reach other planets. Amid a great commotion, Conde and Alex try to escape in the balloon, along with the policeman Azevedo and the balloonist Rodrigo (Alan Fontaine).

When the balloon reaches "80 thousand meters of altitude" (suborbital altitude), the crew members put on oxygen masks in a pathetic attempt to preserve scientific verisimilitude, which will be gone soon after, when the balloon lands on "another" planet. Amid banana trees, the four earthlings are captured by ape men. As in *Planet of the Apes*, the humans of this strange place are dumb, considered inferior, and hunted by the local ape men. The four heroes then escape, locate their balloon, and hide in the "forbidden zone" where several home appliances are stored. On Earth, these appliances had been chosen as pieces for an exhibition in memory of the humans' consumer society prior to the "great catastrophe," around the year 2000. The discovery of these relics by the ape men reinforces the thesis of the monkey scientist, who believes human beings had a complex civilization in the past and are the ancestors of the apes. Here the film alludes to the surprising ending of the original American film.

Conde improvises an electric generator, managing to turn on the appliances, and the apes throw a party with music, a fan, and a full fridge. The bumbling inventor also makes a motorcycle run on banana ("Doesn't banana have sugar? Doesn't sugar make alcohol? Isn't alcohol fuel?," asks Conde, in yet another scientific oversimplification). After many twists and quid pro quos, the heroes finally manage to escape in the space balloon and safely return to Earth, with Alex already restored to his human form.

Any concern with the verisimilitude of the story, its causal logic, or the quality of the sets and costumes is secondary to the main goal of this parody of Schaffner's *Planet of the Apes*, which is to show the faces and acrobatic moves of Didi, Dedé, and Mussum. *The Goofs in the Apes' Plateau* is one of numerous Brazilian films that capitalized on the success of 1970s American SF film productions, by featuring some of the most popular icons of the genre—for example, the mad scientist, the inventor, the spaceship, and the alien—through parody, pastiche, and self-referential jokes about a putative technical inferiority of Brazilian cinema. In a review of the film, José Carlos Avellar (1976) comments, "It is difficult to say what is worse in *The Goofs in the Apes' Plateau*, the clumsy opportunism of the argument, inspired by recent television and cinema successes, the poor quality of the slapstick staging, or the improvised scheme of production." Still according to Avellar (1976), "What could be satire has become just apery. The viewer does not laugh at the original through its caricature, nor do they laugh at the imperfections of the model through a stylized portrait. I laughed at the bad caricature, the inability to portray it properly." In this film review, Avellar aligns with Jean-Claude Bernardet's (1976) ideas on the futility of this kind of pastiche, pointing out differences between satire and parody, and the vices of a cultural subservience underlying the discourse of films like *The Goofs in the Ape's Plateau*.

In *The Goofs in the War of the Planets* (from now on *TGWP*), a 1978 film written by Renato Aragão and directed by Adriano Stuart, Prince Flick (Pedro Aguinaga) comes from space to ask for help in getting back the other half of his "computer brain" held by the evil Zucco (Carlos Kurt), and then free his people from the tyrant's yoke. The Goofs accept the reward offered by the prince (their weight in gold) and board a spaceship piloted by the furry monster Bonzo (Emil Rached), with whom Flick communicates in an alien language. The prince's dress, the characterization of Bonzo, and the landscape of the planet Airus are all crude imitations of

George Lucas's *Star Wars* (1977) and include a scene in which the Goofs are pathetically attacked by the "sand people." The villain Zucco is loosely modeled on Darth Vader, and the famous *Star Wars* scene of the alien-filled bar is also reproduced, mixed with the mood and camera style of the Brazilian soap opera *Dancin' Days*, a major success aired by Globo also in 1978. Naturally, this parody of *Star Wars* featuring the Goofs appears to be closer to films like Kinji Fukasaku's *Message from Space* (1978), the Japanese version of Lucas's film, than the original American model—with the advantage, we must admit, that *TGWP* really does not take itself very seriously. Therefore, the main goal of this production seems to have been fulfilled: to make children and young audiences laugh out loud at the Goofs' acrobatic humor and their incapacity to faithfully reproduce the American blockbuster.

The shoddy visual effects in this film are an attraction that supplements the acrobatics by the Goofs, such as when the heroes are attacked by invisible men. Other scenes are superimpositions, such as the attack of the giant spider. A good deal of metalanguage and anti-illusionism are also present throughout the film. At one point, for example, an enamored alien asks Didi if his impression is right that "Earth is a place where people live happily, safely, peacefully and calmly." Didi answers by addressing the camera, thus breaking the fourth wall in a modern film procedure: "Here I should say a joke, but—" and he opens his arms in dismay.

Zucco, the villain, then kidnaps Princess Myrna and negotiates her release in exchange for the other half of the computer brain, with which he intends to dominate the galaxy. Flick gives him the second half of the brain but is tricked by the villain, who breaks the agreement and captures the heroes. Before being executed, Didi appears with fabulous weapons (disintegrating, paralyzing, and explosive pistols) and saves his friends. The heroes finally defeat Zucco, while Prince Flick takes over the complete computer brain and his power is restored. Eventually, the Goofs' adventure begins winding down, and they are returned to Earth on the spaceship.

Back on Earth, the Goofs wake up outdoors and think everything was just a dream (a narrative artifice very familiar to SF films, especially proto or early SF, such as the Soviet *Aelita*, a 1924 film by Yakov Protazanov). However, a large incandescent mark on the ground and a gold jeep, containing bars of the precious metal, convince them otherwise. The film ends with the spaceship appearing in the sky and the Goofs waving the gold bars.

Shot on videotape and sent to the USA for postproduction and 35mm printing, *TGWP* inaugurates TV Globo's entry into feature film production and is associated with Renato Aragão, as well as being Renato Aragão's first film production (see Biáfora 1978, 46; Sternheim 1978, 26). José Mário Ortiz Ramos notes that, in the documentary *The Magical World of the Goofs* (*O Mundo Mágico dos Trapalhões*, 1981), director Sílvio Tendler acknowledges the hiring of the Goofs by Rede Globo as a "technological leap," and yet he also charges *The Goofs in the War of the Planets* as being an attempt to put a "tuxedo on the humor" of the quartet, thus privileging technique to the detriment of improvisation (Ortiz Ramos 2004, 126).

In his analysis of the Mexican SF film festival The Future in the Tropics: El Futuro mas Acá, exhibited at the 2006 Rio Film Festival, Estevão Garcia compares the film *La Nave de los Monstruos*, directed by Rogélio A. González (1959) to the Goofs' films, especially *TGWP*. According to Garcia, whereas *La Nave de los Monstruos* "is an extremely conscious parody," the SF parodies starring the Goofs "have not yet abandoned their tempting desire to copy. These films are not conscious parodies. *The Goofs in the War of the Planets* is the one that most clearly confirms this idea" (Garcia 2006). Garcia concludes that *TGWP* assumes itself to be a parody (including its title), but it does not adopt a parodic attitude because the yearning to be equivalent to the matrix is greater. "The film eventually becomes a legitimate parody for the simple fact it is not able to decently copy the original in any way. *War of the Planets* ends up laughing at itself" (Garcia 2006).

Indeed, Garcia tackles a central issue in Brazilian parodies, regardless of their box office success or degree of communication with broader audiences. It has to do with "precarious parodies," so to speak, or with the difference between parody and pastiche. But Garcia's analysis may not be totally applicable to the entire filmography starring the Goofs. José Mário Ortiz Ramos, one of the main reviewers of the idea of "precarious parody" in Brazilian cinema, has already demonstrated the heterogeneity within the Goofs' films, despite the recurrence of certain formulas (Ortiz Ramos 2004). Yet, *TGWP* does not assume the same parodic dimension one may find in other films starring the quartet, nor in equivalent foreign films, even in the United States.

Let us compare *TGWP* to *Spaceballs* (1987), a Mel Brooks comedy that shares the same "target" as the Brazilian film: the *Star Wars* film franchise by George Lucas. *Spaceballs* does not initially capitalize on humor based entirely on the impossibility of faithfully reproducing the model. On the contrary, Brooks's film begins by simulating *Star Wars* almost perfectly, from the iconic scrolling introductory text in perspective at the opening to the introduction of the villains' huge (apparently endless) starship. However, at these two moments, Brooks does not miss the opportunity to mock the original, incorporating jokes into the introductory text and exaggerating the cliché about the starship. On these two occasions, Brooks uses the same technology as in the object of parody, in a manner that, unlike *TGWP* comedy, does not spring from the contrast of film style or technique but essentially from the underlying discursive level. *Spaceballs*' spacecraft, for example, could perfectly feature among *Star Wars*'s X-Wings or Tie Fighters, despite its caricatural length and rear "bumper sticker," in the style of big trucks. In other words, there is no significant gap in terms of film style and technical resources, even though *Star Wars* was far more elaborate and costly. Regardless of the obvious difference in terms of budget, directors' film styles, and genre (SF comedy vs. SF space opera), *Spaceballs* lives up to existing more or less "as equal" with *Star Wars*, even though it mostly accentuates caricature as the main strategy of its parody. The qualitative gap is not invoked in Brooks's film as a trigger for humor. At least such a gap does not appear as visibly or intensely as in *TGWP*. In both Adriano Stuart's and Mel Brooks's films, metalanguage is intense (this is a central trait of parody), though in *Spaceballs* it is more refined and directs criticism at the model, such as in the scenes where Yogurt (parody of Yoda) exhibits merchandise with the *Spaceballs* brand, among other scenes.

In addition, *Spaceballs* mobilizes a more robust intertextual repertoire than *TGWP*, not least because it is not limited to *Star Wars*, thus parodying motifs or scenes from other SF films such as Ridley Scott's *Alien, the 8th Passenger* (1979), and Franklin J. Schaffner's *Planet of the Apes* (1968). It is difficult to affirm that the satire put forth by *Spaceballs* is completely beyond the reach of lower-budget cinema. Likewise, there is no way to safely predict that, had it been given a bigger budget, *TGWP* would have gone further. We compare these two productions for the simple fact that they both parody the same object, but the differences in terms of film culture context and film infra-structure between the Brazilian and the American comedies still make this comparison quite complicated.

Directed by Adriano Stuart, *The Incredible Goof Monster* (from now on *TIGM*) features a modest Brazilian scientist called Dr. Jegue (Renato Aragão)—here a pun on Robert Louis Stevenson's character named Jekyll, although "jegue" also refers to donkeys in the Northeast of Brazil—who works with Dedé, Mussum, and Zacarias as the mechanic of the racing driver Carlos, played by Eduardo Conde. Jegue's hobby is chemistry, and he has been doing research on a groundbreaking kind of fuel derived from the quince tree. He also discusses genetics and invents crazy gadgets, such as a "Rainbike" ("Bicichuva"), a covered bicycle for rainy days, among other bizarre inventions. Jegue's relationship with the character Ritinha (Alcione Mazzeo) is one of unrequited love. Inspired by a Superman picture pinned to a wall in his laboratory, the fumbling scientist decides to invent a substance to make him strong and handsome. Nevertheless, after drinking his serum for the first time, Jegue temporarily transmutes into a giant caveman: ugly but gifted with superhuman strength. The misunderstandings pile up, and Dr. Jegue ends up discovering the so-desired quince fuel, much more efficient and valuable than gasoline. It is thanks to this substance that Jegue spectacularly wins a motor race while replacing his boss, Carlos.

The news spreads, and Jegue is hailed as the inventor of a fuel-oil substitute. The Arabs and the Russians are interested in the formula, and an auction is held in which the Arabs top the Russians with an offer of US$100 million for the formula. But before signing the contract Jegue falls prey to his patriotic feelings. The Arabs react aggressively, but Jegue takes his potion and turns into the monster that sends the villains fleeing. Shortly after, the Russians kidnap the heroes' girlfriends and blackmail Jegue and his companions. Thanks to the phone in Jegue's laboratory—a payphone with an "identifier" that shows an image of the place where the call originated—the heroes head to an amusement park named Playcenter,[12] where the girls are held captive.

The amusement park seems to offer the perfect avenue to underscore the corporeal humor of the Goofs, notably Renato Aragão, by providing them a constant position of "pure reaction" (see Benjamin 1999, 18, on the effects of world exhibitions and attractions such as amusement parks).[13] This not only happens in *TIGM*—the musical scene performed by Lucinha Lins in J. B. Tanko's *The Goof Acrobats* (*Os Saltimbancos Trapalhões*, 1981) was set in Hollywood, with film or TV settings repurposed into an amusement park. This "pure reaction" is perhaps at the core of the Goofs' corporeal humor. One of their most frequent sketches on TV featured Carlos Kurt's or Roberto Guilherme's characters reacting to a mischievous Didi who, from a porch or window on a second floor, threw water or bricks (fake bricks, of course) at the heads of his poor victims. Didi himself constantly overreacted to props and characters on the TV comic sketches, as much as in the films, in a rather exaggerated form of slapstick comedy. One may question whether the Goofs' typical mise-en-scène, based on corporeal overreaction, transports to the television or film screen the same industrial/political propaganda referred to by Benjamin (1999) regarding the amusement park's effect.

Also, it is worth noting that the Playcenter amusement park as a whole, but particularly in one scene of Stuart's *TIGM*, pays homage to a famous circus character, a hit in Brazilian itinerant circuses or amusement parks: Konga, the woman who turns into a gorilla. Here, *TIGM* takes advantage not only of the success of the TV show *The Goofs*, but also of Konga, to whom Renato Aragão's character Jegue can also represent as a doppelganger.

The legend of a woman turning into a gorilla arose in the mid-1960s and was often seen in circuses, amusement parks, and freakshows scattered around the world. In Brazil, throughout the 1980s, circuses and amusement parks across the country featured this extremely popular show: a beautiful woman (usually in a bikini) is trapped in a cage, while a narrator explains a sinister transformation. Her hair grows, claws appear, and teeth become fangs. At the climax of this metamorphosis, the monster destroys the bars and "attacks" the spectators. There are several versions of this legend and the origin of such an attraction, which varies from region to region, as does the name (Monga, Conga, Zambora, etc.). In some versions, the girl is lost in the jungle after a plane crash and finds refuge in a temple inhabited by strange apes, dominated by the spirit of a dead emperor. In other versions, the girl may have been bitten by a monkey, was the daughter of Count Dracula, or even cursed by Coffin Joe (Zé do Caixão, the famous intermedial Brazilian character played by José Mojica Marins).

Much like the Konga attraction, *TIGM*'s climactic scenes are set at Playcenter. The Goofs make the expected noise and mess, Jegue turns into the monster once again, and the young girls are saved, while the "foreign" villains flee in terror. In an epilogue, Jegue appears in the Brazilian capital, Brasília, together with his friends, where they are formally commissioned to work on the alternative fuel for the benefit of the country. But the hero declines the invitation and eventually leaves with his girlfriend Ritinha in an old Gordini car with US$200 million in cash and gold bars hidden in a briefcase.

Naturally, R. L. Stevenson's novella *The Strange Case of Dr. Jekyll and Mr. Hyde* (1886) was the inspiration for this film, although its most striking future influence seems to be found in Jerry Lewis's *The Nutty Professor* (1963), as well as in comic book characters, notably Stan Lee and Jack Kirby's *The Incredible Hulk* (1962). Perhaps the most directly recognizable source of *TIGM* is the American TV adaptation of Kirby's comics. Created by Kenneth Johnson and broadcast by CBS from March 10, 1978, to May 12, 1982, *The Incredible Hulk* featured actors Bill Bixby and Lou Ferrigno as Dr. Banner and Hulk, respectively. It ran for five seasons with eighty-two episodes. In Brazil, Globo began broadcasting the series on January 25, 1978. *The Incredible Hulk* was broadcast by Globo, and it aired until 1986, being extremely popular in the early 1980s. The Goof monster in Stuart's film, played by the capoeira master and actor Mestre Touro (Antônio Oliveira Bemvindo), was clearly inspired by Lou Ferrigno's Hulk.

In spite of these Western narrative sources, it is worth noting how in this particular film starring the Goofs, there is a more consistent reaffirmation of national values. Science and technology are featured as 100 percent national and the object of international greed. Some auto-irony or even self-deprecating stances can be inferred in the origin of the alternative fuel—the quince tree—and the name of the inventor-scientist: Jegue. However, "Russians" and "Arabs" both dispute the Brazilian know-how in this *chanchada*-like treasure hunt. The fact that there are no "American spies" may have had something to do with Brazilian foreign policy at the time aligning with American interests, despite previous disagreements between Washington and some leading generals in the regime. Although comic in tone, the patriotic message or reaffirmation of national values is clear in this juvenile film, and notably addressed to children: the prime audience of the Goofs and the main guests at the Playcenter amusement park. This echoes what Ortiz Ramos has already observed with respect to a number of films starring the Goofs (2004, 333). A variation on this curious kind of nationalism is also evidenced by Ortiz Ramos in later popular productions, such as the critically acclaimed TV series *Armação Ilimitada* (2004, 334), broadcast by Globo from 1985 to 88. This ambiguous sentiment of "Brazilianness," therefore, is a relatively perennial trait in Brazilian films or audiovisual media that tackles both the imagery of modernity and foreign cultural inputs, in a constant divide between pride and self-pity.

In summary, the films starring the Goofs were among the greatest box office hits in 1970s and 1980s Brazilian cinema. Most of these films parodied American blockbusters or popular films in some of their scenes and characters, but the three titles commented on above are clearly parodies or simulacra of major American films: Franklin J. Schaffner's *Planet of the Apes*, George Lucas's *Star Wars*, and Jerry Lewis's *The Nutty Professor*. J. B. Tanko's *The Goofs in the Apes' Plateau* and Adriano Stuart's *The Goofs in the War of the Planets* and *The Incredible Goof Monster* were all released after the so-called Brazilian Economic Miracle ("Milagre Econômico Brasileiro"), when Brazil had consistent GDP growth from 1969 to 1973 under the military dictatorship; this was in spite of the crimes against human rights, the murders and torture practiced by both the military and the police, and the slashing of working-class rights and salaries. Unlike the films starring Roberto Carlos, the Goofs' films sometimes addressed, very subtly and obliquely, some of the main problems in Brazil: hunger, the drought in the Northeast, and social inequality. However, all this was extremely subtle and devoid of any clear political discourse. The problems in Brazil, in most of the Goofs' films, are not caused by any identifiable subject or agent. The military regime is never questioned, let alone the predatory elites and the real causes, the long-lasting history of violence, oppression, and social inequality, a reality that is largely attributed to Brazil's slavery. This cautionary stance when it came to social and political criticism makes sense, insofar as both the Goofs and Rede Globo prospered during the most brutal stage of the Brazilian military dictatorship. There would be no TV Globo had the military not come to power, and the same applies to other companies, whereas enterprises that were not supportive of the regime were summarily shut down (see the famous case of the airline company Panair do Brasil).

## Alien Encounters of the Spicy Kind: SF and the Brazilian Erotic Comedy

SF was also explored by the Brazilian erotic comedy genre in the 1970s and 80s, the *pornochanchada*, in films such as Fauzi Mansur's *The Love Insect* (*O Inseto do Amor* 1980), and through Ivan Cardoso's "Laughorror" ("Terrir")[14] in films like *The Mummy's Secret* (*O Segredo da Múmia*, 1982) and *The Seven Vampires* (*As Sete Vampiras*). Targeted at mature audiences, the *pornochanchada* was a very popular Brazilian film genre in the 1970s, especially under the military rule. The films were produced quickly and on a low budget, similar to the original *chanchadas* but emphasizing erotism and sexual jokes. They had plenty of scenes featuring seminaked bodies, particularly women wearing bikinis or topless. Despite the political discourse occasionally embedded in some of the *pornochanchada* films (e.g., the works directed by filmmakers like João Silvério Trevisan, Carlos Reichenbach, and José Mojica Marins, among others), the genre was often deemed as puerile, sexist, and reactionary in both content and form.[15] However, the *porno-chanchada* should not be mistaken for porn movies. There were no explicit scenes, and the scripts were far more complex than any typical porn film, yet still based on the conventional comedy plot verifiable in the previous *chanchadas*. Like in the original *chanchadas*, a star system and film fandom found its place in the wake of *pornochanchadas*, regardless of the general contempt from film critics and film scholars at that time. A paradigmatic case of Brazilian *pornochanchada* that parodied an American blockbuster can be found in Adriano Stuart's *Codfish* (*Bacalhau*, a.k.a. *Bacs*, 1976), a clear pastiche of Steven Spielberg's *Jaws*.[16]

*Codfish* was Adriano Stuart's début directing feature-length films. Produced by Onyx-Havaí Filmes and filmed in Ilhabela, a beautiful island near the coast of São Paulo state, *Codfish*, or simply *Bacs* (an intended pun, in Portuguese, with Spielberg's *Jaws*), is an explicit and exhaustive parody of Universal Studios' world-famous shark. The film's script, written in four days by Stuart, makes use of a plot and characters somewhat equivalent to those in Spielberg's original film, yet using extreme caricature and satire, similar to what *MAD* magazine usually did to Hollywood's summer hits. In Stuart's film, Ilhabela is tormented by a giant cod originating in Guinea, with a particular appetite for beautiful women. The story begins with couples dating on a beach. A young woman enters the sea and shortly after begins to scream for help. She sinks in the water and, in her place, a ridiculous fake skeleton emerges. This is the first attack by the infamous Guinea cod. All the characters appear to be proxies of *Jaws'* original characters but caricatured to the extreme. The mayor (Dionísio Azevedo) is mostly concerned with the resort's revenue, whereas the macho fisherman (Maurício do Valle) believes he can stop the carnage. A confused Portuguese oceanographer (Adriano Stuart himself) and the police chief (Hélio Souto), who intends to close the beach, are direct sendups of the characters played by Roy Scheider and Richard Dreyfuss in the original film. Even critics like Sérgio Augusto (1976) were less tolerant of Stuart's film, with Jean-Claude Bernardet pointing out the contradiction behind the parody in his influential film review titled "The Cod That Sells the Big Sharks' Fish" (1976). According to Bernardet, the degradation of original Hollywood models would actually ratify the logic of dependency, rather than contesting it. Paradoxically, in this apparent attitude of independence, a real attitude of dependence remains, as this kind of parody situates the original as a model. Jaws is confirmed as a model by *Codfish* since its appeal relies precisely on the impossibility of remaking the original spectacle: the codfish must be inferior and degraded. "Under the cover of an irreverent, critical, and aggressive attitude, the oppression of the oppressor and the inferiority of the 'inferior' are confirmed" (Bernardet 1976).[17]

Bernardet's sharp observation could be applied to much of the parodic tendency that long endured in Brazilian SF cinema, of which Stuart's *Codfish* is a good example. The degradation of original models and the well-publicized precarious production can be found in several other films that take foreign SF cinema as a source. Therefore, depending on the opportunity and skills of the filmmakers, the critique of domination and artistic autonomy is more or less evident in the face of the reaffirmation of a logic of dependence. This is what we can see in numerous productions before and after Stuart's *Codfish*.

The decline of the *pornochanchada* in Brazil coincided with the rise of the porn film industry. Hence, some Brazilian porn movies also resorted to popular SF iconography in the mid-1980s, such as in José Rady's *The Test Tube Woman* (*A Mulher de Proveta*, 1984), and Custódio Gomes's *The More Sex, the Better* (*O Etesão: Quanto mais Sexo Melhor*, 1986). Another example of a pornographic film with loose, circumstantial, or accidental references to SF imagery is Levy Salgado's *Punks, Sons of the Night* (*Punk's, Os Filhos da Noite*, 1983), a pastiche of Walter Hill's *The Warriors* (1979), also set in an apocalyptic near future. In general, all these films reveal the internalization of American SF cinema by Brazilian filmmakers and the national audiovisual industry.

But it wasn't just SF comedies and *pornochanchadas* with shallow SF motifs that had prominence in the late 1970s and 1980s Brazilian cinema landscapes. *Voracious Love* (*Amor Voraz*), a 1984 film written and directed by Walter Hugo Khouri, presents an existentialist reflection on "close encounters of the third kind," in a sober, subtle SF film without sophisticated special effects. The film was based on Fausto Cunha's novel "The Kiss before the Sleep" ("O Beijo Antes do Sono"), published in 1974 by ArteNova.[18] Focusing on the relationship between a woman and an alien, Khouri's film represents a more subtle, poetic, and intimate kind of SF&F, along the lines practiced by filmmakers like Andrei Tarkovski, Andrej Zulawski, or Piotr Szulkin.

While recovering from a nervous disorder in a family home outside the city, Ana (Vera Fischer) meets a stranger (Marcelo Picchi), a man of poor health with whom she talks telepathically. She falls in love. This man is an extraterrestrial who traveled through space in the form of a light beam to find a new home for his people, a very advanced and ancient civilization whose planet is about to be extinct. It took him thousands of years to "germinate" as a man in a lake near Ana's house, and his mission is to report data on Earth. Albert Einstein's Theory of Relativity is incorporated into some dialogue in the film. For instance, when Ana explains to Sílvia (Márcia Rodrigues) the origin of the unknown man, or when he informs Ana that he must leave. Ana protests, referring to the years when he would have been "germinating" in that lake, long before she was born, as well as the years he would spend traveling back to his planet, arriving there long after her death. According to Jairo Ferreira, "a [s]cience-fiction film without special or visual effects, *Voracious Love* is a rare example of the inexhaustible power of cinema as a vehicle for poetic suggestions" (1986, 354). It should be noted that *Voracious Love* deals with practically the same subjects as Robert Wise's *The Day the Earth Stood Still* or Steven Spielberg's *ET—The Extraterrestrial* (1982), that is, the contact with an alien and the repercussions of this event on human psychology. However, each of the aforementioned films offers a singular approach to the same theme: in Wise, the alien contact is public and notably political; in Spielberg, the alien contact is with the child, exposing the disparity between the children's and the adults' values; in Khouri, the strange encounter resonates in the psyche of a young, lonely woman.

## Brazilian SF Comedies in the Wake of Redemocratization

At the beginning of the 1980s, Brazilian society underwent important sociopolitical transformations toward the end of the military rule, with the national campaign in favor of direct elections and the ongoing redemocratization. For instance, in 1985, students, educators, and politicians stood up in defense of free public schools. In the same year, *Scalding Sands*—produced, written, and directed by Francisco de Paula—featured a generation of artists from different media: theater, music, visual arts, cinema, poetry, fashion, and television. They represented a young generation that started occupying posts in the so-called productive society. Francisco de Paula himself was part of that young generation and had previously worked as assistant director for the Brazilian directors Ozualdo Candeias, Neville de Almeida (among the cast in *Scalding Sands*), and Carlos Diegues.[19] Despite the fact that *Scalding Sands* was often classified as a comedy, the director explains that initially, his script was not comic at all. It was based on the idea of a terrorist group attacking and blowing up multinational corporations. However, due to budgetary constraints, nonsense held sway in the production: "Humor has saved us from precariousness."[20] In its hint at a dystopian fable, *Scalding Sands* might well be taken as an example of what John Brosnan calls a "fake SF movie" (1991, 359), and the film is justifiably indexed as a "musical" on the Internet Movie Database.[21] Somewhat recalling *RCAR* film language, *Scalding Sands* focuses on rock bands and music hits of the time, while relying on a thin storyline: in a near future (likely the 1990s), in the fictional country of Kali, a group of young terrorists carry out subversive missions that include robberies, kidnappings, and assassinations for the sake of a mysterious boss known as "the Entity." The rebel group is constantly escaping from the pompous and inefficient Special Police.

Francisco de Paula, the director himself, is reticent about labeling *Scalding Sands* as an SF film. According to him, if there is any link to SF iconography, it should be ascribed to the work of his art director, Arturo Uranga (Suppia 2013, 138). Born in Argentina in 1936, Uranga is a visual artist with a career in Brazilian cinema and TV. As a film animator, Uranga introduced some visual effect techniques into Brazil (notably glass painting) while collaborating with directors like Cacá Diegues, Bruno Barreto, Zelito Viana, Geraldo Viana, Paulo Thiago, and Carla Camurati, among others. He produced numerous storyboards, worked as a production designer (see fig. 5.1), and created countless animations for Brazilian TV and the advertising industry before directing his first feature film, *Era Uma Vez*

Figure 5.1. Drawing/sketch for Francisco de Paula's feature film *Scalding Sands* (*Areias Escaldantes*, 1985), by Arturo Uranga. *Source*: *Scalding Sands* (*Areias Escaldantes*). Dir. Francisco de Paula. Prod. Co.: Naive Produções Artísticas Ltda., Brasil, 35mm, COR, 100min. Arturo Uranga (private collection). Courtesy: Francisco de Paula and Cinemateca do Museu de Arte Moderna, Rio de Janiero.

(*Once Upon a Time*, 1994). Uranga introduced the glass painting technique to TV at Globo, and also worked as a set and costume designer in Brazilian theater (Nagib 2002, 496–97).

Directing a truly independent and low-budget film, Francisco de Paula resorted to Uranga's alluring illustrations to achieve the futurist atmosphere in *Scalding Sands*. The drawings appear from time to time, as brief transitions from one sequence to another, thus suggesting that the characters inhabit a futuristic metropolis. Thereby, the dystopian atmosphere and Uranga's art provide the bulk of familiarity between this film and sci-fi, whereas the unfolding story focused completely on the Brazilian pop music scene.[22]

*Scalding Sands* was originally based on a detailed storyboard, created by Uranga and the comic book designer Otto Dumovich.[23] De Paula recalls that "the film was shot in 30 days, with two hours of 35 mm negative. Almost everything was used, and there was no take two."[24] Postproduction was done in partnership with Sky Light Cinema and Álamo Studios. The director comments that distribution and exhibition were disastrous because two actors in the film were arrested for drug possession. However, de Paula himself took the film to festivals in Portugal, Spain, and France and still, according to him, it was well received abroad.[25] De Paula adds that "the film's cinematography, cast, direction of art, set design, costumes, makeup, montage, and soundtrack are featured in an authentic way, in tune with independent film-making." The director stresses that *Scalding Sands* had no direct funding from Embrafilme.[26] Nowadays, rediscovered as a cult film, *Scalding Sands* has been invited to a number of film festivals in Brazil.

One can also notice that, like *RCAR* and *TIGM*, *Scalding Sands* has benefitted from the presence of its stars in television. The mid-1980s set the stage for the ascending art of the videoclip, and many of the singers and bands that appeared in de Paula's film, if not all of them, had significant exposure on Brazilian TV, mostly on the aforementioned magazine program *Fantástico*, produced and broadcasted by Globo since August 5, 1973. Not only *Fantástico*, but various other 1980s TV shows in Brazil featured rock or pop bands.[27] According to Bueno, the video clip aesthetic embedded in cinematic narratives favored the possible insertion of films into the television schedule, as TV was its natural habitat (see Bueno 2016, 191).

Shortly after Francisco de Paula's *Scalding Sands*, in 1986 Uberto Molo's *As Weird as It Seems* (*Por Incrível que Pareça*), written by João Carlos Motta, featured a nuclear power plant employee who suffers an accident and, thanks to the radiation he received, survives his head being severed

Figure 5.2. Film poster of *Scalding Sands* (*Areias Escaldantes*, 1985), directed by Francisco de Paula. *Source*: Courtesy: Francisco de Paula and Cinemateca do Museu de Arte Moderna, Rio de Janiero

from his body. The film opens with quotations invoking SF imagery in the corridors of the atomic power plant, where a metallic voice from a speaker talks about sectors alpha, beta, omega, delta, etc., and serious people wearing lab coats move in and out as if automatons, with the exception of the main character, Marcos Silva (played by the actor, musician, and comedian Tim Rescala). Marcos is in the restroom reading a comic book of *The Incredible Hulk* when the red alert is triggered, and he is injured as the plant collapses. He is finally rescued by an ambulance, which on the way to the hospital is involved in a traffic accident and Marcos's head falls out of the vehicle. The next day, a beautiful young woman named Denise (Thereza Mascarenhas) finds the living head of Marcos and takes him to her apartment. The clearest source for Molo's SF comedy appears to be American SF/horror B movies like Joseph Green's *The Brain that Wouldn't Die* (1962) and perhaps Leonid Menaker's 1984 Soviet film *Professor Dowell's Testament* based on Alexander Beliaev's novel *Professor Dowell's Head*, originally published in the USSR in 1925. None of these creepy "talking heads" appear to be as kind and handsome as Marcos's in Uberto Molo's film.

*As Weird as It Seems* plays out as an absurdist comedy until the moment Denise abandons Marcos's head. Then the film takes a more emphatic philosophical, metaphysical, and melancholic stance, especially concerning the beggar (Jofre Soares) and Marcos's feeling of rejection. Easily classified as SF, *As Weird as It Seems* makes use of the uncanny and the absurd to convey reflections on technology, modern life, urban loneliness, and rejection. On the other hand, it is also possible to identify in *As Weird as It Seems* a touch of Latin American magic realism (*realismo mágico* or, preferably, *realismo maravilhoso*), especially in regard to the narrative treatment after the ambulance crash, when the absurd talking head is "naturalized" in favor of the plot and discussions on human relationships. Then again, unlike films like *The Brain That Wouldn't Die* and *Professor Dowell's Head*, no hint of a life support system is presented in the film: Marcos's head survives thanks to an unexplained phenomenon, or pure magic, and not a single drop of blood is ever spilled. The amalgamation of SF motifs and magic realism, as seen in Molo's film, does not appear to immediately exclude *As Weird as It Seems* from the territory of SF cinema, even though it renders a more local-colored version of the genre.

A little further into the Brazilian democratic period, SF and comedy continue to join forces in *Man in the Box* (*O Efeito Ilha*), a 1994 film written, directed, and starring Luiz Alberto Pereira, alias Gal.[28] According to Pereira, it was the only Brazilian feature film at Riocine and the São Paulo International Film Festival that year (Nagib 2002, 345). *Man in the Box*, Gal's first feature-length fiction film, was supported by PIC (Programa de Incentivo ao Cinema), from the municipal secretary of culture of São Paulo, in addition to funding from the 1994 Pêmio Resgate. Luiz Alberto Pereira's performance garnered some critical acclaim that recognized the filmmaker as a "Brazilian Woody Allen" (André Gatti in Ramos and Miranda 2004, 424).

*Man in the Box* tells the story of TV technician João William (Gal), beginning with an incident in which he is struck by lightning while repairing TV equipment in the RETE studios. The accident does not cause any apparent injury to William, but it does make him the victim of a strange phenomenon: from then on, his image can be seen on every TV channel, 24/7, in a kind of nonstop full reality show and, most fantastically, with no cameras whatsoever. Experts and scientists from around the world are called on to try to reverse the phenomenon, but everyone fails. It is alleged that some kind of "live electromagnetism" makes William's image ubiquitous around the world, without the mediation of any camera. His life is thus wide open to anyone and everyone who has access to a television screen. For example, everything from his relationship with his mistress to his trips to the bathroom all bring about profound change in William's life. His family abandons him, and he becomes more and more isolated. People begin feeling bored with the constant broadcasting of William on every TV channel. It is the time of the World Cup, and there are those who want to see the games or simply watch soap operas—a tradition in Brazilian TV viewing. The press begins to harass William. Soon, an advertising agency, Score and Associates, starts taking advantage of the situation. William becomes a commercial star, incorporating merchandising into his daily routine—or rather, adapting his routine to merchandising. But there comes a time when William no longer tolerates the lack of privacy, nor the futile propaganda tool he has become. By recalling the enigmatic, divine words he had heard when struck by the lightning bolt, he decides to radically change his life, proclaiming himself a prophet. Television becomes his omnipresent electronic church, and William begins working miracles through the TV screen. Political and economic interests are at stake, and with his sudden missionary vocation, William challenges the powerful elites. This deranging "island effect" will only terminate with the assassination of William.

The film's original title (in Portuguese, *O Efeito Ilha*, something like *The Island Effect*) has a number of metaphorical implications, and its origin is diverse. First, we see that it is a contraction of the name "William," since RETE employees when asked by reporters on the phone about the technician's name, answer that he is "Joãuilha" (i.e., João William). The name William, a foreign name, when coupled together with João and spoken quickly in Portuguese, ends up sounding similar to "ilha," or "island." We then see that the word "island" is also justified by the condition of isolation imposed on the main character. William loses his family, his privacy, and his peace of mind.

During the time he is omnipresent in every household with a TV set on, he lives alone, insulated. In a reverie to his ex-wife Fátima (Lígia Cortez), he regrets his current situation, defining himself as an island, an isolated man. Finally, if we consider that William's life is broadcast simultaneously across all TV sets, it is not difficult to associate the character with an "island" as a technical term that designates the place where television programs are edited. William is literally an editing island in the flesh, thus broadcasting his image twenty-four hours a day on all available channels.

Luiz Alberto Pereira comments that the inspiration for the script came from an article on Earth's magnetism.[29] Long before the arrival of the show *Big Brother* in Brazil, Pereira already simulates a radicalized, caricatural reading of the Dutch TV show. The film is based on a very simple yet creative technical artifice: that of constantly reproducing William's image on a TV screen within the shot. On several occasions we see William next to a TV set, also on-screen, reproducing his image. This reinforces the suspension of disbelief necessary for the viewer to accept that William is somehow having his image shown on television without a camera. Sometimes we see the same image/framing, both at the first level (the cinematic image), and at the second level (the on-screen television image), in a type of *mise-en-abyme* (abyss effect). At other times the image of William at the first level (film) and the second level (TV monitor inside the film) do not coincide in terms of framing. On these occasions, the use of two cameras is evident, although the suspension of disbelief continues to be persuasive. Pereira's film is particularly successful in this artifice of persuasion, not only through dialogues between the characters but also through its framing and editing.

Thus, *Man in the Box* puts forth a good-humored critique of the television industry and its relationship with the audience, working off the traditional myth of theft of the soul by image reproduction devices. In this respect, it resembles another 1994 film: *Akumulator 1*, by Czech director Jan Svěrák. Peter Weir's *The Truman Show* (1998) will later use a motif similar to that of *Man in the Box*, to the point that Luiz Alberto Pereira suspected plagiarism of his work.[30] *Man in the Box* also makes fun of the limitations of television technology at the time. In order to recover part of his privacy, at a certain point William paints a room in his apartment all black. The television signal has some limitations in terms of image resolution and texture, at least compared to film. For instance, there is no real true black color on a television screen, especially at the time that *Man in the Box* was released, when LED or OLED TV sets were unavailable in Brazil. Conversely, no conventional television camera (except the ones with night view capacity) is able to broadcast a scene with inadequate or no lighting at all. William takes advantage of this limitation. While he is in the black room, with doors and windows closed, all we see is static on an entirely black spot that covers the entire screen. Only the sound comes through. It is in this room that William will have romantic encounters or business meetings. It will also be his refuge after his conversion into a prophet.

Some supporting or secondary characters intensify the film's overall critique of the television industry and reality shows. Osmar Santos, a well-known Brazilian presenter, plays a cameo in the film as a commentator for RETE. A Catholic Moral League attacks sex on TV (at some point it is inevitable that William will be caught having sex with his mistress), defending the redemption of this medium as a genuine, innocent piece of equipment at the service of family fun. There is also the important performance of the "vidiot" ("vidiota"), the guy who wastes hours watching crappy TV shows. This character always appears talking on the phone in front of the TV monitor on which William's images appear. He talks to a supposed friend, whose voice is not revealed, functioning as an alter ego of the director himself, or a secondary narrator.

When William emerges as a prophet, we have a third and final phase of the film. The first phase, right after the accident with the lightning bolt, sets up the initial conflict: we will see the outcomes of the "island effect" and the disillusionment of William's family. In this first phase the demolition of the protagonist's private sphere begins, and he becomes a widely known personality, an object of widespread consumption. The second phase is that of the "integrated" William, the TV star. The third is that of the prophet William, who works miracles and promotes people's redemption through television. The prophet's mission is to instill in the minds of faithful viewers a change in values. This change in values does not play by the rules of the political and economic status quo and carries the germ of the destruction of popular TV as we know it. William becomes a kind of electronic pastor in a weird mixture of the infamous American Jimmy Swaggart and the Brazilian nineteenth-century prophet Antônio Conselheiro. He works miracles and carries out a mission of redemption for the people alienated by contemporary TV. It is curious that in his preaching he does not offer a more materialistic perspective to his followers, but rather the replacement of a value system based on consumerism by another one, based on New Age religious dogmas. TV continues to be an object of worship, something that reminds us of more unsettling films like David Cronenberg's *Videodrome* (1984). With the assassination of William, the order of consumerism is restored. His image gives way to ads and other TV attractions. The children exclaim, "The TV is back!" The character played by Osmar Santos immediately takes his post, and the event of William's murder becomes the first "post-island effect" television story. The film ends with a *plongée* camera retreating toward the sky, in a zoom out in which William, dead on the ground, is supported by his ex-wife Fátima (Lígia Cortez). The tragicomedy that shook the order of sacred TV finally ends. As in *As Weird as It Seems, Man in the Box* also appears to "flirt" with magic realism. This is evident when, in the film, the (pseudo)scientific explanations fail to provide a useful explanation of the phenomenon, so that the protagonist and the characters begin to naturalize the otherworldliness of their omnipresence.

More recently, another noteworthy Brazilian SF comedy is Claudio Torres's 2011 film *The Man from the Future*. This time travel adventure mixes SF and romantic comedy to tell the story of João alias Zero (Wagner Moura), a brilliant physicist who in 2011 spends his days meditating on the fateful night of twenty years ago, when he was betrayed and publicly humiliated at a college party by his girlfriend, in a scene somewhat reminiscent of Brian De Palma's 1976 film *Carrie*. Although he is directing one of the biggest scientific projects in Brazil, his eccentricities and tantrums leave him on the verge of being fired by his college colleague and current sponsor, Sandra (Maria Luiza Mendonça). Assisted by his best friend and fellow scientist Otávio alias Panda (Fernando Ceylão), Zero activates the unfinished machine he developed to provide a new sustainable energy source to humankind. To his surprise, the reaction caused by the machine proves that he is capable of opening a "bridge" to the past, a "time passage" that takes him back to 1991, in the middle of the traumatic evening when the beautiful Helena (Alinne Moraes) left him for the popular playboy Ricardo (Gabriel Braga Nunes). He then sees that changing the facts will be more difficult and confusing than he thought. Returning to an altered present, Zero discovers that his younger self used his knowledge of the future to become a powerful and corrupt businessman, even further distanced from Helena. He decides to travel back in time once again, to prevent himself from altering the present by trying to avoid the paradoxes of time caused by the presence of three versions of himself in 1991. The plot is clearly reminiscent of Robert Zemeckis's *Back to the Future* film series, notably *Back to the Future—Part II* (1989).

Produced and distributed by Conspiração Filmes, Globo Filmes, and Paramount Pictures, *The Man from the Future* had a relatively good box office draw, though apparently not as good as other similar films produced by Globo Filmes, such as Daniel Filho's extremely successful trilogy *If I Were You (Se Eu Fosse Você*, 2006, 2009, and 2013). *The Man from the Future* spawned no sequels, but it followed the popular revisitation of the old Brazilian *chanchadas* with contemporary casts, crews, and film technology, being a profitable niche exploited by Globo Filmes since its foundation in 1998. All the expertise and the star system accumulated by Globo in its TV soap operas were opened up to the Brazilian film industry in the early 2000s. *The Man from the Future* thus capitalized on that expertise, Globo's masterful marketing techniques, and actresses and actors with careers anchored in TV soap operas. Here, however, Wagner Moura is an exception, whose career began in theater and film and remained deeply anchored in Brazilian cinema. Claudio Torres's film benefits from some futuristic film locations, such as the National Laboratory of Synchrotron Light Laboratory (Laboratório Nacional de Luz Síncrotron), or LNLS, in Campinas, São Paulo state. To a large extent, the contemporary pop-rock music scene is also an asset in the film, much as in Francisco de Paula's *Scalding Sands*, as *The Man from the Future* explores 1990s musical hits, notably songs by the rock bands Radiohead (UK) and Legião Urbana (Brazil). But the film lacks a more consistent and creative screenplay, as well as more familiarity with the possibilities of SF world-building, to the point where there is little or no sense of wonder at all, certainly none based on SF motifs. Torres's film is just another Brazilian time-travel tale, far less ingenious and thought-provoking than Brazilian SF shorts like Jorge Furtado and Ana Luiza Azevedo's *Barbosa* (1988) or Carlos Gregório's *Loop* (2002). Aspects of Brazilian society, and, in particular, of the media industry and consumer society, are discussed through an ironic lens, thus reaffirming the close and enduring ties between SF and satire. Furthermore, these comedies were released after the military dictatorship had ended, when Brazil began attempting democracy once again. Apparently, in accordance with the common knowledge regarding economic neoliberalism, any political dimension in these films does not stretch out far beyond the individual, private sphere. Class struggle, the social history of inequality, and other collective political issues are rarely addressed, or simply not addressed at all. Everything appeared to revolve around the main character's ordinary, petit-bourgeois life, disconnected from any wider scenario. With a few exceptions, politics in Brazilian SF comedy of the 1980s and 1990s tended to be incoherent navel gazing.

6

# The Ghost in the Machine

## Brazilian SF and the Revival of Spiritist Films

In "Reflections on the Seventh Art" (1923),[1] Ricciotto Canudo hailed cinema's power to artistically represent the immaterial world, well beyond its capacity to represent objective reality. In section 5 of his essay "Immateriality in Cinema," Canudo points out that "Camille Flammarion, having witnessed a screening from a film illustrating a soul's survival after death, has once again expressed his long-standing faith in spiritism, with the addition of his new enthusiasm for cinema. He was happily surprised to see the cinema confront the evocation (if no longer the representation) of immateriality. Mr Flammarion's remarks confirm that cinema, *when understood and conceived as an art by artists*, must develop in specific areas that are impossible in other arts" (Canudo 1988, 300). It is worth noting how Canudo, in his strong defense of cinema as an art form, quotes Camille Flammarion, French writer and editor, founder of a renowned publishing house, and a friend of Hippolyte Léon Denizard Rivail, better known as Allan Kardec, the founder of Spiritism. In that same essay, just a few paragraphs ahead, Canudo states that "cinema permits, and must further develop, the extraordinary and striking faculty of *representing immateriality*" (1988, 301; emphasis in the original). Canudo is referring to a particular American spiritualist film: *Earthbound* (1920), by T. Hayes Hunter, based on a story by Basil King. *Earthbound* is about the agony of the disembodied spirit of a man who, after being murdered by his wife's lover, is condemned to roam the Earth until all those he has hurt in life forgive him, and his wife finally recognizes his ghost and his misfortune.

The fact that Camille Flammarion and spiritualist cinema are already mentioned in Canudo's "Reflections on the Seventh Art," first published in 1923, shows that spiritualism in cinema may have a longer history than we usually assume. It is also worth remembering that some spiritualist inspiration, and even diffuse elements of a spiritualist discourse in the broad sense, could already be seen in films such as *Intolerance* (1916), by D. W. Griffith, or Fritz Lang's *Tired Death* (*Der Müde Tod*, 1921).

However, the spiritualist film *lato sensu*, or the cinema of transcendental speculation—a vehicle for fables about life after death, the meaning of life and/or the borderline, a transitory moment between life and death—does not necessarily belong to any given time or nationality, thereby being a worldwide phenomenon. Contemporary examples of films that approach some sort of transcendence (i.e., thus featuring a "dialogue" between a material and a spiritual world), to a lesser or greater degree, can be found in productions of many different nationalities, such as *Biutiful* (2010), by Alejandro González Iñárritu, and *Uncle Bonmee, Who Can Remember His Past Lives* (*Loong Boonmee Raleuk Chat*, 2010), by Apichatpong Weerasethakul, and even the French *Les Revenants* (2004) by Robin Campillo.

In American cinema, a variation of the spiritualist film has already been investigated and labeled as the "*film blanc*." The term refers to an essay by Peter Valenti (1978), who defines the *film blanc* as a cinematic fable with the following characteristics: (1) the death of an individual or his/her transition to an oneiric state; (2) the subsequent presentation of that individual to a kind of representation of the hereafter, generally understood as "Heaven"; (3) a love affair, and (4) finally, the transcendence of mortality to escape the spiritual world and return to the mortal world (Valenti 1978, 294-95). Valenti's cited films are mostly American productions from between 1930 and 1945 (especially between 1940 and 1945), and the term *film blanc* is defined in opposition to film noir: "Just as the best known genre of *film noir* shows the underside, cynical and dark side of human motivation aimed toward death, the *film blanc* portrays the most edifying facet of human nature, our deepest attraction to spiritual transcendence and the luminous side of life" (Genelli and Genelli 2013, 23-24).Valenti's *film blanc* genre has not brought about many in-depth studies, and indeed it is far less well known than the film noir. Nevertheless, once we momentarily accept Valenti's *film blanc*, it is easy to locate an equivalent film production in Latin American cinemas. The Brazilian *film blanc* or *neoblanc* with a touch of local color, so to speak, has been commercially successful in Brazil as well.

In Brazilian films with a focus on the afterlife, Kardecism will be the greatest influence on cinematic fables, many of which are allegedly based on real facts. This chapter presents an overview of the spiritist film, a genre that has garnered the attention of Brazilian film critics and scholars, especially since 2008. The Brazilian spiritist film appears to be wavering between two worlds, between segmented and broader audiences, faith and marketing, religious indoctrination and spectacle.

When it comes to spiritist cinema, we are challenged by the fact that the very definition of spiritism is problematic in itself. Considered less of a religion in the strict sense and more like a scientific doctrine (as its founder Allan Kardec had wished; see Kardec 1998 [1857]; Kardec 1863), the spiritist creed, originally called spiritualist (a title still attributed to more general beliefs in a spiritual world or afterlife) first appeared in Europe in the mid-nineteenth century. As Bernardo Lewgoy (2000, 10) points out, unlike older religions, the spiritualist creed was a phenomenon linked to literate culture, which gave it some very specific characteristics, both in terms of religious practices and related cultural production.

According to Lewgoy, "Kardec's spiritism is not just a book-based religion that maintains an abundant religious literature" (2000, 12). It is also essentially "a literate religion, in the sense of its deep roots in themes and emblems that have characterised Western modernity since the 19th century, such as the Enlightenment's rationalism, scientism, and the novel as a literary genre" (2000, 12). For Lewgoy, spiritism takes over these factors in a kind of desecularizing Christian reading of science and literature (2000, 12). According to its French founder, Allan Kardec, "Spiritism is both an observation science and a philosophical doctrine. As a practical science, it consists of the relationships that are established between the Spirits and us; as a philosophy, it understands all the moral consequences that emanate from these same relationships [. . .]. *Spiritism is a science that deals with the nature and origin of spirits, as well as their relations with the corporal world*" (qtd. in Fernandes 2008, 10; emphasis added). Kardec's doctrine as a whole, which still circulates through a vast international literature, and very prominently in Brazil, has some generic characteristics that should be stressed: (1) the belief in the immortality of spirits; (2) belief in the communicability of these spirits with the living through mediums (generally gifted persons, but occasionally technologic artifacts); and (3) the trust in reincarnation. There are also other beliefs taken up by followers of spiritualism throughout the twentieth century, in particular that the spiritual world would be organized hierarchically in an evolutionary structure that would, at least in its initial stages, include some institutions similar and equivalent to those of the "earthling" culture (schools, hospitals, offices, etc.). We do not intend to describe or discuss the spiritist doctrine in detail in this work but will go over the most widespread precepts or aspects of spiritism in the media and among the general public, inasmuch as these elements end up clearly absorbed and reproduced by both literature and film.

Given the widespread acceptance of spiritism in Brazil, this work also suggests that cinematic representations of this doctrine have been instrumental in adapting the repertoire of Brazilian audiences to allegedly foreign audiovisual genres, such as horror and SF. However, before considering the realm of Brazilian spiritist cinema itself, it is worth remembering some aspects of the arrival of Allan Kardec's spiritism in Brazil. For a more in-depth introduction to the history of Kardec's spiritism in Brazil, see Del Priore 2014.

## The Medium Is the Message:
## Brazilian Spiritism and Twentieth-century Literature

Indeed, Kardecism and its variations found a welcoming environment in Brazilian society, and the popularity of spiritism in Brazil today has been revealed in a variety of cultural products such as books, TV shows (e.g., TV soap operas), theater plays, and films. References to Kardecism—and, under a broader perspective, to spiritualism in a larger sense, sometimes related to Afro-Brazilian religious traditions—can be found in many films throughout the history of Brazilian cinema.

As pointed out by Sandra Stoll (2004), in Brazil the doctrine advocated by Allan Kardec has more clearly taken on the characteristics of a religion. This seems to be reinforced by Brazilian spiritist literature itself, like Chico Xavier's book *Brazil, the Heart of the World, Homeland of the Gospel* (*Brasil, Coração do Mundo, Pátria do Evangelho*, 2014, originally published in 1938), which was allegedly psychographed from Brazilian writer Humberto de Campos.

> While in Europe the spiritualist idea was only the object of observations and research in laboratories, or of big sterile dis-

cussions in the field of Philosophy, despite the moral grounds of the Kardecian Codification, Spiritism penetrated Brazil with all its characteristics of Revived Christianity, raising souls for a new dawn of faith. There, all its institutions were based on love and charity. The very scientific associations that, from time to time, appear to cultivate it, under its metapsychic label, are absorbed in the Christian programme, under the invisible and indirect guidance of the Lord's emissaries. (Xavier 2014, 178)

Deriving from adaptations of evolutionary and positivist theories applied to Christianity, Kardec's doctrine may have found in Brazilian lands some dialogue with Afro-Brazilian religions such as Umbanda and Candomblé, with which it shared ideas such as reincarnation, mediumship, and a complex spiritual world. Such a set of cultural interfaces possibly facilitated the great spread of spiritist ideas across the country. According to Mary Del Priore, "If, in France, Kardecism will be defined as a doctrine and as a science, in Brazil the mystical-religious aspect will predominate. The much desired intimacy with souls, dead, saints, *eguns*, and orishas, and the spread among the most popular segments helped in the expansion of spiritism" (2014, 90). According to data from the 2010 IBGE[2] census, about 3.8 million Brazilians declare themselves spiritists, which works out to be about 2 percent of the population. However, taking into account the number of people attending the more than ten thousand spiritist centers spread across the country, it is estimated that the number of believers and sympathizers (occasional or not) may be much higher. These audiences also attend a large number of lectures, live performances, theater plays, films and, most consistently, they consume literary publications on the subject.

Lewgoy points out that "many spiritists do not declare themselves to the Census as being of a spiritist religion, preferring to think of themselves as a secular movement, which leads to probable under-representation in religious affiliation statistics" (2004, 56). Therefore, it is not unlikely that people who truly believe in a series of precepts of Kardecist spiritism reject the religious affiliation, preferring to identify themselves as spiritualists or esoteric, in a broader sense. We can easily see such a phenomenon in the publishing market and in different shows aimed at audiences potentially interested in afterlife motifs, which creates some difficulties even in the mere classification of certain literary or audiovisual works.

The idea of Brazil as the "land of the future," which would later be the title of Stefan Zweig's book first published in 1941 could already be seen, about four years earlier, in Chico Xavier's *Brazil, Heart of the World,*

*Homeland of the Gospel* (*Brasil, Coração do Mundo, Pátria do Evangelho*, 2014). The myth of Brazil as an Edenic paradise of coexistence between races is at the heart of Zweig's fascination with the country: "Therefore the experiment of Brazil, with its complete and conscious negation of all colour and racial distinctions, through its obvious success, probably represents the most important contribution toward the liquidation of a mania that has brought more disruption and unhappiness into our world than any other" (Zweig 1941, 9). It is this perspective of eternal harmony between peoples that encouraged Zweig to see the future of humankind in Brazil: "So one of our greatest hopes for future civilisation and peace in our world, which has been destroyed by hatred and madness, rests on the existence of Brazil, whose desires are aimed exclusively at pacific development" (Zweig 1941, 13). Xavier's *Brazil, Heart of the World, Homeland of the Gospel* (2014 [1938]) seems to bear the same ideal about the country, with the difference that, instead of an anthropological and sociological "experiment," the project of a peaceful, multiracial society has as its mentors and artisans only God, Jesus, and the angels. In a preface to *Brazil, Heart of the World, Homeland of the Gospel*, Chico Xavier's spiritual guide (*guia*) named Emmanuel announces:

> Our task aims to clarify the general environment in the country, mixing its traditions of fraternity with the cement of pure truths, because, if Greece and Rome of Antiquity had their time, as primordial elements of the origins of the entire Western civilisation; if the Portuguese and Spanish empires spread almost all over the planet; if France, and England have had their prominent place in the timeline that marks the evolutionary stages of the world, Brazil will also have its great moment, in the clock that marks the days of the evolution of humanity. (Xavier 2014, 8)

The teleological perspective of a more evolved nation is intensified in Chico Xavier's 1938 book preceding Zweig's 1941 essay on "the land of the future." The word of Jesus, in *Brazil, Heart of the World, Homeland of the Gospel*, thus confirms the manifest destiny of South America's largest country:

> The tree of my Gospel of piety and love will be transplanted into this wonderful and blessed land. In their very generous and fertile soil, all the peoples of the Earth will learn the law

of universal goodwill. Under these heavens, the tenderest Hosannas to the mercy of the heavenly Father will be sung. You, Helil, will be embodied on Earth, among the poorest and most hard-working people in the West; you will institute a route of courage, so that the immensities of these dangerous and lonely oceans, which separate the Old and the New World, are transposed. We will set up a work tent here for the most humble nation in Europe, glorifying their efforts in God's workshop. We will take advantage of the simple element of kindness, the fraternal heart of the inhabitants of these new lands, and, then I will order the reincarnation of many Spirits already purified in the feeling of humility and meekness, among the oppressed and suffering races of the African regions, to form the pedestal of solidarity of the fraternal people who will flourish here in the future, in order to exalt my Gospel, in the glorious centuries to come. Here, Helil, under the merciful light of the stars of the cross, the heart of the world will be located! (Xavier 2014, 16–17)

Some basic contextual information is called for here while reading the excerpt above. It is from a book first published in 1938, just before the outbreak of World War II and in the middle of the Estado Novo (New State) dictatorship in Brazil, also known as the Third Republic, the dictatorial regime established by Getúlio Vargas[3] on November 10, 1937, which remained in power until January 31, 1946. It was characterized by the centralization of power, nationalism, anticommunism, and authoritarianism. The *Estado Novo* initially sympathized with both Hitler's and Mussolini's regimes, and Brazil was eventually forced to side with the allies, but only in 1942. By the time Xavier's book was released, Brazil had never tasted a great deal of enduring, consistent democracy. On the contrary, it was a distant, unknown political regime, and other dictatorships and martial laws would intervene, a number of times, until the country had its longest allegedly "democratic" times, from 1985 through 2016. *Brazil, Heart of the World, Homeland of the Gospel* also hails the Portuguese origins of Brazil, celebrating the vastness and unity of its territory in the Americas—an accomplishment ascribed to divine providence (Xavier 2014, 24).

In the ideal of the "land of the future," the scourge of slavery, as well as the pivotal role of African culture must be properly accommodated, according to both Zweig's (1941) and Xavier's (1938) ideas on "racial utopia." In such a "racial utopia," slavery is treated as a relic of the past, the result of spiritual misunderstanding on the part of the Europeans and a sacrificial stage in the spiritual evolution of Africans (Xavier 2014, 39).

The indulgent and pacifist discourse in some sort of pseudo-philosophical effort to reconcile Africans and Europeans is clear in Xavier (2014 [1938]). The text both condemns and forgives the "excesses" of European imperialism and its numerous crimes, whereas a new life of peace and prosperity is offered to the African diaspora, as long as its children eventually accept the Gospel. Xavier goes further on to propose a hyperbolic fabulation or, better still, "utopianization" of the history of the African diaspora in Brazil, in clear anti-revolutionary, conservative terms (see Xavier 2014, 51).

The ideal of a leading role as set aside for Brazil in Zweig's 1941 book, was therefore found some years before, in *Brazil, Heart of the World, Homeland of the Gospel*, with particular enthusiasm:

> Our goal, in bringing some notes to the spiritual history of Brazil, was only to enhance the excellence of its mission on the planet, demonstrating, simultaneously, that each nation, as indeed each individual, has a role to play within the concert of the peoples. All have their ancestors in the invisible world, from where they receive the spiritual sap necessary for their formation and conservation. One of the main purposes of our effort was to examine, before the eyes of all, the need for personal and collective education, amidst the unfolding of all the work in the country. After all, the reality is that Brazil, in its very special situation and with its immense wealth, will not be able to isolate itself from the rest of the world or be cast aside in its position as the Fatherland of the Gospel, although the time is one of detestable autarchies, in this period of decay and transition of all social systems. (Xavier 2014, 184)

Thus, the words by Humberto de Campos, as psychographed by Chico Xavier (2014 [1938]), appear to have set the "spiritual bases" for Zweig's "land of the future," which in turn has been translated into several languages. The idea of a Brazilian "manifest destiny" in *Brazil, Heart of the World, Homeland of the Gospel* seems to guide both authors' utopian narratives. It may be reasonable to assume that *Brazil, Heart of the World, Homeland of the Gospel* has contributed substantially to the spread of the ideal of a "land of the future." It is likely that Chico Xavier's book largely exceeded Zweig's in terms of sales, at least in Brazil, excluding the translations of Zweig's book abroad.

*Brazil, Heart of the World, Homeland of the Gospel* ended up recognized as a legitimate work by the family of Humberto de Campos, which led to a lawsuit over copyright, eventually won by Campos's widow in 1944. Since then, the medium and literary works by Chico Xavier and other famous mediums have expanded and diversified, attracting readers seduced by the revelations that mediums brought about the spiritual world and medium techniques such as psychography and the like.

Spiritist literature, mostly psychographed texts, still enjoys great popularity in Brazil. It can be confirmed in Sandra Stoll's *Espiritismo à Brasileira* (2004), in which the author conducts further investigation into different trends within Brazilian spiritism. The first Brazilian spiritist trend, more linked to Christianity, can be epitomized by the public persona of Chico Xavier, the famous medium,[4] who published dozens of psychographed books by great national authors, as well as spirits that would only have become famous after they disincarnated—such as André Luiz, who dictated to Xavier the seminal Brazilian spiritist novel *Our Home* (*Nosso Lar*, 1944). Chico Xavier had his first book published by the Brazilian Spiritist Federation in 1932, *Parnaso de Alem-Túmulo*, a collection of 60 poems attributed to 14 dead Brazilian and Portuguese poets. Xavier, who was to become the greatest medium in the history of Brazilian spiritism, has always admitted the influence of Bezerra de Menezes on his medium work. According to Xavier, the spirit of Bezerra de Menezes was manifested in sessions where patients were being treated. The doctor's spirit was responsible for spiritual cures, homoeopathic prescriptions, and medical advice. Several texts attributed to Bezerra de Menezes were also psychographed by Chico Xavier (Schroder 2014, 13). Over a period spanning almost seventy years, Chico Xavier published 439 books (Lisboa 2014, 45).

A new generation of Brazilian spiritist authors flourished, following in the footsteps of Zilda Gama (2007) and Chico Xavier, with numerous psychographed novels, stories, and biographies. In this regard, another very popular author was medium Zíbia Gasparetto. This writer launched, among dozens of other titles, *A Chat with the Afterlife* (*Bate-Papo com o Além*, 1982), a book of short stories allegedly written together with the spirit of Silveira Sampaio, and *Defeating the Past* (*Vencendo o Passado*, 2008), with short stories assigned to the spirit of Lucius. Zíbia is the mother of another key figure in contemporary Brazilian spiritism,

Luiz Antonio Gasparetto, who opted for a more spectacular—and less monastic—medium career than Xavier's. Luiz Antonio Gasparetto also psychographs paintings by artists like Toulouse-Lautrec and incorporates far more esoteric aspects and elements from New Age religions and self-help literature in his multiple works.

## Beyond the Film Print: Brazilian Spiritist Cinema

Whereas Brazilian mainstream cinema and literature appear to value more sociologically inclined, realist-naturalist approaches to fiction to the detriment of fantasy and SF, popular TV and the book markets are driven by different criteria. Since *The Strangers* (*Os Estranhos*), a soap opera written by Ivani Ribeiro and aired on Excelsior[5] between March and July 1969, many of the most popular TV soap operas and best-sellers in Brazil have significant portions of fantasy, science fictionish elements, and self-help strategies. A more evident, paradigmatic case of spiritism in a Brazilian TV soap opera can be seen in Ivani Ribeiro's *The Trip* (*A Viagem*), produced and broadcast for the first time in 1975, and remade in 1994. *The Trip* was an adaptation of the books *And Life Goes On* (*E A Vida Continua*) and *Our Home* (*Nosso Lar*), allegedly dictated to Chico Xavier by the spirit named André Luiz. More recently, it is worth mentioning Walcyr Carrasco and Thelma Guedes's *Twin Souls* (*Alma Gêmea*), aired on Rede Globo[6] at 6 p.m. from June 20, 2005, to March 10, 2006. Aired from November 3, 2014, to May 9, 2015, Rede Globo's 7 p.m.[7] soap opera *High Spirits* (*Alto Astral*), written by Daniel Ortiz (under the supervision of Silvio de Abreu) also featured mediunity, the afterlife, and communication with spirits.

But talking strictly about film, one of the first appearances of spiritism in Brazilian cinema was probably in a comedy released in the mid-1930s: *The Young Great-Grandfather* (*O Jovem Tataravô*), directed by Luiz de Barros and produced by Cinédia studios in 1936, taps into the quid pro quos resulting from the invocation of a spirit from nineteenth-century Rio de Janeiro in the 1930s, by means of a lackadaisically conducted ceremony of "white table."[8] Supernatural motifs will continue to appear in Brazilian cinema, particularly in comedy films throughout the 1940s.

A more significantly discernible form of spiritism will only reemerge with a stronger emphasis in Brazilian cinema through an early-1950s independent production shot in a small studio on Rua Fortaleza, in the

Bixiga neighborhood in São Paulo, and also in the seaside town of Santos: *The Alley of the Missing Ones, 113 (Alameda da Saudade, 113,* 1951), by Carlos Ortiz, a former priest who, at time of the film's release, was a member of the Communist Party. Ortiz's film plot elaborates on an idea from Santos's folklore, in which a young man dances the whole of Carnival in the company of an attractive young woman, and days later, when he goes to look for her, her mother explains that she died years ago (Máximo Barro qtd. in Silva Neto 2002, 35). Another film about a similar topic, *Maternal Heart (Coração Materno,* 1951), by Gilda de Abreu, presented an otherworldly romantic ending to its heroes (a couple separated in life), showing the reunion of their ghosts in the house where they first met. It was not by chance that *Maternal Heart* was released more recently on DVD as part of a series of spiritist movies in the 2000s, partially because Gilda de Abreu and Vicente Celestino (the film's stars) had been celebrities who publicly declared their belief in Kardecism.

In the 1970s, the show business and the cultural industry's interest in themes that could attract the followers of spiritism—such as reports on spiritualistic contacts through electronic devices of sound and image recording and other paranormal phenomena[9] (like telekinesis,[10] the inexplicable power to move objects, and the so-called *poltergeist* phenomena)—led to some films identified with spiritualism in the broad sense and sometimes with Kardecism specifically.

Among the most famous films with spiritualistic motifs in the 1970s, we could mention *Thrill (Excitação,* 1976) and *The Strength of the Senses (A Força dos Sentidos,* 1979), both directed by Jean Garrett,[11] along with *The Daughters of the Fire (As Filhas do Fogo,* 1978), by Walter Hugo Khouri, and *A Strange Love Story (Uma Estranha História de Amor,* 1979), by John Doo. In these four films, themes like past-life memories and communication with the afterlife—through human mediums and/or gadgets—inspired Brazilian horror stories shaped by international horror cinema, a genre mostly dominated by American and European productions. Since they were prominently commercial films made by independent producers in São Paulo in the 1970s (the so-called Cinema da Boca do Lixo, named after the central urban area in São Paulo where most independent film producers and distributors had their offices), these films also resorted to eroticism and launch strategies similar to those usually associated with exploitation cinema. In the case of *The Daughters of the Fire,* for example, the film was sponsored by publishing house Editora Três and released together with a special offer from the magazine *Planet (Planeta),* a publication focusing on religious and mystic themes that granted prizes to the best supernatural stories sent by its readers (Cánepa 2017).

*Thrill*, a 1977 film directed by Jean Garrett and with photography by Carlos Reichenbach, mixes characteristics of police films, SF, and horror. Renato (Flávio Galvão) is the electronic engineer who wants to get rid of his rich wife, Helena (Kate Hansen), to be with Arlete, his mistress and widow of Paulo, Renato's former business partner. In order to drive Helena crazy, Renato has a hidden computer that turns on and off, moving home appliances in the beach house to where they had recently moved in. The house had belonged to Paulo, and it was in the main hall that he committed suicide by hanging, a victim of a ruse put forth by Renato himself. The image of a woman attacked by home appliances that come to life is very familiar to SF, as in Donald Cammel's 1977 film *Demon Seed*, in which a supercomputer takes over a futuristic house and intends to inseminate a woman in order to create an *Übermensch*. References to SF imagery in Garrett's *Thrill* also lie in some scenes of computers in operation, in addition to the character of the electronic engineer himself, who is passionate about cybernetics and, in this case, a variation on the traditional "mad scientist." According to Renato, electronics can do anything, even "magic." A convinced materialist, the villain Renato did not count on the intervention of the supernatural, with his wife Helena finally serving the revenge plan of Paul's spirit. As the story unfolds, the film oscillates between the fantastic, the crime story, and SF, in fact comprising characteristics of the three genres: the punished soul, the "perfect" crime, and futuristic electronic paraphernalia. Its ending, however, reinforces the prevalence of fantasy or horror. It is curious to note how the soundtrack, an extra-diegetic sound present in the prologue featuring the suicide of Paulo that introduces the supposed manifestations of his spirit, somehow anticipates the diegetic noise of the Alien series' tracking device, as in Ridley Scott's *Alien*. In both films, when the viewer hears the syncopated rhythm, like a heartbeat, something terrible threatens to appear: in one case the alien; the other the soul of a hanged man. *Thrill* also exudes a certain Catholic or spiritualistic morality, much in the style of another, more recent supernatural thriller: Robert Zemeckis's *What Lies Beneath* (2000), in which the husband also sins and ends up being punished, but it is his wife who suffers. Anyhow, Jean Garrett's *Thrill* seems to offer an interesting example of how Brazilian cinema cites SF imagery in tandem with more familiar and widespread beliefs in the afterlife and spiritual punishment.

*The Daughters of Fire* (*As Filhas do Fogo*), by Walter Hugo Khouri, could be located on this borderline area between SF and horror, in which motifs such as parapsychology are emphasized. In this production by César Mêmolo Jr., Lynx Filmes, and Editora Três, with a script by Khouri himself, Ana (Rosina Malbouisson), a young student from São Paulo, visits her friend Diana (Paola Morra), who lives in a mansion in Gramado (a small town in the southern Brazilian state of Rio Grande do Sul), where two employees and a housekeeper work. Sílvia (Selma Egrei), Diana's mother is deceased, and her father spends most of his time traveling on business. Ana and Diana meet Dagmar (Karin Rodrigues), a neighbor dedicated to parapsychology who conducts experiments to capture the voice of dead people. She explains her activity to the two young women, saying that it is "something that many important people, including scientists, have been doing all over the world." A series of strange events starts taking place and has an impact on all the characters. *The Daughters of the Fire* ends up moving away from the domain of SF, even though the genre remains in the film around the "scientific" treatment of paranormality. Rogério Duprat's soundtrack is an additional element of otherworldliness and the usual suspense in mystery and horror films.

In addition to the aforementioned four films, all of which set spiritualism closer to horror and even the SF film genre, at least two productions from the 1980s could be deemed as truly Kardecist films: Paulo Figueiredo's *The Medium: The Truth about Reincarnation* (*O Médium: A Verdade sobre a Reencarnação*, 1980), and Clery Cunha's *Joelma, 23rd Floor* (*Joelma, 23o Andar*, 1980). *The Medium* was written, directed, produced by Paulo Figueiredo (who also costars), with a famous cast that included Ewerton de Castro, Jussara Freire, and Geórgia Gomide. This film is about an arrogant surgeon who is haunted by the ghost of another physician that accuses him of practicing medicine without feelings. After finishing one of his surgeries, the surgeon faints and is taken to a parallel world, where another doctor's spirit explains the origins of his coldness and unhappiness in traumatic events of his past life on Earth. *Joelma, 23rd Floor*, written by Dulce Santucci and based on one of Chico Xavier's psychographic works (published as *We Are Six/Somos Seis*), presents the psychographed memories of young people who died in the Joelma Building fire in São Paulo, a real event that resulted in the death of 179 people on February 1, 1974. Mostly revolving around the report of one survivor, the young Volkimar (in the film, Lucimar), this production intertwines documentary footage from the day of the fire with enacted scenes, in the style of a docudrama. Starring Beth Goulart and Liana Duval, *Joelma* was partially shot in the original building, right after its restoration. The film articulates, in a surprisingly effective way, the sensationalism of exploitation cinema, disaster movie conventions, typical scenes associated with horror cinema (like premonitions and sudden appearances), the docudrama style, and elements from the religious melodrama. As a result, the film may elicit some ethical discussions even today, given its mixture of Kardecist messages, allegedly self-biographic reports obtained by means of supernatural interventions, hints at an ancestral curse, real scenes of the catastrophe, the blur of boundaries between documentary and fiction and, on top of all that, moments of graphic horror. The release of *Joelma* in 1980 was greatly anticipated by the public and the media, and its box office performance was quite impressive, attracting approximately a million spectators to movie theaters. Oddly enough, however, the film was forgotten shortly after its release, being recovered in 2007 by the Video Spirit Collection, under the slogan of "the first spiritualist film in the world." Perhaps the release of *Joelma* in the domestic video market in 2007 has contributed to what we call the revival of Brazilian spiritist cinema, starting in 2008.

It is also worth noting that the majority of Hollywood productions with spiritualistic motifs (despite being significantly different from Kardec's original doctrine) have always been extremely successful at the box office in Brazil. We can think of commercially successful films released in the 1980s, such as Jeannot Szwark's *Somewhere in Time* (1980), followed in the 1990s and early 2000s by Jerry Zucker's *Ghost* (1990), Joel Schumacher's *Flatliners* (1990), Kenneth Branagh's *Dead Again* (1991), Ron Underwood's *Heart and Souls* (1993), M. Night Shyamalan's *The Sixth Sense* (1999), Alejandro Amenábar's *The Others* (2001), and Guillermo del Toro's *The Devil Spine* (*Espiñazo del Diablo*, 2001). One particularly interesting case of commercial success was *White Noise* (2005), directed by Geoffrey Sax. It was the Brazilian market that embraced this film the most: it had been a flop in America. Starring Michael Keaton, *White Noise* is about a widower who believes he can record spirits' voices through electronic devices. The success of Sax's movie in Brazil made its sequel, Patrick Lussier's *White Noise—The Light* (2007), be shown in movie theaters only in Brazil and distributed directly on DVD to the rest of the world.

Cláudio Torres's 2004 feature-length film *Redeemer* (*Redentor*) also deserves mention in this overview. Although not immediately identified with spiritist cinema, much less with the field of religious cinema, this comedy with touches of social criticism and absurdism attempts to capitalize on Brazilian spiritism, inasmuch as the main character (Pedro Cardoso) has the task of "saving the soul" of a corrupt friend (Miguel Falabella), a real estate businessman who intends to make money at the expense of the misfortune of poor people.

Released between 2006 and 2007, at least two Brazilian feature films attained noteworthy commercial success: João Falcão's *Stay With Me Tonight* (*Fica Comigo Esta Noite*, 2006), and Jorge Moreno's *Believe, I Have a Spirit on Me* (*Acredite, Um Espírito Baixou em Mim*, 2007). The former, a romantic comedy starring young actors from TV Globo (Alinne Moraes and Vladimir Brichta), is loosely based on the play of the same name by Flávio de Souza, staged in the 1990s, about a recently deceased man who wants to return to his old body just to say goodbye to his beloved wife. The latter is a comedy about a homosexual dentist who dies in a car crash and then possesses a macho man. *Believe* was also based on a theater play written by Ronaldo Ciambroni and directed by Sandra Pêra; it was a commercial success in the state of Minas Gerais, Brazil, around the early 2000s. This play attracted almost a million spectators and became known as "the Gay *Ghost*," in a reference to the 1990 famous film directed by Jerry Zucker, starring Demi Moore and Patrick Swayze.

João Falcão also directed *The Machine* (*A Máquina*, 2006), an adaptation of one of his plays that could also be studied in the light of Brazilian spiritism. This romantic comedy hinges on the premise of the main character who intends to correct his past in his quest for true love: something akin to the narrative artifice of the "second chance," as in Frank Capra's 1946 film *It's a Wonderful Life*. In *The Machine*, a mixture of fantasy and loose SF based on time travel, a young man (Gustavo Falcão) is instructed by the older version of himself (Paulo Autran) about how to correct his present (and therefore his past). As the story unfolds, it can be interpreted as either a microcosm or a metaphor for belief in the evolution of the spirit by means of reincarnation.

Yet apparently detached from the rest of Brazilian cinema, which often screens comedy-fantasy films without a more direct and in-depth reference to religious aspects (like, for example, in the commercially successful series *If I Were You / Se Eu Fosse Você*, by Daniel Filho, started in 2006), the films mentioned here did not establish a dialogue solely with Hollywood cinema. On the whole, spiritualism *lato sensu* has never been a new development in our audiovisual landscape; much to the contrary, in fact. This is not surprising, as Brazil is likely home to the biggest number of Kardecist followers in the world.

The revival of Brazilian spiritist cinema in the mid-2000s seems to have gained momentum with the commercial success and repercussion of Glauber Filho and Joe Pimentel's *Bezerra de Menezes—The Diary of a Spirit* (*Bezerra de Menezes: O Diário de um Espírito*, 2008), a relatively low-budget production put forth by the spiritist organization called Estação Luz, based in the state of Ceará, in Northeastern Brazil. The film presents an edifying biography of the pioneer of spiritism in Brazil, Adolfo Bezerra de Menezes, through the reenactment of episodes in his life. With actor Carlos Vereza in the title role, the film portrays Bezerra de Menezes's discovery of spiritism, his abolitionist endeavors, his altruistic practice of medicine, and his vocation as an evangelist. In the style of the hagiographic movies (which narrate the life of Catholic saints), the emphasis is on the charitable and pacifist attitudes of the so-called Doctor of the Poor, a personality revered to this day, and whose spirit would have already spoken through medium Chico Xavier—as shown in the epilogue of the film, containing archival footage and real testimonies of believers, along with the final credits. *Bezerra de Menezes* ends with a line dedicating the story to the antiabortion cause, a controversial issue on the Brazilian political agenda.

Following the repercussion of *Bezerra de Menezes*, higher-budgeted productions like Wagner de Assis's *Our Home* (*Nosso Lar*, 2010), and Daniel Filho's *Chico Xavier* (2010), which attracted 4 million and 3.4 million spectators, respectively, capitalized on a new wave of independent spiritist films like Glauber Filho and Halder Gomes's *The Mothers of Chico Xavier* (*As Mães de Chico Xavier*, 2011), André Marouço and Michel Dubret's *The Spirits' Film* (*O Filme dos Espíritos*, 2010), and Paulo Figueiredo's *And The Life Goes On . . .* (*E a Vida Continua . . .*, 2011).[12] These movies represented less impressive box offices, but their commercial careers cannot be underestimated.

Daniel Filho's *Chico Xavier* (2010), a feature film based on Marcel Souto Maior's book *The Lives of Chico Xavier* (*As Vidas de Chico Xavier*, 2003), somewhat repeats the same biopic formula found in *Bezerra de Menezes*, but its far higher budget allows for better script, production, cinematography, and cast. The "Estação da Luz" spiritist society reappears as a partner in this more sophisticated production aimed at broader audiences. In Daniel Filho's film, the path trailed by Francisco Cândido Xavier, the most famous Brazilian medium, is narrated through flashbacks, starting with his famous participation on the TV show *Fire Drop* (*Pinga-Fogo*), aired live by TV Tupi[13] in 1971.[14] Three actors played Chico Xavier's role, each one representing a different stage in his life: his childhood, from 1918 to 1922; his adulthood, from 1931 to 1959; and advanced age, from 1959 to 1975. The actors were, respectively, Matheus Costa, Ângelo Antônio, and Nelson Xavier. Right from its first scenes, the film assumes its spiritist activism by diegetically naturalizing esotericism in the first conversation of the spirit Emmanuel (André Dias) with Chico Xavier, while the medium is getting ready in one of the dressing rooms of Tupi's studios, moments before he is put on stage for the *Fire Drop* live show. The affiliation of this film to the spiritist doctrine occurs through two basic elements: (1) the narrative focus, which lies in Chico Xavier, assuring that the whole story unfolds according to this character's viewpoint, and (2) the subplot about the couple whose child died in a firearms accident. This subplot features the epiphany of the skeptical and atheist husband (Tony Ramos), who happens to be a TV Tupi employee that finally accepts the phenomenon of communication with spirits and the legitimacy of Chico Xavier's mediumship. These two story lines—the episodes in Chico Xavier's life and the conversion of the father whose son died violently—are therefore based on real events: the celebrated TV show *Fire Drop*, where Chico Xavier was interviewed in 1971, and the first case in which a murder suspect was considered innocent by a Brazilian court with the aid of psychographics. As told in the film, the letter psychographed by Chico Xavier during the show, and then given to the skeptical father, ends up being added to the criminal suit, eventually resulting in the acquittal of a young man accused of murdering his friend. The real case took place in the city of Goiânia, central Brazil. The student José Divino Nunes, who in May of 1979 had accidentally killed his inseparable friend Maurício Garcez Henrique in a case known as "Russian roulette," was acquitted by the judge of the Sixth Criminal Court, Orimar Bastos, who considered that the felony was not included under any sanctions of the Brazilian Penal Code since the performed act, for the presented analysis, was not predictable. The judge sent the document to the court for appreciation due to the right of defense (*O Popular*, August 10, 1979). The trial was covered in an article titled "Judge Acquits Based on Psychographed Letter" ("*Juiz absolve com base em carta psicografada*"), published in the newspaper *O Globo* from September 18, 1979.

## All That Is Solid Melts into Air—and Belongs to the Spirits: When Spiritism Meets SF

While extraterrestrial invasions and cutting-edge science and technology portrayed in films appear to be "alien" to Brazilian audiences—something "made by Americans" or associated with Hollywood—stories that feature futuristic spiritual societies or spirits traveling through time in search of their beloved ones do not cause the same kind of "estrangement." This is when religion and SF may merge, resulting in a "familiarizing" process or even "domestication" of an allegedly foreign film genre (SF) then adapted for local audiences.

Wagner de Assis's *Our Home* (*Nosso Lar*, 2010), a film adaptation of Chico Xavier's book of the same name, tells the story of André Luiz in his afterlife, his spirit embarking on a journey of self-knowledge: first facing pain and sacrifice in the purgatory called Umbral, and finally evolving while dwelling in the spiritual city of Our Home. This city hovers over the Earth's atmosphere, in a spiritual dimension, and its communication technology, architecture, means of transportation and social organization are all elements that recall SF iconography and utopian narratives.

*Our Home* the book, first published in 1944, seems to repurpose and anticipate the Utopian dream of a modernist new capital, to be constructed on the Brazilian Central Plateau (*Planalto Central*). This ideal came true with the foundation of Brasília on April 21, 1960, by President Juscelino Kubitschek. Since then, parallels and cross-readings involving both the imaginary city from *Our Home* and the real Brasília have been suggested and discussed in works such as Jonas Staal's book *Nosso Lar, Brasília: Spiritism—Modernism—Architecture* (2014). From a foreign point of view, Staal merges the design of the imaginary city of *Our Home* and Brasília's urban landscape in order to discuss some intriguing similarities but also some discrepancies and ambiguities. In a nutshell, the author suggests that the imaginary city of Chico Xavier's 1944 book *Our Home* might be regarded as a blueprint for Brasília, founded in 1960. No matter how controversial and nuanced this thesis may be, Staal observes that "in a way, it is the people of Brazil that 'perform' the overlaps between Modernism and Spiritism" (2014, 155). Wagner de Assis's film only adds weight to this connection or dialogue between the imaginary city from the book and Brasília based on set designs clearly inspired by Brazilian modernist architecture as confirmed in interviews with the director himself and his film crew. According to art director Lia Renha, Oscar Niemeyer's and Santiago Calatrava's architecture inspired her work with set designer Marcus Ranzani on the creation of a city incarnating the ideals of lightness, fluidity, and simplicity (Assis 2010, 48). Among a number of props, such as communication devices and the like, the film features a floating train that can also be related to typical SF iconography—perhaps considered retro SF by the time the film was released in 2010. Wagner de Assis's comments on the film's production design also evoke the link between *Our Home* and SF:

> At certain moments, the film production had a twist of "fantasy film"—locations did not exist out of computers and set designers' desktops; a great part of the story is set in a city that floats over the Earth (it was necessary to have this geography very clear in mind, how the sunlight reached the surface, whether there was night, how the Earth's reflection affected the city, how the planetary phenomenon and the views of space should be faced, how the life on the streets was, the costumes. In other words, a whole universe needed to be developed, checked and rendered in favor of the story. (Assis 2010, 183)

The visual effects in Assis's *Our Home* were developed by Canadian company Intelligent Creatures, the same one that created the effects for Zack Snyder's 2009 blockbuster *Watchmen*. The Brazilian film's soundtrack is composed by none other than Philip Glass. As Assis himself stated in an interview to *IstoÉ* magazine, he pursued a script as impressive as the original text, with the visual quality to confer more verisimilitude to his film (Rangel 2010).

Antonio Cordoba (2017) compares Wagner de Assis's *Our Home* and Adirley Queirós's *White Out, Black In* (*Branco Sai, Preto Fica*, 2014) to conclude that the former reproduces a conservative agenda, in tune with 2010 "neoliberal transhumanism" (2017, 135), whereas the latter film resorts to a "salvagepunk" (2017, 142) in order to speculate on an Afrofuturistic empowerment scenario, in which the oppressed people from the outskirts take revenge. With regard to Assis's *Our Home*, Cordoba observes:

> It is important to stress that everything in the film can be understood in strictly Spiritist terms. At the same time, Assis' use of science fiction iconography and the words his characters speak in the ideological context of 2010 allow his audience to

> engage in a double reading of the film. This double reading links Spiritism to neoliberalism, and Spiritist emphasis on perfectibility to transhumanist Utopian desires to transcend the human condition. One can conclude that the scriptwriter-director makes an effort to refer to other contemporary discourses to provide his film with a more complex resonance in the audience. (2017, 136)

I could not agree more with Cordoba on the fact that, in summary, *Our Home* remains an extremely conservative piece of cinematic discourse: a didactic film that makes use of SF iconography in order to reaffirm the world as it is and should continue to be. We also agree with Cordoba's remarks on Wagner de Assis's *Our Home* as a twofold film in terms of film reception: "*Nosso Lar* is not a science fiction movie, but an exposition of Spiritist that is fully realistic once we accept the system of belief. However, thanks to its relatively high budget, it can afford to look decidedly futuristic. *Nosso Lar* does feel like a science fiction film" (Cordoba 2017, 135). Notwithstanding, when Cordoba elaborates on my previous comments on *Our Home* (Suppia 2014) and states that the affinity between SF and Assis's film "is more than just an attempt to domesticate science fiction iconography in favour of religious indoctrination and the quest for box office success" (2017, 135), I must object to some extent. Cordoba adds that "on the contrary, it is fully coherent with a retro-futuristic ideology and a forward-looking desire to transcend Enlightenment humanism. This is a desire that, in 2010, seemed particularly in tune with neoliberal transhumanism" (2017, 135). My partial objection is based on two arguments. First, there is a middle ground or a certain link between SF and the bulk of Kardecism that stretches beyond the fact that Camille Flammarion, one of Kardec's main enthusiasts, was also an author of *romans scientifiques*. It has something to do with the very basic assumption, presented by Kardec himself, that spiritism was a "scientific doctrine." To believers or followers, Kardecism or Spiritism is not a fiction: it is the truth, and it explains the whole mechanics and dynamics of the immaterial, spiritual world. It is a whole cosmogony in itself. However, to nonpractitioners or nonbelievers, all the spiritist literature can be regarded as pure fiction: And why not SF? Secondly, Cordoba insists on a "retro-futuristic ideology" and "retro-futuristic landscape," but we ask ourselves to what extent it is a fully reliable "reading" of Assis's film, in so far as it may not be unequivocally accepted as a clear "message" or "intention" put forth by the film's discourse. In other words, was it clear to director Assis and set designers that they were presenting a "retro-futuristic ideology" and "retro-futuristic landscape"? This is really hard to tell because, even if the film's settings, props, and costume design may allude to some sort of "retro-futurism," we cannot be sure whether this "retro-futuristic" atmosphere was really pursued by Wagner de Assis and his crew. On the contrary, and based on the available interviews and bibliography on the film, it may well be that no "retro-," but only "futurism" was attempted. Consequently, one might guess that Assis always pursued futuristic designs for his cinematic speculation on the astral city even though, obviously, contemporary spectatorship and scholarship can see retro-futurism in *Our Home*. Maybe this retrofuturism, partially based on the alleged inspiration on the urban planning of Brasília, is the inherent by-product of merely a conservative approach to SF.

SF and spiritist indoctrination with a more clear touch of New Age imagery can be found in Gérson Sanginitto's *Area Q* (*Área Q*, 2012). Produced by Luís Eduardo Girão, the same producer behind successful blockbusters like the aforementioned films *Bezerra de Menezes* and *Chico Xavier*, among other titles, *Area Q* premiered at the Second International Transcendental Film Festival (*Festival de Cinema Transcendental de Brasília*) in Brasília, 2012. Sanginitto's film is a blend of detective story, melodrama, and SF with spiritist motifs set in the interior of the Brazilian Northeast, in remote landscapes. The story begins with a case of abduction in 1979, and then moves to the contemporary United States, when an American journalist decides to come to Brazil in order to investigate the abductions in the mysterious "Area Q," between the cities of Quixeramobim and Quixadá, in the Brazilian state of Ceará. Needless to say, the days this *gringo* spends in the Brazilian hinterlands will change his life (and afterlife) forever. Although punctuated by references to Rachel de Queiroz's celebrated SF short story "Ma-Hôre" (1960), this film does not go much farther than a pale simulacrum of the *X-Files* series with a stronger twist of New Age esotericism and stereotypical Brazilian motifs.

Random spiritualistic elements and atmospheres have also appeared in films that bear no bond to Kardecism, thus circulating outside the spiritist film circuit, apparently disconnected from any ideal of indoctrination. These recent fantasy films share similarities with the horror genre, revisiting the fantastic much in the style of Jean Garrett's *Thrill*, but with an updated and subtler perspective. For instance, we refer to short films like *A Branch* (*Um Ramo*, 2007), by Marco Dutra and Juliana Rojas, *Red Forest* (*Floresta Vermelha*), by Flávio Soares, *Doomed* (*Encosto*, 2013), by

Joel Caetano, and Marco Antonio Pereira's *Theory on a Strange Planet* (*Teoria sobre um Planeta Estranho*, 2018), as well as Marco Dutra and Juliana Rojas's feature-length film *Hard Labor* (*Trabalhar Cansa*, 2011).

The only Brazilian representative in the official competition in the Cannes Film Festival 2011, Dutra and Rojas's *Hard Labour* emphasizes the working-class conditions orbiting a typical Brazilian middle-class family, thus offering a "kaleidoscopic" perspective on class struggle in Brazil. In *Hard Labour*, the white middle-class husband Otávio (Marat Descartes) loses his job while his wife Helena (Helena Albergaria) initiates her career as an entrepreneur by opening a mini-market. Shortly after, Paula (Naloana Lima) is hired by Helena as a housekeeper to take care of their young daughter Vanessa (Marina Flores). Paula starts working in her new job without proper documentation or rights. Helena offers less than a minimum salary during the test period and promises, if everything works out, a minimum salary plus help with transportation—but still with no proper documentation. Meanwhile, there is a long queue of job candidates in front of Helena's new business, and Otávio runs away from his first job interview based on group dynamics. As time goes by and Otávio fails to find a new job, the relationship with his family deteriorates and mysterious facts start threatening Helena's business: the building where her mini-market is located seems to hold negative spiritual energy. *Hard Labour* mixes a certain social realism with a fantastic twist, in a film style that has not been very common in Brazilian feature-length commercial cinema. The same attitude toward the fantastic, with echoes from Brazilian spiritism lato sensu, seems to persist in more recent movies by Dutra and Rojas, like in *When I Was Alive* (*Quando Eu Era Vivo*, 2014) and *The Necropolis's Symphony* (*Sinfonia da Necrópole*, 2014).

Flávio Soares's experimental short *Red Forest* (*Floresta Vermelha*, 2013) also echoes some Brazilian spiritism in its half-fantasy, half-documentary narrative[15] on the return of a young man, Nikolai (Flávio Kage), to his parents' house in a small town in the Russian countryside after nine years. The reencounter of the young man with his family—the spirits of his parents, or maybe mental projections of his father, mother, and sister—is tense and altogether strange, and involved in a dreamlike or nightmarish atmosphere that somewhat also refers to SF iconography (i.e., the wasteland). An experimentation in open-source filmmaking, *Red Forest* was completely made with free and open software and hardware, using an Elphel camera and benefitting from the support of the international community called Apertus (Open-Source Cinema). Another independent and extremely low-budget short film, Joel Caetano's *Doomed* also echoes Brazilian spiritualism, this time merged with a stereotypical account of African-Brazilian rituals and paying tribute to American B horror movies and the thriller genre.

More recently, Marco Antônio Pereira's *Theory on a Strange Planet* tells the love story of a young woman with hearing impairment (Larissa Bocchino) who is in love with the gas station attendant (Gerson Marques) in the small town of Cordisburgo, in the Brazilian state of Minas Gerais.[16] The girl's family members do not want her to marry the young man, but only he can understand her feelings and thus access the world she belongs to. However, a sad, frightening accident involving a lightning bolt in the midst of a peaceful rainy afternoon suddenly changes the lives of the lovers and shows how special the small moments of everyday life are. This visual metaphor about love, death, and everyday life brings a unique, irreverent, and experimental aesthetic, characteristic of Pereira's film style that merges a latent realism with genuinely popular culture, punctuated by magical realism and hints at SF iconography. The film is virtually about the decisive moment between life and death, and hence it features one of the most curious and striking scenes, in which God is represented by an intriguing countryman, the owner of a picturesque mini-market.

Pereira is a young Brazilian director particularly active in terms of a poetic, fantastic cinema with local colors. His film debut was with an SF short titled *Withdrawal to a Rough Heart* (*A Retirada para um Coração Bruto*, 2017). *A Retirada . . .* tells the story of an old man, Ozório (Manoel do Norte), who lives alone in the rural area of Cordisburgo, in the backlands of the state of Minas Gerais. He spends his days listening to rock on the radio and mourning the loss of his wife. However, a strange incident in the skies breaks Ozório's loneliness and he eventually makes contact with alien visitors. This will change his life forever.

Finally, to give just one single example among the countless spiritualist documentaries that certainly outnumber spiritist fiction films, we would like to mention Rebeca Casagrande, Fabio Medeiros, and Juliano Pozati's *Deadline According to Chico Xavier* (*Data Limite Segundo Chico Xavier*, 2014). Released on DVD and available on the web, this film draws on Chico Xavier's predictions for the day humankind would make contact with an extra-terrestrial civilization. According to the medium, fifty years after humankind set foot on the Moon, "celestial powers" would bring Judgment Day to Earth and finally the human race would have to choose between war and peace. This crucial date would be July 20, 2019, and if no global nuclear conflict had started by then, Earthlings would be eventually accepted in a cosmic community, thus benefitting from unimaginable social, scientific, and technological advances. The film resorts to archival footage from the aforementioned famous TV show *Fire Drops* (*Pinga Fogo*) starring Chico Xavier in the 1970s, edited along with contemporary interviews with an ufologist (Ademar Gevaerd), a journalist (Saulo Gomes), other famous Brazilian spiritist leaders (Geraldo Lemos and Divaldo Franco), two Brazilian generals, and Paul Hilley, former Canadian minister of defense. All speakers, including the Canadian ex-minister, express their belief in the extra-terrestrial concern about the humans' nuclear weapons, an arsenal that might put the universe at risk. Right from the beginning, archival footage of the 1969 American mission on the moon and of Chico Xavier set the "science fictional" discourse or mode of representation, with the most famous Brazilian medium stating that he does believe in extra-terrestrial life. According to the Brazilian journalist Saulo Gomes, friend of Chico Xavier, the medium was convinced about the existence of extra-terrestrial intelligence. Gomes supports that Xavier was the first religious man in the world who dared to defend the existence of other intelligent beings from other worlds live on a TV show. *Deadline* thus explores the eschatological/apocalyptic dimension in Brazilian spiritism based on Chico Xavier's clairvoyant medium capabilities. Words such as telepathy, telekinesis, precognition, extra-terrestrial intelligence, and references to natural disasters and flying saucers landing by the White House, all addressed by the interviewees in the film, clearly evoke at least two familiar SF narratives: Arthur C. Clarke's short story "The Sentinel" (1951), and Robert Wise's film *The Day the Earth Stood Still*, not to mention Susan Sontag's (1990, 209–25) well-known essay "The Imagination of Disaster," first published in *October*, in 1965 (42–48).

Based on this brief overview, we suspect that international SF and horror have mostly been providing a ready-made framework or set of codes for Brazilian directors intending to make film adaptations related to Brazilian spiritism. Nevertheless, and differently from what usually happened in 1970s/1980s cinema (such as *Joelma*), some contemporary films with more overtly spiritualistic motifs have been seeking more consistent recognition as spiritist movies. This means the emergence of a possible new genre or subgenre in the wider field of religious cinema.[17] Both Luiz Vadico's (2010, 2015) and Melanie J. Wright's (2006) works about religious films are based on the taxonomy first established by William Telford (2000; 2005), on the types of religious films. These are films that either

1. make use of religious themes, motifs or symbols in their titles;

2. have plots that draw on religion (broadly defined to include the supernatural or the occult);

3. are set in the contexts of religious communities;

4. use religion for character definition;

5. deal directly or indirectly with religious characters (e.g., the Buddha, or angels), texts, or locations (such as heaven or hell);

6. use religious ideas to explore the experiences and transformation or conversion of characters; or

7. address religious themes and concerns, including ethical issues. (Telford 2000 and 2005, qtd. in Wright 2006, 19)

Even though Vadico's work focuses on Christian movies, it is worth noticing that what he labels as "religious film field" can accommodate several genres or subgenres under this definition, such as the films about the life of Jesus Christ, the life of the saints (hagiography), and movies about sacred appearances or miraculous events, for example. Thus, the most recent new wave of spiritualistic films in Brazil might be one more (sub)genre in this broader field of religious cinema. Moreover, perhaps to better understand the permanence of this constant and diverse public interest in religious motifs (by both spectators and filmmakers), and considering the production of religious dramas in Brazil under the logics of film genre, we would have to adopt an "ecumenical" vision, accommodating not only films with Catholic orientation but also spiritualist, gospel, and African-Brazilian ones. If this is true, a primary aspect must be taken into account: it is not enough for a film to present any religion as a theme or motif in its fictional world; this will not necessarily guarantee its label as a religious film. For this to happen, it is essential that a religious logic be organically linked to the film production, the film's narrative construction, the mise-en-scène, and the way the "real" or the "supernatural" are both shot and presented to the film's spectators. Besides, the truly religious movie tends to integrally—or at least substantially—adopt the vantage point, the worldview, and the assumptions of the religion in focus, without deconstructing it.

Such ecumenical reading rearranges the panorama of religious cinema beyond specific religions and strict approaches. The idea of the "religious logic" as a decisive point in drama (even though it may sound like an oxymoron), as well as the "activism" and "adherence" not only on the level of the film's story, but also the film's discourse, would thus shape the religious film representing any religion, and across film genres. This shaping or configuration of religious cinema also hinges on cultural aspects and can vary depending on the context. For instance, *Ogum's Amulet* (*O Amuleto de Ogum*, 1974), by Nelson Pereira dos Santos might be a case of "transgenre" religious film. On its release, 11 million Brazilians were officially declared as Umbanda believers. In an interview to Jean-Claude Bernardet (*Opinião* n. 119, February 14, 1975), Nelson Pereira dos Santos explained that his concern was to portray Umbanda "with an absolute respect for its theology, rites, formation, and hierarchy." Indeed, the film had the consultancy and participation of a real *pai de santo* (Pai Erley), and the drama integrally assumed the myth of the "closed body" (unbreakable body).

On the other hand (and according to an ecumenical approach to religious cinema), confronting, revisionist, or contesting discourses and attitudes may not necessarily exclude a film from this field. In other words, under a broader perspective the religious film would not need to be necessarily traditional nor conservative: it could also problematize the worldview and system of beliefs it presents, seeking deconstruction to a certain extent. Thus, productions such as Pier Paolo Pasolini's *The Gospel According to Saint Matthew* (*Il Vangelo Secondo Matteo*, 1964), or Martin Scorsese's *The Last Temptation of Christ* (1988) could also be claimed as belonging to the field of religious cinema. This methodology agrees with that of Melanie J. Wright (2006) in her approach to a variety of films under a religious perspective, such as Carl Theodor Dreyer's 1928 *The Passion of Joan of Arc* (*La Passion de Jeanne d'Arc*), Cecil B. DeMille's 1956 *The Ten Commandments*, Robin Hardy's *The Wicker Man* (1973), Udayan Prasad's *My Son the Fanatic* (1997), Edward Norton's *Keeping the Faith* (2000), and Ashutosh Gowariker's *Lagaan* (2001). An even broader perspective might include Glauber Rocha's 1962 Brazilian feature film *Barravento*, perhaps even Zal Batmanglij's more recent film *The Sound of My Voice* (2011). Much in the spirit of this ecumenical approach, Jean-Claude Bernardet recalls that "in the 60's, it is really brought up the religious issue in the Brazilian cinema. One of the most important concepts for the intellectuality in the first half of the decade was the concept of alienation. And also for the *Cinema Novo*, as evidenced in two films, among others: *Barravento*, directed by Glauber Rocha, and *Viramundo*, by Geraldo Sarno, both films about religious issues" (1996, 187). Bernardet states that "the relation religion-alienation is, in Brazilian cinema, a creation of the 1960s. It did not exist in the 50s" (1996, 188). The author splits the Brazilian religious film into two main categories: "the religious movie" and "the movie about religion." An example of the former would be *Anchieta, José from Brazil* (*Anchieta, José do Brasil*, 1977), directed by Paulo César Saraceni, whereas the latter is best represented by Nelson Pereira dos Santos's aforementioned *The Ogum's Amulet* (Bernardet 1996, 190).

Likewise, the spiritist films in this chapter could be initially divided into two major "trends"—sometimes concurrent, parallel to each other, sometimes in confront. I refer to the spiritist or Kardecist films, the ones overtly engaged in indoctrination and usually adapting the most prominent characters and key literary texts in the Brazilian spiritist tradition, and the Brazilian spiritualist films *lato sensu*, hybrid products mixing realism and fantasy, usually making good use of international vocabularies from horror, fantasy, and SF film genres. The Brazilian spiritist film tends to be politically conservative, while the Brazilian spiritualist film can be rather progressive in terms of political subtext. However, the key difference lies in the "religious activism," something overt and often intense in spiritist cinema. In the case of Assis's *Our Home*, for instance, there was the distribution of explanatory folders about the book that originated the film on the occasion of its premiere in theaters. The spiritist films often adapt best-selling books and cast actors associated with spiritism and the spiritist theater, which is fairly popular in the country. Among these artists, Renato Prieto, the main character in *Our Home*, had already taken part in more than a dozen spiritist plays seen by over five million spectators.

Another noteworthy characteristic in these spiritist films is the fact that most of their directors do not seem concerned about the way their works relate to the history of film genres. In some cases, their most apparent goal is chiefly to set a dialogue with people who do follow the spiritist doctrine, or who are just curious about this system of beliefs. Thus, all film genre background and subtext turn out to be circumstantial or secondary, with tropes from comedy, horror, and the disaster movie tending to be eclipsed by religiously engaging approaches, mostly in a fashion very close to the Christian religious melodrama, with stories of learning, overcoming, and transcendence through faith, kindness, and respect for God's will. This aspect may account for the fact that most spiritist films appear to be the same both in terms of content and form, and rife with redundancy or repetition. Moreover, the prevalence of such lack of concern with film genre and the ambition for both formal and narrative innovation could explain the reduction and later stabilization of spiritualistic film audiences between 2011 and 2012, as the overtly religious discourse may have distanced the portion of the audience who might only be interested in casual entertainment.

This duality or diegetic ambivalence verified in the twofold structure of most of the films mentioned in this chapter, with characters moving between two worlds (the material and the spiritual), seems to be reflected in the commercial response to these spiritist films. The tentative affiliation to SF and fantasy film genres is partially justified by the vast filmography that features spirits and/or revelations from other worlds. Nevertheless, an effort in terms of "familiarization" of these ghosts, or the "naturalization" of the uncanny can also be seen in movies such as *Bezerra de Menezes* or *Chico Xavier*. Thus, the handling of generic film codes in these films seems to ultimately aim at the domestication of foreign film genres, repurposed in favor of religious indoctrination. If this is valid for religious movies in a broader sense, there is particularly special attention to ghostly characters in most of the recent spiritist films, with the atmospheres and images lending themselves to proper visual effects/CGI, as in the case of *Our Home*: a film technically and stylistically mirrored in American SF cinema.

In other words, the Brazilian spiritualist film invests in the domestication of the spectacle with indoctrinating purposes, and this maneuver might end up frustrating a mass audience. First, these tactics also seem to indicate a certain indetermination or oscillation between adherence to a set of generic matrices (SF, fantasy, and horror) and a more significant identification with the spiritist cinema as a generic dominant. Such swaying is shown by certain strategies in terms of style and commercial release. Among them, we highlight the effort (not always well dosed) of naturalization of ghosts (i.e., the mise-en-scène involving characters who are "spirits") aiming to reduce the estrangement intrinsic to narratives about the afterlife and other worlds. An example of skillful incorporation of film genre codes can be verified in *Chico Xavier*, directed by Daniel Filho—a more experienced director, with a long career in film and television.

In this contradiction or oscillation between "two worlds" (the spiritist film and other film genres), one can also notice a possible trajectory from the adjective genre to the substantive genre, as proposed by Rick Altman (1999). In this sense, spiritualistic horror films, for example, would become only spiritualistic films and, finally, just spiritist films in Brazil, somehow following what happened with the musical or the western film in American cinema.

In summary, the possible deletion of the pleasure and anxiety typical of horror, the thriller, and SF films in the Brazilian spiritist cinema seem to put forth a strategy of "domestication" at several levels (generic, discursive, spectatorial). Such strategy seeks to efface contradictions that, however, persist and reappear on the surface of the cinematic style, the generic resignification, and the political discourse. The characteristic duality (body and soul) of religion *lato sensu* survives in the spiritist films, thus condemning them to wander across two worlds: the one of repetition and imitation, and the one of a tentatively emerging genre. Waiting for a messiah, the Brazilian spiritist cinema struggles to adapt and translate into cinematic language the faith of an entire nation.

7

# Southern Short Circuits

## Contemporary Brazilian SF Film as Political Film

In the epilogue to her book *Brazil Imagined*, titled "Land of the Future" (an overt nod to Stefan Zweig's famous 1941 book), Darlene Sadlier comments that "Brazil's emergence as a global economic power alongside China, Russia, and India seems in contradiction with its daily media coverage of unprecedented levels of government corruption, rampant poverty, and widespread violence" (2008, 274). Indeed, about five hundred years of acute inner contradictions, social inequality, slavery, and imperialist grip do not melt into the air in just a handful of years. Moreover, unlike China, India, and Russia, Brazilian media today is less coerced by political authorities and any regime than it is shaped by almighty capitalist interest. Among the BRICS, South Africa is perhaps the most comparable to Brazil, with due caution.

However, Sadlier's introductory lines in her epilogue appear to be significantly biased by widespread disseminated feelings, by a "mediascape" or *Zeitgeist* construed by hegemonic media conglomerates and invisible powers that held sway over the nation after the reelection of President Dilma Rousseff in 2015. In reality, this "ghost in the machine" had been lurking in Brazil's social, political, and economic agenda since around 2013, with the first street demonstrations that opened the Pandora's box of fascism and the extreme right.

All in all, since 2013, Brazil has become such a dystopian place that perhaps only the most science-fictional, fantastic, or speculative cinematic experimentation can offer a more faithful portrayal of the country's social, political, and economic scenario. When reality becomes so absurd, it seems appropriate to make even more SF literature and films. Not surprisingly, the last few years have been particularly fertile for dystopian and SF novels if one takes into account recent releases such as Ignacio de Loyola Brandão's *There Will Be Nothing Left of this Earth but the Wind that Blows Over It* (*Desta Terra Nada Vai Sobrar, A Não Ser o Vento que Sopra sobre Ela*, 2018), Bernardo Kucinski's *The New Order* (*A Nova Ordem*, 2019), and Samir Machado de Machado's *Tupiniland* (*Tupinilândia*, 2018).

I believe that the "serpent's egg" brought about in 2013, and more precisely the "first phase" of the coup in 2016 (with the Kafkaesque impeachment of President Dilma Rousseff), were part of the subtext or lurking motif already featured in a number of SF, fantasy, and horror films made in Brazil from 2009 onward. Considering the due proportions and contexts, we also suspect that, like Siegfried Kracauer's (2019) thesis on Weimar cinema as a cinematic "warning" about the rise of the Nazis in the early 1930s, some Brazilian SF films gave "signs" of a possibly emerging dystopian near future in the country.

Some of the most prominent Brazilian directors today—in terms of box office, but first and foremost in terms of their reception by international film festivals, film critics, and scholars—are venturing into the field of SF. We are referring to directors like Kléber Mendonça Filho, Adirley Queirós, Gabriel Mascaro, Karim Aïnouz, and others. It is worth recalling that Ginway's comments on postdictatorship Brazilian SF literature could be applied to post-1985 Brazilian SF cinema in general terms. According to Ginway, "The authors of Brazilian science fiction of the post dictatorship period demonstrate a sophisticated knowledge of the genre, managing to give it a uniquely Brazilian spin. This shows how the Third World can reshape a First World genre the way the feminist revolution transformed Anglo-American science fiction of the 1970s. In both cases the subaltern or outsider position provides this perspective" (2004, 209). Brazilian film studies now seem to be challenged by a new infusion of political engagement in Brazilian cinema and audiovisual media as a whole. On the one hand, as a reaction to the rise of the extreme right and the setting of a conservative agenda, Brazilian cinema seems to have catalyzed not only its power of prediction and speculation but also its vocation to dissect and expose our inner contradictions, violence, and social inequality. Since the early twenty-first century, but particularly since the 2013 street demonstrations in Brazil, social conundrums seem to be under the spotlight in films set in both rural and urban spaces. Brazilian cinema of the 2000s, notably post-2010, appears to have predicted the rise of a "New Order": a regime that is (ultra-neo) liberal in terms of economics, conservative in terms of customs, and uncivilized in both its posture and speech; a kind of "tropical fascism" that arose in the wake of the parliamentary coup against Dilma Rousseff in 2016, along with the fall of both civil and human rights, under fire by the most conservative sectors of Brazilian society. It is important to note how Bolsonaro's administration may have frustrated the market and some of its original supporters as the government gradually shifted from an allegedly neoliberal to a populist agenda, in favor of deep-rooted, systemic corruption. Thereby, much of our disgrace is directly or indirectly addressed by films released over the last 10 years or so: the relentless killing of native Brazilians, Afro-Brazilians, and the peripheral communities in general; the controversial judiciary system; the populist appeal of the sociopolitical "vigilante" character; the persistence of archaisms in our society and its institutions; the sinister legacy of slavery; and the impact of corruption and social inequality. Films like Adirley Queirós's *White Out, Black In*, Affonso Uchôa's *Araby* (*Arábia*, 2017), and Kléber Mendonça Filho's *Neighboring Sounds* (*O Som ao Redor*, 2013), and *Bacurau* (2019, codirected with Juliano Dornelles, art director of the previous films by Mendonça Filho) have provoked new scholarly responses to recent Brazilian movies. Although the Brazilian Cinema Novo and the 1960s context are obviously in the past, Brazil's present situation seems to reinsert politics in the Brazilian film agenda. The most committed auteur filmmakers in Brazil have answered that call.

The success of a series like Pedro Aguilera's *3%* (streamed by Netflix from 2016 to 2020) and films like Adirley Queirós's *Branco Sai, Preto Fica* are illustrative and symptomatic of, among other things, (1) the demystification of SF as a genre inaccessible to low budget independent productions since they are now favored by the popularization of new digital technologies; and (2) the emergence of SF as a "mode of representation" or "decrypting machine" used to decipher the contemporary Brazilian agenda, its main dilemmas, and concerns. Once again, SF cinema in Brazil seems to be a way of expressing the clash between a creative, humanizing conscience and the absurdity or dystopia from the last detour to the extreme right. SF cinema in Brazil today can be the place of expression (and friction) of a dying progressist voice against the wildest neoliberal capitalism and rampant fascism. And at least three Brazilian directors seem to be highly attentive to SF cinema's expressive possibilities in the service of social and political dissection: Adirley Queirós, Gabriel Mascaro, and Kléber Mendonça Filho.

## Redemption is Somewhere in Time: On Traumas and Peripheral Voices

Time travel tales have been instrumental in tackling historical traumas throughout the history of Brazilian SF cinema. Two short films stand out in that scenario: Jorge Furtado and Ana Luiza Azevedo's *Barbosa* and Carlos Gregório's *Loop*.

*Barbosa*[1] mixes SF and documentary to tell a story of two men whose lives were inextricably linked to the historic loss of Brazil to Uruguay in the World Cup on July 16, 1950: a time traveler (Antônio Fagundes) and Moacir Barbosa himself, the goalkeeper of the 1950 national soccer team. In 1950, with the final match at Maracanã stadium in Rio de Janeiro, Brazil's national team was defeated by Uruguay in an unexpected twist at the end of the match. With Brazil winning one goal to nil, Uruguay scored two goals: the second just minutes before the end. Barbosa, the Brazilian goalkeeper, was blamed for the loss. Barbosa himself tells of his personal drama in the film, and how the defeat left an indelible mark on his life and career for years to come. In 1950, Brazil was confident in its future as a prosperous nation and needed the win as a token of self-esteem. The defeat by Uruguay in the World Cup frustrated millions of people. According to some testimonies, when the match ended the stadium was filled with a disturbing and traumatic silence—all except for the euphoria and celebration of the Uruguayan team and supporters. However, and more importantly, it ruined, to some extent, the life of the Brazilian goalkeeper.

Ana Luiza Azevedo and Jorge Furtado's *Barbosa* starts from this premise: in the future, a man who had watched the Brazil vs. Uruguay World Cup final with his father in 1950 decides to travel back in time to "fix" history. The Brazilian press and the general public were so confident of victory that they had already started declaring Brazil the new world champion for days prior to the final match. Brazil had won their last two games with a very attack-minded style of play. Uruguay, however, had encountered difficulties in their previous matches, managing only a draw against Spain and a narrow victory over Sweden. It seemed that the Brazilians were set to defeat Uruguay as easily as they had outplayed

Spain and Sweden. In the eyes of *Barbosa*'s time traveler, the second goal by the Uruguayan Alcides Ghiggia in the seventy-ninth minute of the second half was nothing more than an accident. Once back in time, he could step onto the soccer field and, with discretion, warn Barbosa about the direction of Ghiggia's kick, thus preventing the loss.

The time travel occurs at the beginning of the film, and the traveler is soon walking down the streets of 1950s Rio, in the company of numerous Brazilians already celebrating the expected victory on their way to the stadium. He buys a ticket and finds his seat. Archival footage begins to be interspersed with enacted scenes featuring the time traveler. The time comes to take action, and the hero starts moving toward the restricted area of the soccer field. However, a guard prevents the hero from accessing the area, and he is significantly delayed. Moments before the second Uruguayan goal by Ghiggia, the time traveler loses the guard and runs toward Barbosa. He yells at the goalkeeper, intending to warn him about the kick, but it is this very action that distracts Barbosa. Archival footage of the actual scene appears on screen. The time traveler relives that moment of collective frustration and silence, as Brazil is defeated by Uruguay once again. In a nutshell, the film demonstrates that it is impossible to fix the past. Is Brazil eternally condemned to fail as a nation?

Carlos Gregório's short film *Loop*[2] does not address any collective trauma or key moment in the history of Brazil. Yet, this film can be seen as a delicate allegory of a generation at odds with dictatorial times. It begins quite similarly to *Barbosa* when a middle-aged scientist (Carlos Gregório) is about to test his time machine. The hero is enthusiastic about the possibility to relive his past, re-experience the emotions he felt when he was younger, and re-encounter his loved ones. However, a test must be carried out; he decides to go back in time for just a fraction of a moment. If everything goes fine, then he will be able to go back further and live his best moments again. After much hesitation, the hero finally presses the button, and the machine works. He goes back in time for a fraction of a second, from the moment he presses the button, the rapid travel back through time, to the moment when he decides to press the button. A time paradox then occurs, and the hero gets stuck in this time loop, like a modern Sisyphus. The interspersing of archival footage and "real-time" action intensifies and multiplies as the editing gets faster. There is no way out now for the hero: the time traveler falls prey to the time loop, with some of his most beloved memories becoming the stuff of nightmares. A short SF that began light and nostalgic becomes a creepy, spooky story of time paradox. Perhaps this is an allegory of a country that insists on making the same mistakes, unaware that beloved memories only retain their worth in due time and place and depending on the eyes of the beholder.

In more recent Brazilian SF cinema, the time travel trope continues to provide suitable frameworks for further investigations on some of the most traumatic moments in the country's history, as in *White Out, Black In* (*Branco Sai, Preto Fica*) by Adirley Queirós. This is a speculative fiction that deals with citizenship and civil rights under attack by the state. Winner of the Brasilia Festival in 2014, this feature film used the artifice of a journey through time to face a real-world event in 1986, when the police launched an attack against the Quarentão, a black music ball in Ceilândia,[3] to violently attack the young people in the party. The title of the film refers to an order allegedly given by one of the police officers who had brutally broken into the Quarentão.

First, for a broader understanding of *White Out, Black In* (from now on *WOBI*), we should consider the context of the film's production and the biography of its director. *WOBI* was produced by Ceicine, the Film Cooperative of Ceilândia, and directed by a filmmaker whose profile is at odds with the typical Brazilian director from the country's middle, upper-middle, or economic elite class. A former soccer player in the lower divisions in the Brazilian Midwest, and resident of the periphery of Brasilia, Adirley Queirós didn't have access to higher education until he was thirty years old. He began attending the film course at the University of Brasilia (UnB) after belatedly finishing high school while working a series of typically proletarian jobs. Queirós defines himself as a radically independent and popular filmmaker (Cf. Reis et al. 2013; Suppia and Gomes 2015).

Like Furtado's short film *Barbosa*, *WOBI* seems to reaffirm a trend in Brazilian SF cinema: the time travel trope that allows a fictional character to revisit a moment of trauma in Brazilian history. As in *Barbosa*, real characters take part in the speculative fiction. *WOBI* seems to borrow *Barbosa*'s narrative strategy. Both films explore the issues of race, macro-history vs. micro-history, and use documentary footage in their respective revisitation of national traumas involving Brazil's Afro-descendant population through the lens of SF and time travel. Adirley Queirós's *WOBI* is structured around the following storyline: coming from a far future, the time traveler Dimas Cravalanças (Dilmar Durães) arrives in Ceilândia in the near future, where two characters live: DJ Marquim, played by Marquim do Tropa (a musician who does the vocals in the Elite Squad [Tropa de

Elite]), and Sartana, a mechanic specializing in the maintenance of prosthetic limbs, played by Shockito. These two characters, whose profiles and lifestyles mirror those of the actors, survived the night of police aggression in the Quarentão, their bodies bearing the stigmata of violence (see fig. 7.1). With no means to defend himself against the police aggression, DJ Marquim became paraplegic after being shot. Sartana, meanwhile, lost a leg after being trampled by the police cavalry and now uses a prosthetic limb.[4] Marquim and Sartana's testimonials are interspersed with fictional scenes in which the two characters carry out a plan for taking revenge against the status quo. In this alternate future of Ceilândia, the two survivors of the Quarentão incident are planning to attack Brasília with a kind of sonic bomb. This doomsday device includes varieties of genuine popular music from the outskirts of the capital.

In the dystopia portrayed by *WOBI*, the segregation of center vs. periphery persists and intensifies. Radio broadcasts suggest the existence of a racist police state that excludes peripheral communities from Brasília,

Figure 7.1. Marquim (Marquim do Tropa) and Sartana (Shockito) talk about their past and future plans in Adirley Queirós's *Branco Sai, Preto Fica* (2014). *Source*: *White Out, Black In* (*Branco Sai, Preto Fica*). Dir. Adirley Queirós. Prod. Co.: Cinco da Norte. Brasil, 2014, 95min. Courtesy: Adirley Queirós.

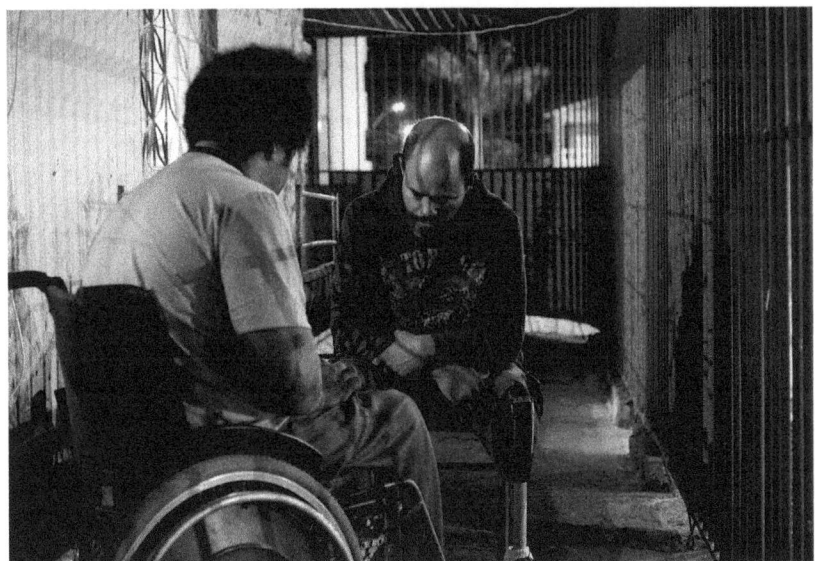

keeping all circulation in the Plano Piloto administrative district under strict surveillance. The time machine used by Cravalanças is an improvised container. As in Chris Marker's *La Jettée* (1962) or Alain Resnais's *Je t'Aime, Je t'Aime* (1968), little or no explanation about technology is presented to justify the time travel. In the case of Queirós's film, rather than bringing a cure for an outbreak or searching for loving memories, the time traveler must gather evidence of the state's responsibility at the Quarentão incident in Ceilândia. In an even more distant future, Brazil is charged with being guilty of crimes against its Black and poor population. Thus, three times or "chronotopes" coexist in *WOBI*: (1) the recent past, when the Quarentão incident occurred; (2) the near future, when the time traveler Dimas Cravalanças is looking for evidence and survivors; and (3) a more distant future, virtually off-screen, where the Brazilian state is being prosecuted for crimes against its people.

The idea of a time traveler who must collect evidence of a crime committed by the state for a future lawsuit is provocative for two reasons. First, unlike other time-travel narratives in which the protagonist needs to act to restore order in the past, present, or future, the time traveler in *WOBI* seems to illustrate something noticed by Roberto Causo's pioneering study on Brazilian SF literature. According to Causo, the characters in Brazilian time travel tales are usually passive observers who can do little or nothing to change the course of history (Causo 2003, 145). As explained by Causo, despite the initial flourishing of natural and human sciences in the late eighteenth and early nineteenth centuries in Brazil, the uneven development of science and technology in the subsequent period was overwhelmed by the need for political and legal order. This factor would have favored the emergence of literature and law sciences as preponderant disciplines. Based on Antonio Cândido's *Literature and Society* (*Literatura e Sociedade*, 2000), Causo argues that "the spirit of the Brazilian bourgeoisie developed under predominantly literary influences, and its way of interpreting the surrounding world was stylized not in terms of science, philosophy or technique, but in terms of literature" (2003, 145).

In *WOBI*, Cravalanças's actions have no effect on the city of Ceilândia, nor on the characters who inhabit that chronotope. I time traveler has no contact with Marquim or Sartana. Cravalanças does not travel back in time to change history or undo any "injustice," rather, he is to collect evidence for a future lawsuit "in progress." The evidence is not specified by the narrative, and the injustice is already carved in history. The only option is to assign responsibility, to find a culprit—admittedly, a significant breakthrough in the context of a society with a "short memory"—in a nation that has been relentlessly punitive toward the poor and historically merciful with corruption and abuses committed by the elite or the state. Accordingly, in a scene where the time traveler curses the virtual oppressors and pretends to shoot at enemies in an abandoned warehouse, he does so in an empty space.[5] Even in the case of *Barbosa*, in which the time traveler does intend to "fix" the past, failure is inevitable: although, as Jean-Claude Bernardet pointed out in his essay "Cinema and Religion" ("Cinema e Religião") (Bernardet in Xavier 1996, 187–94), the action of the time traveler in the short film by Jorge Furtado is not trivial: it represents a decisive step forward in the transition from a stage of "infallible disaster" to "induced disaster." One may wonder if, unlike the typical (Protestant, imperialist time traveler), the Brazilian "chrononaut" with Catholic background has no power in terms of genuine agency or transformative action.

Secondly, the very fact that the time traveler in *WOBI* is on a mission to collect evidence for future legal proceedings against the state seems ironic in itself, given the empirical knowledge of any contemporary Brazilian spectator of the country's judicial system, particularly justice involving powerful people. Timely, if not presciently, the film ends before any note on the outcomes of the future trial that motivated the time travel adventure. Instead, the survivors of the Quarentão incident are the ones who take action. They succeed in their plan to blow up the federal capital, eventually changing the course of history in a sequence narrated by handmade drawings, in the guise of an epilogue. This aesthetic choice might inspire the question: Is this the only way Brazilians can redesign their history? What else could shape people's dream for justice other than low-budget SF featuring amateurish drawings?

## Short-circuiting the Reality Studio: Circuit-Bending, Lo-fi Sci-fi, and the Body in *WOBI*

As a trans-border fantasy, that is to say, a fable that speculates about the transit of characters between restricted or prohibited areas, such as Alex Rivera's *Sleep Dealer* (2008), or even the Brazilian series *3%*, *WOBI* reinserts multiculturalism into the agenda not only of SF film but of Brazilian cinema overall, with peculiarities comparable to other trans-border fables: the rugged geographies and interdiction zones are not restricted to the scenarios or landscapes where the characters transit; they are inscribed in their own bodies, in the mutilation that limits them. Corporeal signs that intensify the documentary appeal of Adirley Queirós's SF, the mutilated bodies in *WOBI* are themselves "cartographies" of violence or "maps" of interdiction, "geographies" altered by the state. These bodies are subjected to a double regime: fiction and documentary. On the one hand, they are legally prevented from crossing Ceilândia's borders, and, on the other, they are no longer able to execute the dance moves they used to perform at the Quarentão music events due to the injuries that resulted from their confrontation with the police. If spatial movement from periphery to center is limited or prohibited, now even dance, the characters' form of expression in their own environment, is finally taken away from the excluded peoples.

The fact that Marquim and Sartana eventually blow up Brasília with a "sonic bomb" seems eloquent in itself and reaffirms the link between *WOBI* and two concepts borrowed from new media art or sound art: *circuit-bending* and *lo-fi sci-fi*. The repeated references to music and sound, as well as metaphors like "the voice from the periphery," publicly stated by Adirley Queirós in interviews (see Suppia and Gomes 2015; Reis, Mena, and Imanishi 2013) and deeply rooted in his films, put *WOBI* even closer to the concept of lo-fi sci-fi. A category usually related to American independent cinema, the lo-fi sci-fi film could be defined as a cluster of "movies that have more speculation than spectacular effects, more focused on big ideas than big budgets."[6] Like other films usually labeled as lo-fi sci-fi, *WOBI* is a relatively low-budget production with a realistic visual style and aesthetics, lacking sophisticated visual effects and making explicit reference to an "analog" paradigm, also alluding to a ruinous low-tech future where the retrofitting and multilayering of industrial waste provides the means for the workers to survive. Thus, *WOBI* renders a "sense of wonder" and/or "cognitive estrangement" based on intellectual challenges that often intriguingly interact with the real world's contemporary agenda. Whereas lo-fi sci-fi has gained momentum over the last ten years or so in the American SF film scene, it seems to be quite common in Latin America's SF cinema history. Does this make lo-fi sci-fi the "norm" in non-Western or Latin American SF cinemas?

Another interesting feature verifiable in *WOBI* is the concept of circuit-bending, the creative modification of internal circuits of electronic devices to create new musical instruments. By modifying toys, cheap keyboards, or essential electronic components, circuit-bending allows new and unexpected sonorities. It is an artistic technique that has been practiced for more than fifty years (Ghazala 2005, 7–12). A pioneer and one of the leading spokesmen of circuit-bending is the American artist Reed Ghazala. In Brazil, artists such as Lucas Mafra, from the Gambiologia[7] group, offer circuit-bending workshops focused on the modification of toys.

Although *WOBI* does not present itself as experimental cinema, Queirós's film can also be seen as a daring case of cinematic "circuit-bending," subverting the established policies of state funding and endowment for the arts in Brazil. In this sense, the concept and practice of circuit-bending, familiar to both electronic and contemporary art, can also be helpful in decoding *WOBI*. The idea of circuit-bending pervades the film at several levels, starting with the fact that it is a hybrid of documentary and SF film, made with public funds granted explicitly to documentary filmmaking (Suppia and Gomes 2015; Reis, Mena, and Imanishi 2013). Circuit-bending as a leitmotif can also be seen in the main characters Marquim and Sartana. The former works on a "sonic bomb" that circuit-bends popular culture by weaponizing the periphery's voice and sounds. The latter takes his prosthetic leg to a hacker, thenceforth obtaining improved performance from the mechanical limb.

*WOBI* also makes use of "circuit-bending" in its settings, narrative, and mise-en-scène, provoking "cognitive estrangement" (Suvin, 1979) out of seemingly ordinary and familiar landscapes and situations. In other words, the film makes use of "circuit-bending" by altering the "meaning" of certain shooting locations or landscapes. The camera angles and lens make a dust road, a favela, a container or a bridge somehow "estranged," alien, futuristic, dystopian. This can be seen, for instance, in the scenes featuring Marquim and Sartana moving around the city or when Sartana is at work in his shop. These scenes highlight bodies in their struggle to move around urban areas clearly marked by social inequality. They feature the mutilated body as an eloquent yet tacit key element of estrangement. In *WOBI*, the geopolitical barrier and political apparatus that separate center and periphery leave their mark on the bodies of the excluded and oppressed people, with even dance eventually being impeded. The bodies become a geography as much violated as the Central Plateau,[8] a metaphor for other Brazilian metropolitan areas.

Consequently, the geopolitical barrier that excludes Brasília's periphery from the Plano Piloto district in *WOBI* leaves its mark on the excluded body: it is more difficult to move around with the need for prostheses or a wheelchair. The body, in *WOBI*, is a "geography" as violated as that of the Planalto Central or other Brazilian urban centers. Moreover, the scenes featuring Marquim and Sartana in transit, as "estranged" by the mise-en-scène as they may seem (the elevator adapted for Marquim's house, the prosthesis workshop where Sartana works), also make for a faithful portrait of our contemporary and very well-known reality: the fact that Brazil physically punishes its marginalized people on a daily basis with accidents at work or on their way to work (commuting in overcrowded trains, for instance). The bodies in *WOBI* represent the reality of the public transport infrastructure in Brazil, the urban planning, the streets, and sidewalks often inhumanely designed, as most people know. Why do so few physically disabled people walk the Brazilian streets compared to developed countries? Because in Brazil, the public space is not yet a safe place for the physically disabled. Unlike the well-known "self-help" or "narratives of overcoming," *WOBI* does not comply. The mutilated bodies do not end up recovering the dance; they do not create new choreographies using wheelchairs or prostheses. Their expression remains restrained. The final result is the explosion of the radiating center of oppression: an explosion expressed in drawings, a vengeance forbidden in Brazilian live-action cinema.

Concerning representation of disability, *WOBI* provides a thought-provoking case study of David T. Mitchell and Sharon L. Snyder's (2008, 203) five methodologies or trends in disability studies (studies of negative imagery, social realism, new historicism, biographical criticism, and transgressive reappropriation). First, one might wonder if these five methodologies can actually be separated, as they seem to overlap and interact with each other constantly. For instance, *WOBI* could be scrutinized under the perspective of New Historicism applied in disability studies. As pointed out by Mitchell and Snyder, "Disability had begun to be recognized as a potent vehicle of political critique at various moments in the literary tradition" (2008, 211). The same could be said about disability in film scholarship. Mitchell and Snyder also remark that, when "the subversive potential of the hyperbolic meanings invested in disabled figures" (2008, 216) is acknowledged, a methodology based on "transgressive reappropriation" takes place. Still, according to the authors: "The power of transgression always originates at the moment when the derived object embraces its deviance as value" (2008, 216). *WOBI* embraces all sorts of deviance, from the disabled body to underrated popular culture, as value: revolutionary value. However, Queirós's film provides a rather challenging account of representation of disability in film, especially from a social realist perspective. It does blur boundaries between positive and negative representations, reconnecting the disabled body to the social (and socially ill) body: the disabled social body. According to Mitchell and Snyder, "Social realist scholarship seeks to decrease the kinds of alienation that pervade social views of disabled people" (2008, 207). The authors cite works by Irving Zola (2003) and David Hevey (1992) to exemplify the social realist approach to representing disabled people in literature and film. Mitchell and Snyder further remark that "the call for action in social realism centers upon a belief that disability will continue to be misconstrued and relegated to the 'dustbins' of history if the able-bodied are left to construct images from their own prejudices" (Mitchell and Snyder 2008, 209). This is precisely what we may see in Queirós's *WOBI*. Its characters are featured in a "visceral way," the representation of impairment becomes a narrative feature, to the point that it effects a different narrative pace/rhythm and time: that of Marquim and Sartana, not of the able-bodied so commonly found in SF or adventure films, nor of the occasional able-bodied spectators. As noticed by Cordoba in his analysis of *WOBI*:

> The disempowering drive of standard supercrip narratives are avoided as Queirós's camerawork eschews tropes that emphasize both tragedy and superlative achievement. At the beginning of the film, a long take follows Marquim as he slowly descends in a clunky elevator to the entrance of his home, gets out of the elevator, and smoothly slides down a ramp. His face while on the elevator suggests boredom; his going down the ramp is not particularly graceful. Both impairment and empowerment are shown under a quotidian light in which they are intricately mixed (as Queirós's continuous take shows) and never enter the sphere of the emotionally extraordinary. Similarly, we spend quite some time with Sartana until we find out that he has a mechanical leg so that it is not the first thing that defines him in the audience's eyes [. . .]. Queirós and his collaborators refuse to participate in discourses of neoliberal perfectibility and individualistic transcendence. The protagonists are neither abject nor superhuman. (Cordoba 2017, 142)

I could not agree more with Cordoba's analysis of *WOBI* in this regard. Moreover, Queirós's film is not centered on disability whatsoever. And yet, it does dig disability out of the "dustbins" of history by allowing the disabled body to make history—or an alternate fictional history. For it is the converging action of disabled bodies that eventually rewrites history in *WOBI*, and thus the disabled characters move away from the mere position of victims or supporting characters to take over leading roles. Still according to Mitchell and Snyder, "The social realist perspective would supply an openly politicized image of disability" (2008, 209).

In this sense, *WOBI* could not be more political. As Cordoba asserts, "There is an intense politicization of disability when the protagonists give testimony about the long history of oppression that causes their condition" (2017, 141). The film undoubtedly provides a politicized image of disability to attain further goals: accountability and action. Moreover, this is the most distinguishing feature in this film in comparison to several other twentieth-century or contemporary Brazilian films: not only are the main characters accountable as agents of social transformation, but their condition is accounted for by the racist police state. One might argue that Marquim and Sartana stand for a negative representation of disabled people (primarily Marquim, perhaps due to his angst and search for revenge). Nevertheless, such an interpretation misses the point. For these characters are not portrayed as ideal characters, let alone heroes or saints: they simply *are*. Furthermore, there is no politics without political will, and no political will comes out of nothing, not without a fight for change. As noticed by Cordoba in his comparison of *WOBI* with Wagner de Assis's *Our Home* (*Nosso Lar*, 2010), "(. . .) The "new paradigm" of *Nosso Lar* is nothing but the reproduction of the hierarchical structures of Brazilian society. The future is the present and the past, and the astral city is oppressively earthly" (Cordoba 2017, 144). Conversely,

> Queirós (. . . .) uses science fiction to work through trauma in order to reclaim the right to the city of Brasília and Ceilândia, even if that new right is the right to take revenge and destroy. In the end, the selves produced by the Afrofuturist urban environment of *Branco sai, preto fica* are the ones who are able to transcend the contemporary reality of Brasília's satellite cities. Excluded because of their race and class, living in a residue of Brazilian past dreams of modernization, they find ways to demand historical reparations, take over the city, and, by radically disrupting the present, make possible a real future for all. (Cordoba 2017, 144)

Moreover, *WOBI* is also a premonitory film insofar as it deals with the long history of Brazilians' plundering. Released in 2014, the film frames a problem that has not been solved thus far. Three years after the release of *WOBI*, following the coup that removed President Dilma Rousseff, a pirate and his entourage took over the presidential office, Planalto Palace[9] in Brasília. At the same time, the Brazilian congress was held by pirates and thieves while the police kept the population under strict control, with the constant menace of military intervention. Every day in Brazil, millions of Marquins and Sartanas lose their dreams, rights, limbs, and lives. As these lines were written, with the Covid-19 pandemic and the genocidal policies/necropolitics of Jair Bolsonaro, hundreds of thousands more Brazilians have died. Through some encrypted language (maybe not very encrypted), *WOBI* foresaw our present and near future: a time of obscure trials, conservatism, violence, and the wholesale denial of civil rights. In this sense, both the film's off-screen trial in a distant future and the final handmade drawings seem to be special warnings and symbols. It is perhaps an interesting case of how Latin American independent lo-fi SF cinema has been decoding our present times. Following the dystopian literary tradition of authors such as Karel Čapek (*RUR*, 1921), Yevgeny Zamyatin (*We*), Aldous Huxley (*Brave New World*, 1932), George Orwell (*1984*, 1948), and Ignacio de Loyola Brandão *And Still the Earth*, I dare say that SF resurfaces, once again, as a privileged locus for representing the current state of Brazilian affairs—and chaos.

Remembering Ghazala's (2005) story about the emergence of circuit-bending in the 1960s, its low-budget context and impromptu tendency as the art of twisting and distorting the material reality in favor of a new and perhaps sublime reality, films like *WOBI* may contribute to the same sensitivity. By twisting audiovisual policies in his favor, re-signifying urban trash and waste, featuring the periphery and its "voice" as a gravitational force in his film, and choosing the unusual combination of SF and documentary, Adirley Queirós seems to play the role of a circuit-bender in the context of Brazilian cinema. A working-class filmmaker speaking about the Brazilian people through codes and conventions seldom seen in Brazilian mainstream cinema. The movies directed by Adirley Queirós, especially *WOBI* and its "sequel," *Once There Was Brasília* (*Era uma vez Brasília*, 2017), seem to support this idea: that of a Brazilian reality untouchable and unrepresentable by canonical or more traditional film vocabularies and conventions. As if only SF, in its most subversive way, could bend and redraw the circuits that have been programming our long history of exclusion and violence.

If cyborgs in Brazilian SF cinema are scarce, represented by a few characters like Joaquim Porfírio in *Stop 88* or Marquim and Sartana in *WOBI*, a different approach to cybernetic organisms can be found in the Netflix film *Bionic* (*Biônicos*, 2024). Directed by Afonso Poyart, *Bionic* is a cyberpunk thriller starring two young Black sisters, both athletes. This story takes place in the year 2035, where sports are dominated by big tech corporations, developers of bionic prostheses. The premise of Poyart's film derives somewhat from the growing success of the Paralympics in Brazil and around the world,[10] as well as the recent advances in the scientific research conducted by the Brazilian neuroscientist Miguel Nicolelis, whose lab at Duke University was stage for some groundbreaking experiments on the control of artificial limbs by brainwaves. Nicolelis and his team developed an exoskeleton that made possible to a paraplegic man wearing an exoskeleton robotic suit perform the opening kick at the 2014 FIFA World Cup in Brazil.

In the fictional universe in *Bionic*, however, instead of inclusion and equity, amputee athletes become great sports stars to the extent that they become icons of the cybernetic market. In this context, *Bionic* presents the story of the rivalry of the Santos sisters, daughters of a great long jump champion in precybernetic times. Maria Santos (Jessica Córes), her mother's would-be successor as long jump champion, dedicated her life to training but now resents the rise of bionic prosthetics. The frustration is intensified by the fact that Gabi (Gabz), her younger sister, an amputee as a child, has become one of the greatest athletes in the world thanks to a state-of-the-art prosthesis from the company Solidlimbs. Gabi is a celebrity, appearing on holographic banners throughout the metropolis (São Paulo assuming its inherent cyberpunk aesthetics). Driven by rivalry with her younger sister, Maria unknowingly becomes involved in a dangerous scheme organized by the mysterious Heitor (Bruno Gagliasso), leader of a supposed movement against the status quo that rewards bionic champions to the detriment of ordinary athletes. Although not free from contradictions and some minor blind spots in the story, *Bionic* has a good script for a science fiction thriller, with typically Brazilian features and a well-constructed critique of the commodification of human bodies, especially black athletes' bodies. As Pedro Henrique Ribeiro (2024) rightly points out, the focus of *Bionic*, clear from the socially charged approach itself, is to discuss classism and moral limits. People born with limb problems or who have been disabled in demonstrably legitimate accidents may have access to robotic limbs if they can afford it. This legal limitation makes the product scarce and difficult to access, giving rise to the police subplot. The film's art direction and cinematography are very well crafted, and nothing in the film purposefully evokes the lo-fi sci-fi aesthetics, at least not for Brazilian film standards. Also, the plot does not consist of obvious, unsuspected characters free of inner contradictions. With clear citations to films such as *Thelma and Louise* (1991), by Ridley Scott, and obviously *Robocop* (1987), by Paul Verhoeven, *Bionic* ends by hinting at possible sequels.

## The "Neon-Pentecostal" future

At this moment in the history of Brazil (early 2020s), is it perhaps time to be carried by a leap of faith? Gabriel Mascaro's *Divine Love* (*Divino Amor*, 2019) is a dystopian SF in which religion encounters futuristic speculation. As we have already commented, the apparent "discomfort" of Brazilian cinema in speculating about the future and alternative realities seems to find a more widely accepted means of communication on the topics of religion and spirituality. Thus, we observe SF in a reasonable number of spiritist or Kardecist films, such as Wagner de Assis's *Our Home* (*Nosso Lar*, 2010). Usually, these Brazilian religious films use SF semantics and syntax (albeit vulgarly or superficially) in their spiritualist fables to convey a rather conformist, conservative discourse. This is very different from Mascaro's *Divine Love*, a confrontational religious film that criticizes religious alienation and its longing for fascism.

*Divine Love* takes a substantially different path in terms of its approach to religion. Mascaro's film presents itself more assertively as an SF film right from the start, both in the opening credits and the opening scene. We see images of an outdoor night party, something like a gospel rave, with a voice-over from a child: "It was 2027. Brazil had changed. The most important party in the country was no longer Carnival. It was the Feast of Supreme Love. The redemption of the body, the purest feeling. The oath of eternal love. The great wait for the Messiah to return."[11] This first scene already features a *novum*, in Suvinian (1979) terms:[12] the narrative element that provokes the "cognitive estrangement" peculiar to SF.

In other words, a discontinuity or distancing from the implicit spectator's reality. Here, however, this "novelty" or strangeness is not radical. It is based on relatively simple extrapolation, given the state of affairs in Brazil in 2019. The child's voice-over will later punctuate several moments in the film.

*Divine Love* tells the story of Joana (Dira Paes), an employee of a civil registry office. Evangelical, she specifically attends couples who intend to divorce, where her personal beliefs and values deeply affect her professional performance. Joana delays divorce proceedings and tries to influence the couples to convince them to stay together. Eventually, Joana invites her clients to her church's worship, Divine Love (Divino Amor), where she and her husband Danilo (Júlio Machado) practice their faith. For the sake of the family, the church promotes evening services that mix decontextualized readings of the Bible, playful activities, self-help sessions, orgies, and the exchange of sexual partners (swinging). The church's décor, its neon lights, and the presence of a doorman reference the stereotype of urban brothels in cities like São Paulo, Rio de Janeiro, or Recife—a small door, guarded by a security guard, with neon on Icade and diffuse lighting seeping from the interior.

While Joana works in the office handling divorces, Danilo makes wreaths for funerals. Both work with the "endings" of something, so to speak, be it marriage or life. The couple has a firm purpose, unknown until this point: to give birth to a child. Danilo seems to have fertility problems, and with Joana's support, he tries a variety of treatments. One of them, in particular, provides comic relief: the therapeutic "fetters," which arrive for the couple in a package with Chinese writing, will be used by Danilo regularly. With this gadget, the user is suspended upside down while the genitals are exposed to a kind of infrared light.

But what kind of evangelical faith appears in the film? As explained by pastor Alexandre Gonçalves (2019) in the article "*Divine Love*: Futuristic Film Is a Criticism of the Hypocrisy of Bolsonaro's Evangelical Brazil" ("*Divino amor*: filme futurista é uma crítica à hipocrisia do Brasil Evangélico de Bolsonaro"), published in *The Intercept* on July 18, 2019,[13] Joana represents the follower of an evangelical religion of the neo-Pentecostal, triumphalistic, and individualistic type, affiliated with the theology of domination. Commenting on Mascaro's film, Goçalves admits: "It may seem like a great exaggeration—and in a way, the intention of the author of the film is really shocking. But in my 25 years as a pastor I have seen things that could also be credited as exaggerations. [. . .] What would be more absurd to believe: in the gospel orgy portrayed in the film or in a mother silent in the face of the abuse committed against her daughter? And all for the same reason: the family" (Gonçalves 2019).

While working and attending the Divine Love cult and their group sex sessions, Joana and Danilo have been trying to have children for some time. Judging by Joana's behavior, giving birth to a child is her life goal, the most extraordinary thing she could ever achieve: to become a mother. Moreover, this anguishing desire introduces another curious novelty in the film: the drive-thru confessional or "spiritual advisory" session set in what looks like a car wash. Akin to an "oil change" procedure, a line of cars waits their turn to enter a small garage where, sitting inside, a pastor (Emílio de Melo) awaits with the Bible in hand. There, Joana will be in her car, more than once, seeking spiritual comfort in the pastor's word. She enters the covered space, shares her anguish, and wins the hymn of praise of that day or night: all without getting out of the car. The dialogue in these scenes is particularly intriguing: to Joana's questions and anguish, the pastor responds like a fortune teller, with evasions or catchwords, such as "you know the answer for everything." The repeated "drive-thru confessional" scene is reminiscent of a sketch in a comic TV show. Gonçalves considers this scene a crude caricature of the individualistic religion, with gospel music and catchphrases such as "no act in the service of the Lord can be called sin." According to Gonçalves, that same faith raised the then-candidate for president, Jair Bolsonaro, to a position of messiah, with neo-Pentecostal evangelicals and even sectors of traditional churches advocating that Brazil needed to become a Christian theocracy (Gonçalves 2019). Gonçalves's judgments sound didactic and premonitory, for if there is not a nationwide evangelical movement underway, it is due to the fact that the most fascist and antihumanist faction is the one that has garnered greater political, economic, and mediatic power. Brazil in *Divine Love*'s near future is a "neo-Pentec" (short for neo-Pentecostal) country or, better still, "neon-pentec"—a juxtaposition of the 1980s neon aesthetic with dark fanaticism, a retrofuturistic nostalgia far more dangerous than any revival of classicist architecture or 1940s costumes. Neither cyberpunk, nor technoir. Neither postapocalyptic (as in the *3%* series), nor postapocalyptic-tropicalist (as in *Who Is Beta?*, the 1972 film by Nelson Pereira dos Santos, or *Nuclear Shelter*, the 1981 film by Roberto Pires). In *Divine Love* the future is "neon-pentec," a futurism where necropolitics will prevail, led by a lumpenproletariat allied to a kakistocracy: the necrolumpenkakistocracy already in power in real-life Brazil under

Bolsonaro's rule. Mascaro's film does not dive deeper into the underground of this "neon-pentec" authoritarian state; reality in 2021 appears to be far scarier than the dystopia in *Divine Love*, and equally prone to neologisms and labels (see fig. 7.2). For instance, journalists Kristina Hinz, Doriam Borges, Aline Coutinho, and Thiago Cury Andries (2021) use terms like "neo-Pentecostal narco-militia" and "narco-Pentecostalism" to refer to new alliances in Rio de Janeiro's organized crime. The journalists explain that drug-trafficking factions, paramilitaries, and evangelical churches have united to fight a "holy war" against their rivals in Rio de Janeiro. According to Hinz, Borges, Coutinho, and Andries (2021), throughout the 1980s and 1990s, drug traffickers in the favelas identified mainly with Afro-Brazilian religions, such as Umbanda and Candomblé. In the 1980s, many police operations brought about evangelical indoctrination, substituting Afro-Brazilian religious symbols and places of worship with Christian-like expressions of faith. Evangelical churches have significantly expanded their influence since the end of the 1990s, thus establishing religious networks that wage a "war against evil," with their roots in the urban peripheries. "Between 2000 and 2010 alone, the number of evangelicals in Brazil increased by more than 60%" (Hinz, Borges, Coutinho, and Andries 2021).[14]

Figure 7.2. A mass celebration in the Divino Amor church, where an initiated couple introduces a new couple to the religious rituals that culminate with swinging. *Source*: *Divine Love* (*Divino Amor*). Dir. Gabriel Mascaro. Prod. Co.: Desvia. Brazil, Denmark, Uruguay, 2019, 99min. Photo by Diego Garcia. Courtesy: Gabriel Mascaro.

It is easy to recall, by watching *Divine Love*, Margaret Atwood's novel *The Handmaid's Tale* (2017), adapted to film by Volker Schlöndorff (1990) and recently released as a series produced by MGM and aired by the streaming channel Hulu. Starring Elisabeth Moss, *The Handmaid's Tale* series (2017–) extrapolates the narrative arc of Atwood's novel and has been a public and critical success, with three seasons already aired. Throughout episodes with scenes marked by violence and terror, in addition to exquisite direction, art direction, and performances, the series narrates the martyrdom of June Osborne (Moss) in a near-future United States that has gone through a civil war and given way to a theocratic and authoritarian state, the Republic of Gilead. *Divine Love*'s 2027 Brazil seems slightly evocative of Gilead from the series, although less stifling and authoritarian. Unlike the American series, weapons and the military do not explicitly appear in the Brazilian film. If the atmosphere of terror in *The Handmaid's Tale* does not seem very distant or absurd, given the rise of the extreme right in various parts of the world, the evangelical nation of Mascaro seems far less surprising to us.

A very realistic "symbol" of *Divine Love*'s dystopian future can be found in the delirious fallacy-ridden speech uttered by President Jair Messias Bolsonaro at the opening of the UN Conference in 2020, when he denied the accelerated environmental devastation in Brazil, placed himself in a position of total subservience to the US president, Donald Trump, and summoned the people of the world to engage in an international crusade against "Christophobia"—whatever that may mean to him. The mention of the fight against "Christophobia" drew the attention of both Brazilian and international public opinion, with a nod that the country truly is heading toward becoming a fundamentalist theocracy and, for some journalists and commentators, a Christian "Taliban."

Another public figure that constantly attacks China, the "red peril," and the secular state, thus promoting a radicalization of Christian fundamentalism, with an evangelical or neo-Pentecostal accent, in Brazil is the diplomat Ernesto Araújo, now ex-Minister of Foreign Affairs in Bolsonaro's government (sometimes referred to by humorists as "the Minister of Foreign Hallucinations.")[15] Judging by the several delusional public speeches by the Brazilian former chancellor, riddled with mentions of God, the dystopian future of *Divine Love* seems even more probable. In a speech by Ernesto Araújo at a graduation ceremony at the Rio Branco Institute in Brasília, on October 22, 2020, the minister stated, among other absurdities, that the predecessors of the Bolsonaro government had been practicing "the utopia of a Brazil without God, of a Brazilian people uprooted from the arms of their Christian faith" (Araújo 2020). In a discourse full of questionable ideological positions, with gross historical and philosophical inaccuracies, Araújo repeatedly criticized the leftist Marxist movements and the communist threat he sees everywhere in Brazil and overseas. The following statement by Araújo corroborates the atmosphere of religious radicalization and reveals something about the state of affairs that Gabriel Mascaro's feature would have previously speculated on:

> As Dostoevsky said, a people without God does not deserve the name of a people, and that is precisely what communists of all ages wanted and want, to destroy the people in their living and sentimental organicity and transform them into a mass. It was like that in the Soviet revolution that destroyed Dostoevsky's old Russia, and they want to do it today, for example, here so close to us, in Chile, destroying churches and images and so they wanted and will always want to do in Brazil. With the perverse aggravation, that in our case, in which they tried to destroy the Christian faith not only from the outside, but also from the inside. (Araújo 2020)

It may seem bizarre or unreasonable to find this type of content in a speech by a minister of a secular federative republic. But this is a clear sign of how the lines between dystopian SF and the Brazilian reality are blurred today. It is the reality of Brazil from 2019 to 2021 that provides the blueprint for the 2027 Brazil in Mascaro's *Divine Love*. The former Foreign Affairs Minister Ernesto Araújo was a critical character in this scenario, prodigal in preaching under the guise of secular public statements. If the delusions paraphrased above were not enough, in an article signed by Araújo in *The New Criterion* magazine in January 2019, upon his inauguration as minister, the diplomat unleashed a cascade of hallucinations. Though quite challenging to select a quintessentially delusional quote among so many available in Araújo's *New Criterion* article, an epigraph that is perhaps perfectly suited to Gabriel Mascaro's film can be found in the following lines: "My detractors have called me crazy for believing in God and for believing that God acts in history—but I don't care. God is back and the nation is back: a nation with God; God through the nation. In Brazil (at least), nationalism became the vehicle of faith, faith became the catalyst for nationalism, and they both have ignited an exhilarating wave of freedom and new possibilities" (Araújo 2019). That excerpt sounds like the same sort of future prophesized in *Divine Love* concerning 2027 Brazil. Araújo was undoubtedly one of the most frightening figures of the Brazilian republic in the Bolsonaro administration, along with the former minister of healthcare, General Eduardo Pazzuelo, the former minister of education, Abraham Weintraub, and the former minister of women, family, and human rights (Ministra da Mulher, da Família e dos Direitos Humanos), the pastor Damares Alves. Apparently, Ernesto Araújo and Damares Alves might be the Adam and Eve of the "brand new evangelical republic," the most explicit heralds of Mascaro's dystopian future. José Fernandes Júnior, on his YouTube channel, comments on Araújo's speech in October 2020, opportunely associating the minister with the figure of Rasputin, the esoteric mastermind behind the last Russian tsarist government.[16] One particular scene in Mascaro's film draws our attention to this point, when Joana convinces a second couple to go to a service at the Divino Amor church. Here, the sequence of the bathing of the naked couple in holy water is visually presented for the first time. It is a group sex scene—the exchange of spouses between Joana and Danilo and the new couple—shown in one long take. Joana gives herself to the man, while Danilo has sexual intercourse with the woman. The voice-over intervenes. Near the moment of ejaculation, each man leaves his partner and returns to his wife to fertilize her. This is done with no apparent use of a condom. Two hypotheses may come to the viewer's mind. Either, in this future, sexually transmitted diseases (STDs) have been completely eradicated, or, what seems more likely, here in the fanatics' circle, STDs are of no concern: syphilis, hepatitis, HIV, none of these illnesses matter. They should not even be discussed publicly. From this perspective, valid among certain sects of present-day society led by religious fanatics and deniers, STDs only affect "homosexuals," "perverts," "sinners," or "infidels." To believers, STDs pose no risk and talking about them is taboo, as much as talking about rape, pedophilia, or abortion. The resourcefulness with which Joana and Danilo relate to other partners suggests that if such STDs continue to infect people in this near future, it is not a concern for the characters, either due to lack of information or the fact that the topic is excluded from matters of conversation in this dystopian society.

Taking as a basis the current state of public health and sex education policies in Brazil in 2020, as well as the difficulties faced by health professionals and educators—not only the severe funding cuts to advertising educational information about STDs but also the constant attacks on children's and adolescents' sex education, often led by the minister of women, family, and human rights, Damares Alves—the near dystopian future of *Divine Love* seems to be more than a possible outcome but an expected one. Adding to this the dismantling of the Unified Healthcare System (Sistema Único de Saúde, or SUS)[17] and the genocidal policy of the federal government concerning the Covid-19 pandemic, we can easily imagine a futuristic scenario in which diseases or epidemics persist. The only difference is that society and the state no longer discuss or take measures against them. Symbolic (or premonitory) events of the day in this sense are the fateful acts of protest by religious fanatics against the termination of the pregnancy of a ten-year-old girl in August 2020 (Jordan 2020),[18] and the constant stifling of sex education in schools promoted by Minister Damares Alves, a staunch advocate of teaching sexual abstinence to young people. In January 2020, Alves declared that she planned to adopt programs to promote abstinence in schools to reduce the incidence of teenage pregnancy in Brazil, which exceeds the world average by 30 percent. On the other hand, according to experts, it is precisely in the school environment that many cases of abuse and misinformation can be remedied or reversed. Sex education in Brazilian schools is provided for in the Common National Curriculum Base (BNCC or Base Nacional de Currículos Comuns) and in the National Curriculum Parameters (PCN or Parâmetros Curriculares Nacionais), documents that guide the performance of all elementary and high school teachers. The latter recommends the topic of sexuality to be treated transversely—that is, across different areas of knowledge—and that it addresses topics such as the use of contraceptives, STI prevention, gender equality, and self-knowledge, among other issues (Fávero 2020). According to a report by Bruno Fávero (2020), systematic reviews of studies of the literature on the subject found no evidence that policies to encourage abstinence have positive effects on the sexual habits of young people, which counterargues Alves's positions. For example, Denford et al. (2017, 33) suggest that interventions based only on abstinence were considered ineffective in promoting positive changes in sexual behavior. By contrast, comprehensive interventions, that is, those that specifically target HIV prevention and clinical initiatives applied in schools were indeed considered effective for improving knowledge and changing attitudes, behaviors, and results relevant to health. Thus, Denford et al. conclude that interventions in the school context aiming at preventing risky sexual behavior may indeed be effective, depending on their design, content, and implementation circumstances (2017, 33).

Another study, by Underhill, Montgomery, and Operario (2007, 1) finds that initiatives that exclusively encourage sexual abstinence do not seem to affect the risk of HIV infection in high-income countries, as measured by self-reported biological and behavioral outcomes.

Brazil, which was at one time praised internationally for its health policies (e.g., our Unified Health System and public policies to fight AIDS), today seems to have regressed to a state of absolute drift when it comes to the health care of its population. Those who still take care of the population and its health are the remnants of successful policies: SUS (Brazil's nationalized, expansive health service) (which has been dismantled year by year), some state governments, and city halls. On the part of the federal government, nothing is expected but necropolitics (Mbembe, 2003).

*Divine Love* ends on a fantastic note. We do not know if the nameless child has a father or if the divine holy spirit itself generated it. The child's voice that is heard in the first scene may, in theory, be the voice of the Messiah himself. Conclusions regarding this ending vary. According to Gonçalves (2019), "In the conflict generated in the heart of Joana with the discovery of her pregnancy and the absence of genetic traits of Danilo's paternity, there is a fervent search for religion, to the point of Joana believing that she is pregnant with God himself." Everything suggests that Joana got pregnant by an unknown father, but the film does not present unequivocal evidence of this more realistic interpretation. Despite its firm anchoring in recent Brazilian scenarios, the film's fable is nonetheless open to divine or fantastical interpretations.

If the child's voice-over can be interpreted as in line with the fable (perhaps the voice of the savior himself, reincarnated after more than two thousand years of waiting), a less hyperbolic and complacent reading may also take place. The child's voice narrates a future in which Brazil, a young nation, regresses even further in its maturity. The adolescent democracy goes back to the infantile stage that only began to crawl in 2019, the year the film was released. The fable's year, 2027, presents an infant nation in which the characters lack defined purpose and self-sufficiency and live under complete tutelage, as devotees of a deceitful faith that automates them in the pure cycle of "grow and multiply." In this respect, the film could be even more radical, more detailed in the construction of its extrapolative fictional universe based on the reality that we know well today: the power of the so-called evangelical bench in the Brazilian congress, the neo-Pentecostal movement with its financial and media tentacles. The furthest the film reaches is the absurdity of the drive-thru confessional and the swing temple itself, which happens to be the Divine Love church. But apart from psychodrama techniques and playful and sexual group activities, little is known about the backstage of the church: Who created it? How is it supported? Are there many others like it? None of this compromises the narrative, of course, but the script, clearly focused on an intimate drama, piques our curiosity about this world, which is simultaneously so strange and so close. In this sense, the narrative option of the film seems to echo Éric Dufour's thoughts on the SF cinema focused on totalitarian dystopias. Dufour explains that Orwell's post-*1984* futuristic dystopias (1948) bring an ominously innovative idea, visually developed by films such as George Lucas's *THX 1138*, Michael Anderson's *Logan's Run* (1976), or K. Wimmer's *Equilibirum* (2002): "that the totalitarianism of tomorrow will be religious or it will not exist" (Dufour 2011, 223).[19] According to Dufour,

> If the religious is so important in many cinematographic fictions devoted to totalitarian society, it is because totalitarianism is responsible for generating the totality of the individual's life, thus appropriating the private space, which is precisely represented, in our societies, by the freedom of cult. A society in which there is not only a state religion but, above all, religion is politically generated, where religion is a political issue, so that there is no longer a difference between the political and the religious, because the religious becomes a way to control the individual, [this] is really [a] totalitarian [society]. (Dufour 2011, 223–24)

Curiously enough, in *Divine Love* this state of absolute indistinction between politics and religion does not seem to have been reached, as Joana's official superior in the office has a dialogue with her, in one particular scene, expressing her disapproval concerning her behavior at work whenever she tries to persuade couples not to break up. The hierarchical superior makes it clear to Joana that her job is to carry out divorce proceedings, not religious indoctrination. That scene suggests that *Divine Love*'s dystopian future is not yet that of an absolute totalitarian theocracy but one with a certain degree of secularism, even if tenuous, underlying the institutions. This pulls *Divine Love*'s dystopian future even closer to our current reality, where the slogan often expressed by Bolsonaro (loosely inspired by Nazi slogans like *Deutschland über alles*) is "Brazil above everything, God above all" ("Brasil acima de tudo, Deus acima de todos"), and a crucifix is kept hanging on a wall in the Supreme Court, not to mention the countless Brazilian forums or public offices that display religious relics or symbols in contradiction with the country's political laicism. However, even in the 1988 Constitution, a rather progressive document, the prevalence of Christian ideology can be gauged, as it hails the Christian god on at least one page. Still according to Dufour, "The totalitarianism that constitutes the threat or possible terror of our liberal democracies is precisely totalitarianism without an apparent party or ideology. It is the totalitarianism of effectiveness, of profitability—where, under cover of productivity, the totality of what is provided for is submitted to the public, and the individual is domesticated and watched even in its most secret recesses" (Dufour 2011, 226).

The quotation above aptly illustrates a worldwide trend but one that has found in contemporary Brazil its most promising test tube. We speak not only of Bolsonaro's Brazil here. Needless to say, Bolsonaro came to power by constantly declaring he was an "outsider," not a politician, much like Trump in the United States. But in Brazil, Bolsonaro managed to deceive his voters by eliding the fact that he was an ineffective congressman for about thirty years, never working on a single law or act. Over 2020 and 2021, he was a president unaffiliated to any political party: a quite atypical situation in the history of Brazilian democracy. But this ruse, Dufour's "management of politics," and totalitarian tendencies with no apparent ideology can also be applied to the public persona of the governor of the Brazilian State of São Paulo, João Dória, who during the 2018 elections did not hesitate to link his name to the then-candidate for presidency, Jair Bolsonaro, launching the infamous slogan "Vote for Bolsodória." It should be remembered that while Dória was mayor of the city of São Paulo, he tried to implement a public food policy reminiscent of the dystopia of Richard Fleischer's *Soylent Green*: he intended to distribute to the poor and homeless people the infamous "farinata," that became known as "human ration," a nutritious meal made of residue from the food industry. The popular idea that the alternative to totalitarianism is "pure" neoliberalism is nonsense. Neoliberalism in late capitalism has often gone hand in hand with fascism, hiding the relationship, only denying it when caught by the *paparazzi*. In this sense, the religious dystopia designed by *Divine Love* is in no way radically opposed to the rising economic neoliberalism of the 1980s and perhaps the other way around. Religious fanaticism fills the vacuum of the trivialization of life and death; it may play the role of the "goat in the room" of the famous parable. We do not insist on the premonitory character of *Divine Love* because the film so closely reflects the current Brazilian reality, at least for the majority of the population. The phenomenon of neo-Pentecostalism has been seen as a reaction to economic neoliberalism, and indeed it may have been at some point. Nevertheless, the system is agile and malleable enough to co-opt it in its favor. As Mark Fisher reminds us, "The limits of capitalism are not fixed by fiat, but defined (and redefined) pragmatically and improvisationally. This makes capitalism very much like the Thing in John Carpenter's film of the same name" (Fisher 2009, 10–11). If at any time religious fanaticism served as a reaction to neoliberal pragmatism, now that is a thing of the past. In the 1960s and 1970s, capital envisaged a "solution" for Latin America in dictatorial regimes, hence the successive military coups on the continent. Today, perhaps they can be replaced by hybrid war techniques, widespread misinformation, and the funding of new think tanks and new religions. The corporate functioning of the largest and most famous Brazilian evangelical churches seems to signal this. Neoliberalism and totalitarianism, whether political or religious, are not divergent. They are not "alternatives," but intertwined, indivisible branches. Perhaps the slogan "Bolsodória" would never be more precise and prophetic.

In any case, we can infer, of course, that *Divine Love*'s plot stems from an extrapolation of the state of affairs in 2019, based on the assumption that the situation would have expanded: a national congress wholly taken over by political representatives from the so-called three B benches (the bullet bench, the Bible bench, and the bull bench), the expanding reach of the neo-Pentecostal churches in the media,[20] and the waiving of millions in tax debts that have not been paid by those same churches. The 2027 Brazil of *Divine Love* is a reborn, infantile nation, where life is reduced to domestic chores, sex in the name of the family, and religious worship in leisure hours, after working hours in the public office or one's own small business. External scenes in *Divine Love* are scarce and subtle, for reasons that can be ascribed to production contingencies. And yet this makes a lot of sense considering its script: in the Brazil of the future, there is little to be seen outside one's home, work, and church. The rare external scenes take advantage of a certain Brazilian modernist architecture, that of the molded concrete, that in its shades of gray acts as a metaphor and commentary on the souls of characters living in a dystopian nation.

Though perhaps the most unsettling, *Divine Love* is not the only religious dystopia in Brazilian SF cinema. Anita Rocha da Silveira's film *Medusa* (2022) conveys a similar sectarian religious dystopia complete with a cult of young fanatics, somewhat echoing the neon-fascist or neon-Pentecostal aesthetics of *Divine Love*. A mixture of Atwood's *The Handmaid's Tale* and Kubrick's *A Clockwork Orange* with Brazilian colors, *Medusa* features two lifelong friends, Mari (Mariana Oliveira) and Michele (Lara Tremouroux), whose church vocal group Michele and the Treasures of the Lord sings political propaganda and gospel love songs in the style of 1960s girl groups, while awash in purple-pink neon. The same group moonlights as antifeminist masked vigilantes who roam the streets at night beating up women they deem as sinful (Gates 2022). *Medusa* seemingly belongs to the same fictional universe of *Divine Love*, and it could well be seen as a prequel or spin-off of Mascaro's film.

## Cities under Siege, Again and Again

The third Brazilian feature-length SF film that completes a "holy trinity" of politically engaged cinematic SF, and perhaps best symbolizes the recent state of affairs in Brazil, is Kléber Mendonça Filho and Juliano Dornelles's *Bacurau* (2020). Along with Adirley Queirós's *White Out, Black In* and Gabriel Mascaro's *Divine Love*, Mendonça Filho and Dornelles's *Bacurau* stands out as one of the most controversial works in contemporary Brazilian film. Urban violence, social inequality, and the legacy of slavery had already been addressed by Mendonça Filho's *Neighboring Sounds*, with a Western and thriller twist. His second feature, *Aquarius* (2016), concerning the life of a lone middle-class woman struggling against the greed of real estate developers in the city of Recife (capital of Pernambuco State, Brazil), was interpreted as a symbol of the ruin of Brazilian democracy during the Kafkaesque impeachment process of President Dilma Rousseff.

Within Brazilian documentary film, works like Maria Ramos's *The Trial* (*O Processo*, 2018) and Petra Costa's *The Edge of Democracy* (*Democracia em Vertigem*, 2019) further scrutinized the parliamentary coup that removed President Rousseff and paved the way for the rise of an extreme-right civil-military government. Taking into account the Bolsonaro administration's attacks against culture, Ariel Schweitzer (2019) posed the question: What is the strategy against a government that does not disguise its hostility toward cinema and its intention to control film culture? Based on interviews with Brazilian filmmakers, Schweitzer observed directors were hesitant during the Bolsonaro era. They foresaw a cleavage between an official cinema for the status quo, centralized and largely funded by public money, and a regional cinema, politically engaged, primarily independent, or self-sustained (Schweitzer 2019, 84). Still, according to Schweitzer, "The evolution of regional cinema in Brazil comes in tandem with films dedicated to racial, social and sexual minorities, people relatively overlooked in the history of Brazilian cinema" (2019, 82).

Created by two celebrated contemporary directors, *Bacurau* is focused on racial, social, and sexual minorities but divided the opinions of spectators while collecting prizes at international film festivals like Cannes and Munich. The impact of *Bacurau* among popular audiences and film scholars alike has not been trivial. The film was given the cover of the September 2019 issue of French magazine *Cahiers du Cinéma* and has triggered passionate discussions on social media and academic forums. *Bacurau* can be seen as a powerful allegory of Brazilian society in the present day—even though the project began ten years before its premiere, with the final script finished three years before the film's release. *Bacarau* is a dystopian thriller that utilizes genre conventions such as SF, the Western, and the thriller and resignifies a cinematic vocabulary already present in films like Irving Pichel and Ernest B. Schoedsack's *The Most Dangerous Game* (1932), Clint Eastwood's *High Plains Drifter* (1973), and Gary Ross's *The Hunger Games* (2012). *Bacurau*'s vast array of sources and intertextual references include the SF dystopia of "human safaris" and the Zapata Western of films like Damiano Damiani's *Gringo* (*Quién sabe?*, 1967). The final scene in *Bacurau* is quite evocative of *Gringo*, when El Santo (Klaus Kinski) takes revenge on soldiers who have oppressed vulnerable people in a small village. The "burial" of the villains in an underground cage creates the contours of a political allegory in both *Gringo* and *Bacurau*. As Camille Bui points out, "In the wake of the ideology of the conquest of the west, *Bacurau* redirects the avenging and playful energy of the Western by targeting the America of devourer capitalism and rampant fascism" (2019, 8). This is not the first time *Bacurau* is referred to as an SF film or read through the lens of the SF film genre (see Suppia 2020; Dias Jr. 2020). In a review of *Bacurau*, Jocimar Dias Jr. suggests that seeing the film "through the lens of the sci-fi genre may help" (2020) to further understand the intensely divided reactions to its potential subtexts and some exasperating Tarantino-esque scenes of graphic violence. Drawing on ideas from Adilifu Nama (2015, 94), Dias Jr. compares *Bacurau* with Quentin Tarantino's *Inglourious Basterds* (2009) to conclude that both films can be seen as SF fantasies set in alternative worlds or parallel universes

(Dias Jr. 2020, 85). Furthermore, Dias Jr. refers to John Rieder's analysis of Neil Blomkamp's *District 9*, James Cameron's *Avatar* (2009), and again *Inglourious Basterds* as "spectacularly violent, realised revenge fantasies directed against white-male representatives of organised racial injustice" (Rieder 2011, 41). Thereby, according to Dias Jr.,

> *Bacurau* could easily be included in this category, since it allegorically revisits Brazil's colonial history and its open wounds in Brazilian society today. The attack on Damiano [Carlos Francisco] and Deisy [Ingrid Trigueiro] reenacts the violent encounter between white colonizers and non-white native peoples in Brazilian lands; the couple's nakedness and use of psychotropics corroborate such a reading, while their triumph over an intended genocide acquires the status of historical reparation. When Michael (Udo Kier), the hypermasculine white-supremacist leader of the snipers, is finally buried alive by Lunga (Silvero Pereira), a queer person of color, isn't it also *Bacurau*'s attempt to bury this foundational colonial violence, as currently revived through Bolsonarism? (Dias Jr. 2020, 85)

Dornelles and Mendonça Filho admit their identification with a generation of cinephiles strongly influenced by genre films screened in movie theaters. In an interview with Camille Bui and Joachim Lepastier, Mendonça Filho remarks that "the genre film gives us a good excuse to exaggerate, to go further," while Dornelles explains that genre films "allow us to talk about politics by disguising very subversive thoughts in a kind of innocent way" (Bui and Lepastier 2019, 10). In addition to Zapata Western and SF, *Bacurau* can also be seen as a cinematic manifestation of the recent Brazilian SF trends called Cyberagreste and Sertãopunk.

All in all, the semiarid hinterlands in Northeastern Brazil have generally been a particularly intriguing locus for Brazilian SF stories. Gerson Sanginitto's *Area Q*, for example, capitalizes on legends about UFO sightings in the skies over the state of Ceará, with the "Q" in the film's title standing for the cities Quixadá and Quixeramobim, areas supposedly visited by aliens. In the same vein, a series of Brazilian SF shorts have told stories of alien visitors and alien abductions. Severino Dadá's *A Nave de Mané Socó* (2019) mimics the famous radio adaptation of H. G. Wells's *The War of the Worlds* (1898) by Orson Welles and his Mercury Theater in 1938, adapting this leitmotif to a very small town in inland Pernambuco. Mané

Socó is Manoel Zoroastro, a local radio MC who narrates a threat from space that has been terrorizing the small and peaceful town of Pedra, in the backlands of Pernambuco. In a sensational tone, he comments on the mysterious abductions that take place after a red light is emitted by the UFO. Veteran Brazilian filmmaker Severino Dadá is almost eighty years old and was the celebrated editor of several films directed by Nelson Pereira dos Santos and Rogério Sganzerla. When *A Nave de Mané Socó* premiered at the Brasília Film Festival, Dadá introduced his film on stage. After recalling part of his many decades-long history in Brazilian cinema, he warned that if Spielberg and Lucas create SF cinema, he, a Pernambucan filmmaker, makes *"fuleiragem* fiction," that is, an intentionally poor, artisanal—but wholehearted and very amusing—*fuleira* SF (Caetano 2019).[21]

The Cyberagreste aesthetic seen in these films started with Vitor Wiedergrün's series of illustrations by the same title (see Paiva 2019). The artist mixed two aesthetics he was fond of: cyberpunk's dystopian futurism and the Northeastern Brazilian culture of the *sertões* (hinterlands). Thus, Wiedergrün so created illustrations of futuristic *cangaceiros*,[22] cyber accordion players, and androids inspired by historic Brazilian characters like Lampião and Maria Bonita. Literary counterparts of Wiedergrün's Cyberagreste can be found in works like Laísa Ribeiro's short story "Sons of Metal and the Caatinga" ("Filhos do Metal e da Caatinga," in Zuin 2019), and Roberto de Sousa Causo's "The Fight of the Jedi Cangaceiro" ("A Luta do Cangaceiro Jedi" 2020). Zé Wellington and Walter Geovani's graphic novel *Cangaço Overdrive* (2018) is also considered a key work in the emerging Cyberagreste (or Sertãopunk) movement. Notwithstanding, as a response to Cyberagreste and the predominance of Southern Brazilian artists in the trend (the exception would be Zé Wellington, born in the state of Ceará), Alan de Sá and Alec Silva's Sertãopunk (see Sá 2019) appeared to exhort Northern Brazilian artists to support an SF trend more in tune with the actual cultural roots of the region. According to Sá, Sertãopunk is far more suitable as a name than Cyberagreste and, as a literary movement, it aims to elaborate on the following topics: (1) a Northeast where technological advances, especially ecological ones, provided a high quality of life for the Northeasterners; (2) the social disorder spurred by an emerging *coronelista*[23] elite financed by powerful groups; (3) the reconfiguration of Brazilian migratory fluxes; (4) the Northeast as an independent center for intellectual and cultural development; and finally, (5) the use of orality, cultural elements, and the various legends and religions of the region in fictional works. The Sertãopunk movement is illustrated by works like the collection of short stories and essays edited by Alan de Sá, G. G. Diniz, and Alec Silva's *Sertãopunk: Stories from a Northeast of Tomorrow* (*Sertãopunk: Histórias de um Nordeste do Amanhã*, 2020), but is still meager in comparison to the Cyberagreste it confronts and previous trends such as the Tupinipunk.

The controversy between Cyberagreste and Sertãopunk somewhat mirrors the discussion between the Manguebeat[24] in music and Ariano Suassuna's Armorial Movement (Movimento Armorial)[25] in literature and other arts. The Manguebeat movement, led by artists like Chico Science and Fred 04, elaborated on the globalization of Northeastern culture, amalgamated with more universal icons or cultural symbols such as the parabolic antenna and cyberspace. By contrast, the Brazilian poet, playwright, and writer Ariano Suassuna saw in the Manguebeat movement a mischaracterization and the disempowering of the actual Northeastern culture, as though Walt Disney had invaded our precious and original cultural heritage.[26] Dornelles and Mendonça Filho's *Bacurau* stages a dialogue with Cyberagreste (or Sertãopunk) in the way the film orchestrates both local (Brazilian Northeastern) and globalized icons or cultural symbols, including an SF iconography, to portray a clash of civilizations—the bellicose white aliens vs. the backlands' people. Naturally, apart from *Bacurau*, several other Brazilian SF shorts could be even more easily identified with either Cyberagreste or Sertãopunk, such as Renata Mourão's short film *Abjetas 288* (2020), Matheus Farias and Enock Carvalho's *Unliveable* (*Inabitável*, 2020), Henrique Arruda's *The Last Romantics of the World* (*Os Últimos Românticos do Mundo*, 2020), or the web series *Stufana* (2010).[27]

As pointed out by Bui and confirmed by the directors themselves, *Bacurau* escalates conflicts already suggested by *Neighboring Sounds* and *Aquarius*. It is set in the near future and tells the story of characters who inhabit a remote town called Bacurau, in the countryside of Pernambuco. As explained by one of the characters in the film, the name of the village refers to a bird. Mendonça Filho, however, says that "Bacurau" is simply the nickname given to the last buses at night in Recife (Bui and Lepastier 2019, 11).

This small community struggles to survive with the lack of proper infrastructure, water, and medical supplies, not to mention the political abandonment of a mayor whose only interest in the people of Bacurau revolves around election times. The film opens with Teresa (Bárbara Colen) arriving in Bacurau for the funeral of her grandmother Carmelita (Lia de Itamaracá). She also brings with her some vaccines and supplies to help the community. Thenceforth, strange events take place and create an atmosphere of eeriness and menace. These events include the sudden erasure of Bacurau from online maps, a truck that periodically brings potable water is riddled with bullet holes, the visit of two strangers riding motorcycles, and the massacre of a family on a nearby farm. It soon becomes clear that Bacurau is under attack by a mysterious power. Here, the film echoes a tradition in Latin American SF films, such as Alberto Pieralisi's *The 5th Power* and Hugo Santiago's *Invasión*. The citizens of Bacurau have been hunted and killed by foreign visitors (presumably Americans) engaged in some sort of human safari led by Michael (Udo Kier). Once aware of the attack, old rivalries and internal disputes are put aside while the villagers organize a resistance. Acácio (Thomas Aquino), a former hitman under the nickname of Pacote, seals a pact with Lunga (Silvero Pereira), a fugitive from the police who lives with his acolytes in a dry, abandoned dam. Lunga's gang then returns to Bacurau to help the community resist and avenge the murder of their people. Eventually, violence erupts in the town, and the villagers take extreme measures to survive. Camille Bui recognizes two primary spatial relationships in the film (inhabiting and predation) as follows: "The territory of Bacurau seems to be a public good, threatened to disappear due to the private madness of corrupt politicians and American paramilitary. The foreigners' relationship with that land, be it the ludicrous mayor, North-Americans or Southeastern Brazilians, is marked by predation" (2019, 8).

By resorting to SF tropes and thriller conventions, *Bacurau* translates some of the horrific problems of Brazilian society today into a divisive film. The film is naturally subject to multiple interpretations. However, whereas leftists tend to praise it as a cinematic manifesto against fascism and submission to imperialist rule, conservatives have condemned the film as an outrageous call to insubordination, sympathetic with outlaws and so-called second-class citizens (e.g., women, prostitutes, transvestites, gays, and lesbians—all of whom are the primary victims of violence in Brazil today). All in all, *Bacurau* seems to prod a sensitive spot in the decomposing organism that is Brazilian society right now: it demonstrates how the history of violence and inequality in Brazil owes so much to Brazilians who hardly see themselves as a whole nation and community. This is didactically exposed in the scene where the pair of motorcyclists, Brazilians who had visited Bacurau in the service of the foreign invaders, participate in a meeting with them. They pathetically try to convince Michael and the Americans that they are "different" from the villagers of Bacurau; they are "whiter" and closer to Europeans. This particular scene, pathetic and outrageous at once, is drastically representative of the true feelings of certain Brazilians toward "other" Brazilians, and not surprisingly is a highly unsettling scene for most spectators. Another crucial point addressed by *Bacurau* lies in its fierce call to resistance to the current sociopolitical situation in Brazil and revenge by those excluded from dominant societal practices. While the effectiveness of this approach might be debatable, the film sets a thought-provoking dialogue with 1960s and 1970s Latin American film manifestos such as Fernando Solanas and Octavio Getino's "Toward a Third Cinema" ("Hacia un Tercer Cine," 1969/1997) and Glauber Rocha's "An Aesthetics of Hunger" (1997) ("Uma Estética da Fome," a.k.a. "Estétyka da Fome," originally published in 1965)—notably with Glauber's ideas, in which violence is claimed as an aesthetic value.

The dystopian character of the film is, nevertheless, ambiguous. As confirmed by the directors (in Bui and Lepastier 2019, 12), the small community of Bacurau represents a relentless utopian spirit. It could be regarded as a society reminiscent of an old *quilombo*.[28] Among the most prominent characters in the film is Plínio (Wilson Rabelo), a teacher in Bacurau and the person who most explicitly stands for the community's utopian drive (see fig. 7.3). Plínio is one of the first to perceive the alien

Figure 7.3. Plínio (Wilson Rabelo), the only teacher in town, provides a lucid voice for the community while the eerie events take place. He is the first to find out that Bacurau had been erased from the internet maps. *Source*: *Bacurau*. Dir. Kléber Mendonça Filho. Prod. Co.: Emilie Lesclaux, Saïd Ben Saïd et Michel Merkt. Brazil, France, 2019, 131min. Courtesy: Kléber Mendonça Filho (private collection).

invasion, and is mainly a sensible and peaceful voice as the story unfolds. Echoing Glauber Rocha's *Antonio das Mortes* (*O Dragão da Maldade contra o Santo Guerreiro*, 1969), Plínio, the intellectual character, cannot ultimately refrain from using violence against both the local and foreign aggressors: "We're under the effects of a powerful psychotropic . . . and you're gonna die,"[29] he finally says to the mayor toward the end of the film. This character provides one of the clearest links to the Brazilian Cinema Novo, especially Glauber Rocha's film *Antonio das Mortes*.

A focus on Plínio—as a symbol of the power and faith in free education as an instrument to defeat obscurantism, violence, and authoritarianism—might also be interesting for an approach to *Bacurau* against the backdrop of the recent rise of the extreme right in Brazil, tracing the ruin of rational thinking and the collapse of a faith in a more inclusive, peaceful, and progressive future.

Today, *Bacurau* seems to stand out in a group of aesthetically innovative and/or politically engaged *auteur* films that critique the conservative turn in Brazil, a group that includes Juliana Rojas and Marco Dutra's *The Good Manners* (*As Boas Maneiras*, 2017), Adirley Queirós's *Once There Was Brasília*, and Affonso Uchôa's *The Hidden Tiger* (*A Vizinhança do Tigre*, 2016), among others. Adirley Queirós's films, it is worth repeating, are essentially political films, and his more recent works, coauthored with the Portuguese director Joana Pimenta, only accentuate this political drive. Pimenta and Queirós's *Dry Ground Burning* (*Mato Seco em Chamas*, 2022), is one of their latest near-futuristic dystopias. The film mixes SF, western, and documentary, with a touch of George Miller's *Mad Max* universe, to portray class struggle, sexism, and "the survival of the misfits" in the periphery of Brasília. Here a "wild bunch" of women (the "Gasolineiras de Kebradas") seize power over their town after finding an oil well in the backyard of one of the local homes. The film is a tour de force that alternates between memorialism, documentary, and utopianism while featuring a group of unprecedently empowered women.

In terms of politically engaged SF cinema in Brazil, Thiago Foresti is perhaps one of the most promising young filmmakers. His latest short, *Algorithm* (*Algoritmo*, 2020), is a dystopian speculation about the near future in which the police state restricts rights, harasses, hunts, and eliminates political dissidents. Young people who venture into critical and libertarian thinking, simply by reading "subversive" works and participating in political or interrogative discussions about the system, thus become preferential targets for the police state, empowered by the use of an almighty algorithm that operates in an omnipresent surveillance structure (perhaps not very distant from reality) (see fig. 7.4). The reference to works like George Orwell's *1984* (1948), as well as his adaptations for film and television, seems natural and immediate. Films such as *Grayish Morning*, by Olney São Paulo, or *Punishment Park*, by Peter Watkins, also seem to be part of this cinematic lineage from which Foresti's *Algorithm* arises.

As Éric Dufour rightly recalls, "The camera that observes, records, and controls people (video surveillance) is a constant in the cinema which is interested in totalitarian societies or in the totalitarian transformation of society" (Dufour 2011, 228). Curiously, Dufour does not mention the French feature *Futuristic Disillusions* (*Le Couple Témoin*, 1977), directed by William Klein. A parody of totalitarian dystopias like *THX 1138*, where the boundaries between public and private simply disappear, *Le Couple Témoin* somewhat anticipates Peter Weir's *Truman Show* (1998), by presenting a young "model" couple who volunteer to live in a modern house, built as the backdrop for a prolonged televised experiment, an initiative of the "Ministry of the Future." *Algorithm*, though, goes far beyond the camera

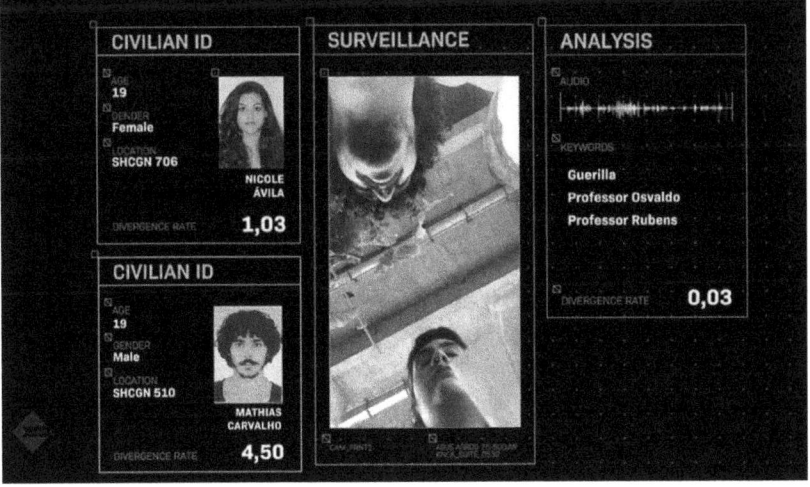

Figure 7.4. Nicole (Agda Couto) and Mathias (Pablo Magalhães) are surveilled by the omnipresent panopticon in Thiago Foresti's *Algoritmo* (2020). *Source*: *Algorithm* (*Algoritmo*). Dir. Thiago Foresti. Prod. Co.: Foresti Comunicação. Brazil, 2020, 20min. Courtesy: Thiago Foresti (private collection).

as an icon of totalitarian surveillance. The film is able to summarize, in effect, a situation of constant multimodal or multimedia surveillance, where all communication tools can be reframed or reobjectified for the sake of behavioral or ideological control. In this, too, Foresti's film does not appear to be radically imaginative; it just creatively extrapolates the current conditions of surveillance.

Furthermore, perhaps the most reiterated or common likeness in the dystopian fable of this short film is the phenomenon of social networks, the accumulation of information about individuals (let us remember the case of the company Cambridge Analytica and the elections in Brazil and other countries between 2016 and 2018), as well as the escalation of a police-corporate state of unlimited surveillance, as it is reported by Shoshana Zuboff, professor at Harvard Business School, in Jeff Orlowski's documentary *The Social Dilemma* (2020). Zuboff is the author of *The Age of Surveillance Capitalism* (2019) and, in Orlowski's documentary, she explains that "Facebook conducted what they called a 'massive-scale contagion experiment.' How do we use subliminal cues on the Facebook pages to get more people to vote in the midterm elections? And they discovered that they were able to do that. One thing they concluded is what we know now. We can affect real-world behavior and emotions without ever triggering the user's awareness. They are completely clueless."

In this sense, the vigilant dystopia described by *Algorithm* seems to echo Jean-Pierre Vernant's idea of "totalitarianization," taken up by Éric Dufour (2012) in his analysis of SF cinema. According to Dufour,

> In short, the totalitarian society that we must fear today is perhaps not that of fascism, nazism, or the different forms of communist societies after the Second World War, but that of our liberal democratic societies, much more discreet because it does not present itself as such, and because it is not a proven fact, but a process that is set in motion—which is why it is better to speak of *totalitarianismization* than of totalitarianism. *Totalitarianismization* is based on the installation of techniques and devices that we can approve [. . .] to favor our autonomy and facilitate and improve our daily life. On the other hand, and from another angle, these techniques set control over the individual who, in this sense, can no longer dispose of himself, insofar as he is instrumentalized by a device in whose

installation he participated. (Dufour 2011, 226; emphasis in the original)

Nevertheless, *Algorithm* engenders an outcome that beckons with resistance, possibly inspired by the contemporary hacktivism of organizations like Pirate Bay or young people like Alexandra Elbakyan, Kazakhstan programmer and creator of the *Sci-Hub* website. Elbakyan fights the capitalist voracity of scientific publishing market giants, like Elsevier, through their work of free and wide dissemination of scientific knowledge. Foresti's *Algorithm* won Best SF short in the 2021 CineFantasy (Festival Internacional do Cinema Fantástico), among other prizes in different film festivals. The latest movie by Foresti, *A Guide for the Post-Truth* (*Manual da Pós-Verdade*, 2022), follows the despair of a journalist drowned by fake news and post-truths in an allegorical film set in a vaguely near-future Brasília. Foresti's refined irony and sometimes acid humor reappears in *Manual da Pós-Verdade* as in previous works like *Space Invasion* (*Invasão Espacial*, 2019) or *Nonsemsical School* (*Escola Sem Sentido*, 2019).

Another recent short film clearly inspired by the current state of political affairs in Brazil, the detour to the extreme right and the impact of big data, biometrics, and new digital technologies is Julio Urbano's *2030* (2019). In *2030*, a mysterious blackout occurs in São Paulo, the most technologically advanced urban area in the country, generating a wave of protests and operational problems that bring disorder to the capital. Upon requesting a ride in an app, Débora is surprised to find a supervisor inside the self-driven vehicle she ordered. In this short trip, certain events reveal who are the true enemies in a closely watched society. In *2030*, the dystopian "city under siege" trope is metonymically subsumed to a "car" interior, while a futurist version of an Uber driver is serving a client. They end up stuck in a traffic jam due to power shortages that affect the AI in charge of urban circulation. However, toward the end of the "ride," off-screen sounds and confusing commands from the AI make the characters suspect a confrontation is occurring on the streets, with soldiers shooting to kill the rebels. Filmed in a single internal location, in the guise of this futurist "car" with no windows or view of the surroundings, the film alludes to a near-future dystopian police state based on strict surveillance. Yet again, films like *Algorithm* and *2030* depict the idea of a city under siege with citizens being constantly monitored by invaders or the authoritarian state, evoking previous SF feature films like Alberto

Pieralisi's *The 5th Power*, Hugo Santiago's *Invasión*, and Fernando Spiner's *The Sleepwalker* (*La Sonámbula: Recuerdos del Futuro*, 1998), to name just a few. Suffice it to say that short films like Thiago Foresti's *Algorithm* and Julio Urbano's *2030* are symptomatic of the societal backlash and tense political situation in early-2020s Brazil.

In the wake of short films like *2030* and *Algoritmo*, a feature-length film titled *The Second Man* (2022), directed by Thiago Luciano, takes place in an indeterminate near future, when the Bolsonaro government's gun policies have reached their peak. Streamed on Star Plus, the film extrapolates the history of violence and problems with organized crime that afflict Brazilian society to depict a country in collapse in terms of public security, with the population subjected to the power of militias. Violence prevails at all levels. From the first scenes, shootings and free movement of armed groups outline a dystopian society where everyone survives at their own risk. In this scenario, a lower middle-class family moves from São Paulo, the capital, to a smaller city in the countryside, Sumaré, with the aim of escaping violence. The idea of taking his wife and daughter to Sumaré comes from Miro (Anderson di Rizzi), the family man who fears for the safety of his dearest ones.

Now settled with his family in Sumaré, with a slightly more peaceful life, Miro contacts a unit of the Foreign Legion. Enlisting in the Legion comes to mean a double salvation for Miro: he will finally learn to shoot, be trained militarily and be able to defend his family, as well as having the opportunity to emigrate to France or another country under the best institutional conditions in Brazil. Miro symbolizes the middle-class white man in crisis, powerless in the face of violence and working underpaid jobs. Despite his wife's distrust, Miro enlists in the Foreign Legion with a view to realizing his dream of taking his family out of Brazil. He manages to complete his training and travels to Paris, where he will finally be incorporated into the French mercenary group (interestingly, not far from a militia). But Miro's plans for himself and his family are at serious risk after the mysterious murder of one of his colleagues in arms, one of the most outstanding soldiers in training. The local police intervene and begin investigating the case. The film starts from a familiar exposure to science fiction, in dialogue with the Brazilian reality of the time, but soon gives way to the thriller or the whodunnit-style police genre. *The Second Man* benefits from reasonable-to-good cinematography, editing, soundtrack and performances, although it is quite inconsistent in the sum of its parts, resulting in a mediocre film.

Another example of Brazilian science fiction cinema with engaging political discourse is *Tremor Iê* (2019), a film contemporary with the rise of the Bolsonaro administration, directed by Elena Meirelles and Lívia de Paiva, and produced by the independent production company Tardo Filmes, based in Fortaleza, Ceará. Starring young women, mostly non-professional actresses playing Black and peripheral characters, *Tremor Iê* departs from the story of Janaína (Lila Salú), arrested in a 2013 popular demonstration in Fortaleza. While Janaína was imprisoned, a coup d'état establishes some sort of Orwellian regime in Brazil, also based on some kind of religion. The social order is guaranteed by the "soldiers of Good," while voices of command echo from loudspeakers throughout the city. When Janaína escapes from prison, she reconnects with her friend Cássia (Deyse Mara), who faces the authoritarianism of the dystopian government daily. Gathered again, they remember the stories they lived, stories of violence suffered before and during the rise of the military-religious dictatorship. Along with other women, Janaína and Cássia steal the remains of former dictator Castelo Branco[30] as a bargaining chip for the release of other political prisoners. Meirelles and Paiva's film seems reasonably influenced by Adirley Queirós's and other Brazilian artistic collectives' films in which female characters lead the resistance against patriarchal authoritarianism. This low-budget film finds clever ways to build its dystopian world and blurs the lines between science fiction and docudrama. But differently from other films analyzed in this chapter, where political criticism and science fiction are more skillfully orchestrated, in *Tremor Iê* and *The Second Man*, science fiction appears in a very superficial way, nothing much beyond the frequent intro: "in the near future . . ." *Tremor Iê*, however, stands out for being a low-budget production, a lo-fi sci-fi film made mostly by women and featuring marginalized female characters, thus confirming the ever more frequent use of science fiction vocabularies on the part of peripheral artists to address sociopolitical contradictions in Brazil—something unthinkable in the country in the late twentieth century, when SF cinema was regarded as a "foreign" genre, extremely expensive and unattainable by the Brazilian audiovisual industry, despite counter-examples.

This chapter has attempted to demonstrate that the dystopia imposed by the Bolsonaro (mis)government provoked cinematographic and audiovisual responses in the same tone, films that resorted to the semantics and syntax of science fiction cinema to come to terms with the absurdity that Brazilian society has been plunged into since the coup that deposed President Dilma Rousseff in 2015.

8

# Find Your Escape Pod

Afrofuturism, Amazofuturism, and Queer Sci-Fi

Over the past decade, a constellation of films of varying budgets, visual effects, political discourse, and narrative complexity seems to confirm both the interest and familiarity of a new generation of Brazilian filmmakers with SF.[1] Short films like *The Flying Man* (2013), by Marcus Alqueres, and *Lunatique* (2016), by Gabriel Kalim Mucci, feature young filmmakers particularly attentive to the quality of visual effects as a quintessential trait of SF cinema. *Lunatique*, for example, is a postapocalyptic short film with eye-catching and meticulous art direction and visual effects, about a woman fighting for her survival among the rubble of a shattered metropolis shrouded in a poisonous atmosphere and inhabited by strange radioactive and carnivorous creatures. Despite a satisfactory editing, good pacing, and well-crafted costumes, cinematography, sets, and effects, films like *Lunatique* lack a more compelling and cohesive storyline. With a plot reminiscent of formulaic postapocalyptic movies such as Fede Álvarez's Uruguayan short film *Panic Attack* (*Ataque de Pánico*, 2009), *Lunatique* consists of isolated scenes that do not stand on their own as a unique, robust story to be told. The drama is kept to a minimum, and the action is limited to a mere sequence of images following a superficial cause-and-effect logic: something akin to a teaser for a lengthier film. Its main narrative function seems to rely on demonstrating the filmmaker's expertise with visual effects and his ability to emulate an "SF-model" or canonical cinema, an ersatz Brazilian knock-off of North American or European SF cinema. *Lunatique*, like many other visually polished SF shorts available on YouTube, such as the channel *Dust*, can thus be regarded as a "portfolio film." But it was not just good graphics and CGI that fueled Brazilian SF cinema in the 2000s.

Even so, the neoliberalism that befell Brazilian society and the slight detour to the political left in 2003, with the election of President Luís Inácio Lula da Silva, seem to have momentarily quieted ecodystopias in Brazilian cinema for some twenty years or so. The documentary treatment of favelas and urban violence in Brazil thrived during that first decade of the twenty-first century in a myriad of films that attempted to combine humanistic, sociological, investigative, or simply ecstatic approaches to social inequality and the massacre of subaltern peoples in Brazil. Some of the most remarkable movies from the period include Walter Salles's *Central Station* (*Central do Brasil*, 1998), João Moreira Salles's *News from a Personal War* (*Notícias de uma Guerra Particular*, 1999), Kátia Lund and Fernando Meirelles's *City of God*, José Padilha's *Bus 174* (*Ônibus 174*, 2002), and Hector Babenco's *Carandiru* (2003), among others. As if the reduction in environmental issues and symbols addressed by ecodystopias had made room for the perhaps more visible perils of urban violence exploited by the media, audiences saw themselves lured by controversial films like José Padilhas's *Elite Squad* (*Tropa de Elite*, 2007) and *Elite Squad 2* (*Tropa de Elite 2*, 2010). A blend of environmental concerns and political criticism—a sort of eco-social criticism[2]—ecodystopias reappeared more explicitly in short films no earlier than 2009, with Kléber Mendonça Filho's *Cold Tropics* (*Recife Frio*, 2009), and in feature-length films in the 2010s like Luiz Bolognesi's animation *Rio 2096*.

## Tales of Ice and Fire

Shot on 35mm, Kléber Mendonça Filho's *Cold Tropics*, the seventh short film in his career, is a mockumentary that simulates an Argentinean television show covering an unprecedented climate change in Recife following the fall of a meteorite. Without obvious explanation, Recife, a once tropical city in northeastern Brazil famous for its coastal landscapes and beach lifestyle, begins registering temperatures more suited to a quasi-European winter. The narrative discusses the impact of this "climate catastrophe" on the city's population and its cultural and economic backdrops. By resorting to a self-ironic documentary style, *Cold Tropics* joins a seemingly contemporary trend or revival in world SF cinema, one that serves as an eloquent reconciliation of SF with the long tradition of satire (see Booker and Thomas 2009, 98).

Other examples of this combination A (SF tropes) + B (documentary rhetoric) revival can be found in Neill Blomkamp's *Alive in Joburg* (2005), a short about the nonpeaceful coexistence of aliens and humans in Johannesburg, South Africa, an apartheid allegory disguised as SF, and *Why Cybraceros?* (1997), directed by Alex Rivera, in which archival footage of the 1940s US Bracero program gives way to speculations on the future of labor in the age of cognitive capitalism.[3] Rivera's feature film *Sleep Dealer* stems from the original idea of *Why Cybraceros?*, while Neill Blomkamp's *District 9* (2009), in turn, further develops some of *Alive in Joburg*'s plot ideas. In the last twenty years or so, this artifice seems to have been intensified in SF cinema: the use of documentary rhetoric, through inspired mockumentaries, as a laboratory for more ambitious feature films.

Set in a near future, Mendonça Filho's *Cold Tropics* opens with scenes of a rescue team working in an isolated area of Maria Farinha Beach where a meteorite has fallen, killing three people. An Argentinean narrator, Pablo Hundertwasser, reporter for the Argentine TV show *The World in Motion* (*El Mundo en Movimiento*), comments on the images in Spanish, explaining that, according to scientists, there is no relation between the fallen meteorite and the sudden climate change. However, some weeks later, he continues, the penguins began to arrive. The reporter explains that he is now in Recife to investigate an interesting phenomenon: a case of climate change that is disrupting a whole society, leaving the international scientific community struggling for answers. Images of a sunny Recife recall the city's tropical climate and beach lifestyle. At this point, however, the narrative criticizes the real environmental degradation affecting the city, introduced by Pablo's comments on the Capibaribe River: "This 'Brazilian Venice' is crossed by a dark sludge that was once a river . . . the Capibaribe." The reporter further explains that the average maximum temperature in the area has always been around 30°C in the summer, while the minimum was rarely below 22°C in winter: "In other words, Recife was unfamiliar with the concept of being cold." After a cut to black and the sudden interruption of the dancing soundtrack, the narrator declares: "Today, this is all part of history." For about seven months, Recife and its entire metropolitan area have received no sunlight. Massive gray clouds and continuous rain shroud the entire region, making it "the independent republic of cold weather amidst a tropical country." Scenes

190 | Brazilian Science Fiction Film

of locals on the streets ensue: people are buying scarves and sweaters, while a street vendor announces an expected minimum of 6°C for the night. The current maximum temperature, according to the narrator, does not exceed 14°C (see fig. 8.1). The urban landscape has changed due to a spectacle of lights and smog from the myriad bonfires set in the city streets at night by the homeless trying to keep warm. The narrator then tackles a crucial issue that emphasizes and deepens the sociopolitical overtones of this science fiction satire: "The nightly bonfires reveal one of the many problems caused by the cold: social injustice and homelessness are now particularly cruel."

Like other Brazilian SF movies, *Cold Tropics* presents a dissertation on the history of Brazilian social inequality under the guise of an ecodystopia. The most deep-seated contradictions of Brazilian society—the remaining acute class struggle as a constantly silenced driving force, the persistence of archaic social structures, and the legacies of slavery in contemporary Brazil—seem to be constant themes in Kléber Mendonça Filho's filmography. To address such issues, stories focusing on Recife or the Brazilian real estate market are instrumental, as they provide perfect scenarios and characters for an intensive discussion on Brazil's reckoning

Figure 8.1. When Recife is trapped in a weather akin to that of Northern European cities, the people long for a ray of sunlight. *Source*: *Cold Tropics* (*Recife Frio*). Dir. Kléber Mendonça Filho. Prod. Co.: Cinemascópio Produções. Brazil, 2009, 35mm, COR, 25min. Courtesy: Kléber Mendonça Filho (private collection).

with its history of violence, exclusion, oppression, and abuse of power. *Cold Tropics* can thus be regarded as a "blueprint" or "tutorial text" for all Mendonça Filho's cinematographic oeuvre, in the sense that it condenses, in a short film and for the sake of an ecodystopia, the director's interest in the SF genre, irony, and satire at service of exposing social inequality in contemporary Brazilian society. We must note that *Cold Tropics* came to light in an apparently stable period in the history of Brazilian democracy, with no explicit criticism directed at any particular government. Instead, the film's overall criticism seems to target a long history of social inequality and the prevalence of a neoliberal logic that dehumanizes cities and social relations. *Cold Tropics* criticizes the system; it opposes the status quo regardless of who is in power.[4]

Nostalgia for the sun, longing for the night. If in *Cold Tropics* the sudden low temperature exposes an unequal society, in Raul Lemos Arthuso's short SF film *Master Blaster—Hans Lucas's Adventure in Nebula 2907N* (*Master Blaster—Uma Aventura de Hans Lucas na Nebulosa 2907N*, 2013) the opposite occurs: it is endless daylight and heat that denounce capitalist exploitation. *Master Blaster* is a parody of Jean-Luc Godard's *Alphaville* (1965). In the Brazilian short, an intergalactic agent is sent to Nebula 2907N to collect information and find a solution for the mysterious appearance of a second reddish sun in the sky. The film repeats the general formula used by Mendonça Filho in *Cold Tropics*, a film style whose origins can be traced back to Jorge Furtado's short films *Isle of Flowers* (*Ilha das Flores*, 1989) and *Barbosa*. In *Master Blaster*, however, instead of a time traveler or a journalist, our hero is special agent Hans Lucas (Rômulo Braga), an ersatz copy of Godard's Lemmy Caution (Eddie Constantine). The appearance of the second sun helps "Work-Town" ("Cidade-Trabalho") fulfill its manifest destiny: with sunlight twenty-four hours a day, the inhabitants of Work-Town and Nebula 2907N are doomed to work incessantly. As in *Cold Tropics*, *Master Blaster* makes use of an absurd scenario to critique neoliberal capitalism. The businessmen in the film give cheerful interviews, as the economy grows ceaselessly with the uninterrupted production cycle. Restless workers, however, express their discontent. The film also takes a Foucauldian approach when its voice-over narrator (Hans Lucas) discusses the role of schools, how they keep children safe and train students to join the workforce in the future, while their parents spend their entire lives working.

A parody of George Lucas's Master Yoda or the Wachowskis' Oracle (Gloria Foster) in *The Matrix* can be found in Pepita, the "mentor," whose empty advice barely helps Hans Lucas. As in John Carpenter's *They Live!* (1988), Hans Lucas puts on sunglasses he finds in Pepita's place and has a sudden "epiphany" regarding the true origin of the red sun. As unveiled by Hans Lucas, the second red sun was artificially projected into the sky by a "power plant" antenna; part of a ploy put forward by the city's powerful businessmen, allied with the petty bourgeoisie and some "double-agent" workers to economically "develop" Nebula 2907N, thus keeping it forever as a "Work-Town." The film ends by reaffirming its debt to the French Nouvelle Vague, but especially to the Brazilian Cinema Marginal, and the night-and-day cycle is eventually restored to Nebula 2907N.

Hence, a fantastic event highlights the class struggle, which seems to be a systematic strategy in recent Brazilian SF cinema (mostly from 2009 onward). Environmental dystopias, or ecodystopias, underpin the political argument in films like *Cold Tropics*, *Master Blaster*, and Leonardo Martinelli's *Gray Lives* (*Vidas Cinzas*, 2020).

Martinelli's short mockumentary makes a social critique based on a surrealist premise, mixing real and fictional characters. The plot revolves around a "law" that prohibits color in Rio de Janeiro, leaving the city restricted to shades of gray.[5] Narrated by a female voice that speaks fluent French and evaluates the situation from a Eurocentric perspective, conceiving a heterogeneous and exotic reality, *Gray Lives* focuses on artistic and political protests and resignifies several real demonstrations as though people were protesting the color ban. The scenes are interspersed with speeches and interviews made by public figures such as actor Wagner Moura, Senator Lindberg Farias, journalist Glenn Greenwald, filmmaker Petra Costa, Senator Flávio Bolsonaro (eldest son of President Jair Bolsonaro), State Representative Marcelo Freixo, and Councilwoman Marielle Franco, who was assassinated on March 14, 2018. The film takes advantage of a rather tense political scenario in Brazil and in the city of Rio, making explicit references to the rise to power of militias and the murder of Marielle Franco—a crime with worldwide repercussions that is yet to be solved. *Gray Lives* pays tribute to the councilwoman and caused an uproar at its screening sessions.

## Rethinking Our Heroes and the Water Conflict

A hodgepodge of ecodystopia, social issues, and historical traumas (again, social-environmentalist cinema) appears in Luiz Bolognesi's *Rio 2096*.

Produced by Buriti Filmes and Gullane, *Rio 2096* revisits the history of Brazil over the last six hundred years. The narrative follows Abeguar (Selton Mello), an Indigenous man from the Tupinambá nation and an immortal character who lives through the centuries searching for reincarnations of his beloved Janaína (Camila Pitanga) while fighting in defense of the oppressed. Abeguar's immortal journey and his pursuit of Janaína's reincarnations suffuse the story with the kind of spiritualism that often appeals to Brazilian audiences—although this time also inspired by Indigenous legends. At the beginning of the film, Abeguar, in his "original" appearance, battles against the Portuguese and the Tupiniquins in 1565.[6] A few centuries later and under a new identity, Abeguar leads the Balaiada, also called the Bem-te-vis War, one of the most remarkable popular revolts of enslaved and oppressed people in Brazilian history, which took place in the state of Maranhão between 1838 and 1841. Still young and motivated in the mid-twentieth century, Abeguar joins the resistance against the military dictatorship in the 1960s and 1970s. Finally, in the late twenty-first century, the still youthful Brazilian continues to fight against the status quo in the water conflict of 2096, when Rio de Janeiro is a futuristic megalopolis where private militias exert power over the life and death of poor people. Drinking water has become a precious commodity worldwide: a few drops are more expensive than gallons of whiskey or gasoline. In Brazil, a company called Aquabrás (most likely a parodic version of the national oil company Petrobrás) owns the Guarani aquifer and therefore makes astronomical profits at the expense of people's suffering. In this scenario, Janaína works as an agent for the clandestine organization "Water for All" ("Água para Todos") and, like any rebel, is considered an "aquaterrorist." The idea of corporate water control reminds us of Alex Rivera's Mexican American film *Sleep Dealer* (2008), while the postapocalyptic Rio de Janeiro echoes Francisco de Paula's *Oceano Atlantis* (1993), as well as the futuristic Bogota atmosphere of *In August* (*En Agosto*, 2009), a Colombian short animation by Andrés Barrientos and Carlos Andrés Reyes. *In August* follows two characters living in two different periods, a fable that also mixes Indigenous legends with futuristic dystopia. On the references to Brazilian Indigenous mythology in *Rio 2096*, Bolognesi explains that he sought inspiration in Tupinambás's legends, especially in the tales about their good and evil deities, Munhã and Anhanguá (see Merten 2013).

Still, according to Bolognesi, *Rio 2096* fuses Brazilian history with a graphic novel aesthetic to tell an unofficial history of resistance in the country (Merten, 2013). Thus, a revision of Brazilian history that emphasizes deconstructing national myths and heroes in favor of speculating on the heroism of ordinary people constitutes the backbone of this film's script. The critique of field marshal Duque de Caxias, for example, serves this purpose.

Shortly after its premiere in Brazil in April 2013, Bolognesi's animated feature—made in the classical animation style—won one of the most important awards in animation: Best Film at the 2013 Annecy Film Festival in France. Considered the "Cannes" for animation, the Annecy Film Festival selected only nine films for competition, among hundreds of entries from all over the world. This was the first time in fifty-three years that a Brazilian film was selected.

As previously discussed in relation to ecodystopian films released during the military dictatorship or shortly after, nostalgia remains a visible trait in Brazilian cinematic approaches to social-environmentalism. Thus, *Cold Tropics* features a nostalgia for the sun, for a tropical past, while *Rio 2096* romanticizes a "Golden Age" represented by Brazilian Indigenous characters and their communion with nature. *Cold Tropics*, in its nostalgia for a "brighter" past, also evokes the "green" victimized by uncontrolled urban expansion.

Environmentalism and the rights of minorities and marginalized peoples are often, if not always, inseparable issues. Hence, aside from Afrofuturist films (or rather Brazilian SF films with a touch of Afrofuturism), the emergence of a "Fourth Cinema" (see Murray 2009)[7] or, more often, SF films starring Indigenous individuals or focusing on Indigenous issues, must be further examined. The animation *Rio 2096*, for example, already featured an Indigenous hero. But what about live-action movies?

## Amazofuturism: Native Replicants, Alien Invasions, and Reconnecting with Earth

If Bolognesi's *Rio 2096* can be seen as a cinematic example of Roberto Causo's Tupinipunk, the film's main character—the immortal Tupinambá—predicted, in a way, the newest trend focused on futuristic landscapes and characters set in the Amazon: Amazofuturism (Amazofuturismo), a new subgenre in Brazilian SF visual arts, literature, and cinema that began with João Queiróz's illustration "Cyberamazon" (see Dutra 2020).[8] As Queiróz explains (in Zuin 2019), "Cyberamazon was my first attempt to insert a character close to my ethnicity in a work of SF, something that I had never seen properly represented."[9] Literary Amazofuturism followed in João Queiróz's visual art footsteps in works such as Mário Bente's short story "The Pajemancer" ("O Pajemancer"; Zuin 2019) or Rogério Pietro's film *Amazofuturismo* (2021). Unlike Tupinipunk, which despite referencing a Brazilian Indigenous nation, does not necessarily focus on Indigenous communities, Queiróz's Cyberamazon and Amazofuturism elaborate a futuristic vision of the Amazon rainforest and its cultures and were also inspired by solarpunk, a subgenre that opposes the darkness and pessimism of cyberpunk by imagining a more sustainable future. The movies discussed below seem to illustrate or establish a fruitful dialogue with Queiróz's Amazofuturism in Brazilian cinema.

Produced by Capivara Filmes and written and directed by Portuguese artist Pedro Neves Marques, the 2017 short film *YWY, The Android* (*YWY, A Andróide*) is of particular interest here. Despite its minimalism, this short film presents an eloquent and thought-provoking experience, thus holding unprecedented symbolic power. Shot in the Brazilian southern state of Rio Grande do Sul, mostly in long and medium takes, this film features the Indigenous android YWY as she talks to a GMO (genetically modified) corn plantation in the Brazilian agricultural countryside. In an intimate moment, the artificial woman speaks to the plants about the "nature" of "artificiality," the manipulation of sexuality at the hands of white men, reproductive rights, infertility, labor, and agricultural monoculture, explaining that she is just as "artificial" as the manipulated GMO corn seeds. The implied spectator is unable to hear the voice of the corn; thus, the dialogue between android YWY, played by Indigenous actor Zahy Guajajara, appears to be a monologue. Some of Guajajara's lines and attitudes toward the camera, however, are quite ambiguous, and what at first seems to be a dialogue inferred by a monologue or soliloquy, can be also perceived as a conversation involving three "characters"—the android YWY, the corn plants, and the implied spectator. The film is inspired by the work of Brazilian writer José Guimarães Rosa, in which dialogues are commonly expressed by the voice of a single character—a narrative device often explored in powerful film adaptations or original works, such as the 2018 Oscar-nominated short film *Mother* (*Madre*), written and directed by Rodrigo Sorogoyen.

While watching *YWY, The Android*, it is impossible not to be reminded of movies like Ridley Scott's *Blade Runner*, Marek Piestrak's *Inquest of Pilot Pirx* (*Test Pilota Pirxa*, 1979), or Michael Crichton's *Westworld* (1973)—as well as the latest version of Crichton's original story, the HBO series *Westworld* (2016–). Yet, one crucial aspect gives Pedro Neves Marques's short film an unsettling and thought-provoking quality: the very presence of a nonwhite, female, artificial sentient being as the main character, unlike traditional SF cinema. By featuring a female Indigenous android, the movie points to a variety of related issues: the genocide of these original peoples (as already suggested by films such as Walter Lima Jr.'s *Brazil Year 2000*) and the "incongruity" behind an artificial human being that identifies with Nature, one that coexists peacefully with the environment. As Ginway notes, "As Haraway predicted, YWY is capable of subversion, since she is neither the mother of the past nor a prostitute of imperialist technology: she sets out to dismantle the traditional divisions between nature and technology. Neves Marques's Indigenous hi-tech cyborg also recalls Oswald de Andrade's concept of the "bárbaro tecnizado" [technofied barbarian] ("Manifesto antropófago" [Cannibalist Manifesto] 14), which implies a new paradigm that combines technology with the utopian sensibilities of Indigenous Brazilian cultures" (Ginway 2021, 95).

Oswald de Andrade's "Cannibalist Manifesto" ("Manifesto Antropófago")[10] was first published in May 1928, in the *Anthropophagy Review* (*Revista de Antropofagia*). Its first and third aphorisms are among the most famous statements made by Oswald and the Brazilian Modernist Movement: "Only cannibalism unites us. Socially. Economically. Philosophically," and "Tupi, or not Tupi, that is the question" (Andrade 2017, 49). Despite aphorisms like "But we never admitted the birth of logic among us" (Andrade 2017, 52), the manifesto unwittingly beckons some science fiction imagery in passages such as: "We had no speculation. But we had guesswork. We had Politics, which is the science of distribution. And a planetary social system" (Andrade 2017, 56). Brazilian SF writer Ivan Carlos Regina, in his "Cannibalist Manifesto for the Brazilian SF" ("Manifesto Antropofágico da Ficção Científica Brasileira," 1988), reappropriates Oswald's highly influential manifesto and criticizes the lack of imagination in the Brazilian SF literature, arguing that "we are not here to criticize the role of the machine, but to propose the aesthetics of man. We urgently need to devour, after Bishop Sardinha, the laser gun, the mad scientist, the nice alien, the invincible hero, the space warp, the evil alien, the girl with perfect legs and walnut brain, the flying saucer, which are as distant from Brazilian reality as the farthest stars. Brazilian science fiction does not exist" (Regina 1988).[11] Regina cites here the historical episode in which the Catholic clergyman Sardinha, a first bishop in Brazil, was killed and eaten by Indigenous people of the Caeté nation after his ship sank in the Coruripe River in 1556. Originally published in the fanzine *Somnium*, n. 30 (June 1988), Regina's manifesto concludes as follows: "We emulate technologies without knowing them. . . . Every day man proves that he is not worthy of technology. We want to awaken the iconoclast that lies in every Brazilian breast. Death to machine worshipers. A green-yellow caipora devours hamburgers, destroys satellites, swallows weapons and wrecks technologies. An Indian will descend from a bright, colorful star" (Regina 1988).[12]

SF and Indigenous futurisms meet once again in Pedro Neves Marques's *YWY*, this time featuring an Indigenous person as a human-made machine. Ginway further observes that "I subversion of coding, be it biological or cybernetic, seems to be at the center of Neves Marques's argument. It is an argument that questions traditional dichotomies and paradigms of the artificial and natural, showing that, with the breakdown of borders, ethical choices and agency become ever more critical. YWY embodies both Indigeneity and rebellion, helping us to imagine a future in which biological, political, and ontological categories will inevitably merge" (Ginway 2021, 98). Despite its short length (about seven minutes), carefully polished lines provide the film with a powerful discourse that reasonably extrapolates its frames and timespan. Several questions may come to the viewers' minds: for example, who created YWY, the Indigenous android? Additionally, toward the film's end, an ironic and unsettling line "plants" a question that anticipates the ending titles. When commenting on her staple food, YWY says that she eats that same GMO corn; she eats her "sisters" ("sisters" in artificiality), but not raw. She eats the corn after it is processed and becomes "energy," that is, fuel. A clear nod to the world energy industry, but above all to the American and Brazilian energy matrices, in which sugarcane and corn are processed to provide fuel for automobiles and other machinery. *YWY, The Android* is a strong example of minimalist, lo-fi Brazilian SF cinema infused with powerful philosophical stakes.

In fact, *YWY, The Android* is derived from an ending sequence of Marques's short film *Exterminator Seed* (*Semente Exterminadora*, 2017). In it, YWY (Zahy Guajajara) shares the lead role with Capivara (Luiz Felipe Lucas), an offshore oil rig worker who has been evacuated back to Rio de Janeiro, where the locals remain oblivious to an oncoming disaster: the massive oil spill that is contaminating the coast. Mixing documentary and SF, *Exterminator Seed* begins by introducing the oil spills in a clear documentary fashion, using news broadcast for voice-over narration. The ecological disaster immediately reminds us of similar, real catastrophes in Brazil, such as the oil spills that began in 2019 near the coast of Northeastern states. More than a year after the accident, 130 cities in 11 Brazilian states have suffered damage, and no culprit has been found. As Ginway puts it, "The on-location documentary style manages to evoke futuristic landscapes by using oil platforms and mechanized granaries as *mise-en-scène* for the two main characters as they share conversations about their lives" (Ginway 2021, 93). Despite the danger on the rigs, Capivara wants to return to the offshore oil fields. In the city, he meets and is aided by a woman, YWY, who convinces him to travel to her homeland in Mato Grosso do Sul to search for work in the soy and corn monocultural plantations. There, YWY tells him about the infertility characteristic of these transgenic plants and of an android such as herself. The focus shifts from oil spills and disasters related to humanity's constant quest for fossil fuels during the Capitalocene to inland plantations, notably agribusiness that revolves around soybean and corn exports.

As a longer short film, at twenty-seven minutes in length, *Exterminator Seed* seems to be less direct in its environmentalist and political discourse, and a bit more erratic in terms of pacing and focus. The movie also expresses a certain anachronistic quality in its worldbuilding, with an energy matrix still based on fossil fuel extraction and old trucks that transport soybeans and corn. The SF in the film is construed by dialogues and allusions to the off-screen "world," rather than truly estranging images and sounds. It relies on the notion of lo-fi sci-fi to build its speculative fictional world, which is not an issue, but compared with *YWY* and considering that *Exterminator Seed* features more characters and clearly invests in a more complex fictional world, its construction seems to lack the strength to pull the film out of the documentary gravitational pull. It is only in the final sequence featuring YWY's monologue that Pedro Neves Marques employs SF sound and imagery. Nevertheless, *Extermination Seed* retains a great deal of symbolism and speculation by alluding to contemporary Brazilian issues that, although mostly off-screen, are also addressed throughout the characters' conversations and the documentary-style footage.

The casting of Indigenous actors in SF films has increased in recent years. The 2018 feature-length film *The Kawa's Black Earth* (*A Terra Negra dos Kawa*) is perhaps the most ambitious attempt at Indigenous futurism in recent Brazilian cinema, being widely indexed and advertised as Brazilian-Indigenous SF—though the film was directed by a non-Indigenous, but Amazonian filmmaker, Sérgio Andrade. *The Kawa's Black Earth* tells the story of a team of scientists who, while excavating land in the Amazon in search of fertile black soil used for agricultural purposes, arrive at the land of the Kawa people and realize that the land possesses energetic and sensory powers.

Much like in his short *Cachoeira* (2010), and feature-length movies *Jonathas' Forest* (*A Floresta de Jonathas*, 2012) and *Time Was Endless* (*Antes o Tempo Não Acabava*, 2016), Amazonian director Sérgio Andrade resumes working on Indigenous motifs. In *The Kawa's Black Earth*, Andrade invents the Kawa (allegedly a branch of the real Tukano people, according to one of the dialogues) as a metaphor for all tribes. The plot revolves around a nuclear Kawa family—an older couple, Uçana (Severiano Kedassere) and Turyná (Ermelinda Yapario), and their children, siblings Kandra (Kay Sara) and Gatowo (Anderson Kary Báya)—who, throughout the movie, meet people from different backgrounds and ethnicities, including a group of Haitians. The dialogues recount Haiti's earthquake, a humanitarian disaster that ravaged the country, and the recent history of Haitian refugees in Brazil. Such an "ecumenical" attitude reminds us of cases like the Black Seminoles in Florida.

The peaceful and tolerant Kawa family lives in an area where the black earth, besides being highly fertile, has aphrodisiac and hallucinogenic properties, seen by the Kawa as linked to a spiritual rather than purely recreational experience. The relationship between the family and their land is key throughout the film. While the older couple has an organic relationship with the black earth, their son and daughter show different interests. Kandra shares the black earth with the scientists and ends up in a love triangle. Gatowo, in turn, tries to use the energy of the soil to create a machine capable of communicating with his "relatives" from other galaxies, in a clear reference to cosmologies common to several real Brazilian Indigenous ethnicities. The Kawa's black earth also functions as a natural energy source, as seen in scenes where the young son conducts experiments with spotlights, salvaged computer parts, and TV screens: when connected to the earth the electronic pieces turn on. Such scenes clearly evoke an Indigenous Brazilian cyberpunk or scrapper punk, perhaps even Roberto Causo's Tupinipunk (1996, 2015). Gatowo collects all the mechanical and electrical parts he finds around the region, including parts from an "aircraft graveyard" he and her sister happen to visit. Some of the scenes featuring Gatowo and his experiments are evocative of João Queiróz's Amazofuturism.

Played by Mariana Lima, Felipe Rocha, and Marat Descartes, the scientists orbiting the Kawa family seem to have different interests in exploring the Kawa soil. While a *deus ex machina* resolves the situation and restores protection to the Kawa's site, thus preserving their vital relationship to their land, the Kawa family welcomes apparently vulnerable people searching for shelter. Finally, they all engage in a communal ritual, and the film ends on a rather optimistic note. Once again, the general character of the Kawa family in Andrade's film presents a cinematic representation of João Queiróz's Amazofuturism in Brazilian cinema.

One of the most recent cinematic approaches to social-environmentalism in Brazil with a speculative and fantastic touch can be found in a short film that mixes documentary and SF, resulting in a creative work, as uncanny as the reality it tries to investigate. Released in 2019, Thiago Foresti's *Space Invasion* (*Invasão Espacial*, 2019) had a successful run in national and international film festivals, winning important awards in Brazil, such as the Best Editing Award at the 47th Gramado Film Festival. Written and directed by Foresti, *Space Invasion* came about while he and his film crew were shooting commissioned work in Lençóis Maranhenses. On their days off, they found the "seed" for *Space Invasion*. This SF short documentary discusses the impact of the Alcântara Military Base in the State of Maranhão, a rocket-launching site built within an inland quilombola community. The film makes extensive use of the syntax and iconography of SF cinema, including quotes from Robert Wise's 1951 film *The Day the Earth Stood Still*, to tell a story of alien invasion based on true events. On the one hand, the way Foresti and his team approached the occupation of the Alcântara base region—first by the Brazilian military, then by the US Army—seems very amusing. On the other, it acquires even more ominous and prescient tones with the Bolsonaro administration's open submission to Washington and Donald Trump. It's a movie about a double alien invasion. As the Brazilian Indigenous philosopher Aílton Krenak argues, "From the Northeast to the eastern border of Minas Gerais, where the Doce River flows through the Krenak Indigenous reserve, and in the Amazon, where Brazil meets Peru and Bolivia along the upper Negro River, in all of these places our Indigenous families are experiencing moments of great tension in their political relations with the Brazilian State. This tension is nothing new, but it has worsened because of recent political changes that have severely affected Indigenous communities" (Krenak 2020, 41). Brazilian SF ecodystopia, therefore, forcefully addresses an inseparable issue: the survival of Indigenous Brazilians and Afro-Brazilians, inasmuch as their relationship with the planet is radically different from that of the European colonizers and their descendants. Brazilian Indigenous Futurism and Afrofuturism are indelibly linked to SF ecocriticism in Brazilian SF cinema. For pre-Columbian Amerindians and Africans, SF happened not as a thought experiment but as a real in vivo experiment hundreds of years ago. This "real SF" involved alien encounters, alien invasions, abductions, slavery, pandemics, sinister technologies, and more. Hence Aílton Krenak calls our attention to the fact that

> a European adventurer arriving on a tropical beach left a trail of death in his wake, and he did so without knowing he was a walking plague, a two-legged weapon of mass destruction, an angel of the apocalypse. He had no idea, nor did his victims.
> For those visited by these wayfarers, the world ended in the sixteenth century. I'm not exonerating anyone from blame, or relativizing the gravity and brutality of the machine that drove the European conquests. I'm merely pointing out that the events that ensued were the great disaster of that time, much as the conjuncture of factors labelled the Anthropocene by a select few is the disaster of ours. For most of us, however, that abyss goes by other names—social chaos, generalized misgovernment, loss of quality of life, degraded relationships—and it's swallowing us whole. (Krenak 2020, 69)

On this note, Krenak (2020) ends his book *Ideas to Postpone the End of the World*. At the same time, Latin American SF cinemas, Afrofuturist cinemas, and Indigenous futurisms have been translating into movies the apocalypses and postapocalypses already experienced by Africans and Amerindians, when these peoples faced the horrors of "real SF" at different times and places.

## Toward a Brazilian Afrofuturist cinema

Several of the films mentioned above, along with *Bacurau* by Juliano Dornelles and Kléber Mendonça Filho, and *White Out, Black In* by Adirley Queirós, can also be regarded as preliminary and introductory examples of Brazilian Afrofuturism in cinema, considering their script, political discourse, and characters. The term "Afrofuturism" first appeared in 1994, when critic Mark Dery interviewed SF writer Samuel R. Delany, Greg Tate (frontman of the band Burnt Sugar), and Professor Tricia Rose. On this occasion, Dery used "Afrofuturism" to define the "Speculative fiction that treats African-American themes and addresses African-American concerns in the context of 20th century technoculture—and, more generally, African-American signification that appropriates images of technology and a prosthetically enhanced future" (1994, 180). Later in his interview, Dery also explained that "African-American voices have other stories to tell about culture, technology, and things to come. If there is an Afrofuturism, it must be sought in unlikely places, constellated from far-flung points" (1994, 182). From a more ecumenical and universal perspective, films like *Bacurau* and *WOBI* can also be understood as Brazilian Afrofuturist proto-manifestos. These movies feature Afro-descendants as their main characters, a group that represents most of the excluded and marginalized people in Brazil since colonial times. In both *Bacurau* and *WOBI*, it is the Afro-descendant characters who drive the stories, make the most meaningful decisions, and offer another possible "future." We could add to these two feature films a handful of Brazilian short films more overtly associated or identified with Afrofuturism, such as André Novais Oliveira's *Backyard* (*Quintal*, 2015) and Grace Passô's *Republic* (*República*, 2020).

Brazilian Afrofuturism gained more visibility throughout 2020. For example, the Scotland-based "Africa in Motion" festival (October 30–November 29, 2020), organized the session "Afrofuturism in the Brazilian Way," featuring Ana do Carmo's *The Woman at the End of the World* (*A Mulher No Fim do Mundo*, 2019), Leon Reis's *Cartuchos de Super-Nintendo em Anéis de Saturno* (2018), Diego Paulino's *Negrum3* (2018), Sabrina Fidalgo's *Personal Vivator* (2014), and Renata Martins's *Sem Asas* (2019).

*Personal Vivator*, for instance, is based on a slightly similar premise as Jonathan Glazer's *Under the Skin* (2013), with extraterrestrial visitors intent on investigating (and perhaps taking advantage of) human society. The alien who sets out into the field to film a documentary has seventy-two hours in the form of a Black man posing as a "gringo" filmmaker named Rutger (Fabrício Boliveira). The field is the city of Rio de Janeiro, a landscape encompassing both bourgeois middle-class apartments and the favela. The first "specimen" that attracts the interest of "documentary filmmaker" Rutger is a white woman from a middle-class family, but soon the alien turns his attention to the family's maid, Marinalva (Ana Flávia Cavalcanti), a young Black woman. Fascinated by Marinalva, Rutger admires people like her: Afro-descendants who work hard for the delight of their white bosses. According to Rutger, Afro-descendants are "personal vivators," workers who take care of their white employers. Soon after, while recording an interview with Marinalva on the *laje* (open-air rooftop) of her house in a favela, Rutger discovers that the maid had also hired a nanny, and so she too aspires to be a boss. This Afrofuturist social SF short film is punctuated by a series of social, political, and economic commentaries, particularly on the legacy of slavery and the economic and educational rise of the poorest under the Workers' Party (PT) administrations. Somewhat like Kléber Mendonça Filho's *Cold Tropics*, in which the fantastic climate change in the city of Recife serves to expose the racism, socioeconomic inequalities, and real estate speculation in Brazil, *Personal Vivator* uses the semantics and syntax of SF to reflect on Brazil's social contradictions from a more overtly Afrofuturist perspective.

Another strong example of Brazilian Afrofuturist SF cinema is Rossandra Leoneé's *Blackout* (2020), in which a Black, female hacktivist has found ways around the system, to "circuit-bend" it and "turn the tables" in favor of the oppressed in a style similar to the Wachowskis' *The Matrix*. The film thus presents a preamble to a near future in which cyberhactivism can finally undermine the long history of inequality and violence against the Afro-Brazilian population. *Blackout* is a feminist Afrofuturist Brazilian film where cyberpunk and the favela short-circuit the system once again.

But among the best representatives of Brazilian Afrofuturist cinema, one film that caught our attention is Grace Passô's *Republic*, due to its eloquent minimalism, the performance of its star and director (Grace Passô), and the juxtaposition of dystopia and dream. In *Republic*, a work made during lockdown in early 2020 following the outbreak of the Covid-19 pandemic, Grace Passô plays a character dealing with a disturbing dystopian reality, or a dream she cannot escape—in that it is "a shaman's dream." The short film begins with Grace's character (named Grace) waking up alone in her apartment when she receives a call informing her that Brazil does not really exist, that it is just a dream. Visibly moved, Grace opens the window of her apartment and cries out into the cityscape. An aerial exterior shot reveals poverty and vulnerability on the streets. From Grace's perspective, we find her döppelganger screaming in the streets. Back at the apartment, Grace calls her mother and asks her to turn on the television immediately. She explains to her mother that "Brazil is a dream," that the country does not exist, that nobody really exists, that the house is a dream, and that everything is a dream—a shaman's dream. "The world exists, except Brazil." "Someone is dreaming of Brazil," she adds, "soon the person who is dreaming may wake up," and when that happens, she and her mother will be free. Dystopia is portrayed as a nightmare. As in Adirley Queirós's *WOBI*, *Republic* can be seen as another eloquent "outcry" toward the history of exclusion in Brazil, amplified through the prism of a Brazilian cinematic Afrofuturism.

Another excellent example of recent Afrofuturistic Brazilian lo-fi sci-fi can be found in Ary Rosa and Glenda Nicácio's feature film *I'm Back!* (*Voltei!*, 2020), a minimalist tale about the reunion of three sisters in Brazil in 2030. Filmed in the state of Bahia, *Voltei!* presents a dystopian story that extrapolates the social and political context of Brazil in 2021: the pandemic persists while an authoritarian government remains in office. The situation has become so chaotic that electricity is no longer supplied to the population. The entire film is set in a single location, a kitchen in the apartment of two sisters, Alayr (Wall Dias) and Sabrina (Mary Dias), who meet at home at the end of the day. Amid gas lights, the two sisters decide to have a beer while listening to a political trial broadcast on the battery-powered radio. It is a trial that may change the course of a "powerless" country. The sisters share a conversation about their day and the past, with memories of their dead mother and missing sister, Fátima (Arlete Dias).

*Voltei!* presents a near-future Brazil in which political repression has only intensified. The movie alludes to both the recent far-right and the military dictatorship (1964–1985) by mentioning two "absent" characters: the mother, who was arrested and murdered by the military regime somewhere between the 1960s and 1970s, and the third sister, who has been missing for eight years since she sang a censored song in the streets during the Brazilian Carnival. As Alayr and Sabrina continue talking, pro- and antigovernment politicians vote on a trial that could result in the impeachment of the authoritarian leader. Though no name is mentioned, we infer from the sisters' dialogue that it is probably Jair Bolsonaro who remains president in 2030. By the time the viewer is reasonably familiarized with the two absent characters, victims of authoritarian governments, a strange event occurs. Frantic knocks on the door surprise the two sisters, and they discover that Fátima has come back from the dead to mingle on this historic night.

At this point, the film could take the horror route, but directors Ary Rosa and Glenda Nicácio instead use identification and sympathy tactics to provoke further engagement, employing a minimalist and realistic approach reminiscent of cinema vérité. After the initial shock, Fátima tells her story, and the sisters discover that she was not murdered by the state. She was in fact arrested by the military police along with other "rebels" and sent to a distant "ghost town." Though for a long time they believed themselves to be under strict surveillance, the state simply abandoned them. Eight years is indeed a long time, and one may wonder why only now Fátima has returned to her sisters. Based on the history of the Brazilian military dictatorship, however, one could accept the argument that Fátima stayed away from her sisters while living underground. But the explanation remains murky throughout the movie, as its most crucial allegory depends on Fátima being reunited with Alayr and Sabrine at this decisive moment—when politicians are deciding on the fate of the dystopian country in a political trial held in the capital, Brasília. The film continues, the three sisters delving deeper into their memories and affections, concluding that "Brazil hurts" ("O Brasil machuca"). What initially resembled a comedy or comedy-horror film turns into a lo-fi Afrofuturist sci-fi, deeply anchored in the current Brazilian reality.

The historical racist stigmata are exposed once agIin in Matheus Moura's allegorical *Purple Dictatorship* (*Ditadura Roxa*, 2020), a dystopian short film featuring Yeda (Meibe Rodrigues), a green-faced woman that sells bread to provide for her sick husband Goulart (Paulo Trindade). In the context of the "green people," one may grasp the reality of those who live on the margins of a conservative "purple society," where an opportunity makes Yeda rethink her identity and values.

Moura's short invests in metaphors and allegories to represent Brazilian apartheid, the country's history of segregation that reactionaries have tried to negate lately. The movie is quite effective in its social criticism, even if it subsumes the cleavage in two colors whose symbology are not, in principle, antithetical. Greens constitute the lowest and lower medium strata of society, both economically and socially speaking: they are drivers, street musicians, cooks, residents of poor and peripheral neighborhoods. Purples make up the elite, middle, and upper-middle classes, consisting of liberal professionals and authorities. Is it possible to change from one color to another? Yes. Greens are allowed to participate in a contest known as "Mega Loto," whose prize is the possibility of undergoing surgery that changes the person's face permanently, from green to purple—a passport to a new life, the social ascension so desired by all. A prize that Yeda wins.

Matheus Moura's choice of Black actress Meibe Rodrigues to play Yeda overlaps reality and fiction. Over time, the film shows the existence of purple-faced Black people, a fact that makes the whole situation of social inequality more complex, as in fact happens in Brazil. Ascension opportunities are indeed allowed as exceptions, but under the strict management of the ruling classes. In *Purple Dictatorship*, the only instrument of ascension is the "Mega Loto," an allegory of the possibilities of social ascension in real Brazil. Matheus Moura's film thus reminds us of somewhat similar Brazilian futuristic dystopias, such as *3%*.

The scene where Yeda attends a dinner party with three "purples" after winning the lottery is particularly eloquent. At the table, the hosts congratulate the "Mega Loto" winner while being served by "green" servants. One of the purple-faced men in attendance appears to be a doctor and turns out to be Dr. Indigo (Marcus Labatti), the surgeon who will be responsible for Yeda's surgery. The process, he explains to the future patient, is called "transpigmentation," and she will have to take some precautions right after the surgery, such as avoiding direct sun exposure for a few days. But as a poor woman who takes care of her bedridden, wheelchair-using husband, Yeda explains that she no longer intends to undergo surgery so that she can continue to care for him. The three "purples" express great disappointment and try to persuade her otherwise, talking about the opportunity that she would be giving up. Yeda then asks if she could continue to care for her companion even after taking on a purple face, but the hosts immediately refute such a possibility.

Interestingly, while the speech of Yeda and the green characters is fully understandable, the purples remain unintelligible throughout the film. They emit a distorted noise, mixed with children's babbling and birdsong, as if speaking another language. Subtitles are required to understand what any purple-faced character says. This linguistic mismatch seems to represent the same disagreement observable between the lower and upper classes in Brazil: each speaking a completely different "language," despite sharing Brazilian Portuguese as the official language.

After dinner, a pensive Yeda takes a bus home. The next scene shows a priest celebrating a Catholic religious ceremony. He's purple. Yeda then tries to get her sister-in-law to care for her husband Goulart, which she refuses, condemning Yeda for wanting to throw her life and marriage away, completely disregarding her husband's feelings. Here, guilt and resentment seem to fill the atmosphere of the scene. Guilt and resentment, both such powerful feelings in the Brazilian social context.

In the scene where Yeda decides to euthanize Goulart by suffocation so she can undergo "transpigmentation," the brutal action is eclipsed by images of Catholic saints pinned to the walls and pictographic representations of biblical passages where the illustrated characters have purple-dyed faces. This suggests that the color purple, a symbol of social superiority, finds moral support or justification in the hegemonic religious dimension of that society: Catholicism. The purple human being mirrors the image of God and holiness, while the greens find no parallel in the pantheon of saints—they are given no narrative of transcendence. This is an allegory of a well-known fact throughout human history: the "official" religions, which support and are supported by the state, prevail. In recent Brazilian history, Catholicism has often been touted as the country's official religion, although Christianity is, in reality, more likely to be the most popular, owing to the fact that neo-Pentecostalism, or evangelical religions that branched off from Protestantism, appear to have accumulated the most political, economic, and even paramilitary power (remember the militias in Rio de Janeiro). Strictly speaking, evangelical religions condemn depictions of God, Jesus, and sanctified figures in images (paintings or statuary), thus *Purple Dictatorship* seems to underline Catholicism as the religion of the ruling class. But the film's message could also be interpreted more broadly. Although based on secularism like all modern states, this principle is largely ignored in Brazil, even by the authorities. Recall that a Catholic crucifix hangs on the wall of the highest court in the country, the Supreme Court. *Purple Dictatorship* is another dystopian Brazilian SF film that, following the example of Gabriel Mascaro's *Divino Amor* (2019), uses Brazilian religiosity to make an acid critique of Brazil's disparity and long history of inequality, referring in allegorical terms to the social, political, economic, moral, and sanitary upheaval that has recently befallen the country.

But, to date, one of the most meaningful parables against structural racism (Almeida 2020) deep-rooted in Brazilian society and the historical social and economic debt to African-Brazilians publicly appeared in 2021 as a feature-length film that conveys an alarming dystopian tale. *Executive Order* (*Medida Provisória*, 2020), an adaptation of Aldri Anunciação's play "Namíbia, No!" ("Namíbia, Não!"), is actor Lázaro Ramos's début in film direction.

Directed in collaboration with Flávia Lacerda (co-director), *Executive Order* is set in a near-future Rio de Janeiro, when the Brazilian government is sued by the young, successful lawyer Antônio Gama (Alfred Enoch) and eventually condemned to pay massive reparation to all descendants of enslaved Africans in the country (echoes from Adirley Queirós's 2014

*White Out, Black In* may be heard in this fictional premise). The authorities see the just reparation as the state's utter financial doom. Thus, the authoritarian government responds by signing a decree that enforces the exile of all Black citizens (now addressed as "accentuated-melanin citizens") to Africa as an excuse to repay the debts of slavery—this operation immediately reveals itself as a new wave of eugenics with the "desirable" whitening of Brazilian society. Citizens are measured by their skin color, captured, and sent to Africa against their will. While the army and police enforce the law, Antonio, the lawyer, gets involved in a personal drama as he, his uncle André Rodrigues (Seu Jorge), and his wife Capitu (Taís Araújo) become victims of the authoritarian state among millions of other people. Capitu, a doctor who goes missing after her shift at a hospital amid the announcement of the decree and the beginning of the find-and-capture operation, eventually finds an underground resistance known as the "Afrobunker." The trio (Antônio, Capitu, and André) fights the madness that has taken over the country and joins the resistance that inspires the people.

Obviously, this nationwide state operation is not free from opposition. Many "accentuated-melanin citizens" refuse to be banished, and "partisan" cells begin to appear. The most significant is the so-called Afrobunker, an underground community shaped after the old Brazilian quilombos that provided safety for runaway enslaved people. As a "neoquilombo" (Ramos 2022, 19) that appears in only five scenes of the film, the Afrobunker is one of the most exciting and stimulating fictional worlds within *Executive Order*. It is a place of resistance that had once served as a gathering spot for lovers and Carnival party-goers; in this futuristic dystopia, Carnival is forbidden by the authoritarian state. In the wake of the decree, the Afrobunker now stirs a peaceful communal strategy for resistance that reminds us of the long-lasting "institution" of Brazilian Carnival, the quilombos, and even contemporary favelas and urban "occupations." It is worth noting, as highlighted by Ramos (2022, 78), how Black people in *Executive Order* do not handle firearms with ease, as is shown in countless other films set in favelas with Black actors as drug dealers. The Afrobunker and the main characters' acts of resistance are primarily peaceful and not driven by revenge. Though André Rodrigues does come to the verge of bursting out in rage, the trio's reactions often assume a naïve perspective.

But first and foremost—as can be seen in a pivotal scene set in the Afrobunker toward the end of the film—the characters' choice is for civilization instead of brutality, collective engagement, empathy, and solidarity as a more profound and successful response to state authoritarianism and the long-lasting history of racial inequality. The trio of main characters performs a final scene that stresses this choice, eventually resorting to ingenuity instead of violence. The film's ending remains open to further speculation with a clear nod at a promising future that encompasses a kind of national epiphany.

As told by Lázaro Ramos (2022), *Executive Order* was derived from his experience as director of Aldri Assunção's play "Namíbia, No!," originally written as a dialogue for the stage. Excited with the play's repercussions and potential, Ramos decided to adapt it into a feature-length film along with screenplay co-authors Aldri Assunção, Lusa Silvestre, and Elísio Lopes Jr. The film entered the production stage in 2019, before the outbreak of the Covid-19 pandemic and during the first months of Jair Bolsonaro's administration. However, as Lázaro Ramos (2022, 76) explains, the film was never made to attack the current government overtly. "Yet, if some of the attitudes of this government bear similarity to our story, the problem is not fictional, it's reality." (2022, 76).[13]

*Executive Order* was completed at the beginning of 2020 and was ready to be theatrically released. However, the outbreak of Covid-19 profoundly impacted the film's career. When the world's film festivals and film markets eventually began to adapt to the pandemic, bureaucratic problems involving the National Film Agency (Ancine) and the Tribunal de Contas da União (TCU) further delayed *Executive Order*'s premiere in Brazilian theaters. The press and public opinion expressed suspicion about possible censorship imposed by Bolsonaro's administration. *Executive Order*'s avant-premiere took place at the South by Southwest Film Festival in Austin, Texas, in March 2020. The film was screened on-site at the Indie Memphis Film Festival in Moscow and Havana in the same year. In 2021, with the Covid-19 pandemic still spreading, Ramos (2022, 70) says that he and the producers had to opt for online screenings in several film festivals worldwide.

If, on the one hand, the pandemic was highly unfavorable to the film's career, it may have, on the other hand, made *Executive Order* seem to be even more "attached" to reality. For instance, due to budgetary restraints, Ramos decided to reduce the number of police officers involved in scenes of the deportation operation enacted by the "Ministry of Return" ("Ministéro da Devolução"). Ramos envisioned a future in which all law enforcers work masked, optimizing the reduced number of actors playing these agents (2022, 69). This visual motif is reminiscent of previous cinematic dystopias (e.g., George Lucas's 1971 film *THX-1138*) and immediately addresses the pandemic's reality.

Ramos (2022) and film critics often mention highly successful dystopian films or streaming series such as *Black Mirror* and *The Handmaid's Tale* while addressing *Executive Order*. However, it is worth recalling more radical, experimental cinematic approaches to near-future utopias/dystopias, such as Lizzie Borden's *Born in Flames* (1983) or Peter Watkins's *Punishment Park*. Aldous Huxley and George Orwell's creative lineage is also frequently evoked in Lázaro Ramos's film reviews. As in Ed Rampell's review for the *Hollywood Progressive*:

> Despite—or because—of its vast Black population, in 1888, Brazil became the last nation in the Western Hemisphere to abolish slavery, a quarter century after Lincoln signed the Emancipation Proclamation. As one can imagine, racism remains an issue for contemporary Brazilians, whether they are aboriginal peoples or of African descent, etc.
>
> All this is backdrop for the gripping plot of *Executive Order*, which like George Orwell's *1984* and Aldous Huxley's *Brave New World*, is a dystopian look at a futuristic society. (Rampell 2021)

*Executive Order* was screened for the first time in Brazil during a tense session at the Rio Film Festival on December 15, 2021, where it won the Jury's Special Award, though it had not been authorized to be commercially released by that time. Finally, *Executive Order* was theatrically released on April 14, 2022. Since then, it has divided critical opinion. The film script, direction, and final cut demonstrate some irregularities in pace, rhythm, mise-en-scène, and "organicity." These ups and downs could be ascribed to the neophyte status of Ramos as a filmmaker. Sometimes, a "second hand" or "second mind" is perceived in the script, but mainly in the mise-en-scène and edit—likely Flávia Lacerda's.

Notwithstanding, *Executive Order* galvanized attention due to its contemporaneity. It was released around the end of Bolsonaro's military administration. Regardless of the power of *Executive Order* as a cohesive artwork, it found its place as the cinematic outcry of a people on the brink of irreversible destruction. According to Katiúscia Vianna (2021), "At the end of the day, *Executive Order* is a film as paradoxical as Brazil. It is a horror film, although it will make you laugh. Moving, yet it also yields an intensely rational debate. Imperfect, yet unmissable."[14]

The controversial term "accentuated-melanin citizens" adopted by the authorities to classify and exile African-Brazilians in *Executive Order* directly resembles the issues addressed by Shalini Kantayya's documentary *Coded Bias* (2020). A similar term, if not verbatim, also appears in Kantayya's documentary that focuses on how racism and sexism remain in facial recognition algorithms. These algorithms, designed mainly by white developers, transport old, archaic, racist worldviews into artificial intelligence. The parallelism between two contemporary films, *Executive Order* and *Coded Bias*, a fiction film and a documentary, is an alarming harbinger of dystopian SF approaching our daily lives.

*Executive Order*s can be seen as a thought-provoking parable that may illustrate some of Sílvio Almeida's main concepts in his book *Structural Racism* (2020). According to Sílvio Almeida, since the work of thinkers such as Frantz Fanon (1986 [1952]), Abdias do Nascimento (1966), and Alberto Guerreiro Ramos (1957), not to mention several others, a theory on racism has evolved throughout three stages: (1) the individualistic approach to racism; (2) the investigation of racism in institutions, as an institutionalized mechanism; and (3) structural racism. The first, the individualistic approach to racism, is very limited in scope and accuracy and focuses on the relations between racism and subjectivity. It tends to criminalize racism by subsuming it to individual attitudes, with no further investigation of the roots of racism, the racist social machine, or how racism can be instrumental in the history of capitalism. The second, the concept of "institutionalized racism," delves further into the problem by addressing the relations between racism and the modern state. How institutions can be racist despite racism being a crime is a central issue in this approach. The third, structural racism, encompasses all three linkages (racism-subjectivity; racism-state; racism-economy) to analyze in more detail the roots, the platforms, and the structures that sustain racism in the institutions and individual or collective behavior (Almeida 2020, 35–57). As Almeida remarks, it is impossible to fully understand racism as simply prejudice or an individual or collective deviating behavior. History, politics, and, notably, economics are crucial factors in structuring racism worldwide, even though each nation has developed its own particular kind of racism. For instance, racism in Brazil is significantly different from racism in the United States. However, both are equally catastrophic and have left indelible marks on their respective societies.

Almeida's book (2020, 20) revolves around two main arguments: first, contemporary society cannot be fully understood without the concepts of race and racism. Second, to fully understand race and racism, it is crucial to master social theory. Almeida contends that racism is always structural, an inseparable element that constitutes a society's economic and political organization. In other words, racism is "normal," that is, it ordinarily emerges in any given society not as a pathological phenomenon expressing any kind of abnormality. Racism provides meaning, sense, logic, and the technology for the reproduction of violence and inequality that shapes contemporary social life. Thus, any other approach to racism that does not deem it as a structural phenomenon, constitutive of our economic and political system, is incomplete as an ad hoc or limited theoretical approach to a far more deep-rooted phenomenon (Almeida 2020, 20–21). Drawing on Giddens (1984) and other authors, Almeida explains that institutions are just the materialized surface of a given social structure or mode of social life that finds in racism one of its constituent, organic elements. In other words, "The institutions are racist because the society is racist" (Almeida 2020, 47). Still according to Almeida, "*Racism is a systematic form of discrimination that has race as its foundation, and that manifests through conscious or unconscious practices that culminate in disadvantages or privileges for individuals, depending on the racial group to which they belong*" (2020, 32; emphasis in the original).[15] In summary, Almeida pragmatically considers racism as a "technology" that is instrumental to modern states under capitalism throughout its colonial and imperialist phases. Such "technology" still impregnates judicial systems and state administrations worldwide, justifying governments' reproduction of violence and guaranteeing the economic elites' hegemony.

Indeed, structural racism as a theory is far more complex than any single film. *Executive Order* is one of many other cinematic representations that partially address the issue. Ramos's film could be added to a "constellation" of short and feature-length films that revolve around this problem, in part or integrally, directed by either white or Black people. To name just a few: Sabrina Fidalgo's *Personal Vivator*, Eduardo and Marcos Carvalho's *Chico* (2016), Diego Paulino's *Negrum3*, Grace Passô's *Republic*, and even the streaming series *3%*, produced by Netflix. Films like those from Kléber Mendonça Filho can also tackle structural racism, yet from a white director's perspective.

However, in *Executive Order*—perhaps more explicitly than in any comparable feature film targeted at broader audiences—one can find a patchwork of allegories addressing the three approaches racism (individualistic, institutionalized, and structural racism). Contemporaneous with the launch of Sílvio Almeida's book, *Executive Order* may be one of the first films that overtly address structural racism in Brazil, at least among the films with the most prominent box office draws and significant production budgets.

The fictional premise that fuels the film's narrative concerns both institutionalized and structural racism. The financial reparation for descendants of enslaved Africans, a penalty imposed by the judiciary system on the Brazilian state, not only presents the admission of a historically racist nation but also a possible "dilution" and "filtration" of such racism by the state apparatuses. The subterfuge employed by the government to escape the penalty, that is, the substitution of financial reparation for a one-way trip to Africa (in fact, exile), only stresses the racist policies internalized by the institutions and paves the way for the disclosure of structural racism. The Afrobunker scenes are perhaps the most telling passages that suggest Brazil's structural racism in the film.

Taking a closer look, under a "microscope," some characters are stereotyped to emphasize the individual approach to racism. This is the case for Izildinha (Renata Sorrah), Antônio and Capitu's neighbor, and Isabel (Adriana Esteves), a public servant working for the "Ministry of Return." Isabel's character is the most complex in this regard, as she cannot disguise her racist mindset while doing her job in the "acceptably" racist manner. As the lens pulls back and focuses on a bigger picture, the racist mechanisms within the institutions become more visible. By looking at the film from a broader perspective, exploring the entire plot and the scenes in their respective connections, structural racism can be found: no wonder the Afrobunker is set underground, apart from the institutions. In *Executive Order,* structural racism provides the rationale and technology for the institutions/state apparatuses' policies concerning African-Brazilians. However dystopian it may be, the film's plot could not hold up if Brazil were not a racist state. It does not matter if racism is a crime and the Brazilian state is charged as guilty in Ramos's dystopian film. The similarity with the "real" Brazil is astonishing. The "return policy" put forth by the government is just the alibi, a slightly odd situation that justifies the story. It is far from being completely absurd, nonetheless.

It is worth noting that Sílvio Almeida's approach to structural racism in Brazilian society draws on a wide array of authors, but first and foremost Florestan Fernandes (2017), Guerreiro Ramos (1957), Michel

Foucault (1997), and Achille Mbembe (2003). Almeida points out that Florestan Fernandes had already established that the (false) dilemma "class struggle" vs. "race struggle" are not mutually exclusive, and neither struggle exhausts the other (Almeida 2020, 188). In addition to Fernandes's (2017) accurate analysis of the legacy of slavery and racism as a constitutive element in the broader structure of Brazilian socioeconomic relations, Almeida's theory is also substantially based on Mbembe's (2003) concepts of "necropower" and "necropolitics." Mbembe's own ideas take shape in their dialectical relation to Foucault's concept of "biopower" and the neoliberal, contemporary globalized world. *Executive Order* provides an interesting cinematic example of Mbembe's necropolitics when the state's "final solution," the deportation of African-Brazilians to Africa, is contested or simply refused by the people being exiled against their will. These descendants of enslaved Africans start resisting, and those who do not accept their exile are simply hunted and killed by the police forces. Leave or die are the options. The film then presents a cinematic equivalent to Mbembe's "colonies," particularly the Palestinian cases of Gaza and West Bank. Despite the good humor and irreverent approach to the "entrapment" of African-Brazilians, *Executive Order* provides us with a thought experiment: what if there was an entire Algeria inside Brazil? Since not all African-Brazilians accept being "sent back" to Africa, a new Palestine-like cartography takes place, with African-Brazilians being hunted or confined to ghettoes like the Afrobunker. The Afrobunker in Ramos's film may be seen as a metaphor for some of the clearest examples of necropolitics: the South African apartheid and the Palestinian situation in Gaza. The bunker works as a haven in the midst of a city under siege, a "colony." According to Mbembe, the colonies' usual lawlessness stems from the racial denial of any common bond between the conqueror and the native (Mbembe 2003, 24).

Lázaro Ramos and Flávia Lacerda's film thus exacerbates and fictionally parabolizes Mbembe's necropolitics and, by extension, Almeida's analysis of Brazilian structural racism. Antônio, Capitu, and André, as well as all the other African Brazilians (once simply Brazilians) thenceforth become strangers in a strange land, foreigners in the very country where they were born. As put by Almeida, racism does not hinge on the fact that one is an immigrant or not, but on one's connections to a given ethnic group or minority, even though the members of such a group are officially recognized as national citizens. Thereby, the order produced by racism does not only impact society in its external affairs, as in the case of colonization, but it affects, first and foremost, its inner configurations, by setting hierarchical patterns, naturalizing historical forms of domination and justifying state intervention on discriminated social groups, as one can see in the daily lives of Black and Indigenous peoples (Almeida 2020, 178).

The film's accentuated colors, though, are remarkably familiar, as if the story might happen in Brazil just the day after tomorrow.

## Afrofuturism and Environmentalism

Shot in Chapada dos Veadeiros National Park (a region of exuberant nature in the state of Goiás, Midwestern Brazil), Tiago Esmeraldo's *At the Edge of the Universe* (*À Margem do Universo*, 2017) mixes Afrofuturism with aspects of Indigenous culture and overtly ecological discourse. This short film features a Black protagonist (astronaut Awada, played by Cameroonian-Brazilian actress Petra Sunjo) in a utopian tale of space exploration spoken in Portuguese and Suruwahá, an Indigenous Brazilian language with fewer than 150 speakers alive today. The Suruwahá people (also known as Zuruahãs) are an Indigenous group totaling around 130 people, which inhabit the Zuruahã Indigenous Area of southern Amazonas and speak a language of the Arawá family. In *At the Edge of the Universe*, Adawa is introduced as an "organic unit" sent to explore "Planet X33-1," supposedly uninhabited and located in a remote area at the edge of the galaxy. Once "awakened" by her commander and wearing her astronaut "armor," Adawa begins to fulfill her mission. She explores the lush landscapes to collect data and samples, according to her commander's instructions. Adawa is put in danger, though, when the mission is hacked or sabotaged, with limited life support systems and the risk of missing her extraction. On her way to the extraction point, Adawa finds a male "organic unit" who had lost consciousness by a pond (see fig. 8.2). She rescues him, and the pair continue to search for an escape plan. Near the end of the movie, Adawa has no more oxygen or power supply, and the male unit refuses to follow the order to leave her behind. Finally, they realize the planet's atmosphere is breathable and, in fact, the planet is inhabited by humankind, a species that became intergalactic, as in the series *The Expanse* (2015–). Planet X33-1 is actually Earth, and the two explorers had been taken to an uninhabited region as a precaution by the Earthlings. The end credits report that 12 billion people live on Earth, 79 billion humans inhabit the solar system, and 436 billion humans populate the entire Milky Way. *At the Edge of the Universe* is a good example of Afrofuturism mixed with Indigenous culture in recent Brazilian SF cinema, reminding us a bit of previous Afrofuturist works like Cristina De Middel and Pep Bonet's *Afronauts* (2014). Despite the strong influence of an Afrofuturist perspective on the art direction and costume design, as well as on the role and casting of Adawa, *At the Edge of the Universe* ends with the portrayal of a colonial language as Earthers' language, with Adawa and her off-screen hostess both speaking Portuguese. As the movie's multicultural worldbuilding and narrative universe cannot be contained in just one single short SF film, chances are that Esmeraldo may further expand his work into other media, such as a graphic novel.

As part of a global definition of the phenomenon, Freitas and Messias (2018) sustain the notion of a Brazilian Afrofuturism, stating that "the future will be black, or it won't be" (2018, 423).[16] To distinguish between Afrofuturism and Afropessimism, the authors take the Brazilian short film *Chico* as an example. Set in 2029, *Chico* presents a deeply dystopian

Figure 8.2. Adawa (Petra Sunjo) finds another astronaut on the mysterious planet. Source: *À Margem do Universo* (2017). Courtesy: *At the Edge of the Universe (À Margem do Universo)*. Dir. Tiago Esmeraldo. Brazil, 2017, 20min. Tiago Esmeraldo (private collection).

Brazil where the federal government's authoritarian and technocratic policy authorizes the kidnapping of Black children living in peripheral areas to contain crime. In this regard, *Chico* echoes Tadao Miaqui's *Projeto Pulex* (1991), a Brazilian short animation in which the authoritarian government's technocracy carries out Black genocide by infesting peripheral communities with fleas.

Traits of Brazilian Afrofuturism can also be found in Pedro Aguilera's series *3%* (2016–2020), the first original Brazilian production by Netflix and the second produced in Latin America. The series' first season aired in November 2016, becoming a hit. Aesthetically close *basurapunk* (a Latin American cyberpunk in which garbage provides raw materials for technology and anti-establishment mobilizations), *3%* can also be illustrative of the lo-fi sci-fi aesthetic mode. According to Amauri Terto in a *Huffpost Brasil* article (2017), *3%* was "the most watched non-English series in the US"[17] at the time of its release.

The series piques our interest not only as the most-watched Latin American production among Netflix audiences in 2016 but also because its international release took place after the "white" coup that overthrew President Dilma Rousseff (democratically elected in 2014 for a second term) in a broad maneuver involving lawfare and palace intrigues. *3%*, therefore, makes its debut on Netflix in a political environment shaken by a coup d'état that marked Brazil's turn to the far right and paved the way for the rise of Bolsonaro. In other words, the show's four seasons were streamed while Brazilian citizenship and democracy were being hijacked and undermined, from the 2016 coup to the tragedy of over six hundred thousand deaths in 2021. Today, it is clear that the genocidal policies of the Bolsonaro administration, its neglect of the pandemic, and its omission and direct interference during the spread of the virus have led to thousands of preventable deaths among the Brazilian population, particularly among the most vulnerable—Blacks, Browns, homeless, favela residents, Indigenous populations—who lack access to information and Covid-19 prevention. Unfolding over four seasons, *3%* presents itself as one of Brazil's potentially most popular SF parables. A futuristic adventure that embodies an allegory of the history of slavery, inequality, exclusion, violence, and authoritarianism that mark the country's five-hundred-year history.

Over the first three seasons, the series follows the trajectory of characters who move between two worlds: one utopian, the island of Maralto, and the other dystopian, the desertified, unhealthy, and collapsing Continent (identified with Brazil). The plot revolves around a trial known as

"The Process" that each year selects 3 percent of all twenty-year-olds for immigration to Maralto, an island of prosperity and ecological balance that maintains, through the use of force, a mass of excluded people on the impoverished continent. In addition to the sea, the notorious Process and a fascist military police force guarantee access for only a few to the technological wonders, abundance, and harmony of Maralto. Throughout the three first seasons, characters' actions at times strengthen or weaken this unique system of concentrated prosperity. Once again, we see the environmental theme being juxtaposed or confused with a revision of Brazil's history, its past and present of inequality, violence, and exclusion, with few exciting prospects for the future. In the fourth episode of the second season, for example, directed by Jotagá Crema, the character Marco (Rafael Lozano) recalls the history of his family, the Álvares, when each of his ancestors got their ticket to Maralto. This episode, perhaps one of the best in the entire series, recaps the central argument of Sérgio Buarque de Holanda, among other authors, who criticizes the perpetuation of a false meritocracy in Brazil, all against the backdrop of ecodystopia. Its third season, perhaps the weakest, most irregular, and disheartening of all, coincides with the first year of Bolsonaro's presidency.

The series' last episode, released in 2020 during the pandemic, may seem overly synthetic, naïve, or dependent on a *deus ex machina*. Unlike many recent Brazilian films such as *Bacurau*, *3%* abandons violence in favor of a peaceful, optimistic resolution. Characters who, up to this point, had opposed each other never come to blows; even the oppressed people of the continent, represented by main characters such as Joana (Vaneza Oliveira), Rafael (Rodolfo Valente), and Xavier (Fernando Rubro), renounce violence as a legitimate form of upheaval. It may seem indefinable, naïve, and conformist, but we can look at this ending with more complacent eyes and ears, less indoctrinated by a narrative "logic" widely infiltrated in action, fantasy, or SF movies (especially from the US), in which gunshots, blood, and brutality abound, and revenge is the main driving force behind the characters. In this more optimistic light, the resolution of *3%* "breaks" that logic by investing in congregation and pacifism as a way out of a historical and structural impasse, at least symbolically. Instead of blood and violence, we see fraternity, a parade, and a song performed by Brazilian singer-songwriter Chico César in a very Brazilian contribution to the genre—for better or worse.

All in all, the conclusion of the saga offers a pacifist discourse, pointing to tolerance and the need not only for action but also congregation:

Antonio Carlos Belchior's[18] song interpreted by Chico César underlines such ideas, dictating the pace for society's reorganizing movement. This message clearly speaks to the Brazilian scenario, dominated by political polarization and intolerance. The ecological dimension is added to the political substrate: 3% concludes that it is not possible to survive, nor build a future, based on authoritarian caesuras. Environmental issues cannot be compartmentalized, nor remain infinitely restricted to a specific geographic space or social stratum. Rather, they are a global challenge compounded by conflicts of race, class, or nations that will have to be overcome. Taken together, the four seasons of 3% seem to suggest that the environmental problem will never be solved definitively and exclusively by cybernetic or computational science and technology. Such a state, supported only by technology and optimization of resources, is fragile—a simple electromagnetic pulse puts an end to Eden and promotes the return of fallen angels. Society must rise to a new level of social advancement. Resolution needs to be sought by means of more advanced, humanistic, and inclusive science and social technology: something attempted within the third season, which despite being the weakest, introduced an alternative community, the Concha, located on the continent and dependent on more sustainable technologies. The future is in humanity, rather than beyond it. To a certain extent, 3%'s environmental discourse nods to Afrofuturist ideals adapted to the Brazilian context, while incorporating a recycling aesthetics originally associated with cyberpunk but also present in Brazilian Tupinipunk and in postapocalyptic narratives that seek in ruins, garbage, and waste a premonitory iconography of the future. Its inclusive cast, featuring trans characters and characters with disabilities, as well as a female Black protagonist, seems to emphasize the ecological message underlying the series' central political plot.

3% is also one of the few series representing true diversity on screen. Its characters are extremely varied when it comes to color and ethnicity, gender, political stance, and creed, and all of this is plainly evident in the final season. Characters include Black, Brown, white, heterosexual, queer, and trans profiles, among others. This can be another positive contribution to global audiovisual SF: real plurality beyond the frequent paternalistic gaze toward minorities and the oppressed.

The importance of Black or Brown characters and Afrofuturistic speculation in 3% are inseparable from the ecological/environmental issue that permeates all seasons and explains much of its dystopian atmosphere, making the series a true, contemporary example of Brazilian SF ecodystopia.

Such leitmotif is most evident in the first few seasons, notably the first, when the fictional world is introduced to viewers: a vast number of people of all ethnicities and colors live in huge favelas in the continent's wasteland, while a small fraction of this population lives on the island Maralto, a wealthy utopia with plenty of water, food, and cutting-edge technology.[19] Reminiscent of the US film franchise *The Hunger Games* (2012–2015), every year Maralto offers young people from the continent the opportunity to "cross the border" and embrace a "new life" on the island. To do so, the twenty-year-olds must pass a series of psychological, mental, and physical tests, after which only 3% will be admitted into "paradise." This concept of "testing" young people of all origins and colors evokes the Brazilian educational practice of the "vestibular," a test that grants individuals admission to public state universities, allegedly the best higher education institutions in the country. The "vestibular" and types of competition evoked by 3% address the long history of false meritocracy and social inequality in Brazil, with the white elite always starting the race miles ahead of the Black and poor populations.

## Somewhere Over the Rainbow— or under the Sun: Queer Futurisms

Another example of Cyberagreste or Sertãopunk can be found in the psychedelic, queer SF road movie *Rodson (Rodson ou Onde o Sol não tem Dó)*, 2018–2020) by Cleyton Xavier, Clara Chroma, and Orlok Sombra. Shot in the northeastern state of Ceará, *Rodson* depicts a future near the turn of the twenty-second century where reading is forbidden, and any kind of artistic expression is considered a crime. Only mass production and consumption are allowed. Rodson (Orlok Sombra) is a young man who feels out of place in this repressive society controlled by the "Anarcocrente" government, a theocratic police state. His creative mind conceives Caleb, Rodson's alter ego, who takes him out on the road without the comfort of air conditioning. The duo goes on a journey in search of the perfect hallucination, under the merciless "2,000° C sun." Along the way, they meet "good citizens" like the traditional middle-class family, the sadomasochistic police, the militia, a TV pastor, and the digital influencer Evy Topstar. Eventually, Rodson meets the rebel leader Cavalona Dishavada (Lyna Lurex) and her cyborg gang—public enemy number one. In the end, Rodson finds refuge in another dimension.

This anarchic-cannibalistic-carnivalesque-psychedelic SF film establishes a dialogue, voluntarily or not, with the late 1960s Cinema Marginal and mid-1970s Brazilian experimental cinema, notably with movies such as Rogério Sganzerla's *The Red Light Bandit*, André Luiz Oliveira's *Meteorango Kid—Herói Intergalático*, Ozualdo Candeias's *Zézero* (1974), and Luiz Rosemberg's *A$suntina das Amérikas* (1976). In *Rodson*, however, the ludic, carnivalesque, chaotic narrative inherent to experimental cinema's usual iconoclasm is catalyzed by electronic music, circuit-bending, and contemporary hacker culture.

Somewhat eschatological, *Rodson* is also representative of the *basurapunk* aesthetic in which trash is resignified by peripheral hackerism. To some extent, it reminds us again of artistic collectives such as the aforementioned Gambiologia, a Brazilian group based in the state of Minas Gerais. Gambiologia is a contemporary approach to *gambiarra*: an untranslatable word from Brazilian Portuguese that means "shoddy improvisation," broadly speaking. "Gambiologistas" research how the Brazilian tradition of adapting, improvising, and finding simple and creative solutions to small, everyday problems can be applied to contemporary art and digital culture. "Gambiologistas" define their movement as "Art, Design, Technology, Invention, Reuse, Education—with a Tupiniquim accent."[20]

Alongside *Rodson* as a northeastern Brazilian postapocalyptic SF, or simply Sertãopunk film, with references to the electronic music scene and Queer and hacker culture, is the short film *Abjetas 288* (2020) by Júlia da Costa and Renata Mourão, shot in Aracaju, state capital of Sergipe. In a dystopian future, Joana and Valenza travel aimlessly across a northeastern city. Inspired by electronic music and a noisy soundtrack, the characters walk the streets while physically performing their feelings on being misfits in a repressive society. *Abjetas 288* tackles issues as varied as territorialities, identities, and meritocracy, all with an ironic tone and using allegorical elements that reference the popular history of Aracaju.

Brazil's only representative at the 2021 Sundance Film Festival, Matheus Farias and Enock Carvalho's *Unliveable* (*Inabitável*, 2020), a short film from the state of Pernambuco, features a desperate mother searching for her transgender daughter, mysteriously missing for days. The movie mixes a thriller atmosphere with SF, especially around the abduction plot, which can be interpreted both literally and metaphorically. Farias and Carvalho's short film uses SF iconography or tropes to address a particularly sensitive issue in Brazil: the rights of transgender people.

In *Unliveable*, Marilene (played by Luciana Souza) searches for her daughter Roberta, who had gone out partying. Injecting social issues into a suspenseful plot, the short follows the journey of a mother worried about her child amid the genocide of Brazil's trans population. As pointed out by Mendes and Silva, "Brazil is the country with the highest number of lethal crimes against LGBT people in the world" (2020, 1709). Although referring to a recent era, the film's production began three years prior to its 2020 release. According to *Unliveable*'s writer and director Enock Carvalho, the work on the film script started in mid-late 2017, when Brazil was already going through serious political destabilization. Carvalho recalls those were times of great fear and uncertainty. The script kept changing, in parallel to the political events, until it was time to shoot the movie. *Unliveable* was shot in December 2019, and postproduction work continued over the following months (Carvalho qtd. in Vinicius, 2020).

As Vinicius (2020) notes, *Unliveable* works as a synthesis of the symbolic and structural violence inflicted against the LGBTQIA+ community in Brazil. The story is not an isolated case, and Roberta's disappearance translates to feelings of fear, violence, and lack of protection that queer individuals experience. As director Matheus Farias explains, Brazil has never been a safe country for LGBTQIA+, especially for trans people. But since the 2018 elections, the country had been taken over by an even more worrying hostility. Brazil is the leading country in terms of murder of transgender people. In the film, Roberta's disappearance is the driving force of the story, since their disappearance is not considered an ordinary event. There is always much violence orbiting the disappearance of a trans person. This state of emergency may account for a constant sense of fear and threat to which LGBTQIA+ people are subjected every day (Farias qtd. in Vinicius 2020).

*Unliveable* is particularly successful in its approach to an extremely sensitive social issue, the genocide of the LGBTQIA+ population in Brazil, via SF tropes and syntax, evoking an atmosphere of otherworldliness reminiscent of alien abduction stories, but with local colors. The movie also adopts a narrative pace and aesthetics that evoke Todorov's theory of the fantastic in literature, as the story unfolds with increasing hesitation on the part of the characters, but shared with us, the viewers.

Another example of female-focused, feminist SF can also be seen in shorts like Maria Leite's *Tarik's Puzzle* (*O Quebra-Cabeças de Tarik*, 2015). With meticulous art direction and skillful visual effects, *O Quebra-Cabeças de Tarik* is a delicate stop-motion animation with a well-written script, reminiscent of something from the Eastern Europe school of animation (e.g., Jan Švankmajer), in its poetic use and crafting of small wooden or metal objects not to mention its use of nuts or chestnuts as constitutive elements of the scenes, the action, and the characters. *O Quebra-Cabeças de Tarik* seems to be a free adaptation of Mary Shelley's novel *Frankenstein* (1818), with a feminist slant and simple ingenuity. It is a delicate film that activates a whole repertoire or iconography of SF cinema, starting with James Whale's *Frankenstein* (1931) and its sequel, *Bride of Frankenstein* (1935), by the same director.

Another paradigmatic case of feminist SF in Brazilian cinema is Clarissa Campolina's *Solon* (2016). The film in some ways provides an SF visual elaboration of the ancient prophecy attributed to Antônio Conselheiro:[21] "and then the backlands will turn into seacoast and the seacoast into backlands" ("O sertão vai virar mar e o mar vai virar sertão"). Campolina's 2016 experimental short film establishes a fruitful dialogue not only with environmentalism but also with visual arts, dance, and SF, in a dreamlike cinematic fable of the world's creation through the appearance of a mysterious creature amid a wasteland. Inhabiting an extremely arid and barren landscape, the creature Solon gradually assumes different shapes as she learns to move and explore her body, gradually diverging from the background. The creature pours water from her limbs, thus "nourishing" the once dry and smoking land. As the landscape changes, so do the characters. Eventually, a world is born: likewise, a woman is born. Shot in the state of Minas Gerais, the film recalls the Mariana ecological disaster on November 5, 2015, with the collapse of the "Fundão dam" belonging to the Samarco mining company (controlled by the multinational companies Vale and BHP Billiton). In addition to nineteen people, thousands of animals were killed. The dam failure released 45 million m$^3$ of toxic mining waste, causing short and long-term effects on the environment and affecting the lives of thousands of people, including the Krenak Indigenous reserve (see Krenak 2020, 45–46). Opening with eerie imagery and accompanied by an intriguing musical score, *Solon* takes on a dreamlike, otherworldly atmosphere that not only revisits the biblical myth of Adam and Eve (perhaps prompting us to inquire "what if Adam *were* Eve?") but also seems loosely inspired by the Greek myth of the Phoenix, with the possibility of countless rebirths.

*Solon* and other world SF movies that rethink our relationship with the planet are highly in tune with new horizons of SF art in any medium, counterbalancing Aílton Krenak's (2020) criticism of the most popular type of SF cinema: the American blockbuster. In discussing conversations between Brazilian Indigenous leader and Yanomami Shaman Davi Kopenawa and the French anthropologist Bruce Albert, published in a recent book titled *The Falling Sky: Words of a Yanomami Shaman* (2013), Krenak explains that

> people can live in the spirit of the forest. With the forest and in the forest. I'm not talking about the film *Avatar*, but about the lives of twenty-odd thousand people—some of whom I know—who inhabit the Yanomami homeland on the Brazil-Venezuela border. This territory is being destroyed by roving prospectors and threatened by the mining industry and by the perverse corporations I mentioned before, which have no tolerance for our kind of cosmos—for the imaginative capacity and existence of a people like the Yanomami. (Krenak 2020, 31–32)[22]

Contemporary Brazilian and Latin American cinema has been helpful in restoring one of SF's most fascinating vocations: the ability to genuinely speculate about alterity and about possible encounters with other cosmic views and other cosmoses—not necessarily relying on pure spectacle and visual effects to achieve more plural and thought-provoking speculations.

Alternative views inspired by SF on the relationship between humankind and the planet also appear in a very short film that mixes ecological awareness, nativism, electronic music, and psychedelics. Produced by Cria_Ciber Research Group (Grupo de Pesquisa Cria_Ciber) from Universidade Federal de Goiás (Federal University of Goiás, UFG), and directed by Ciberpajé (Cybershaman) Edgar Franco, Luiz Fers (Luiz Carlos Ferreira da Silva), and Amante da Heresia (Léo Pimentel Souto), *(In)Finitum* is a psychedelic, hypnotic short film composed of an explosion of shapes and colors suggesting altered states and otherworldly landscapes. According to its synopsis, *(In)Finitum* features a posthuman Horus who reintegrates into nature after the collapse of the human species, living a psychedelic experience of reconnection with the cosmos. Made with digital rotoscoping, this posthumanistic SF presents a humanoid figure wearing a mask reminiscent of those worn by black plague doctors in sixteenth-century Europe. The character is barely distinguishable from the colorful background, but we can see that he is at peace with his environment. Subverting the conventional contrast between form and content, figure and background, the film thus suggests a full integration between the human being and the environment, as if a living being could not be separated from its surroundings whatsoever. It appears, therefore, to evoke a posthumanist spirit in tune (or at least partially in tune) with some Indigenous futurism, and the critique of prevailing white ideologies realized by Aílton Krenak's ideas. To some extent, *(In)Finitum* seems to converge similarly on issues also addressed by Clarissa Campolina's *Solon*, particularly the relationship between body vs. environment, which in both cases turn out to be body + environment. With a soundtrack by Posthuman Tantra, *(In)Finitum* has one brief spoken line: "Only Experience knows! Only Eternity is!"[23] The end credits explain that this movie is a "short-aphorism" ("curtaforismo") authored by Ciberpajé.

Another example of art from Cria_Ciber Research Group is *The Burial of Gods* (*O Enterro dos Deuses*, 2020), the first Brazilian animation to utilize the DeepDream neural network in post-production. The video was produced, directed, and animated by Diogo Soares, alias Caos Nechrofagos Soturnums (CNS for short), who was also responsible for the venture into DeepDream. *The Burial of Gods* was written by Edgar Franco (Ciberpajé) and Diogo Soares (CNS), and the duo also created the film's soundtrack. Conceptually hybrid, the video can be seen as an animated short or as video art for Ciberpajé's musical project.

This DIY animation uses visual metaphors and hermetic/occult symbols to reflect on the recent explosion of Christian monotheistic religions that have allied with neo-fascism to maintain the status quo. Its overall concept was inspired by the following aphorism by Ciberpajé: "When all the gods are buried with their so-called holy books, humanity will awaken. Empathy and love will reign in post-humanity!"

Set in a desert with an occult pyramid symbolizing the cosmic tomb of the gods, *The Burial of Gods* creates a retro 1990s digital aesthetic. Post-production required a slow process of inserting each of the base frames of the video into the Deep Dream neural network to obtain the final frames. The result is an intense digital "psychonautic" journey, and the video should be watched in the dark to better visualize the effects. Franco and Soares's *O Enterro dos Deuses* is a good example of Brazilian experimental SF cinema with cross-cultural imagery focused on posthumanism.

Written and directed by Henrique Arruda, *The Last Romantics of the World* (*Os Últimos Românticos do Mundo*, 2020) is a pearl in the latest of Brazilian SF cinema; a contemporary queer version of Jean-Luc Godard's episode in *Ro.Go.Pa.G.* (1963), "The New World" ("Il Nuovo Mondo"). As a "Queer-fi" short film, *The Last Romantics in the World* tells the story of lovers Pedro (Carlos Eduardo Ferraz/Gilberto Brito) and Miguel (Mateus Maia/Sóstenes Fonseca). The night before the world ends due to a mysterious, lethal pink mist spreading across the planet, as in Iuli Gerbasi's *The Pink Cloud* (*A Nuvem Rosa*, 2021),[24] Pedro, frontman "Magexy" of the band Magexy and the Lunatics, falls in love with Miguel and the couple decides to spend their last hours together. The next morning, they jump into an old convertible and hit the road, heading out into the wild. Pedro and Miguel will spend the last minutes of their love story closer than ever, surrounded by nature as the hazardous pink mist approaches.

*The Last Romantics of the World* is a highly metatextual work. It simulates the neon aesthetics of the 1980s and the tube TV image texture typical of late twentieth-century television channels. The film even emulates the subtitles often featured in movies aired by TV Globo in the 1980s and 1990s, indicating "Part 1," "Part 2," and "Finale"—a partition imposed by TV advertising. The characteristic TV or VCR "noise" is present throughout the film. *The Last Romantics of the World* also employs what is now called *vaporpunk*, a nostalgic style that emulates 1980s electronic music, CGI, and retro aesthetics (see fig. 8.3).

Toward the end, Pedro and Miguel ask each other: What if this was all just a moving picture? What if the pink mist was nothing but visual effects? One of the best SF love stories ever made in Brazil, *The Last Romantics of the World* then delivers a brilliant plot twist that subverts the original trope, expanding the notion of SF outlined initially. Its overall message and ending titles ("Love Yourselves!"/ "Amem-se!") reiterate the political stance taken by the film: *The Last Romantics* was released in 2020, under a solid conservative wave in Brazilian society and in the wake of the 2018 presidential election, which voted a self-declared racist and homophobic man into office. Today, Brazil is considered one of the most unsafe countries for LGBTQIA+ people by NGOs, with one death per day and high rates of hate crimes against queer people (see Sousa and Arcoverde 2019).[25] Produced by Filmes de Marte in partnership with Portela Productions and Tarrafa Productions, *The Last Romantics of the World* was supported by the State of Pernambuco (FUNDARPE) and the Brazilian Culture Secretariat (11th FUNCULTURA/AUDIOVISUAL).

The central themes of racism and homophobia in Brazil are at the core of another brilliant Brazilian SF film, a recent case of lo-fi sci-fi that magnificently utilizes SF tropes to address the country's widespread and enduring record of crimes against Blacks, homosexuals, and Black gay

Figure 8.3. Pedro and Miguel (Mateus Maia and Carlos Eduardo Ferraz) wait for the end of the world, as the pink cloud falls from the skies. *Source*: *The Last Romantics in the World* (*Os Últimos Românticos do Mundo*). Dir. Henrique Arruda. Prod. Co.: Filmes de Marte, Portela Produções, Tarrafa Produtora. Brazil, 2020, 22min. Photo by Barbara Azevedo / Filmes de Marte. Courtesy: Henrique Arruda (private collection).

men. Drawing on Spielberg's *Close Encounters of the Third Kind* (1977) and *The X-Files* series (1993–2018), Susan Kalik and Thiago Gomes's *Above our Heads* (*Sobre Nossas Cabeças*, 2020) tells the story of two young men who go to an abandoned mansion on the outskirts of Salvador to make contact with UFOs.

As Alfred Hitchcock once pointed out, it is better to start with a cliché than to end your film with one (cited in Carrière and Bonitzer 1990, 88).[26] Jean-Claude Carrière and Pascal Bonitzer also said that "the cinema is a man who arrives on horseback in a town in the West, and we know nothing about him. He will define himself little by little, by his gestures, by his looks" (1990, 40).[27] Susan Kalik's excellent script gradually unveils the "mystery," as the story unfolds, taking on different contours shifting as the characters talk and react. First, we have a seemingly banal tale of two nerds seeking contact with aliens; then, a love story subtly seems to emerge from the connection between the two characters. Third, we discover another third character that, although absent, is of great importance and was loved by both Cícero (Dan Ferreira) and Alexandre/Xande (Danilo Mesquita). Fourth, we confirm the presence of a love story, but one in the past: Xande had a relationship with Cicero's older brother George, who was murdered. Cícero lost his brother to racial hatred, and perhaps also to homophobia, and he reminds Xande of his beloved George. SF then returns to the story as Xande tells Cícero that he has bargained with extraterrestrials so that they would both be rescued, then and there, by a UFO. Xande wants to save Cicero from George's fate by forcibly taking him to another planet, but Cícero vehemently refuses, and the two have an argument that escalates. Xande grabs Cícero, who then pushes him to the ground. Finally, the story gains a "sixth hue," so to speak, with that ominous light from above (typical of abductions) appearing behind Cícero. Xande exclaims in excitement: "Cícero. I knew it! Our time has come, Cícero." Cícero stands up, turning his head to the skies, but we never see the true source of the light. Finally, he walks away, leaving Xande lying on the ground. The film ends according to Todorov's (1975) fantastic: we will never know if there was indeed a close encounter, a UFO in the skies. Unlike Andrew Patterson's 2019 feature film *The Vast of Night*, which pays homage to Rod Serling's *The Twilight Zone* and also *The X-Files*, no flying saucer ever appears in *Above our Heads*. But the SF dimension is key to Kalik and Gomes's film: it underlines the brutal reality of an extremely racist and homophobic society. Brazilian structural racism, described by several authors, including Silvio Almeida (2020), is a central topic lurking on the surface of *Above ur Heads*' SF narrative. Its lo-fi sci-fi quality, benefitting from a well-crafted script, seems to be symptomatic of a realist SF cinema from the Global South, an often-political, socially minded SF cinema. The "escape" envisioned by Xande can be interpreted as a dead end, a conundrum, but also as a seductive symbol of alternative futures. Despite its degree of mourning and melancholy, the film is far from a conformist piece: both characters take action, each choosing and doing the best they can. Cícero says emphatically: I'm not George! George was him, and I am me! I have a whole life ahead of me, are you insane?" In deciding to stay and face his reality, Cícero also carries the promise of an alternative future, regardless of the aliens' providence (or not).

This brief overview of Brazilian Queer SF ends with a leap of faith: a rather modest independent production, yet rife with powerful cinematic poetry on "what if" another Brazil had been possible. Produced by Mariana Zani, written and directed by Joel Caetano, the animated short *Splendid Cradle Mission* (*Missão Berço Esplêndido*, 2021) presents a thrilling time-travel tale in which a Black woman changes the future of Brazil by providing new origins for its political leader. Set in a near future where the totalitarian government leader is an immortal head kept in a "cyber jar," our heroine is a time traveler whose mission starts on the two hundredth birthday of this "Supreme Leader" (see fig. 8.4). A TV show hails the leader by recounting his memoirs, the importance of his strict upbringing, and his stern father who helped him build a country dedicated only to "good citizens." For a moment, behind the TV host, we can see that the Brazilian flag has turned into a simulacrum of the US Star-Spangled Banner, in yellow and green. The TV host further explains that today's perfect regime of civil obedience began with the population-wide implantation of a neural control microchip the moment its citizens are born. This microchip, explains the TV host, allows the Supreme Leader to rule over the entire country with an iron fist, through a network connecting all citizens to its "lethal" mastermind. The TV show is suddenly interrupted as the "Splendid Cradle Mission"[28] is initialized. Its success depends on the proper relocation of the leader as a child, 199 years ago: any resemblance to James Cameron's *Terminator* franchise is no coincidence. The heroine is the leader of a group of "non-microchipped"

Figure 8.4. The time-traveling-heroine watches the TV show that celebrates the 200th birthday of the "Supreme Leader" of a dystopian Brazil, in the far future. *Source*: *Mission Splendid Craddle* (*Missão Berço Esplêndido*). Dir. Joel Caetano. Prod. Co.: RZP. Brazil, 2021, 4 min. Courtesy: Joel Caetano (private collection).

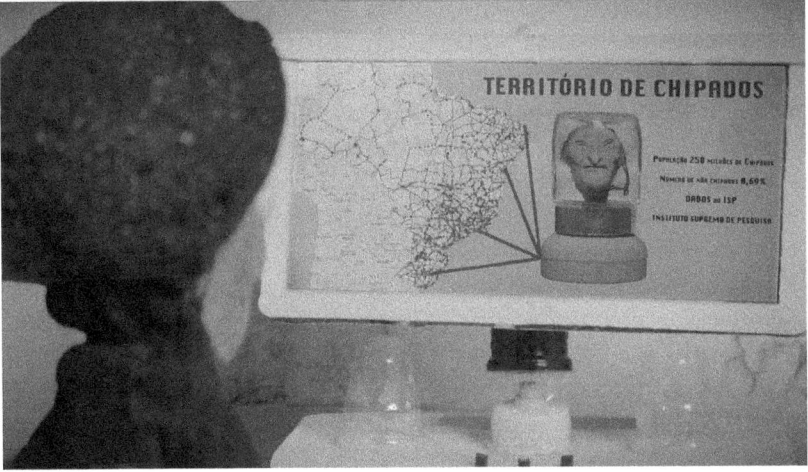

rebels who are constantly hunted by the police state. As she is initiating her time-travel mission, a "police drone" (creatively made from a microphone attached to two mic jackets, somewhat evocative of the ED 209 police robot in Paul Verhoeven's 1987 film *Robocop*) appears and opens fire, but it is too late: the "time jump" has already started and the heroine escapes, arriving at apartment no. 66 in an old, decaying building. Bleeding from a bullet wound, she manages to enter the apartment where an old man is sleeping on the couch and a rifle is hanging on the wall. The old man sports a mustache reminiscent of Adolf Hitler's and does not wake up as the heroine steps inside. A baby's cry grabs her attention and she moves into one of the rooms. The AI guiding her confirms: "target locked" and "execute mission." She approaches the baby's crib, and a flash of light follows. Over a black screen, the voice of a TV host announces the two hundredth death anniversary of an important leader who had a beautiful life story. The same TV host from earlier reappears on the screen but this time speaking in a less aggressive tone. He explains that two hundred years ago, the leader was left as a baby on the doorstep of a couple, Isabela and Melissa, who decided to adopt him. In his inauguration speech, he emphasized how his mothers had always taught him about sympathy, equal rights, inclusion, empathy: all values that he praised in his government, resulting in the creation of one of the most socially and economically balanced countries in the world, with one of the highest HDIs, and an example for future generations. Our heroine bleeds to death as the TV host finishes his tribute to the leader and, in the usual journalese, adds: "and now, sports. . . ." Cut to black. Ending credits.

*Splendid Cradle Mission* is a spark of wit and hope amid the dystopian reality of Brazil in 2020–2021. This (very) short stop-motion animation, with an extremely creative script, brilliantly synthesizes the general zeitgeist and the need for change that many of the aforementioned feature-length films have elaborated on in more detail. Despite the film's clear nod to Hollywood SF films like the *Terminator* series, the film is far from a mere simulacrum; rather, it revisits and resignifies well-known SF tropes, giving them renewed character. The heroine in *Splendid Cradle Mission* travels back in time to fix the future, changing the history of the "Supreme Leader": in this "fixed" future, no longer a "Supreme Leader," but a true leader. By changing the child's environment and moving him from a repressive and intolerant home to that of two tolerant and loving mothers, the heroine changes the trajectory of an entire nation. As naïve as this kind of thought experiment may be, it provides a breath of fresh air in the often bleak atmosphere of several recent Brazilian SF films, offering a time-travel tale that fills the genre with hope and high levels of creativity and craftsmanship dedicated to low-budget SF cinema.

## Winds of Change? Eco-Social-Criticism Again and Again

As these pages were being written, the world was enduring the Covid-19 crisis. With poorer and underdeveloped nations more severely impacted by the pandemic, in Brazil an antiscience and negationist federal government only made things worse. Besides the expected economic crisis, political persecution and attacks against culture, education, and freedom of speech in Brazil have further weakened numerous previously lagging industrial sectors, such as our audiovisual and film industries. With the film industry struggling under the Covid-19 crisis and far-right federal government, Brazilian SF has been kept alive by a new generation of Brazilian filmmakers who see the genre as a flagship of change. Young directors like Thiago Foresti, Leonardo Martinelli, Marco Antônio Pereira, Mariana Zani, Joel Caetano, and Matheus Moura, among many others in the most diverse states of Brazil, have been tackling issues such as class struggle, gender, Afrofuturism, environmentalism, and democracy through their invaluable contributions to Brazilian SF cinema.

The titles mentioned in this chapter, especially Henrique Arruda's *The Last Romantics in the World*, Iuli Gerbase's *The Pink Cloud*, Clarissa Campolina's *Solon*, and Cyberpajé's experimental films, among many others in this book, could be related to Mark Bould's *Anthropocene Unconscious* (2021) insofar as climate change often propels their narratives, literally or symbolically.[29] However, the following movies are more overtly focused on climate change and the Anthropocene.

*The Pleasure of Killing Bugs* (*O Prazer de Matar Insetos*, 2020), by Leonardo Martinelli, addresses climate change and the current Brazilian political scenario as a real threat to the global environment. The short film starts as a documentary, with voice-over narration in several languages warning about the risk of a worldwide ecological catastrophe caused by the disappearance of entire insect lineages. As the narration explains, insects are instrumental to the survival of the planet and are being killed off in increasing numbers by global warming, pesticides, and deforestation. Soon after, *The Pleasure of Killing Bugs* becomes an SF movie, a dystopian tale about a near-future world without insects, in which humanity is living its last generation. In this rotten, insect-deprived world, a nun and a priest mourn a human civilization on the brink of extinction. The third part of Martinelli's film revels in the fantasy genre, embracing the poetic license and metaphor at its core.

Some of the first scenes featuring the nun, set in Rio de Janeiro, suggest rising water levels. When she takes a ferry, the constant noise of rain reinforces this atmosphere of climate change. When the nun meets a priest in a seaside church and they engage in a dialogue about their current situation, the scenes are interspersed with images of cloudy skies. She asks him, "Is it true that there are still bees here?" "I don't know," he replies, "I heard something about it a few months ago, a buzz, but I wasn't sure what it was about." She then talks about her past, about the time she frequented that place, and how many bugs lived there. She asks the priest about God's intentions, whether such extinction was part of His plan. The priest replies by saying he does not know, and that his only certainty is that God created humans like clouds. And, like clouds, we humans do not know where we are destined to go. But we keep on going, though we are destined for the end. "So, all the clouds are in the wrong place?," asks the nun. Immediately following this question, a long shot of a clock tower by the sea rotates 360° clockwise, perhaps as a metaphor for the passage of time. The nun then looks up to the windy sky and both characters begin to pray, in a seemingly desperate attempt to "stop the clock" and reverse the extinction event. This scene also nods to the usual reference to faith and religion in Brazil as, for the most part, the only "lifeboat." Faith and religion are believed to be the only ways to prevent catastrophes in a society that often lets the course of natural events run free, with neither precaution nor communal effort or political will to prevent disasters like the annual landslides, dam collapses, oil spills, airplane crashes, etc., etc. Then again, "God is Brazilian" is a popular motto throughout the country, as a convenient alibi for all sorts of negligence, omission, and crimes.

The role of faith, divine providence, or simply luck, is made clearer in the following scene, as the nun walks along a coastal dirt road and eventually meets a young boy sitting on the sidewalk with a bug in his hands. A new beginning? A leap of faith? Time-lapse shots of cloudy skies ensue, followed by an image of Jesus Christ in flames, and takes of the nun running through the streets. A long take of a tree by the sea, an image that opened the short, reappears a bit differently, interspersed with more shots of the cloudy sky and images of Jesus and Mary. A storm brews on the horizon, and the nun eventually reaches a house, possibly the priest's home. After knocking and receiving no answer, she forces the door open and enters the house, finding a miniature cloud floating by a closed window. Has the priest turned into the cloud? A boom of thunder marks the cut to black, in this final scene that ends the story's circle, a parable in three acts: documentary, SF, and fantasy.

No matter how fantastic the film ends, it is in fact deeply anchored in SF, regardless of its poetic atmosphere and experimentalist traits. It speculates on a real and scientifically based premise: the threat of climate change and pesticide use resulting in the extinction of insects and, consequently, of humankind. The SF dimension of this Brazilian short film lies precisely in this speculative approach to the problem, translated into a kind of poetic SF that also incorporates Brazilian religiosity as a deep-seated cultural factor in national dystopia—as in other films discussed here. For SF, metaphor, and poetry are not mutually exclusive; on the contrary. *The Pleasure of Killing Bugs* can thus be regarded as an eloquent example of contemporary Brazilian ecodystopian film.

Another noteworthy example of environmentalist discourse wrapped in political criticism is Karim Aïnouz's *Persephone Mission (Missão Perséfone*, 2020). This short film presents a "second chance" for humankind on a new, distant Earthlike exoplanet. Made in lockdown during the Covid-19 pandemic, the movie is set in the year 3020, when humanity has completed a thousand years on a planet outside the Solar System, called Super Earth. In 2020, a catastrophic event caused the extinction of animal life on Earth and precipitated the exodus of the human species. The opening credits explain this premise more precisely: "The move to the new planet ushered in the end of the commodity empire and Capitalocene, and the beginning of a new era." Still, according to these opening lines, "the Persephone Mission is the effort of this new, just and egalitarian civilization to build an archeology of its past on the blue planet, so that the heavens shall never fall again." By collecting images from the most diverse origins, such as long shots of landscapes, water, land, and air, indoor and outdoor shots, CGI, as well as archival images (and ones vaguely inspired by Brazilian Indigenous legends), *Persephone Mission* construes the memoirs of our existence on Earth. In this regard, it resembles Carlos Canela's *Paths in Search of a Time (Not Yet Cataloged)* (*Caminhos em busca de um tempo (ainda não catalogado)*, 2001), which is supposed to resemble a documentary from the future, using domestic Super-8 archival footage, repurposed and re-signified by an original voice-over that alludes to a broad range of human history, emotions, and meanings for life. With a clear message of ecological awareness, Aïnouz's *Persephone Mission* is one of the most evident ecodystopias in the recent Brazilian filmography. It is proof that this subgenre subsists, therefore, as one of the most structured and enduring driving forces in Brazilian SF cinema.

Several other contemporary Brazilian SF films that we have already discussed, such as Adirley Queirós's *WOBI* and *Once There Was Brasília*, and Marcelo Pedroso's *Brasil S/A*, take on an ecodystopian perspective or "anthropocene unconscious" (Bould 2021). In *WOBI*, for example, such perspective is latent in the fractured cityscape, a kind of Brazilian apartheid, and also in the rough and mutilated geography of its characters' bodies, which bear the marks of exclusion and authoritarianism: the failure of a modern urban project that always postulated "the land of the future." In its own (related) way, it is the capitalist machine in *Brasil S/A*—the engine of unbridled exploitation of natural resources and concentration of wealth—that promotes the economic inequality and social divide that suggest the bankruptcy of the future. *Brasil S/A* opens with *plongée* shots of seawater swept across the bow of a ship delivering tractors destined for a sugarcane plantation, this commodity so central to Brazil's economic history—and slavery. Water and land are the predominant motifs at the beginning of the narrative. More and more machines appear throughout the film and gradually take over from the characters, sharply transforming the landscape. The final scenes alternate *plongée* and *counterplongée* shots, searching the sky for an ambivalent perspective of the future. But the sunlight is blinding: it crosses the center of the national flag, and the vision is impaired by a strange, perhaps premonitory, eclipse.

These films resume a critical discourse on the historical exclusion and violence in Brazil with a broad impact on the environment and urban experiences in different regions of the country. This becomes more evident when the government ostensibly turns its back on the environment, our biodiversity, our natural reserves, and Indigenous nations, instead encouraging land grabbers, ignoring crimes against our environmental heritage, and reducing the supervisory power of IBAMA (Brazilian Institute of Environment and Renewable Natural Resources).[30]

Just a few years ago, Bolsonaro's Economy Minister Paulo Guedes repeated in a simplistic and biased manner the old 1970 thesis that environmental degradation supposedly stems from poverty. Guedes stated, during an official presentation at the World Economic Forum in Davos, Switzerland, on January 21, 2020, that "people destroy (*sic*) the environment because they need to eat."[31] As if rampant deforestation is not the responsibility of the agribusiness industry or greedy farmers who multiply their profits by violating the law, or as if massive air and water pollution should not be attributed to big industries and mining companies. To cite a recent example, mining giants Samarco and Vale do Rio Doce are respectively responsible for the two massive, consecutive ecological disasters in Mariana and Brumadinho.³² They were responsible for the deaths of hundreds of Brazilian citizens, countless animal and plant deaths, and unprecedented destruction of regional ecosystems: the collapse of the Samarco and Vale do Rio Doce dams represent two of the biggest ecological disasters in human history.

According to scientist Paulo Artaxo (member of the IPCC [Intergovernmental Panel on Climate Change] since 2003), Paulo Guedes is entirely wrong, as "[most] deforestation is done by companies and wealthy individuals who hold power in the region, who have major influence in the Judiciary and the Executive Branch. They simply invade public lands, and the Public Prosecutor's Office and the police do not investigate them" (Artaxo qtd. in Linder 2020). Furthermore, Ricardo Abramovay shows that reduced deforestation does not result in decreased production: agricultural GDP in the Amazon increased by about 300 percent between 1999 and 2013, regardless of the approximately two-thirds reduction in deforestation in that same period (2019, 38–39). According to the author, while only 1 percent of the Amazon rainforest had been destroyed by 1960, by 2020, under Bolsonaro, deforestation affected approximately 20 percent of the rainforest (2019, 34). Abramovay further notes that in 2016, under President Michel Temer's administration, Brazil was the seventh largest emitter of greenhouse gases (2.278 billion tons), of which no less than 51 percent were caused by deforestation (Abramovay 2019, 32). He explains that, according to the UN IPCC, the decrease in deforestation in Brazil between 2004 and 2012 (under Presidents Lula and Dilma Rousseff) was considered the greatest national contribution against global warming. Between 2003 and 2009, 75 percent of the increase in all protected areas worldwide occurred in Brazil (Abramovay 2019, 17). Since 2012, however, this trend has been reversed with increases in rates of deforestation, all of which is unlawful.

Unfortunately, since the rise of a far-right government in 2019, any achievements in Brazilian diplomacy and environmental policies have been compromised. As Ivo Lesbaupin states, in "the first months of the Jair Bolsonaro administration, we see a total lack of control by the Brazilian authorities, favoring a process that could end in the savannization or desertification of the Amazon" (in Abramovay 2019, 8). Within a few months, Bolsonaro's government destroyed an image that had been built over some thirty years. His speeches and public policies, all related to loose environmental surveillance and protection, leniency to farmers and poachers, and hatred of Indigenous people and the environmental movement, have repositioned Brazil once again as one of the planet's greatest climate offenders in the eyes of the world. In an article published in the *New York Times*, Londoño and Casado (2019) report that the Brazilian Amazon rainforest lost an area equal to about twelve times the size of New York City between August 2018 and July 2019. Nicolas Bourcier (2019), in *Le Monde*, analyzes "Bolsonaro's incendiary policy in the Amazon" noting that deforestation in Brazil increased by 222 percent in August 2019, compared to the same period in 2018. *Le Monde* (2020) also reports that, according to the National Institute for Amazon Research (Instituto Nacional de Pesquisas da Amazônia, INPA), 1,202 km$^2$ of forest disappeared between January and April 2020.

Immediately following his inauguration, Bolsonaro restricted IBAMA's power to inhibit and punish deforestation and crimes against Indigenous populations, meanwhile, illegal rainforest burning and violent attacks on national reserves, including murders of environmental and Indigenous leaders, were on the rise. Films like Claudinê Perina Camargo's *Túnel 93º* and José de Anchieta's *Stop 88—Alert Limit*, made during the military dictatorship, therefore seem to have renewed significance some fifty years later, with their powerful critique of a regime that once again scorns life and the environment.

Almost thirty years after Brazil's redemocratization, ecodystopian imaginary continues to fuel debates on the day of reckoning with a history of authoritarianism and the growing inequality favored by neoliberalism. This can be seen in films like *Cold Tropics*, *Rio 2096*, and *White Out, Black In*, all of which condemn long-term authoritarianism and the dues never paid to most Brazilians (Blacks, browns, and Indigenous peoples). As these movies seem to suggest, exclusion, maintenance of privileges, and intolerance make sustainable development unfeasible, ruin urban projects, and accentuate the damage to nature. Social ills result in environmental scourges, and the unsustainability of cities spreads voraciously into regions once protected. After a brief period of social advances in this regard between the late 1990s and the 2000s, the return of the far-right to power prompts review of the films mentioned here, as the warnings they convey are valid and current. Ecodystopia seems to loathe neoliberalism and governments dictated by its logic, as well as authoritarian or nondemocratic regimes, which have always despised environmentalism. As these pages were being written, the Amazon and the Pantanal were on fire. The federal government had dismantled all environmental efforts promoted by previous administrations: from the modernization of INPE (National Institute for Space Research) and its monitoring tools to IBAMA's inspection. As confessed by the former environment minister, Ricardo Salles,[33] the Covid-19 outbreak was the perfect storm, the moment to "steer past" deregulation.[34] This means encouraging environmental crime and impunity for the advancement of industry and economy. An article published in *Jornal da USP* (Escobar 2020) states that the destruction of the Amazon rainforest continues at an accelerated rate in Brazil. Satellite monitoring data released on August 7, 2020, by the INPE show that the deforestation rate in the Amazon increased by 34 percent over the previous twelve months, compared to the same period the year before. It was the second consecutive increase in the first two years of Jair Bolsonaro's mandate.

While Indigenous populations continue to be victimized by federal neglect, with exposure to Covid-19 and scarcity of resources or proper medical care, the greed of large soy producers and ranchers is also growing in the Pantanal. Bolsonaro had already indicated how he would handle the environment when, in a moment backstage at the 2019 World Economic Forum in Davos, Switzerland, the Brazilian president was approached by former US vice-president and environmentalist Al Gore, who expressed his concern for the Amazon. Bolsonaro replied that "the Amazon cannot be forgotten (*sic*). We have many riches. And I would love to tap into the Amazon's natural resources together with the United States."[35] Astonished, Al Gore expressed his confusion. When the explanation only accentuated the outrage, Gore simply walked away. The scene, which has only recently entered a wider public debate following the release of Marcus Vetter's film *The Forum* (2020), has caused worldwide outrage.[36] This collective indignation provoked reactions in the form of international campaigns, such as #DefundBolsonaro, which sought to discourage the purchase of Brazilian products by citizens of other countries until the government's environmental policy changes.[37] As Aílton Krenak notes,

> When people speak of imagining a new possible world, it's in the sense of rearranging relations and spaces, introducing new understandings of what we recognize as nature, as if we

were not nature ourselves. In truth, all they are invoking are the same old ways people have always had of coexisting with the metaphor of nature, which they created for their own consumption anyway. All other human beings who fall outside of the established "we" can be eaten, beaten, broken, packed off someplace else. The state of the world we are living through today is the very same one our recent forebears ordered for us. (Krenak 2020, 65–66)

All the films discussed in this chapter make us further reflect on Krenak's words concerning the imagination of new possible worlds and the enduring human divide between "us" and "them." Brazilian SF and other Latin American SF cinemas often remind us how many of "them" are spread across the world, and how often "them" can be one of "us"—how easily "us" can become "them." The current scenario, therefore, highlights the revival of interest in ecodystopia, given the global union that simultaneously aggregates the epidemics of obesity, malnutrition, and climate change (Swinburn et al. 2019), in addition to the Covid-19 pandemic, the largest global health crisis since the early twentieth century. Perhaps more than ever, environmentalism and the dangers of climate change are on the world's political agenda. Decades of research and accumulated scientific knowledge have exposed the urgency of the issue: an advance compromised by the rise of far-right governments. Meanwhile, the world's cinemas have provided some of the most provocative comments on the economic, social, political, and individual impacts of environmental crimes, negationism, or simple omission or negligence toward the well-being of the planet. Many of the films cited here indicate that, beyond individual and sporadic initiatives, environmental issues need to be faced globally, as an effort by the human species to fulfill its responsibility to the planet. The environment can only be saved if we profoundly transform our economic existence—the "capitalocene" that currently rules us, as Karim Aïnouz suggests in his short *Persephone Mission*. Another system must be possible for the sake of survival.

Consequently, the ecodystopian images of Brazilian SF cinema must not be overlooked: they are valuable tools for environmental awareness and a constant reminder that a just society does not exist without sustainability. Earth's environmental collapse is perhaps the possible "extinction event" about which we have speculated most in the history of art: from poetry to cinema. We thus close this chapter with the first and last verses of a poem by Carlos Drummond de Andrade, published in 1984 in the newspaper *Cometa Itabirano*. The poem seems to foresee those two devastating ecological tragedies: the collapse of the Mariana and Brumadinho dams (2015 and 2019, respectively), both in the state of Minas Gerais: events that resulted in the deaths of countless people and animals and the irreparable destruction of the environment, and yet for which, to date, no one has been duly held accountable for (Câmpera 2019). Drummond's verses (qtd. in Souza 2019) in "Lira Itabirana" (1984) sound like a requiem, a lament for the lives lost and the environmental crime committed:

> The River? It is sweet. Vale? Bitter.
> Oh, how it could have went
> Had the load been lighter. (. . .)
> How many tons are for exportation
> Of iron?
> How many tears are a dissimulation
> With no bellow?[38]

If reality shall not change, let the artists' images denounce the horror.

# 9

# A Strange Object South of the Equator

Hypotheses and Investigations about Restraints against SF Literature and Films in Brazil

According to Brazilian writer and journalist Zuenir Ventura (2013), "Brazil is a country where surrealism did not succeed as an artistic movement, but as a lifestyle." With due regard, the same could be said about Brazilian SF in a broad sense. The "land of the future" would already be an SF per se—considering its history and its modernist, "artificial" capital, Brasília. No wonder Terry Gilliam gave the name *Brazil* (1985) to his futuristic dystopia.

Apropos, it is worth contextualizing the idea of Brazil as the "land of the future," an epithet whose origin refers to the 1941 book by Stefan Zweig. In a preface to the 2013 Brazilian edition of Zweig's book, published by L&PM, Brazilian journalist Alberto Dines explains that "to this day, it is not known exactly what Zweig intended to say with this suggestive and enigmatic play on words (*a* land or *the* land, *from* the future or *of* future?). The idea was not his, but James Stern's (incidentally, Andrew St. James), the English translator of the original German, who fished it in French in the epigraph of the work" (Dines in Zweig 2013, 7; italics in the original). It is a fact that the future envisaged by Zweig in Brazil was based much more on an alleged fascination with a hypothetical "racial democracy" than any state of industrial, scientific, or technological progress *stricto sensu*. In other words, in his book Zweig exalted a "social engineering" that would have been unique in the world, a society virtually free from racial and religious conflicts or tensions, a very different scenario from Europe's. Thus,

Zweig refers to the success of "the experiment of Brazil, with its complete and conscious negation of all color and racial distinctions, represents by its obvious success perhaps the most important contribution toward the liquidation of a mania that has brought more disruption and unhappiness into our world than any other" (1941, 9). Based on such assumption, Zweig comments on his eagerness to travel back to Brazil "better prepared and for a longer stay, to once more experience this sensation of living in a world that has a future and the security of peace, to enjoy with even greater awareness its hospitable atmosphere" (1941, 4). The truth is, Zweig did need to come to Brazil in order to escape the Nazis in Europe, and the South American country appeared to be, at that point, the safest and most convenient option.

However, despite Zweig's personal history and fight for survival during World War II, his book advocates that the technological, scientific, and industrial advances in Western civilization had been overvalued at the time, and these "modern wonders" were not able to avoid chaos in Europe. The true future should be sought in peaceful coexistence between peoples, as in the "Brazilian experiment" (1941, 9). Needless to say, there is much fable and imagination in Zweig's "land of the future." Nevertheless, he desperately needed at least two things by that time: a welcoming place and the belief in such a welcoming place that it was somewhere he could settle and survive. At present times, sociologists, anthropologists, historians, and philosophers have proved beyond any reasonable doubt how this myth of racial democracy was a sinister device deployed by the dominant ideology. On this topic, see Sílvio de Almeida (2020), Djamila Ribeiro (2019), and others. Notwithstanding, every now and then the idea that there is no racism in Brazil resurfaces, such as in some public speeches given by unreliable authorities (e.g., Vice President Hamilton Mourão).

Therefore, no matter how lasting and widespread the concept of Brazil as "the land of the future" may have been, for quite some time we had the impression that the Brazilian SF cinema was a sort of "exotic" organism struggling to survive in a rather rarefied atmosphere. As if only the country could be seen as "the land of the future," whereas any speculation, fabulation, or futurism in Brazilian cinema tended to be impaired or made "invisible." In the early 2000s, the number of Brazilian SF films in peoples' minds was very small, even among film scholars. Some people could barely remember having seen one single Brazilian SF film, and most people could not remember any at all. In fact, the impact of the suffocating climate prior to the Retomada (1993–94 onward)—with successive economic crises in the 1980s, culminating with the dismantling of Embrafilme—led to a conjuncture of rarefied atmosphere for a number of cultural initiatives, especially filmmaking. Brazilian SF cinema, in this case, was just the most fragile film organism in a cinematic environment already poorly oxygenated.

The metaphor of the rarefied atmosphere seeks not only to contextualize the object but also pays tribute to one of the rare texts on SF studies in Brazil, written by critic and writer Fausto Cunha. "Science fiction in Brazil: an almost uninhabited planet" ("Ficção científica no Brasil: um planeta quase desabitado," in Allen 1976, 5–20), served as a starting point and parameter of comparison in our first critical inventories of SF in Brazilian cinema. From an almost uninhabited planet to a rarefied atmosphere: it was not necessary to go very far. Even though we continue to believe in the validity of both metaphors, our first investigations, between 2003 and 2007, revealed that, although there are fewer films than we would like (hence a "rarefied atmosphere"), they are also more of them than we sometimes expected. Thus, Brazilian SF films are like "spectra" or "electromagnetic radiation," which we can only see with the aid of some "special instruments." What would these "special instruments" be? In short: (1) goodwill and resilience in the investigation; (2) a good amount of disregard for Eurocentrism; (3) skepticism regarding the canons; and, finally, (3) some flexibility in the approach to film genres and the history of Brazilian cinema, in line with the most contemporary research methodologies.

Thus, this chapter seeks to carry out an introductory investigation into alleged obstacles hindering the development and consolidation of SF in Brazil, especially in the Brazilian cinema and audiovisual industries. In this regard, we will analyze aspects such as the influence of the US model of literary and audiovisual SF, the role played by special effects in films of this genre, scientific culture, and public perception of science in Brazil. At the end of this path of investigation we suggest more systematic studies on the theme due to the complexity of the issues and possible connections between them.

Despite the growing number of experiences involving SF cinema in Brazil, the notion of the Hollywoodian super production being a model still remains reasonably widespread. If, on the one hand, the reduced costs and increased popularity of digital technology in the art of film production have increased access for new film directors (many of whom have shown interest in SF), on the other hand, such accessibility does not always lead to an expansion of creative horizons. This means that films directed by Brazilians, including both short and feature-length films, such as Flávia Moraes's *Acquaria* (2003), Marcus Alqueres's *The Flying Man*, or Gabriel Kalim Mucci's *Lunatique*, have employed digital effects in an evident attempt to mimic foreign standards. Even films that had more elements of visual effects often end up emulating the Hollywood model, not only in their plots and art direction but also in resorting to some well-known formulas—often somewhat clichéd. Films that could exemplify the persistence of North American SF being adopted as a model include the feature-length film *The Man from the Future*, by Cláudio Torres, or the short film *The Return* (*A Volta*, 2020) by Flávio Langoni, among many others. According to Márcio Napoli, producer, scriptwriter, and director of the medium-length film *Sooty Skies* (*Céus de Fuligem*, 2005), the practice of overvaluing a certain type of SF—appearing in super productions from Hollywood—is still prevalent among the younger generations.[1] The case of the Uruguayan short film *Panic Attack*, by Fede Álvarez, which was a viral phenomenon on the internet, seems to illustrate this "Holy Grail" sought by Latin American film directors: the SF film that is almost indistinguishable—in terms of semantics, syntax, and visual effects—from Hollywood blockbusters. *Ataque de Pánico* even resulted in contracts with Hollywood producers and film studios, with Álvarez later directing US productions with reasonably large budgets; however, there has been no news that the Uruguayan film director managed to attain the same importance as Mexican film director Guillermo del Toro in the Hollywood film industry. The moral of the story: having talent and mastery of narrative techniques, aesthetics, and designing the production of SF cinema according to the US model does not always ensure that a Latin American film director will have a prominent career in Hollywood. This is also because the best of world SF film production may not even arise from Hollywood but from other parts of the enormous and heterogeneous industry of North American film production (including Mexico), Latin America, Africa, Asia, and even Europe.

Fortunately, at least over the last ten years, we have seen an expanding industry of Brazilian film production, of both short and feature-length films, with low budgets but high levels of creativity. In addition to some unforgettable examples of the sheer quality of Brazilian cinema in the SF genre throughout its history—as in the case of Jorge Furtado's short film *Barbosa*—arguably, at least since 2002, with the modestly funded yet creative short film *Loop* by Carlos Gregório, followed by a string of successful short films such as Kléber Mendonça Filho's *Green Vinyl* (*Vinil Verde*, 2004) and *Cold Tropics*, a whole new generation of Brazilian fantasy filmmakers has produced highly original SF films, providing a genuinely Brazilian contribution to the genre. In this regard, some examples are: Afrofuturist films, such as Eduardo Carvalho and Marcos Carvalho's *Chico*, Diego Paulino's *Negrum3*, Sabrina Fidalgo's *Personal Vivator*, and Grace Passô's *Republic*; LGBTQ+ SF films (or "Queer sci-fi," according to film director Henrique Arruda), such as Arruda's *The Last Romantics in the World*, Mozart Freire's *Janaína Overdrive* (2016), Susan Kalik and Thiago Gomes's *Above our Heads*, and Joel Caetano's *Splendid Cradle Mission*, this also being an Afrofuturist film); Tupinipunk or Amazofuturist works, that is, SF films with narratives and characters who are Native Brazilian in origin, feature-length films such as Luiz Bolognesi's *2096: A Story of Love and Fury* and Sérgio Andrade's *The Kawa's Black Earth*, the short film *Exterminator Seed*, by Pedro Neves Marques, or the hybrid Afrofuturist and Amazofuturist film *At the Edge of the Universe*, by Tiago Esmeraldo. Highly creative short films, with careful use of visual effects, can be observed, such as Raul Lemos Arthuso's *Master Blaster*, Marco Antônio Pereira's *The Last Song for a Rude Heart*, Thiago Foresti's *Space Invasion* and *Algorithm*, while dystopias and provocative intellectual experiments found their place in political SF: feature-length films such as Gabriel Mascaro's *Divine Love* and short films like Matheus Moura's *Purple Dictatorship*. Moreover, we note the repercussions of the *3%* series, which ran for four seasons (2016–2020), created by Pedro Aguilera and produced by Netflix. In other words, the above filmography, together with the growing publication of studies on SF in Brazil, show that the obstacles discussed below have been slowly overcome or reconfigured, despite some complexities and reminiscences of old ideologies regarding SF and economic development.

Nevertheless, it is a fact that, while in Hollywood (or more contemporary media conglomerates) SF is the business of major studios, being almost synonymous with special effects, in Brazil this genre is underexploited commercially. However, it is worth noting that, even in a period with scarce production (as after the most recent "death" of the film industry in Brazil, with the closure of Embrafilme, the Brazilian Film Company, in 1990), SF has been present. Here, we should note works such as Francisco de Paula's *Oceano Atlantis* and Luiz Alberto Pereira's *The Island Effect*.

The most common justification for the limited history of Brazilian cinema in the SF genre is based on lack of funding. According to this explanation, the SF genre would require sophisticated settings and special effects. For instance, Paulo Bastos Martins, director of the 1970 feature-length film *The Messenger: The Man from the Storms*, believes that the main obstacle hindering the development of this genre in the Brazilian film industry would be "the financial issue. That is because SF is expensive: settings, costume design, special effects, and the like."[2] Consistently, historian Eduardo Morettin (University of São Paulo) believes that the lack of resources should account for much of the inhibition of film producers or executives with regard to fantasy or SF cinema.[3] Film director Carlos Canela—author of three SF short films—also agrees with this hypothesis: "In truth, the view that SF is expensive still holds today and it is, in my opinion, one of the main restrictions blocking its growth in countries other than the United States. Even though technology has opened many doors, the use of special effects is still always expensive if we wish to bring a minimum standard of quality into film production."[4] On the other hand, Canela notes his own experience in the production of short films on very small budgets, which did not lead to anything "as terrible as one could imagine." This makes him confirm that "SF is there for anyone wishing to use it. We just need to cast ideology aside and move toward pure and simple creation, which is where everything should converge at the end of the day."[5]

## The Wrangle about Visual Effects

For us to better understand the reasons for the "lag" or "underdevelopment" of SF within the Brazilian film industry, it is essential that we look into the role of special effects (more recently known as "visual effects") within the development and identification of audiovisual SF as a whole.

The notion that economic and infrastructural deficiencies inhibit a greater production of SF in the Brazilian film industry helps to cement a situation that had been identified by film critic Paulo Emílio Salles Gomes during the era of silent films in Brazil. In his opinion, "One thing that prevented the development of the film industry in Rio de Janeiro, and also in the more archaic remainder of the country, was the insufficiency of electricity supply" (Salles Gomes 1997, 9).

The fact is that, even today, the Brazilian film industry still suffers from infrastructural shortages that effectively prevent its full development. If yesterday it was the lack of electricity that limited Brazilian cinema as a whole, today it is the lack of investment in areas such as computer resources and the technologies of special effects that could block the development of a certain genre of films.

According to Adam Roberts, SF in the cinema is synonymous with special effects: "Critics, and particularly film reviewers, sometimes complain about the dominance of special effects, but that misses the point. The special effects in any given SF film—and, in a slightly different way, technical marvels of more conventional written SF—*are* the point" (Roberts 2000, 152–53). Peter Nicholls seems to agree with this view, suggesting that special effects are essential within the film, being the core element in the cinematographic art, technique, and language:

> Film snobs often talk as if special effects were somehow vulgar—at best, the icing on an otherwise realistic cake. It probably makes more sense to regard special effects as completely fundamental to film, the cake itself. After all, the language and grammar of film is nearly all "special effects," but most of the tricks are now so familiar that we pay them no more attention than people just talking pay to nouns, verbs and adjectives. Montage (juxtaposing different images in quick succession), cross-cutting, close-ups, panning and tracking shots, zooms and all the rest of the film-maker's vocabulary, were all in their day special effects. Now we take them for granted, but in the earliest days of film-making they did not exist; the camera was plumped down in the visual equivalent of the front row of the stalls, and there it stayed. This did not last long. (Nicholls 1984, 12)

In his statement, Nicholls disregards an entire realist tradition film theory or film art, headed by French film critic André Bazin, also completely ignoring the work of Christian Metz in his "'Trucage' and Film" (1977),[6] where the French film semiotician scrutinizes and offers an opportune type of special effects—such as profilmic trucage vs. cinematographic trucage, as well as the peculiarities concerning visible, invisible, and imperceptible trucage. Certainly, special effects for Nicholls—those Metz defines as visible and as fundamental for full fruition of the show—are present in a wide range of films that extend well beyond the limits of SF. However, it is supposed that Roberts, in turn, is referring to a more specific and sophisticated type of special effects, characteristic of fantasy cinema or more precisely of SF cinema, which makes it stand out from a realist-naturalist style of film production. Therefore, we have to ask: Does the genre depend that much on visual effects? And, as a result, does making SF films cost much more than other genres? And what can be said about those SF films that renounce the presence of sophisticated special effects and employ other means to make "spectacle" or "seduce" film audiences? Is it really the case that every *novum* (Suvin 1979, 63–64) transposed to cinema is visually materialized only through sophisticated special effects?[7] J. P. Telotte (2001) agrees with Nicholls. According to Telotte, SF is the film genre that relies the most on special effects for ontological reasons. SF films would be all about technological development and cinema itself as a technology. In other words, we could say that technology—in SF films—is always manifested at two levels: at the diegetic level (of the fictional universe itself) and at the extradiegetic level, that is, at the level of the medium, or of how a given fable is "materially" presented. In a given SF film, the technology that makes it feasible is often "mirrored" in its own story and vice versa. In short, according to Telotte (2001, 28), technology contributes to the creation of an essential SF identity in cinema: "A specific issue concerning representation and mechanical reproduction that we might see as a kind of birthmark of the genre" (2001, 28).

If throughout the twentieth century SF in cinema proved a great showcase for economically powerful cinematographies, in the transition to the twenty-first century, the genre shows signs of being the most illustrative locus of what Tom Gunning (1990) has pointed out as a resumption of the cinema of attractions. Gunning explains that the "cinema of attractions" is a kind of film production that was popular up until 1906–1907, after which "narrative cinema" would become dominant. A good example of the cinema of attractions is the work of French filmmaker Georges Méliès. According to Gunning, "To summarize, the 'cinema of attractions' directly requests spectator attention, inciting visual curiosity, and supplying pleasure through an exciting spectacle—a unique event, be it fictional or documentary, that is of interest in itself" (1995, 58).

This time, however, far from the PMR (Primitive Mode of Representation)[8] proposed by Noël Burch (1987), the attractions "reloaded" (see also Strauven 2006) are properly "tamed" by audiovisual industry and enhanced by a broader range of technological resources compared to the original "cinema of attractions" that preceded the rise of narrative cinema in 1906–1907 (Gunning 1990). Hence the criticism of "pyrotechnics" in

SF films, cinematic spectacles that offer impressive imagery where the narrative pace and script quality are often secondary—or tertiary.

This criticism is related to one of the two possible paths pointed out by Shilo McClean (2007, 36) in the use of special effects. In a first case, the effect is used as a self-reflection, seeking to draw attention to itself so viewers examine it and assess its verisimilitude, distracting themselves from the narrative—which would correspond to the "attraction" that interrupts the story. In the other approach, the effect is transparent, used to hide its own production while trying not to draw attention. In a way, all (or at least most) of the special effects are diegetic, fully integrated into the fictional universe and, therefore, the narrative. However, in the case of the first path pointed out by McClean, the effects can be so intense and purposefully emphasized that they translate as "attraction," also resulting in a mode of particular enjoyment that could be approximated or provisionally described as *mise-en-phase* (Odin 1983, 213–38; Buckland 2000, 77–108). It should be noted that McClean (2007) defends the second option (for the "transparent" or "discrete" effects), emphasizing that the use of technology to produce special effects is only relevant when it supports the story told. Obviously, this predilection suggests an underlying ideology, a preference for narrative cinema, and the transparency or invisibility of the procedures of audiovisual discourse. In a way, Shilo McClean's (2007) predilection meets David Hutchison's observations: "A special effect should always be a means to an end. A film tells a story in a series of images; the job of special effects is to make the visual storytelling effective and economical" (1987, xvi–xvii). According to Hutchison, special effects in cinema are inspired by magic and pioneered by the French magician-filmmaker Georges Méliès. On the other hand, Hutchison (1987, xviii–xix) notes to the differences between cinematic special effects and the magic show:

> Special effects in the movies have an advantage over those used in traditional magic shows. On stage a magician entertains the audience with a series of well-performed tricks. The show is no more emotionally involving than an ordinary exhibition of gymnastics, for example; nor is it supposed to be. In the movies, in contrast, the magic of special effects is called upon to help tell a story, which can simply entertain or stir our deepest emotions. Movie special effects are not an end in themselves, like stage magic. To subvert story to effects is to undercut

the power of the film medium severely. Georges Méliès never realized this. He was content to continue making little trick films, relegating the art of filmmaking to the status of a toy. In a very short time, the cinema outgrew him. (Hutchison 1987, xviii–xix)

Needless to say, such a statement is quite biased. In this excerpt, Hutchison reveals his ideological option for narrative-dramatic cinema: the defense of cinema's alleged intrinsic narrative vocation. He is mistaken, perhaps, to claim that Georges Méliès did not realize this. The French filmmaker may simply have resisted market trends at the time. Clearly, McClean and Hutchison's positions both agree that (1) film is a narrative medium and (2) visual effects serve narrative functions.

On the other hand, Barry Keith Grant (1999, 16–30) criticizes the surrender of the SF film industry to the overenthusiasm for special effects and the prominence of the visual spectacle, to the detriment of a thought-provoking SF cinema. Grant comments on a childish movement in mainstream SF cinema that impedes the intellectual power widely observed in a great deal of the world SF literature.

According to Grant, the special effects in contemporary SF cinema would be at the same time a differential (a "Holy Grail"), a factor of greater appeal to the broader audiences and the Achilles' heel of the genre. Grant (1999, 23) opportunely comments on eschewing the complexity of a novel like *Frankenstein* (2003 [1818]), by Mary Shelley, for its most famous film adaptation, directed by James Whale (*Frankenstein*, 1931). To name just a single aspect of this process (perhaps the most relevant), "The creature is transformed from a nimble and articulate being, an effective metaphor for Romantic hubris and encroaching industrialization, into a lumbering, grunting monster" (Grant 1999, 23). The emphasis on the visual aspects, Grant suggests, overshadows the potential of SF cinema: "Because film is primarily a visual medium, it tends to concentrate on the depiction of visual surfaces at the expense of contemplative depth" (1999, 23). Grant further observes an "invasion" of children as characters in SF cinema from the 1970s, under the influence of George Lucas and Steven Spielberg (1999, 25). The children in SF films would be symptomatic of a broader process of infantilizing the spectator, rooted in classic Hollywood cinema, which would have taken SF cinema by storm (Grant 1999, 25).

This process of infantilization, significantly favored by the rise of special effects technology as a major attraction of the genre, characterizes the SF cinema's movement (of return?) from narrative to spectacle, from thought-experimentation to mystification. It is no wonder that one of the most prominent special effects companies—owned by George Lucas—is called Industrial Light and Magic. "Magic," in a work of making visible that which is imagined, "repressed," or impossible, as widely seen in the subgenre known as "apocalyptic," or simply "catastrophe film" (Grant 1999, 22).

It is worth pointing out that the discussion about the exaggeration in special effects in the contemporary cinema industry—and notably in the SF cinema—is related to the rise of computer-generated imagery (CGI) or digital effects. However, the infantilization of the spectator and the SF cinema itself and the mystifying and spectacular orientation of the genre today cannot be understood as a mere result of the expansion of visual effects in the film industry—especially digital effects. The emphasis on visual spectacle in mainstream SF cinema has an ideological and stylistic motivation. We are not certain about whether cinema, (also) due to its representational character, its ability to register the physical world and its emphasis on the body, is definitely a poorly fertile medium for the symbolisms and intellectual speculations that are characteristic of SF literature in general (Grant 1999, 23-4).

Nevertheless, Grant seems to make the mistake of drawing a relationship of opposition or cause and effect between two incommensurable elements: visual *vs.* intellectual; special effects = infantilization. Thus, the author seems to be a victim of the very object he criticizes: the excessive emphasis of the SF film industry on special effects.

We have insisted that, contrary to the claims of Roberts (2000, 152-53), SF is not synonymous with special effects—in other words, special effects are not a fundamental requirement of the genre, not even one of its most essential characteristics. What about films such as Chris Marker's *The Jetty* (*La Jetée*, 1962), Jorge Furtado's *Barbosa*, and Darren Aronofsky's *Pi* (1998), and other films in which visual effects are invisible, imperceptible, or simply pointless? Would it be possible to make an SF film without special effects typically associated with the genre? We would answer yes to this question. A movie like *Barbosa*, for instance, employs the same class of visual effects observed in a melodrama or documentary. Its "special effects" most directly identified with SF are, in fact, based on modest film settings. And yet it is, without a doubt, an SF film.

Even international SF films that unrestrainedly adopted the "Hollywood-standard" SF cinema (albeit with far more modest budgets), reworking the genre from a cross-cultural perspective, provide solutions to the process of "infantilization" pointed out by Grant. We refer to films such as *Code 46* (2003), by Michael Winterbottom, *Children of Men* (2006), by Alfonso Cuarón,[9] or *Sleep Dealer* (2008), by Alex Rivera. All these SF feature films have not required extremely sophisticated special effects, and the fascination they may stir arises, above all, from speculations on contemporary agendas with a particular target: the spectators' intellect, worldviews, beliefs, and cultural backgrounds.

Furthermore, Mark Bould notes the greater inventiveness of some low-budget films that, sometimes, have found creative solutions for the problem of lack of funding (2003, 79–95). In this regard, he agrees with our standpoint, that there is a whole production of low-budget SF that is relevant for the history of the genre (Bould, 2003). According to writer Gerson Lodi-Ribeiro, the poor development of SF cinema in Brazil "could perhaps result from the persistence of a mistaken concept that grandiose special effects are essential in order to tell a good SF story. This is an incorrect notion, typical of those people who are not familiar with the genre."[10] I believe that the budget for settings and special effects is not necessarily linked to any film genre a priori. Indeed, there are certain epic films, westerns, and action films that spend a lot more on special effects compared to the average SF film budget. In Brazil, with budgets available to "historical" films such as Guilherme Fontes's *Chatô, the King of Brazil* (*Chatô, O Rei do Brasil*, 2015), Sérgio Rezende's *The Battle of Canudos* (*Guerra de Canudos*, 1996),[11] or *Mauá: The Emperor and the King* (*Mauá—O Imperador e o Rei*, 1999), it would surely be possible to produce a Brazilian SF film that might be highly competitive on the global market.

A film like Andrei Tarkovsky's *Stalker* (1979) is celebrated as an SF masterpiece, even though there was no "pyrotechnics" (abundant special effects) as would be typical for this genre. *Solaris* (1972), also by Tarkovsky, spent a fraction of what had been spent in the production of *2001* (Stanley Kubrick, 1968)[12] to adapt such complex work as the book by the same name by Polish writer Stanislaw Lem, and even so it led to a great SF film—despite any controversy involving the author of the original work. Even works such as Stanley Kubrick's *A Clockwork Orange*, or Andrew Niccol's *Gattaca* (1997)—both acclaimed SF films of acknowledged quality and produced with American money—are not really based on sophisticated special effects. Wouldn't this be an exemplary case for the Brazilian film industry, that is, to be attentive to the good SF stories, casting aside the excessive preoccupation with special effects?

In Argentina, Gustavo Mosquera adopts this posture in his film *Moebius* (1996), similar to what occurred in Spain with Alejandro Amenábar in *Open your Eyes* (*Abre los Ojos*, 1997) and Nacho Vigalondo in *Timecrimes* (*Los Cronocrímenes*, 2007). Before all these, Hugo Santiago had already produced an intriguing cult film, often considered SF: *Invasión* (1969). Also in Argentina, in the 1980s, Eliseo Subiela directed an SF film without any special effects yet full of mystery and awe: *Man Facing Southeast* (*Hombre Mirando al Sudeste*, 1986). One might say this film would be a "pseudo-SF" (Brosnan 1991), as it lacks the successive "attractions" that have made cinematographic SF more popular. But we prefer to consider Subiela's film as a sort of "subtle SF," "realist SF," or even a "Third SF Cinema." All these labels might be just another way to refer to what Alex Rivera once called "Science Fiction from the South" (Rivera qtd. in Lim 2009).

Another moniker designating a film style characterized as a more independent and authorial SF—which forgoes sophisticated special effects and the Hollywoodian spectacle to favor more modest productions, whose narrative in some cases is much more creative and intriguing than any blockbuster—is lo-fi sci-fi, a type of film production based on low-fidelity SF. Many Latin American SF films might also fit in the idea of lo-fi sci-fi, whereas examples of lo-fi sci-fi abound especially in the US independent cinema. The website *Taste of Cinema*[13] lists twenty-one SF films considered lo-fi sci-fi: *Computer Chess* (2013), by Andrew Bujalski; *The American Astronaut* (2001), by Cory McAbee; *Mars* (2010), by Mark Duplass, *Christmas on Mars* (2008), by Wayne Coyne; *Primer* (2004) and *Upstream Color* (2013), both by Shane Carruth; *Antiviral* (2012), by Brandon Cronenberg; *Science of Sleep* (2006), by Michel Gondry; *Monsters* (2010), by Gareth Edwards; *Another Earth* (2011), by Mike Cahill; *Sound of My Voice*, by Zal Batmanglij; *Moon* (2009), by Duncan Jones; *Safety not Guaranteed* (2012), by Colin Trevorrow; *Europa Report* (2013), by Sebastián Cordero; *La Jetée*, by Chris Marker; *Pi*, by Darren Aronofsky; *Take Shelter* (2011), by Jeff Nichols; *Beasts of the Southern Wild* (2012), by Behn Zeitlin; *Melancholia* (2011), by Lars von Trier; *Her* (2013), by Spike Jonze; and, finally, *Beyond the Black Rainbow* (2010), by Panos Cosmatos. Based on this list, we could pin down Chris Marker's 1962 film *The Jetty* a source or pioneering enterprise in terms of lo-fi sci-fi aesthetics. Such a list interests us in terms of possible comparisons with Latin American films: perhaps several Latin American SF films have always been lo-fi sci-fi *avant la lettre*. Thereby, here we could add to the lo-fi sci-fi cinema and Alex Rivera's "SF from the South" the hypothesis of a "Third SF Cinema"[14]—by parodying Fernando Solanas and Octavio Getino's "Third Cinema" (in Martin 1997, 33–58). This "Third SF Cinema" would be more representative of narratives addressing the world's minorities and peripheral nations, with a rather realist and sometimes minimalist style.

In Brazil, it seems that Carlos Pedregal and Alberto Pieralisi in *The 5th Power*, as well as Walter Hugo Khouri in *Voracious Love*, tried to make a more subtle style of SF cinema based on "atmosphere" and plot rather than the visual spectacle normally present in American SF films, even the so-called B movies. However, based on *Acquaria* and other films, the still prevailing trend in the audiovisual market seems to be that of fascination with sophisticated effects, which continues to limit the development of SF in the Brazilian film industry, restricting it to more expensive productions and shifting interest from ideas to the available technology. This is how film director Clóvis Vieira views one of the major obstacles hindering the development of the SF genre in Brazil. According to Vieira, one of the pioneers of digital cinema, with the feature-length animation film *Cassiopéia* (1996), Brazilian producers are usually quick to reject SF projects due to the fear of launching oneself into the odyssey of special effects.[15] We must remember that the issue of special effects in the SF film is at the heart of the debate about the restoration of a "film industry of attractions," as observed by Tom Gunning and Geoff King, among other specialists.

According to Gregg Rickman, "Geoff King and other contemporary theorists suggest that in films such as *Twister*, *Titanic*, *Independence Day*, *Jurassic Park* and others 'that the cinema of attractions . . . has made its comeback, displacing the centrality of narrative" (2004, xv). Gunning himself already acknowledges reminiscences of the "cinema of attractions" in the spectacle cinema of New Hollywood and after, in what can be called the "Spielberg-Lucas-Coppola cinema of effects" (1995, 61). Certainly, ever since the 1920s and through to the present day, SF cinema seems to be an important showcase for the film industry in general and for the technological expertise of a given national film industry (e.g., the American, French, or German film industries, among others). As recalled by Gregg Rickman, "Méliès is the father of the special effects film, and from its inception science fiction cinema has been a leader in the presentation of the latest "trick effects"—from the Schüfftan process first used in *Metropolis*, through Ray Harryhausen's models in the 1950s, Douglas Trumbull's effects in *2001: A Space Odyssey*, *Star Wars* and *Blade Runner*, and digital effects today" (2004, xv). On assigning the paternity of special effects to

Méliès, however, Rickman forgot the fact recalled by Paulo Emílio Salles Gomes (1981, 162–66): that the Spaniard Segundo de Chomón[16] could be put alongside Méliès and Zecca[17] in a "tripod" of the first "fantasy cinema." Indeed, the "cinema of visual spectacle" had pioneers beyond this famous trio Méliès-Zecca-Chomón. In his approach to scientific cinema or the popular science film, Oliver Gaycken (2015) also comments on the contributions by other filmmakers such as Charles Urban, Percy Smith, Francis Martin Duncan, and Louis Feuillade. Scientific cinema and the popular science film are closely tied to technical creativity and partake greatly in the cinematic aesthetics observed in SF cinema. For example, *The Cheese Mites* (1903), produced by Charles Urban and directed by F. Martin Duncan, or *Le Scorpion Languedocien* (1913), by the French company Éclair, among many other examples where the visual spectacle, whether in a large or small scale, plays a key aesthetic role.

The Soviets ventured into SF cinema in sophisticated productions such as Protazanov's *Aelita* or Tarkovsky's *Solaris*. The histories of film and SF film in circulation in the West tend to overlook or minimize the role of filmmakers like Pavel Klushantsev who, in films like *Road to the Stars* (*Doroga k zvezdam*, 1957), *Luna* (1965), or *Planeta Bur* (1961), was already employing techniques that would be hailed as groundbreaking in *2001: A Space Odyssey* (1968) (Barker and Skotak 1994a, 78–83; Barker and Skotak 1994b, 77–82). In what is probably the most typical case of advertising and ideological capitalization on a super production of the SF genre, UFA[18] mentioned the financial investment and technical quality in Fritz Lang's *Metropolis* (1927). However, it is worth remembering that, in 1927, Luís Buñuel wrote a critique of *Metropolis* concluding that film art is not all about money (Buñuel in Rickman 2004, 15). In this text, originally published in *La Gaceta Literária*[19] in 1927, Buñuel concludes with the following words: "In comparing *Metropolis* and *Napoléon*, the two greatest films that modern cinema has created, with others far more humble, yet also purer and more perfect, we may draw the useful conclusion that money is not the most essential ingredient in a modern cinematic production. Compare *Rien que les heures: Nothing But Time* (*Rien que les heures*, 1936) which cost only 35,000 francs, with *Metropolis*. Sensitivity first; intelligence first; and everything else, including money, comes after" (Buñuel in Rickman, 2004, 15). In other words, the cutting-edge special effects (in *Metropolis*) did not distract Buñuel from the sensitivity and intelligence found in a modest documentary (*Rien que les Heures*)[20]—which was directed by a Brazilian with an infamous career in Europe: Alberto Cavalcanti. In a nutshell, if, throughout the twentieth century, SF arguably proved a major showcase to publicize economically powerful film industries in the transition to the twenty-first century, the genre showed signs of being a locus for the phenomenon that Wanda Strauven (2006) and others defined as the "cinema of attractions reloaded." However, these attractions have now been far more domesticated by the film market. Hence the criticism of "pyrotechnics" in SF films, spectacles that afford impressive moving images in which narrative and plot are relegated to secondary or tertiary roles. Robert McKee, the author of *Story* (1997) and one of the main gurus on "how-to-write-your-screenplay" in the United States says that "the biggest problem, not only within Hollywood but also in most of the film creators these days, is the emphasis on the surface rather than on the substance. Many film directors spend their entire creative energy in a move to enhance the photography or the special effects, instead of writing stories that show the rich complexity of human nature" (McKee in Essenfelder 2006, E4).

McKee is not referring to SF in particular, but his comment fits perfectly into a contemporary analysis of the genre. Would it be a call for Brazilian film directors with an interest in fantasy cinema or SF to turn their attention to plots that are really creative and interesting, instead of often (pointlessly) taking Hollywood blockbusters as role models? In Brazil, and in other film industries outside Hollywood, it is quite possible that this paradigm shift could indeed improve the feasibility of more consistent national SF cinemas. Certainly, most of the best world SF filmmakers are pretty aware of this, consciously or intuitively. SF in the Brazilian film industry usually fails when it tries to emulate the American model (more precisely, the Hollywood model). This long-standing discussion even surpasses the borders of the SF film genre. The fact is that nobody makes American films better than American film producers, regardless of their nationality, or the nationality of their directors. Likewise, Brazilian filmmakers are experts in Brazilian cinema (no matter how obvious and silly this statement may sound), and the ones interested in Brazilian SF cinema should approach it with clarity. This problem affects not only the Brazilian film industry but also European productions that attempt to "emulate" American SF cinema. Let's consider the example of French film director Luc Besson: films such as *The Fifth Element* (1997) try to emulate the Hollywoodian model for SF, also including participation of American actors, and the result is a controversial SF film that spurs a tremendous feeling of déjà vu. This is not a matter of requesting a national "stamp" of authenticity on the production of a given film, but rather a matter of demolishing the parameters that have been deeply cemented. When the Brazilian film attempts to create an ersatz copy of another national film style chances are it may end up as a *kitsch* film, for obvious reasons. This is what happens in some films of the famous comedy troupe the Goofs (Os Trapalhões), many *pornochanchadas*, and even certain passages in genuine Brazilian SF films like Roberto Pires's *Abrigo Nuclear* (1981). In the Brazilian film industry, SF does not have to be picturesque, caricatural, folkloric, or anything along those lines. We have enough cultural diversity to create good plots in a wide range of different scenarios, something that can be attested by our SF literature. Besides, the Brazilian film and audiovisual industry should take advantage of the quality of our (SF) writers. We believe that it is fundamental to instill in the minds of Brazilian film producers our potential and possibilities. Fortunately, the intrinsic universality of the genre has been acknowledged by more and more Brazilian producers and filmmakers over the last twenty years or so. To some extent, Brazilian audiovisual SF has gained momentum also thanks to the acceptance of foreign producers and decision-makers: let us think of *3%*, the series, among other examples. As already stated by Rivera (in Lim 2009), SF does not occur only in Washington, New York City, or Los Angeles but also in São Paulo, a city that is even more associated with the most recent trends in SF literature. From this standpoint, spectacle films are nothing more than a brand of SF film.

## Literature and the Film Industry

The argument based on lack of funding could partly explain our film industry having only rare instances of SF films. But what about our SF literature? Just like the film industry, literature can also be subject to market demands; however, it cannot be denied that, strictly speaking, making a film is much more expensive than writing a book, and in the latter option the issue of special effects does not exist. Even so—and this is proven by the article penned by Fausto Cunha (Allen 1976, 5–20)—Brazilian SF literature sometimes faces rarefied atmospheres, despite the efforts of some of our publishers (e.g., Gumercindo da Rocha Dória, owner of the publishing house known as GRD) and internationally acclaimed authors. Gerson Lodi-Ribeiro argues that the poor expression of SF in the Brazilian film industry is also a consequence of the poor profitability of this genre in our literature.[21]

In addition, by examining this in greater detail, one could see that the argument based on lack of money is no longer sustainable as the main obstacle that hinders the development of SF in the Brazilian film industry. The advent of more affordable digital technologies, changes in the structure of public endowment for the arts, and international co-productions have mitigated the unfavorable economic circumstances.

So, would there be some other factor, besides the economic aspect, that could discourage our production of SF in any medium? We also ask if there is consistent demand for SF films and literature in our country and, if the answer is yes, then why is this not matched by the production of films, books, graphic novels, and video games in the same genre?[22] It is quite likely that cultural aspects compound the economic factors in the alleged unfeasibility of Brazilian SF films, obstacles that have been addressed in Ginway's *Brazilian SF: Cultural Myths and Nationality in the Country of the Future* (2004), and which would have some connection with the overvaluation of the realist novel and the Brazilian history of underdevelopment. I therefore risk saying that, in addition to the financial issue, a myriad of cultural factors are also involved. Notwithstanding, according to Andrea Bell, "The good news is that the pairing of the phrases 'Latin America' and 'science fiction' no longer provokes the denial or dismissal it once used to. The bad news is . . . it has yet to break through the cultural and economic barriers that keep it from a wider readership at home and abroad" (Bell qtd. in Ginway 2004, 212).[23]

## Scientific Culture and Public Perception of Science

In addition to financial difficulties, film director Clóvis Vieira mentions two cultural factors that hinder the development of SF in the Brazilian film industry: the alleged limited scientific and technological tradition of the country when compared with more developed countries (something that, in theory, would impact people's interest in SF) and also prejudice in the Brazilian film industry in relation to this genre. According to Vieira, the more a nation invests in science and technology, the greater the chance that it will develop a consistent national SF film industry. Certainly, the interest of film artists in SF might be greater if there were more scientific and technological enthusiasm in the country. In this regard, Vieira agrees with film director Elie Politi, who believes that an alleged scarcity of Brazilian scientists would impact the development of the genre.[24] This reasoning, regardless of its good intentions, reinforces certain prejudices in relation to underdeveloped or developing countries, such as "there is no SF in places lacking scientific and technological development." As remarked by Ginway, "The presence of science fiction in Latin America, not only in Brazil, belies David G. Hartwell's statement that, 'there is not yet a really identifiable third world SF. The underdeveloped countries have not responded to the technologically optimistic appeal of SF, perhaps because that visionary future filled with mechanical wonders seems so far beyond their present resources'" (Hartwell qtd. in Ginway 2004, 219, n. 2).[25] Oversimplifying and materialist *in extremis*, this notion establishes a direct link between base and superstructure, neglecting other means and ways a given nation builds up its self-image and speculates on its future. The following words by Brazilian director Clóvis Vieira cast more light on this controversy:

> There is some prejudice within the Brazilian film industry against SF films. They do not consider SF films made in Brazil as serious films. In serious films, you need to address social issues. Even if you make a light film—a romantic comedy, for example—you are also discriminated against. These films—normally made and shown on Globo, light-hearted comedies, some of which were very well made, such as the recent *Se Eu Fosse Você*[26] (2006)—are discriminated against, not being considered serious films. Science Fiction (SF) is included in this category.[27]

At this point, we should briefly recapitulate the discussions on the image that Brazilians have of their own society, in scientific and technological terms. A survey published under the title of *Public Perception of Science—Results of a Research Study in Argentina, Brazil, Spain and Uruguay (Percepção Pública da Ciência—Resultados da Pesquisa na Argentina, Brasil, Espanha e Uruguai)*, by Carlos Vogt and Carmelo Polino (2003), provides data that could be useful for our thoughts and considerations. First, the authors make a distinction between "public perception of science and technology" and "scientific culture." According to Vogt and Polino, "In general terms, the concept of public perception harks back to the processes and mechanisms of social communication and the impacts that these have on the formation of content, attitudes, and expectations of the members of a society, with regard to science and technology" (2003, 41). On the other hand, "The concept of scientific culture has much more complex roots and composition, being identified as a more structural aspect of society, even though a certain type of literature of the last few decades has considered this as a synonym of it [the public perception]" (Vogt and Polino 2003, 41). The authors also observe that "scientific culture is a condition of society, and not an attribute that is expressed in terms of stocks of knowledge as individually expressed by individuals in isolation." So they subdivide it into "scientific culture in a broader sense" and "in a narrower sense" (Vogt and Polino 2003, 65). Thereby, Vogt and Polino blend the discussion concerning a "scientification" of culture as follows: "The 'scientification' of culture is, without any doubt, and among other processes, the result of the social communication of Science, as also the population's level of schooling, the extent of participation—often conflictuously [sic]—in the processes of making decisions about science and technology, tensions and resolutions of problem situations that a society faces (nuclear accidents, wars, epidemics, and so on), regarding which science and technology are able to conceive culturally formative arguments" (Vogt and Polino 2003, 65).

In the United States, the UK, Japan, Australia, Canada, and China, among others, regular research on public perception of science and scientific culture is carried out quite often (Vogt and Polino 2003, 35). In Brazil and in Latin America, however, only recently has this kind of concern gained greater attention. The authors also write that, according to a 2000 informative document of the National Science Foundation (NSF),

> The relation between most people from the US and Science and technology can be characterized by a strongly positive attitude, together with a poor understanding of the content of scientific knowledge and particularly the methods of science. According to the NSF, the fact that a society with little scientific literacy or a lack of ability to show critical thinking may mean that many Americans are not ready to make well-informed choices in the polls or in private life. (Vogt and Polino 2003, 53)

Such a fact jeopardizes the notion that highly developed countries always have populations that are much more informed about science and technology. Nevertheless, the findings do not deny the fact that, in these societies, science and technology are often well accepted by public opinion, or have a prominent place on the social, economic, and political agenda of the country. Notice that Vogt and Polino (2003) worked on evidence collected mostly in the late 1990s and early 2000s. Brazil under the Workers' Party administrations saw a significant increase in terms of scientific production (articles published in academic journals, international cooperation, etc.). However, after the election of Donald Trump in the United States and Jair Bolsonaro in Brazil, followed by a global rise in terms of science negationism and antivaccine movements/organizations in the wake of the Covid-19 pandemic, the Brazilian scenario changed. Bolsonaro's administration was responsible for some of the biggest budgetary cuts in the history of Brazilian science and technology.

What really makes our analysis of the development of SF in the Brazilian film industry more complex is the fact that, according to the study published by Vogt and Polino, research in Brazil has some surprising elements, quite unexpected and different from those found in other countries that took part in the research study (see fig. 9.1). The Brazilian research sample, for example, shows a more evident "pro-science" attitude than that of Argentina, Spain, or Uruguay (see Vogt and Polino 2003, 99, graph 13 in the original book).

As for the perception of "local science and technology," Vogt and Polino note that "in the four countries, there is prevalence of an image of local scientific and technological development according to which there is 'a bit of science and technology in some (thematic) areas'" (2003, 115).

Figure 9.1. The development of science brings problems for society (%). *Source*: Vogt and Polino 2003, 99, graph 13. Used with permission.

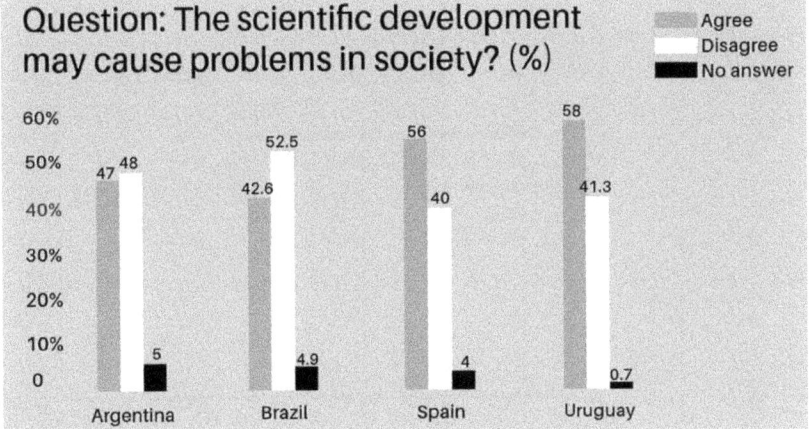

The research also shows that, in Brazil, in contrast to the other countries analyzed, there is a significant adherence to the notion that local science and technology are "highly developed" (see fig. 9.2). The percentage of those who believe that "there is no" local scientific and technological development is very small in all the countries as analyzed here (Vogt and Polino 2003, 115, graph 21 in the original).

According to some writers and filmmakers interviewed for this book (e.g., Gerson Lodi-Ribeiro, Roberto Causo, Carlos Canela, Clóvis Vieira, and Elie Politi, among others), the unsteady performance of the SF cinema in Brazil would result from a rarely or poorly publicized scientific culture, which in turn results from poor governmental investment in consistent, long-lasting scientific or technological policies.[28] Vogt and Polino, however, have confirmed that, even though the large majority of those interviewed in the four countries covered by the research consider that state financing of scientific research is "insufficient," "Brazil once again shows a different pattern of behavior (see fig. 9.3), with a much higher percentage when compared to other countries (27.8 percent), believing that the state machine finances scientific research to a 'reasonably scientific extent' in the country" (Vogt and Polino 2003, 117, graph 22 in the original).

The respondents in the research project conducted by Vogt and Polino recognize that the "little State support" is the main factor that hinders

Figure 9.2. Do you believe there is science and technology in the country? *Source*: Vogt and Polino 2003, 115, graph 21. Used with permission.

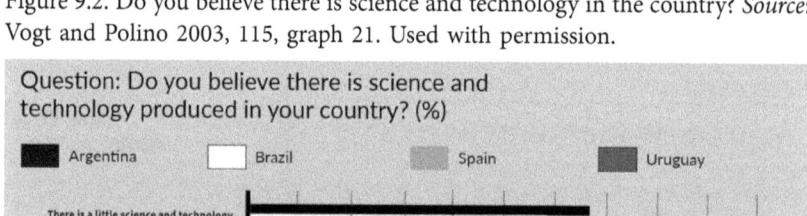

Figure 9.3. In your opinion, to what extent do you feel that the state finances scientific research? *Source*: Vogt and Polino 2003, 117, graph 22. Used with permission.

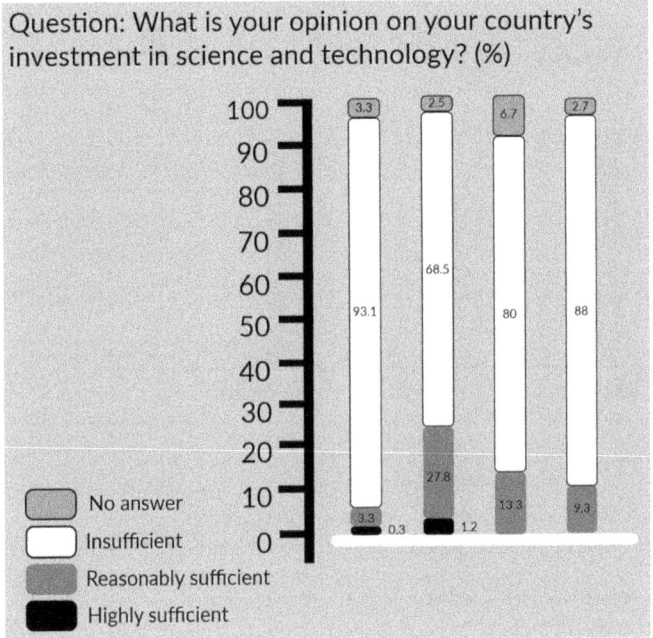

further scientific and technological development in their countries, even though the fact is that, in the case of Brazil, the percentage of those who blame the private sector is somewhat higher than in the other countries considered (Vogt and Polino 2003, 119–21) (see fig. 9.4). The authors also highlight that "most Brazilians highlight the practical application of knowledge as being a positive element of the scientific system in the country (54.9%)" (Vogt and Polino 2003, 121) (see fig. 9.5).[29]

The research study released by Vogt and Polino displays some characteristics of the public perception of science and technology in Argentina, Brazil, Spain, and Uruguay that could make the scientific culture issue more complex, perhaps as a supplementary factor that impedes greater development of SF in the Brazilian film industry or reinforces the notion that SF only flourishes in countries that stand out as scientific and technological centers. The evidence shown by Vogt and Polino presents a panorama that is probably different from the panorama that Brazil experienced fifty

Figure 9.4. Why is there no more development in science and technology? *Source*: Vogt and Polino 2003, 119, graph 23. Used with permission.

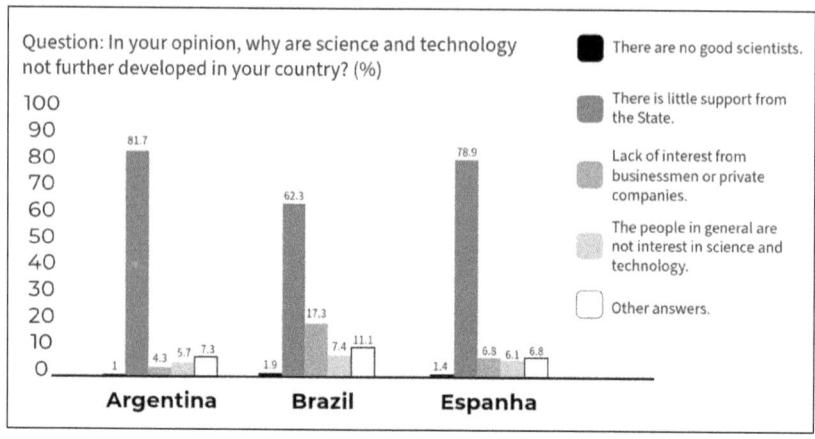

Figure 9.5. What do you think of the results that scientists obtain? *Source*: Vogt and Polino 2003, 119, graph 24. Used with permission.

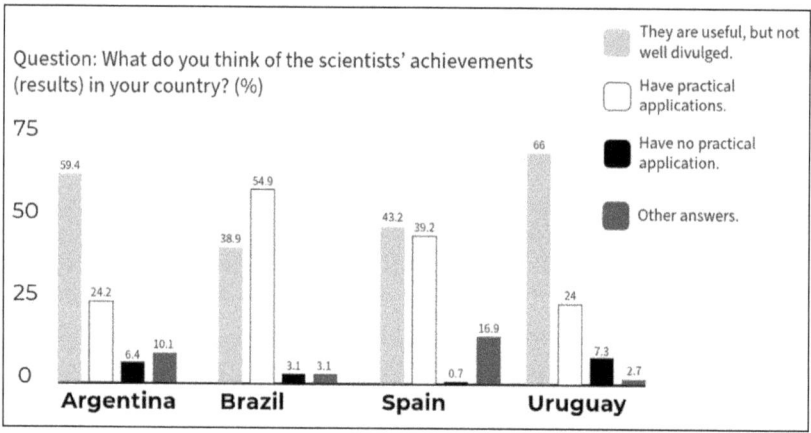

years ago, for example. However, the data must be taken with a pinch of salt, as the authors themselves warn, due to their poor representativeness and provisional nature (Vogt and Polino 2003, 77).

Even so, we must also point out a gradual change for the better, considering the Brazilian scientific and technological productivity over the last thirty years (see fig. 9.6), with a resulting impact on the scientific culture of the country, albeit a gradual one.[30]

Figure 9.6. Brazil: scientific articles published in international journals indexed by the Institute for Scientific Information (ISI), 1981–2004. *Source*: Brazilian Ministry for Science and Technology, Brazil, http://www.mct.gov.br/index.php/content/view/9256.html.

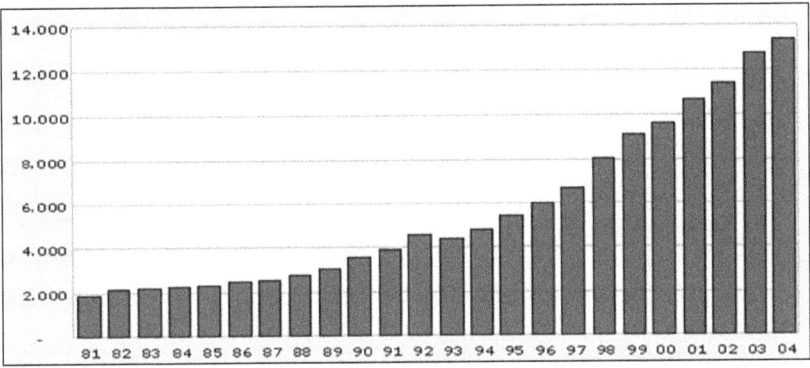

The findings of Vogt and Polino (2003) are naturally out of date now in 2023. After 2003/2004, academic/scientific productivity improved significantly, as a series of public policies were implemented while the Workers' Party (PT) occupied the presidency of the Federative Republic of Brazil (2003–2016)—programs such as PROUNI,[31] REUNI[32] and "Borderless Science" ("Ciência Sem Fronteiras")[33] among others. After the judiciary and parliamentary coup that deposed President Dilma Rousseff in 2016, to this day, all governmental policies to foster education, science, technology, and innovation have been gradually wound down, stopped, or discontinued entirely. A clearer picture of this scenario is provided by an article titled "Intensity of Research & Development in the Countries' Productive Structure" ("Intensidade de P&D na estrutura produtiva dos países"), published in *Pesquisa Fapesp* 307 (September 2021, 11) and based on data from the National Science Foundation: Science and Engineering Indicators, 2020. According to *Pesquisa Fapesp*, in the ranking of the twenty countries with the greatest EVA (Economic Value Added) in knowledge intensive sectors (2002–2018), Brazil occupied the fourteenth position in 2002. It went up to the eighth position in 2010, during President Lula's administration, then fell to eleventh position in the ranking under President Michel Temer. Until 2011, Brazil's performance in the knowledge intensive segments surpassed that of the world's total. It lost dynamism after that year and stabilized as of 2015, at a level slightly higher than in 2002. Even so, in 2018, it accounted for 1.3 percent of the value added worldwide in the knowledge intensive segments and was in the eleventh position. In other words, in 2018 Brazil still retained complex segments in its productive structure, despite the difficulties faced by the economy and industry (*Pesquisa Fapesp* 2021).

However, even though nominal competition may still be low if compared with more developed countries, the rates of scientific and technological production in Brazil, or by Brazilians, still hold a prominent place within Latin America, and a position that must not be disregarded on the global scene. The idea that "there would not be any SF in Brazil due to the lack of science and technology" has therefore totally bitten the dust: even though, considering the population, the sheer size of the Brazilian territory and shortcomings of the education system, the aspect of scientific culture in the country still appears as an obstacle hindering greater prominence of the genre. In addition, in a more globalized context, with intense information flow, it is estimated that a population could easily become aware of the world's scientific and technological imagination without having a significant industrial base.

According to Francisco Alberto Skorupa, "In Brazilian film and television, science fiction is usually an accident, not a goal." (2002, 4). The author further notes that "the role currently played by scientific and technological development in the production of SF is somewhat controversial" (Skorupa 2002, 93). Skorupa says there is strong evidence that points to a link between scientific/technological development and SF production, especially after the Industrial Revolution and the significant scientific development of the nineteenth and twentieth centuries. In this regard, the examples of the United States, the former Soviet Union, the United Kingdom, Japan and Germany stand out; on a smaller scale, Australia, Canada, and Italy are also examples of the close relation between scientific development and SF (Skorupa 2002, 93). On the other hand, Skorupa notes that this argument can appear mistaken at first sight, as, even though technology has a nationality and even an owner, "free imagination is not nationalist,"[34] meaning that it extends outside national borders and can be inspired by foreign stimuli (Skorupa 2002, 316). Claude Lévi-Strauss (1978) has already demonstrated that techno-economic infrastructure and ideology bear no cause-and-effect relationship in a strict sense. On the contrary, Lévi-Strauss defended the entanglement of infra- and superstructure by commenting on the Seechelts and the fishing of salmon: "The empirically lacking salmon is made present by the myth" (Lévi-Strauss 1986, 163). However, Skorupa does not resort to structuralist anthropology to make his point—he actually refers to Fausto Cunha's opinion about the issue. Cunha argued that Brazil could be an example that would jeopardize the equation on science+technology vs. SF: "Technological support is what matters least (after all, we have São José dos Campos,[35] Barreira do Inferno[36] [and] many scientists)" (Cunha qtd. in Skorupa 2002, 93). By extension, India, China, and South Korea would be consistent with Brazil as other examples proving that an industrial or technological base does not necessarily mean development of SF. This is something that is not observed in fact. Out of all members of the BRICS plus South Korea, Brazil is the only one where an SF film industry still seems exotic to a large portion of the population. This scenario has been changing, however, as Brazilian audiences gradually get acquainted with Brazilian SF in film festivals and streaming platforms around the world.

Moreover, Skorupa suggests some subtleties behind the arguments raised by Fausto Cunha. He notes that countries such as Brazil, India, China, South Korea, and Argentina have had centers for scientific excellence approximately since the 1960s, "yet this is not true in the case of daily viewing of technological projects completed within the realm of science, as also for the experience of a consistent policy for education and diffusion of knowledge and scientific concepts" (Skorupa 2002, 93).[37] This means that Skorupa associates SF not only with scientific and technological development but also with policies for fostering and improving public perception of science in the countries concerned. According to the author, "The routine viewing of technological novelties and an educational policy aimed at Science are situations that instrumentalize the imagination and, consequently, the writing of SF" (Skorupa 2002, 94). Still according to Skorupa, "One cannot not ignore that a cultural environment that adds value to research and scientific education is directing or guiding perception and individual sensitivities to an idea of technical and scientific progress" (Skorupa 2002, 316). The author further observes that, specifically in Brazil, not only the process of modernization and industrialization but also the "construction of a new and bold city for the capital of 'a country of the future" and the start of the Brazilian space program show the organization of an environment that is ideal for the development of SF (Skorupa 2002, 94). On the other hand, also according to Skorupa, the lack of readers, which are often poorly encouraged and unprepared for scientific and technological debates, along with a weak editorial market, tend to answer why, for instance, is there no consistent production of space opera in Brazil (Skorupa 2002, 94). If we replace "editorial market" with "film industry," the same could be applied to Brazilian cinema. Skorupa goes one step further in the discussion about the obstacles hindering the development of SF in Brazil, addressing the issues related to government policies and the public perception of science, which takes us back to research studies such as that published by Vogt and Polino (2003). According to Skorupa, the "modernity of underdevelopment" as proposed by Marshall Berman (1998) helps understand the movable bases on which SF is constructed in Brazil. Modernity, in countries like Brazil, would be shown in "islands," and as a (calculated) imposition of the elite on the country. This means that the development assumes "a characteristic of fantasy, as it is forced to feed not on social reality, but on fantasies, mirages and dreams" (Berman 1998, 224). In other words, in a country like Brazil, modernity would be something from far away, yet so close; something present and visible, yet exclusive, isolated, and seldom tangible. This could contribute to a better understanding of the fact that SF in Brazil, whether in literature, the film industry, or television, is often regarded as a "misplaced idea" (paraphrasing the Brazilian literary critic Roberto Schwarz 1992), even by those people responsible for its production, leading to questionable ideas like the one in which Brazilian authors would lack intimacy, familiarity, or the skill to work with SF (Skorupa 2002, 281). In summary, Skorupa equates the problem of the "rarefied atmosphere" for the proliferation of SF in Brazil as follows: "The increase in icons of technological modernity helps to explain the emergence of science fiction in Brazil, whereas the absence of a serious policy of education and democratization of knowledge complements the explanation of why this initiative did not flourish with more vigor, remaining as a literary enclave constantly isolated from the common interest" (Skorupa 2002, 94). In short, the public perception or even the prominence of science and technology in Brazil have not yet reached the same levels as in Europe, the United States, or Japan, even though science and technology in Brazil has attained international visibility. In this case, it is consistent with the proverb that says: "It is not enough for Caesar's wife to be honest; she must be seen to be honest." The lack of widespread public knowledge regarding the Brazilian scientific and technological production may be a variable in the equation, a variable responsible for the lack of a cultural background that would be more inspiring for and more receptive to SF.

## Imperialism and SF

Nevertheless, would there be other variables and hypotheses, other factors that would lead us along another path fraught with questions? What do countries like the United States, Great Britain, France, and Japan have in common, as opposed to China, India, and Brazil, for example? The very mention of space opera in Skorupa's text is highly suggestive. In fact, space opera is an SF subgenre that is significantly inspired by an ideology of colonization that celebrates the notion of the self-made human and the superiority of the Western white ethnicity. We could engage in a lengthy discussion on the issue of scientific and technological development in countries like Brazil (whether we have sufficient scientists or not, etc.). However, there is one element observed in the history of countries such as the United States, France, and the United Kingdom (and also Germany and Japan) that places these countries within a well-defined category: these are all nations that have engaged in serious imperialist projects.

If, on the one hand, we partially disagree with Adam Roberts when he states that SF *is* special effects, on the other hand we partially agree when the same author says that not only the ideology of the Industrial Revolution but also that of imperialism has supplied the cultural melting pot that has encouraged the spate of SF (Roberts 2000, 65) in Western countries (plus Japan). According to Roberts, "SF as a distinctive genre comes out of the Age of Empires precisely because it is necessary for the official ideology of Empire-forming that difference needs to be flattened, or even eradicated" (2000, 65). In his discussion of SF as a subconscious expression of the imperialist ideology (2000, 65), Roberts analyzes the classic *The War of the Worlds*, by H. G. Wells (Roberts 2000, 63–7). According to the author,

> My point is that science fiction first emerges as the underside to this set of cultural dominants; as, in a sense, the dark subconscious to the thinking mind of Imperialism. Where much mainstream Victorian culture, for instance, is about the patent rightness and decency of 'civilisation' as it was then conceived, science fiction explores the problematics of that term. [. . .] It is no coincidence, the argument would go, that British science fiction experienced a burst of inventive creativity at around the time of Wells, Bram Stoker (1847–1912), Olaf Stapledon

(1886–1950) and Rider Haggard (1865–1925); because this period saw the high summer of the British Imperial adventure. Similarly, the rise to world domination of the USA after the Second World War saw a cognate flourishing in American SF, the so-called 'Golden Age' of Science Fiction, leading through the 1950s and 1960s both to SF texts that articulated Imperial anxiety (for instance, *Invasion of the Body Snatchers*, 1956) but also to works (such as the ongoing *Star Trek* series) that are all about exploring the new frontier, transferring the colonisation of the American continent directly onto the galaxy. (Roberts 2000, 66–67)

Therefore, a certain "endogenous" imperialist ideology has thrived for quite some time within SF cinema, not only in terms of tropes, motifs, and inspiration behind the films but also in their very mode of production. There has already been a discussion of the colonialist postures of the European filmmakers who traveled around the world making films with their cinematographs. The SF cinema made by powerful film industries like Germany's in the 1920s or present-day America repeats this attitude by operating, as already mentioned, as a kind of "shop window" or means of propaganda of the scientific and technological expertise and industrial power of some nations. Countries such as Brazil, Argentina, or Mexico, without any significant imperialist history, have no equivalents of *Metropolis*, *Aelita*, Irving Pichel's *Destination Moon* (1950) or Kubrick's *2001* in their filmographies, which could justify the lack of a more consistent boost to SF in these Latin American nations.

For some decades now, we cannot deny that Brazil is an industrialized country. However, our SF cinema is yet to find the same fertile ground as found in the United States, UK, France, Japan, or South Korea. This could also be due to the geopolitical situation of Brazil in the global context; according to Roberto de Sousa Causo, this is because Brazil is a nation in a minor role, rather than a leading player, on the world stage (Causo 2003, 145). But is it really true? Roberts's commentary on SF and imperialism is simply conjecture. However, the notion that imperialist nations have developed more prominent SF still is food for thought. On the other hand, Ginway shows a specific aspect of our culture that can supplement the notion proposed by Roberts, possibly working as an element constitutive of a typically Brazilian SF: "While American science fiction generally embraces technology and change, but fears rebellion or invasion by robots and aliens, Brazilian science fiction tends to reject technology but embraces robots and finds aliens to be generally indifferent or exotic. These differences, I believe, reflect Brazil's colonial and neo-colonial experience, its legacy as a former slave society and its diverse, racially mixed population" (Ginway 2004, 39).

Ginway also asserts that one of the reasons for the limited visibility and production of Brazilian SF is the power exerted by the realist/naturalist tradition that predominates in Brazilian literature, television productions, and the film industry (Ginway 2004, 29). From this perspective, Brazilian works that address social conditions or political and economic issues receive priority in production or distribution and generally appeal to critics and academics, much more so than fantasy or utopian works, which are often considered juvenile or escapist. This attitude may also explain why certain texts with SF premises written by Machado de Assis (2015), such as the short stories "Captain Mendonça" ("O Capitão Mendonça," 1870) or "The Immortal" ("O Imortal," 1882)—the latter was originally published as "Ruy de Leão" in 1872 and later as "O Imortal" (1882) (Causo, 2008)[38]—, are generally less known by the public and receive less attention from critics.

## Brazilian SF Cinema: A Spaceship with Extra Load

Within the scope of the Brazilian film industry, SF inherits the sheer weight of the difficulties common to genres of Brazilian national cinema in general, in addition to the obstacles affecting the Brazilian literature of the genre. Many people are totally unaware of the Brazilian production of SF in terms of literature, sequential art, and visual art, and the works by Brazilian authors (even the ones who had their works published internationally) end up ignored by the Brazilian film industry, which seeks to produce films of this genre.

Currently, however, SF has been increasingly rediscovered outside the map comprising the US, Canada, and Europe thanks to the work of authors who are well aware of the limitations of the Eurocentric approach, including Americans or Europeans such as Rachel Haywood Ferreira, who feels that "in the North, especially in the United States, we suffer from a certain myopia in our perception of the world and its literatures" (2007, 456). Haywood Ferreira mentions Argentine critic Pablo Capanna, who described this phenomenon as "the incapacity, characteristic of all imperial centers in history, to understand what occurs far from the center of power, or how those who live in the periphery think" (Capanna qtd. in Haywood Ferreira 2007, 456).

According to Ginway, Brazilian SF literature may offer significant contributions to the genre globally, in so far as "in their reformulation of the tropes of science fiction, Brazilian writers offer the perspective of the 'outsider,' reinterpreting familiar traditions from a Third World perspective" (Ginway 2004, 209). What Ginway observes in Brazilian literature also occurs, in due proportion, in the Brazilian film industry. In fact, on some occasions SF provided the Brazilian cinema with the atmosphere and the instruments appropriate for social and political critique, especially in the period known as *anos de chumbo*,[39] or "years of lead." About the literature under military rule, Ginway says that "in general, Brazilian dystopian texts portray a rebellion against a technocratic regime as an allegory of the Brazilian people's protest of the military dictatorship" (2004, 33).[40] In a period very dangerous for individual liberties and freedom of speech, when art and media often used metaphors or allegories, SF was very important in films with a reasonable content of social and political protest. This is what we can confirm in a variety of both short and feature-length films, including Olney São Paulo's *Grayish Morning*, Walter Lima Jr.'s *Brazil Year 2000*, Paulo Bastos Martins's *The Messenger: The Man of the Storms*, José de Anchieta's *Stop 88*, and Roberto Pires's *Nuclear Shelter*, among others.

# 10

# Do Brazilians Dream of Edenic (or Industrial) Futures?

The Brazilian anthropologist Darcy Ribeiro reminds us that one of the most notable distinguishing traits that may singularize Brazilians is their extraordinary cultural homogenization. However, "This nation-people did not arise in Brazil from the evolution of previous forms of sociability, where human groups were structured in opposing classes that join to attend to survival needs and progress. It came from the concentration of a slave labor force alien to it, recruited to serve mercantile aims. It arose through processes so repressive and violent in governance that they constituted a continuous genocide and an implacable ethnocide" (2000, 4). Still according to Ribeiro, Brazilians are the byproduct of a collision between bureaucratic rationalism aimed to carry out the official agenda in the new land and the spontaneity shaping it haphazardly, under the constraints of tropical ecology and a despotic world market (2000, 172). Ribeiro constantly blamed the country's extremely unequal society and unbalanced economic development on the Brazilian elite and its exploitative modus operandi. Thus, the way the nation was inserted into the global market appears to be in tune with an economic model based on plantations and slavery that dictated the country's history for so long, "modernized in a reflexive way in spite of its being yoked to this retrograde institutionality, Brazilian society is not configured as an archaic remainder of the western civilization that gave it birth but as one of its external proletariats (. . .)" (2000, 175). Hence (and unsurprisingly), such a controversy between archaism and modernization impacts the country's culture in the broadest sense. Still, according to Darcy Ribeiro,

> Resistance to the innovative forces of the Industrial Revolution and the fundamental reason for the tardiness of the latter cannot be found, however, in the people or in the archaic character of their culture but lie rather in the resistance of the ruling classes. This is particularly so as regards their interests and privileges, founded on an archaic structural order, and an unfortunate method of articulation with the world economy, which act as factors for backwardness but are defended wholeheartedly against any change. (2000, 174)

With due proportions, this "will to inertia" already appears itself as an obstacle to any utopian genre, such as SF. As if Brazil, despite being a "young" nation, was one of the most conservative societies in the world, averse to changes. This national trait appears to emerge in Brazilian SF films of any era, as well as in the way the Brazilian film industry and audiences treat vernacular SF with skepticism in any medium. As Csicsery-Ronay observes, SF keeps contact points with Marxism precisely in its utopian drive and critique of social reality (2003, 113–24). Therefore, would such a will to inertia and resistance to change—stemming from the deeply rooted archaic structures and privileged castes, the scarce, virtually null social mobility, in addition to the fact that Brazil was one of the last countries to abolish slavery—be responsible for the "invisibility" of SF in Brazilian culture? Could the fact that Brazil is a country of unequally balanced modernization, with science and technology still below their full potential, be considered another factor that impedes the development of SF across different media? Could the invisibility or timidity of national SF be ascribed to the significant flaws in the country's educational system and, consequently, in scientific education?

Nearly twenty years after my first investigations into Brazilian SF cinema, all these questions have only been met with incomplete, unsettling answers. In summary, and for the sake of simplification, the barriers to further development and visibility of Brazilian SF cinema are undoubtedly varied. Moreover, once dissociated from one another, none of them provide a satisfactory explanation for the past and present scenarios. Perhaps a good metaphor for the Brazilian SF film might be that of an obsolete and overweight spaceship. This excess load is made up of items as diverse as old artistic prejudices, lack of more long-lived and consistent public policies focusing on scientific and technological development, problems in the public perception of science and technology, absence of a "culture of invention" (or innovative culture), low self-esteem, excessive appreciation of realism at the expense of other styles or aesthetics, cultural elitism, deficiencies in the educational system, and vices as well as feebleness in the Brazilian editorial and audiovisual markets, among other issues.

Nevertheless, since 2007 the panorama of SF in Brazilian film and audiovisual media has changed significantly, and it continues to change. The present book is an attempt to demonstrate how substantive and complex Brazilian SF has become. Many young filmmakers have ventured into SF, fantasy, and horror in contemporary Brazilian cinema with unprecedented success: if not commercial success, at least a very welcoming critical reception, both in Brazil and overseas.

The success of a series such as *3%*, as well as both artistic and scholarly recognition of Brazilian films like Adirley Queirós's *White Out, Black In*, Gabriel Mascaro's *Divine Love*, and Juliano Dornelles and Kléber Mendonça Filho's *Bacurau*, comes down to—or is imminently representative/symptomatic of—the following aspects: (1) the demystification of SF as a genre inaccessible to independent or low-budget productions; (2) the role of new digital media and technologies that have been favoring the venturing into SF on the part of both young and veteran filmmakers; (3) the rediscovery of SF as a "representational mode" or "decoding machine" put at the service of a better understanding of our contemporary agenda along with its main dilemmas and anxieties, and (4) the ever-growing and unneglectable artistic contribution of non-Western artists and filmmakers to the world SF cinema.

In other words, in the early twenty-first century, SF cinema reached a saturation point in terms of the limited visions of "white" futures in New York, Washington, or London. The futures of women in Tanzania or Indonesia, for instance, also matter to us. As well as the futures of rice farmers in Vietnam. The future of Black kids in a favela of Rio de Janeiro in the year 2096 is as worthy of our attention as the future of fishermen in Thailand, Maori hackers in New Zealand, Seminole ranchers in Florida, or Yanomami women in the Venezuelan Amazon, among thousands of other futures. All futures matter. We undoubtedly want to know about them and further discuss our own futures and not only the futures sold by Silicon Valley, Wall Street, Nasdaq, Tesla, Space X, or Virgin Galaxy. Aílton Krenak has somehow warned us in this regard:

> In fact, we spend our lives complaining, but the world we have was made to order. It arrived gift-wrapped and labeled "non-

returnable once opened." We've been waiting two hundred, three hundred years for just this world, and now all these people are moping and moaning: "This is the world they lump us with? This? What sort of world are you boxing and wrapping for future generations? You keep talking about another world, but have you asked the generations of tomorrow if the world you're building is the world they want? (Krenak 2020, 66)

Moving toward a conclusion, but without any presumption to provide final answers, we would like to retrieve some of Paulo Emílio Salles Gomes's ideas as a key for decoding Brazilian SF cinema. As Salles Gomes asserted, "We are neither Europeans nor North Americans. Lacking an original culture, nothing is foreign to us because everything is. The painful construction of ourselves develops within the rarefied dialectic of not being and being someone else. Brazilian film participates in this mechanism and alters it through our creative incapacity for copying. Cinema in Brazil witnesses and delineates many national vicissitudes" (Salles Gomes, qtd. in Martin 1997, 263).

This book is somewhat influenced by metaphors such as Fausto Cunha's "semi-deserted planet" and Salles Gomes's "rarefied dialectics"—but only as a departure point. Salles Gomes's thoughts have always been relevant in our attempts to investigate the allegedly "rarefied" SF in Brazilian cinema. However, many years later and due to present-day research, we can see more clearly that such a "rarefied atmosphere" is less ascribed to the number and consistency of Brazilian SF films than to the way this film corpus is addressed by traditional film scholarship.

As John Rieder writes, "Genre, therefore, is always found in the middle of things, never at the beginning of them" (2017, 20). Rieder also reminds us that the "*attribution of the identity of sf to a text constitutes an active intervention in its distribution and reception*" (2017, 25; emphasis in the original). In his essay "On Defining SF, or Not: Genre Theory, SF, and History," John Rieder (2017, 13–31) scrutinizes SF through the lens of five different positions as follows: (1) SF is historical and mutable; (2) SF has no essence, no single unifying characteristic, and no point of origin; (3) SF is not a set of texts, but rather a way of using texts and of drawing relationships among them; (4) SF's identity is a differentially articulated position in a historical and mutable field of genres; and, finally, (5) attribution of the identity of SF to a text constitutes an active intervention in its distribution and reception (Rieder 2017, 16). Before he delves into the analyses of each position, Rieder opportunely quotes Paul Kincaid's 2003 essay "On the Origins of Genre" along with his proposal, according to which one can neither "extract a unique, common thread" that binds together all SF texts nor identify a "unique, common origin" for the genre (Kincaid 2003, 415 qtd. in Rieder 2017, 20). As Kincaid wrote: "Science fiction is not one thing. Rather, it is any number of things—a future setting, a marvelous device, an ideal society, an alien a creature, a twist in time, an interstellar journey, a satirical perspective, a particular approach to the matter of story, whatever we are looking for when we look for science fiction, here more of overt, here more subtle—which are braided together in an endless variety of combinations" (Kincaid 2003, 416-17 qtd. in Rieder 2017, 14).

As I often try to remind myself, a Brazilian SF film is never just an SF film. Instead, it is a cluster of multiple elements and various sources of inspiration, including SF. Therefore, Kincaid's proposal and the third position investigated by Rieder ("SF is not a set of texts, but rather a way of using texts and of drawing relationships among them") is of primary interest to us here, since we understand SF as a universal macrogenre. Its raw material is the exotic, the exogenous, the unusual, the different, the queer, the chimeric, or everything that may challenge boundaries and definitions. John Baxter (1970) had already claimed SF cinema as an essentially American cultural manifestation by stating that "most countries have attempted sf, some have succeeded to an extent, but the form remains aggressively American, an expression of a national impulse that, like the Western, lies too deep under the American skin ever to be revealed by any but a native son" (Baxter 1970, 208). Even though we do understand the reasons behind such a stance, we could not disagree more with that statement. The insistence on "nationalizing" SF by claiming its patent or copyright seems to contradict the universalizing nature of the genre itself, its intrinsic speculative or experimental vocation. Yet, it does make sense insofar as this rationale echoes not only an international division of labor, but also an international division of intellectual property, so to speak. There is plentiful imagery and iconography reassuring this ideology, such as in the case of Edwin Blashfield's paintings on the domed ceiling in the US Capitol, Washington, DC. Bashfield painted "Human Understanding" as twelve seated figures, male and female, arranged against a wall of mosaic patterning. These godlike human figures represent countries or epochs that, in 1897, when the dome was being built, were thought to have contributed the most to the evolution of "Western civilization." Egypt represents Written Records. Judea represents Religion. Greece represents Philosophy. Rome represents Administration. Islam represents Physics. The Middle Ages represent Modern Languages. Italy represents the Fine Arts. Germany represents the Art of Printing. Spain represents Discovery. England represents Literature. France represents Emancipation. Finally, America represents Science, which is of utmost importance to us here, in the twenty-first century. Why does America represent Science with a capital S? In other words, and under a historical, larger-than-human-lifetime scale, why does America represent Science any more than Egypt, Italy, Spain, or the Arab countries? Naturally, we cannot delve any deeper into this question here, but it is worth posing nonetheless.

The power of such imagery or iconography cannot be underestimated for it represents what we have been calling "cordial iconoclasm":[1] a superstructural or social engineering device that has been important in the history of Brazil, yet equally present in many other national narratives, under different guises and functions. Blashfield's paintings on the dome ceiling illustrate our cordial iconoclasm in the sense that it "kindly" deletes huge portions of human history in favor of a narrative, the one according to which the West is heir to ancient knowledge and wisdom and America represents the most scientific and technologically advanced country in the world.

Iconoclasm refers to the feeling of hatred for specific images and the action of destroying them. However, the relationship is complex since the destruction in most cases is directed to the medium (physical support) through which the idea is conveyed and not to the image itself. For example, in 2001, the Taliban destroyed two Buddha statues (one 53 and the other 34 meters tall) on the mountains in the Bamiyan Valley, Afghanistan. Those specific images were destroyed, but Buddha keeps on existing in both collective and individual imagery. Every image has a material aspect (its support or medium: canvas, sculpture stone, photographic paper, TV, film, digital media, etc.), but it also has an immaterial source; it inhabits an imaginary, a collective "mindscape," so to speak. Thereby, iconoclasm may assume manifold facets in addition to its traditional sense of physical destruction—therefore "cordial iconoclasm."

The descriptive term in our "cordial iconoclasm" refers to Sérgio Buarque de Holanda's (2012a) concept of "cordial man" ("homem cordial") developed in his book *The Roots of Brazil* (*Raízes do Brasil*), whose first edition was published in 1936. According to Buarque de Holanda, the hospitality and generosity so praised by foreigners who visit Brazil define the Brazilian character. Nevertheless, it would be a mistake to suppose that these virtues could mean "good manners" or civility. This ordinary form of social interaction is precisely the opposite of politeness. It can be deceptive in appearance, and this is explained by the fact that the polite attitude consists of something like a deliberate mimicry of spontaneous manifestations in the "cordial man": "it is the natural and living form that has become a formula" (Buarque de Holanda 2012b, 53). "Furthermore, politeness is, in some way, organizing a defense before society. It stops at the outer, epidermal part of the individual, and can even serve, when necessary, as a piece of resistance. It is equivalent to a disguise that will allow everyone to preserve their sensitivity and emotions intact" (Buarque de Holanda 2012b, 53).

The "cordial man" here stems from Latin *cor* (genitive *cordis*), meaning "heart," "of or pertaining to the heart," and Medieval Latin *cordialis*, "of or for the heart." The word also remotely refers to "strings" and, in Buarque de Holanda's specific context, it concerns affection, endearment, family relationships, things from the heart. It means that apparent politeness is equivalent to a disguise that allows everyone to preserve their sensitivity and emotions: "Armed with this mask, the individual manages to maintain his supremacy over the social. And, in fact, politeness implies a continuous and sovereign presence of the individual" (Buarque de Holanda 2012b, 53).[2] The "cordiality" described by the author makes the individual feel, at the same time, the desire to establish intimacy and the horror of any conventionalism or social formalism. This cordiality makes family relationships further expand as the model of any social composition. For this reason, in general, Brazilian individuals do not understand the fundamental distinction between public and private spheres, mainly between state and family. "In the 'cordial man,' life in society is, in a way, a true release from the dread he feels about living with himself, in supporting himself in all circumstances of existence. (. . .)" (Buarque de Holanda 2012b, 53).

Therefore, the "cordial man" is a deception, a psychological and behavioral mechanism fundamental to Brazil's social structure and the Brazilians' formation as a people. In iconoclasm *tout court*, the legacy of any given culture, notably its material, tangible manifestation, is simply destroyed. For instance, over the last few years in Rio de Janeiro, temples devoted to African-Brazilian religions have been invaded by iconoclasts (i.e., evangelical drug dealers and militia) who destroyed idols, demolished monuments, and buildings. Conversely, in cordial iconoclasm, the "other" is destroyed by assimilation. It is silenced and de-individualized when it starts enjoying calculated benefits that only a cordial relationship of closeness or familiarity can provide. Yet the American historian Brodwyn Fischer does not use this term, the overall idea of "cordial iconoclasm" converge with Fischer's thoughts when she applies her concept of "hyperreal ideas" (Mota 2021) in her course at the University of Chicago.[3] Recent events that took place in the wake of the murder of George Floyd in the US may be representative of straightforward iconoclasm that ensued the Anglo-Saxon version of our "cordial iconoclasm." We are referring to protesters tearing down the statue of Edward Colston in Bristol, UK (Bland 2020), and the removal of the statue of the American former Vice President John C. Calhoun in Charleston, North Carolina (Holcombe 2020). In both these cases, narratives construed by some kind of "cordial iconoclasm" suffered a counterstrike in the form of a more straightforward, evident iconoclasm.

To a large extent, we believe that the automatic alignment between SF and American culture masquerades some form of cordial iconoclasm. By the same token, many Brazilian SF films have further demonstrated, through SF vocabularies, semantics, and syntax, how much our cordial iconoclasm has shaped our society and favored the mechanisms of social exclusion, privileges, oppression, and concentration of wealth. Thus, John Baxter's standpoint appears to be the byproduct of an ideology inherently opposed to recent critiques of Eurocentrism (e.g., Shohat and Stam 2013). As put by Aílton Krenak, "The notion that white Europeans could jump in their ships and go colonizing the rest of the world was based on the premise that there was an enlightened humanity that had to go in search of the benighted humanity and bring those savages into their incredible light. This call to civilization was always justified by the idea that there is a right way of being in the world, one truth, or concept of truth, that has guided the choices made down through history" (Krenak 2020, 14). Complying with the claim that SF cinema is inherently American is nothing more than accepting uncritically the most controversial and reactionary international division of culture. This hegemonic strategy appears in tandem with the international division of labor—and wealth. To say that there is no SF in the so-called Third World since non-Western countries would lack the proper scientific and technological infrastructure is a rather ideological, political position that has been adequately deconstructed by several other works and scholars (e.g., Said 1979; Stuart Hall 2007; Shohat and Stam 2013; Fanon 2005; Appadurai 1996; Mbembe 2003, etc.), and by visible facts themselves.

Likewise, defending that SF films *are* special effects (as in Roberts 2000, 152–53) means that only a specific "system" in the vast "galaxy" or "supercluster" of the world's SF is being taken into account (i.e., Hollywood SF cinema and its international simulacra). Thereby, the automatic linking of SF cinema to sophisticated visual effects without any attention to the global history of the genre means denying off-Hollywood and non-Western film industries the access to a universal mode of representation: SF as a macro-genre. The meretricious reasons behind such an opinion (and imposture) are quite understandable.

As everyone knows, not only is SF claimed as a privilege of Western hegemonic powers, cinema has always been assumed as such. It is not by chance that one of the most famous film festivals in the world distinguishes the "best foreign film" from the "best film." To paraphrase Paulo Emílio Salles Gomes once again, it is not surprising for the "colonizer"[4] to propagandize it like this. The problem appears when the "occupied" complacently reproduces such an ideology uncritically. Fortunately, however, and perhaps for the first time in a long history, the one-sided relationship dictated by the colonizer's flagship being welcomed by the colonized is truly showing signs of fatigue. After insisting on surviving in a rarefied atmosphere for quite some time, lurking underground and sometimes rendered "invisible," Brazilian SF cinema is now not only being noticed but is making itself blatantly visible: it is speaking out loud. It is virtually impossible to deny its existence any longer. Brazilians are preproducing, producing, and postproducing SF in film and television, in literature and comics, in theater, on the web, and in video games, notwithstanding the persistent (yet dwindling) obscurantism in the national market. Academic works on Brazilian and Latin American SF have also multiplied over the years to demonstrate that even the old conservative Brazilian academia has gradually yielded to the multiplicity of texts that characterize the SF phenomena in contemporary Brazil.

The increasing number of Brazilian SF, fantasy, and horror films, as well as the festivals that spring up around this film culture, can confirm this significant gamechanger over the last twenty years or so. Brazilian SF films can be seen in various traditional film festivals across the country, such as the Brasília Film Festival, the Rio Film Festival, the São Paulo Film Festival, the Gramado Film Festival, and the Tiradentes Film Festival, among several others. However, some Brazilian film festivals primarily dedicated to SF, fantasy, and horror, have also played an essential role in showcasing and recognizing new generations of filmmakers. Some of these film festivals have transcended the mark of ten annual issues, such as Fantasporto, in its forty-first edition, or Cinefantasy, in its thirteenth edition in 2023. Lastly, new film festivals or special exhibitions specialized in Brazilian or international SF, fantasy, and horror have also gained momentum, such as the Dystopian Brazil Film Exhibition (Mostra Brasil Distópico, in 2017), and Antropokaos: Brazilian Science Fiction Exhibition (Antropokaos: Mostra de Ficção Científica Brasileira, in 2019 and 2021).

The Dystopian Brazil Film Exhibition appeared in a rather tense political moment in Brazil, back in 2017. The show took place in Rio de Janeiro from August 15 through 27, 2017, at Caixa Cultural. Produced by Dora Amorim and Thaís Vidal, with support by the Goethe-Institut, and curated by Rodrigo Almeida and Luís Fernando Moura, the show screened Brazilian SF feature films that catalyzed symptoms of the greatest Western crises in the twentieth century, such as the Cold War and the Brazilian military dictatorship. Among the shorts, the show screened films as diverse as *X-Manas* (2017) by Clarissa Ribeiro, *Flash Happy Society* (2009) by Guto Parente, *The Adventures of Paulo Bruscky* (2010) by Gabriel Mascaro, *Cold Tropics* by Kleber Mendonça Filho, *Zigurate* (2009) by Carlos Eduardo Nogueira, *Éternau* (2006) by Gustavo Jahn, *Hiperselva* (2014) by Helena Lessa, Jorge Polo, Lucas Andrade and Pedro Lessa, *Waiting Room* (*Quarto de Espera*, 2009) by Bruno Carboni and Davi Pretto, *Janaína Overdrive* by Mozart Freire, and *Pacífico* (2010) by Jonathas de Andrade. The curators and organizers of the Dystopian Brazil film festival managed to locate and borrow the few surviving copies in both 16mm and 35mm of some of the 1960s, 70s, and 80s films mentioned in this book, with high-quality screening sessions. It was undoubtedly one of the most comprehensive and thought-provoking Brazilian SF film events in the last few years. The whole show resulted in an exciting print catalog containing essays by film critics, curators, and scholars focusing on the Brazilian SF cinema (Almeida and Moura 2017).[5]

Antropokaos: Brazilian Science Fiction Exhibition (Antropokaos: Mostra de Ficção Científica Brasileira) began its history in 2019 in an action to occupy the film theater at Galpão Cine Horto, in the city of Contagem, state of Minas Gerais. In 2021, Antropokaos gained a second edition with the support of the Aldir Blanc Law[6] and a free online film exhibition. Created by Lea Monteiro and Luís Oliveira, the show took place from March 6 through 28. The feature films exhibited by the show revisit the history of Brazilian SF cinema, while the short films demonstrate how contemporary Brazilian independent cinema has been creating new narratives and realities based on SF, albeit usually with far fewer economic resources. Antropokaos also resulted in an e-book by the same name (Monteiro et al. 2021), a collection of essays on both Brazilian and international SF cinema.

Contagem, in the state of Minas Gerais, is a hotspot in terms of film culture and film production. In addition to the exhibition named Antropokaos, it was home to the independent film production company Filmes de Plástico. Created in 2009 in Contagem, Filmes de Plástico is today headquartered in Belo Horizonte, capital of Minas Gerais. Directors André Novais Oliveira, Gabriel Martins, Maurílio Martins, and producer Thiago Macêdo Correia form the film company. Its movies have been selected in more than two hundred festivals in Brazil and worldwide, such as the Directors' Fortnight in Cannes, Locarno Film Festival, Rotterdam Festival, FID Marseille, Indie Lisboa, BAFICI, Cartagena Festival, Los Angeles Brazilian Film Festival, Brasília Film Festival, and Tiradentes Film Festival, winning more than fifty awards. Some of the Filmes de Plástico's associates did venture into SF cinema with local colors, such as André Novais in his short film *Backyard*. The film tells the story of just another ordinary day in the life of an elderly couple living in the suburbs of Contagem, but with a plot twist in which an alien force eventually changes the lives of these characters forever.

Brazilian spiritist films have one of its most widespread showcases in the Brazilian Transcendental Film Festival (Festival Brasileiro de Cinema Transcendental), created in Brasília-DF more than ten years ago. Organized by the Brazilian spiritualist society Estação da Luz, the Transcendental Film Festival aims to present films with messages of peace and spirituality, regardless of religion, as well as to reward and encourage the best short films with spiritualist motifs. Among the films yearly presented by this festival, some productions can be considered spiritist SF.

The Film & Transcendence Festival (Festival Cinema & Transcendência), created in 2013, also explores the crossroads between science and imagination, capitalizing on Brazilians' widespread spirituality. Some interfaces with SF cinema can also be seen in various films screened in this festival whose 2020 edition featured, among other attractions, the lecture "Dreams, psychodelics and transcendence" ("Sonho, psicodelia e transcendência"), by the Brazilian neuroscientist Sidarta Ribeiro, and Chilean cult director Alejandro Jodorowsky's latest film, *Psychomagic: A Healing Art* (*Psicomagia: A Arte da Cura* 2019), an adaptation of his 2004 book *Psicomagia*.

All these events and the bulk of the Brazilian SF film production have demonstrated, over the last twenty years or so, the increasing relevance of the speculative genre for artists, audiences, and film scholarship in Brazil.

# Final Remarks

## or Hurry Up! We are Dreaming!

> And I won't travel from "thought to thought" but from attitude to attitude. We shall be inhuman—as humankind's greatest conquest. To be is to be beyond the human. To be a human being doesn't do it, to be human has been a constraint. The unknown awaits us, but I sense that that unknown is a totalization and will be the true humanization we long for. Am I speaking of death? No, of life. It isn't a state of felicity, it is a state of contact.
>
> —Clarice Lispector, 1988

As mentioned more than once throughout this book, we are living in an age when science and technology have become fundamental assets to human civilization.[1] Humans reached a point of no return in terms of their dependence on science and technology a long time ago (see Clark 2003). In the Anthropocene, or Capitalocene, global crises such as climate change and pandemics can only be solved with science, technology, and social engagement. Notwithstanding, conspiracy theories, dogmas, and science negationism have shown how deep-rooted irrationalism and destructive drives have plagued people worldwide. The Covid-19 pandemic in the early 2020s has made it even more evident how unbalanced and biased the economic system and our lives are and how much we need science and education in order to form a new humankind in harmony with the planet.

SF may be a superstructural manifestation of this scenario. The genre has always been identified with science or, at least, with an "esthetics of science" (Carr 2019), some level of rational thinking. If a term like lo-fi sci-fi is too restrictive, whereas scientific realism may sound too ambitious and perhaps stigmatized, we would propose something in between, another way to address both Latin-American SF and Brazilian SF cinema. I would suggest the term "science drama" (dramaciência)[2] as an amalgam of SF and melodrama.[3] This category, if used to name a vast body of Latin American films defined as SF, yet hardly visible as such, would take into account the legacy of melodrama in Latin American fiction, herein integrated to speculations on discontinuous chronotopes. Science drama would be, therefore, a subgenre of SF in which the realist approach with a touch of melodrama prevails or guides the speculative dimension in the fiction.

No matter how SF can distance itself from the scientific method, the word "science" is constitutive of the genre; it is there to constantly remind us of an "idea" of science that, somewhere in time, had been there and often returns. However, according to Aílton Krenak, "It's been a long time since there was anyone who really thought with the freedom of what we've learned to call a scientist. There are no more scientists. Everyone capable of innovating is swallowed up by the thing-making machine, turning out more merchandise" (Krenak 2020, 63). Ergo, where to find real innovation? How to retrieve the true freedom of thought of pioneering science unchained before science and technology fell prey to capitalism? In dreams, perhaps?

In his 2023 feature film *Pictures of Ghosts* (*Retratos Fantasmas*, 2023), Kléber Mendonça Filho states that "futuristic films are also documentaries." Mendonça Filho's comment is about the film *The Sect* (*A Seita*, 2015), directed by André Antônio.[4] If there is any link between *The Sect* and *Pictures of Ghosts*, this lies in the fact that both films construe a cinematographic portrait of Recife focusing on memories, ghosts, meaningful territories, urban ruins, and dreams.

*The Sect* is a queer postapocalyptic SF film in which a privileged immigrant from the "space colonies" returns to Earth to live in the decadent capital of Pernambuco, Recife in the year 2040. The film maps Recife's territories as the main character wanders through the city's streets, amid dilapidated buildings, ruins, and deserted areas. The city's desolate exteriors contrast with the interior of his apartment, filled with nineteenth-century furniture and kitsch iconography. As time goes by in Recife, the main character interacts and has sex with different partners. This routine makes him resume the "old" habit of sleeping. In 2040 in the space colonies, he explains, a vaccine had allowed humans to stay awake 24/7. Sleeping became useless, same with dreaming. While roaming the city streets, he finds out about the existence of "the Sect." Longing for dreams, the main character attends one of the Sect's ceremonies. There he will be able to dream plentifully in the company of fellow dreamers.

As remarked by Krenak, dreaming is a practice perceived by many different cultures and peoples, not merely as part of the daily experience of sleeping and dreaming. Unlike the white, Western capitalist culture where dreams often have no further relevance nor impact, numerous non-Western peoples find in dreaming a disciplined guidance for actions in their daily lives (Krenak 2020, 52). "For some people, to dream is to step outside of reality, relinquish the practical meaning of life. For others, however, there is no meaning to life unless informed by dreams, the place we go in search of songs, cures, inspiration, and even solutions to practical problems that befuddle and elude us in the daytime, but which are laid out in all their possibilities in the realm of dream" (Krenak 2020, 52–53).

According to the Brazilian neuroscientist Sidarta Ribeiro (2019) and other authors, dreams have likely played a vital role in the evolutionary history of the human species. Dreams, from this perspective, are immaterial "tools" capable of preparing (or training) our species for the future. Ribeiro explains that about seventeen thousand years ago, in the Lascaux caves in France and in Altamira, Spain, humankind likely had to deal with three types of daily "problems," very "simple" or objective issues, but with inexorable consequences: drink, eat, and avoid predation (2019, 39). Dreams may have been, at that moment, fundamental for the human mind to get around these problems by dreaming of "probabilities" and "hypotheses" (i.e., "testing" worst-case scenarios). Ribeiro refers to this period as an essentially "Darwinian" context. "The dream was the cinema of our ancestors, far more fascinating because it was potentially real" (Ribeiro 2019, 42). With natural selection and the passage of time, today, each individual must deal with a myriad of minute, medium, and large problems together, both short and long-term, confronting dozens of issues to be solved on a daily basis. To prey on and to be preyed upon may still be a problem for humans in some regions of the world, but not in cities with relatively high HDI, for example. Thereby, our dreams are now populated by these "little" problems, such as paying the bills, studying for a test, moving to another home, applying for a job, etc. However, these dreams keep playing a "pedagogical," "training," or "essayistic" role in many ways. As Ribeiro summarizes: "Long before Freud, dreams were believed to be about the future. After him, dreams came to be seen as an inaccurate but significant reflection of the past. Almost eighty years after his death, the accumulated evidence demonstrates that both conceptions are correct. Step by step, through a winding journey, a general theory of sleep and dreams takes shape. It combines past and future to explain the dream function as a crucial tool for survival in the present" (2019, 33). Ribeiro (2019) also defends the idea that the study of human dreams must encompass a wide array of knowledge and sciences. Dreams cannot be entirely understood only through the lens of biology or neurosciences. In a virtual meeting[5] organized by the Brazilian publishing house Companhia das Letras titled "Ideas to Postpone the End of the World" ("Ideias para Adiar o Fim do Mundo"), Ribeiro's thoughts on human dreams converged with Aílton Krenak's philosophy. In the company of Krenak and repeating the main arguments of his 2019 book, Ribeiro explains that humankind as the species we know has been around for approximately three hundred thousand years. It means that, in terms of "hardware," the human body and mind are relatively old, but in terms of "software," that is, culture, everything has been changing fast. The last two hundred years have had a tremendous impact on the way we dream. Broader contexts, such as the industrial revolutions and particular events like the invention of the electric bulb, all left an indelible mark on our lives while we have been either awake or sleeping. Radio, film, television, the internet: the changes keep accelerating and impacting the way everyone sleeps and dreams. Ribeiro considers our cultural contexts and the advent of new techniques and habits the "software" capable of changing our dreams. Here, we suspect that SF could be regarded as part of the "code" in that broader "software": a very relevant, influential part of the code.

According to Ribeiro, while dreaming, the human brain recycles memories and other data from the past to speculate on possible futures: *"the dream prepares the dreamer for the next day"* (2019, 36; emphasis in the original).[6] This is what Ribeiro calls a "probabilistic oracle" ("oráculo probabilístico") (2019, 279), a kind of embodied technology or ability that granted a considerable advantage to our species, even though it is far from being an exclusively human gift. When Ribeiro refers to dreaming as a "probabilistic oracle," we cannot refrain from thinking of SF literature (and audiovisual SF) as "filtered," "refined" forms or byproducts of such a probabilistic oracle, produced and put in circulation while we are awake. This link appears to be even more evident when Ribeiro mentions Jorge Luis Borges's short story "The Library of Babel" ("La Biblioteca de Babel") (2000) as a metaphor. According to Ribeiro, "Likewise, a dream is a possibility of imagining potential futures through a mechanism capable of prospecting past experiences and forming new psychic conglomerates, bringing together old ideas in a new way. Everyone who had successful ideas and transformed the world, those who managed to transform themselves into what they wanted, all those people, without exception and by definition, lived the days and nights when they had not yet done any of that. And then they dreamed" (2019, 99). In this sense, all art by definition, but particularly SF (including folk tales, the utopian genre, and everything else that preceded SF but shared a similar purpose or aesthetic effect), could be imperfect fragments or residues of Ribeiro's "probabilistic oracle." As Ribeiro states in the virtual meeting with Krenak, by dreaming we can speculate on or apply critical scrutiny to an imagined future. Obviously, most of our dreams will never really come to fruition; they are not even close to any possible future reality we may end up experiencing in the flesh. However, as Ribeiro further explains, the simple fact that we dream of something that may not happen does impact our lives in some way. Any dream can potentially change our way of thinking or our feelings, and this can be an actual, tangible, and material effect that stems from the simple act of dreaming. So, what if we adopt the same rationale in creating SF? What if, *mutatis mutandis*, the simple fact of reading or watching SF impacts our future: the way we build up expectations concerning our futures, both individually and, most importantly, collectively?

Ribeiro underscores that Western societies lost their ancient knowledge about dreaming over the last few centuries and embraced science and technology as the Holy Grail, a new totem. As he explains in his book (2019), the relevance of dreams lost ground to the capitalist society based on material productivity, market value, technique, and utilitarianism. Ribeiro also explains that the roughly one billion nights during which humans had dreamed were put aside over the last five hundred years or so, particularly in the last hundred years, when the marriage between capitalism and science overtook dreaming as a survival strategy, a means of acquiring knowledge. For a long time up until the present, sleeping and dreaming have been considered a necessary but undesired "break," literally a "non-time" or "non-life," in so far as sleeping and dreaming do not generate any profit nor surplus according to our mode of production or economic system. However, this significant change, the hegemony of the capitalist society underpinned by science and technology, appears to have entered a downward phase. As remarked on by Ribeiro in the memorable online talk with Aílton Krenak, the five hundred years of modern and contemporary Western societies made us stop dreaming about possible futures, which does not make sense, insofar as we live today in a world full of possibilities favored by all the knowledge we have accumulated over hundreds of thousands of years. Incidentally, David Fisher's "capitalist realism" (2009) may be one way to put it, referring to Sidarta Ribeiro's dream-blindness, so to speak. It is easier to imagine the end of the world than envision a system other than capitalism (Fisher 2009).

Hence, what if SF could be regarded as a "return of the repressed" to some extent? Is it possible that SF has become the means through which Western societies or Western-modeled societies reconcile dream and logos, dream and technique? Could SF be considered the means that Western societies or Western-modeled societies found to (day)dream collectively, in a "scientifically" acceptable manner? As recalled by Ribeiro and Krenak, many Amerindians are still capable of collective dreaming. By contrast, the Western capitalist society not only underrates dreaming (sleeping does not make any money, in principle), but it barely allows individual dreams. Again, let us imagine for a moment the possibility of SF opening the door to possible collective dreams.

Moreover, it is perhaps in this way that SF, and particularly SF cinema, could be closer to the dream—or to this contemporary idea that science has of human dreams and their function. As a species, we cannot all have the same collective dream—or share a dream in real time, like in Christopher Nolan's film *Inception* (2010) or the Mercerism[7] in Philip K. Dick's well-known novel *Do Androids Dream of Electric Sheep?* (1968), among other examples. Art has always played this role of a collective, communal dream, be it in literature, painting, theater, sculpture, architecture, performing arts, and so on. Any work of art can be regarded as such, as an engaging collective dreaming, regardless of authorship. It suffices to accept the notion that, once created, a work of art belongs to its readers, viewers, or listeners. However, these days we would like to further emphasize that, potentially, the SF genre in film, literature, video games, etc., may be the most proficient form of collective dreaming, insofar as SF dreams in a semantics, a syntax, and an overall aesthetics that are organically, straightforwardly linked to our present mindset and our way to live in the world of today. This is the aesthetics of science and technology, as described by Terry Carr. One of Carr's more accurate insights is that

> the essence of science fiction is not that it presents the likeliest futures, but rather that its futures are plausible for the duration of each story. Like all fiction, science fiction is built on aesthetics more than anything else, and that's as it should be.

Fiction is about people's responses to life's problems, ironies, and ambiguities; at its best, any kind of fiction is directed at the emotions. Science fiction has gone further than most fiction in realizing that intellectual interest is a form of emotion, that science can be the basis of good stories because its fascination is a strong emotional response that blends with feelings of hope, fear, and beauty.

Science fiction isn't really about science—in truth, it's about the aesthetics of science. Logic has its own beauty: the neat symmetry of Newton's Laws of Motion, or the cool equations of evolution. Plato's ideals were an early attempt to celebrate the logic of the universe; and since his time we've learned that the universe is infinite and so is the delight of its expanding possibilities.

Even pure fantasy stories, at their best, show the fascination of logic. The best fantasies present readers with a single fantastic concept and proceed to explore its consequences as rigorously as any science fiction story would; a writer who presents a vampire on page one and then tells us on page twenty that the vampire can also teleport is cheating readers, because the rules of the story are lost. As H.G. Wells said, "If anything is possible, nothing is interesting." (Carr 2019, 269)

In times like ours, when a pandemic has had such an impact on human life (and death) and politics worldwide, we can more precisely gauge how much our existence depends on science and technology. Whereas every single individual in the world may dream of the cure for cancer, HIV, or Covid-19, SF provides us collective dreams related to all these concerns and much more. Moreover, the idea of SF as a collective dreaming "software" herein is not unrelated to poetry and Seo-Young Chu's idea of lyricism as a driving force in the genre (2010). Chu underlines the scarcity of studies on SF poems and how poetry is rarely seen as a suitable medium for the genre. Indeed, from a narrow, orthodox perspective, the SF dimension of poetry is often underrated in favor of more "SF-friendly" media or languages, for example, the novel, the short story, film, video games, and sequential art. Nevertheless, non-Western SF production may signal otherwise. In Brazilian SF, for instance, much of the genre can be found not only in teledramaturgy but also in poetry and, thereby in music, notably the Brazilian Popular Music (Música Popular Brasileira, or simply MPB for short). The study of SF in MPB is still an area where much more work has yet to be done.

Modernist writer and poet André Carneiro is often celebrated as one of the greatest Brazilian SF authors of all time. But also the finest mainstream Brazilian poetry also sometimes featured SF tropes or motifs (either explicitly or indirectly), as in João Cabral de Melo Neto's "The End of the World" ("O Fim do Mundo," in Bishop and Brasil 1997, 120–21), Carlos Drummond de Andrade's "The Machine of the World" ("A Máquina do Mundo" 2015, 240–9), or Manuel Bandeira's "Pasárgada" (2021[1930]).[8] Often considered the greatest Brazilian poet of all times, Carlos Drummond de Andrade wrote several poems with an SF touch, such as "It Lacks a Flying Saucer" ("Falta um Disco," in Andrade 2015 [1972], 54–56), "The Greatest Train in the World" ("O Maior Trem do Mundo," in Souza 2019 [1984]), "Lira Itabirana" (in Souza, 2019 [1984]), "The Bomb" ("A Bomba," 2012), and "Science Fiction" ([1962] 2015, 299).

Yet, why is that important? So what if some of the finest Brazilian poets indulge in SF imagery in their poetry? According to Chu, "SF cannot be understood as *narrative* without concurrently being understood as *lyric*" (2010, 67; emphasis in the original). The author further explains, "Hence the moment when a humanoid robot comes alive is not only a narrative event but also a spatiotemporal trope—a *twist*, a *turn*, in space-time—charged with the lyric energies of personification. Within the narrative universe of SF, the literal and the metaphoric share ontological status. As a figurative discourse whose grammatical mood is indicative, SF can provide a representational home for referents that are themselves neither purely literal nor purely figurative in nature" (Chu 2010, 67; emphasis in the original). In what realm do "the literal and the metaphoric share ontological status"? In what domain are "referents (. . .) neither purely literal nor purely figurative in nature"? When the principle of the excluded third (*principium tertii exclusi* or *tertium non datur*)[9] frequently nullified? In dreams. And perhaps in SF as well.

In addition to the well-known proximity between cinema and dreams, SF films could perhaps be considered artifacts "specialized" in an intellectual kind of "experiment" that provides us with audiovisual blueprints for possible future choices and actions. Somewhat similar to the way we usually try to "rationalize" dreams and interpret them in some way, SF films often present themselves as "previously organized dreams," a mass of conjectures or hypothetical scenarios that, for the sake of an escape valve or thought experiment, can further contribute to the constant exercise of "daydreaming" at the collective level of spectatorship. Hence, there is a "nodal" situation in Brazil today (Bode and Rainer 2013),[10] in which the country can choose between utopia or dystopia, or even choose none of them and prepare itself for a more feasible reality and a more tangibly egalitarian future society at ease with the planet and the environment. We firmly believe that Brazilian SF cinema has rehearsed possible scenarios, possible options, and likely actions. While writing these lines, the options still seem to be open; there are real chances that Brazil will return to the path of more sustainable development and give up on the quest for a fascist and/or religious fundamentalist state. Grace Passô's *Republic* best synthesizes our idea of audiovisual SF as collective dreaming or a collective lucid dream. For Grace Passô's character in the film proposes precisely this: (1) Brazil is a dream, (2) it has been dreamt of by a shaman, (3) at any moment the dreamer can awake and, thereby, (4) Brazil will be no more. The Brazilian dystopia in which a Black human being lives in confinement due to a pandemic, isolated in her tiny apartment in São Paulo, the biggest city of Latin America, can only be fully fleshed out with a touch of SF: with the due cognitive estrangement (Suvin 1979) provided by an apparent trivial chat on the cellphone between daughter and mother, in which the former explains to the latter that we are simulations (i.e., characters in a dream). The fable told by *República* also reminds us, in the present day, of the role of dreaming in ancient societies. As Sidarta Ribeiro explains in his archeology of dreams in human history, "The successful navigation of this new universe turned out to be a social specialization. It was the embryo of shamanism, the great-great-grandfather of religion, medicine and philosophy" (2019, 43). Ribeiro also remarks that in Umbanda—a highly syncretic Brazilian religion also influenced by Christian dogmas on the afterlife—it is believed that dreams are the portal to enter into communication with deities and the people's souls (2019, 51).

Grace Passô's *República* subtly evokes all this background amidst an SF atmosphere in tune with the ideas of low-fi sci-fi. No need for special effects to provoke cognitive estrangement beyond orthodox SF storytelling. Drawing on Chu's (2010) ideas on a "science-fictional theory of representation," one could also see Grace Passô's character in *República* as a "metaphor," a "dream of literal sleep"—or vice versa. Passô's film is the eloquent outcry of a reality that can be no more; it can only be accepted as a dream, a simulation, a transitional state. The bellow of the excluded catalyzes cognitive estrangement in non-Western, peripheral SF, which, as remarked by Alex Rivera, best represents the majority of people in the world: the "SF from the South" (Lim 2016).

The queer, chimerical kind of SF of Clarissa Campolina's *Solon*, in turn, offers an intriguing reflection on our relationship with the environment, the fragility of human existence, and its organic relationship with the world we live in. The strange creature in *Solon* initially stands for a clueless human species that, step by step, tries to find its role in the world. The encounter of earth and water, favored by the creature, gives way to a new reality when a woman is eventually born. Thus, Campolina's *Solon* also provides a sensuously cinematic elaboration on Ailton Krenak's ideas regarding the gradual divide between humankind and its planet: "For a long time we have been alienated from the organism to which we belong—the earth. So much so that we began to think of Earth and Humanity as two separate entities. I can't see anything on Earth that is not Earth. Everything I can think of is a part of nature" (Krenak 2020, 22).

SF films like Grace Passô's *República* and Clarissa Campolina's *Solon*, among many others, could ultimately be regarded as "rationalized dreams." As the future is constantly being built, tomorrow can start being designed now. If, on the one hand, according to some neuroscientists, dreams can play this cognitive, pedagogical function (the function of making us work on hypotheses and problem-solving techniques), on the other hand we can recognize in SF cinema something a bit similar or equivalent to that, but on a collective, superstructural level. Perhaps it can be thought of as collective dreams—just as other forms of art, obviously—but specialized in problem-solving techniques related to our present and future as a species. Our present, both in Brazil and in the world, is full of uncertainties. Beyond Hollywood spectacle and matinees, the world's SF cinema, including Brazilian SF cinema, has helped us face these uncertainties.

Hence, we are here partially inspired by Vint and Bould's ideias (in Gunn, Barr, and Candelaria 2009, 43–51), for example, but largely provoked by the empirical observation that a great deal of global SF cinema has shortened the distance between reality and fabulation. SF has become more and more relevant, to the point that the mere predicament "in the near future" often sounds redundant: the future (or lack thereof) is already happening. In other words, the most recent or contemporary Brazilian SF cinema seems to inspire and even justify—along with international SF cinema—a variety of memes in the form of diagrams that seek to demonstrate how much humankind in 2021, for instance, is in the grip of more than one dystopian universe as described by SF literature.

Films like Adirley Queirós's *White Out, Black In*, Gabriel Mascaro's *Divine Love*, and Juliano Dornelles and Kléber Mendonça Filho's *Bacurau*, among several other titles, point in this direction, as they "shorten" the gap between dystopian SF and empirical, tangible reality. These films' impact and exoticism appear to rely on a curious sense of "proximity," an unfathomable sense of "realism." This is not exclusive to Brazilian or Latin American SF cinema; on the contrary, it looks like a global phenomenon: the path of extrapolation, in international SF cinema, seems to be getting shorter and shorter: the future is "right around the corner" and, different from Sérgio Buarque de Holanda's (2012b) "cordial man," it is blatantly inhospitable.

Another central argument derived from the investigations contained in this book concerns a possible social function of speculative fiction, particularly SF cinema. In times of social and/or political unrest, SF (cinema) can be as eloquent or elucidative as realist fiction, realist films, or documentaries. By the same token, of course, any genre or mode of expression can also lapse into conveying less progressive discourses. However, in Brazilian SF cinema, it is more frequent that the genre offers critical readings of a gloomier and unfathomable reality in moments of greater political and social tension.

The tense political and economic situation, the recent detour to the extreme right, and the Covid-19 pandemic have all rarefied the air, but Brazilian SF cinema has been finding a way to take a deep breath and keep going. Brazilian SF cinema is breathing; it is perhaps more alive than ever. As Aílton Krenak recalls, in Guarani the word *nheẽ* can mean "life breath."[11] Valéria Macedo observes that León Cadogan (1959) translated *nheẽ* as "soul-word," whereas Pierre Clastres (1990) translated *nheẽ* as the "inhabitant word" (2017, 518). León Cadogan (1959), Bartolomeu Melià ([2010]1979), Elizabeth Pissolato (2007), and other authors have often translated *nheẽ* as "soul-word." However, as a Native Brazilian academic Sandra Benites explains, *Nheẽ porã* has plenty of meanings. Still, one of its prime significations is "the good word," "beautiful words": "It is often used to give advice, to address the person who is emotionally upset or angry" (Benites 2020, 38).[12] Benites further explains that *Nheẽ* is the foundation of the Guarani person—"for us Guarani, only after a child starts walking she has *ã*, that is, *ã* is something of the earth, of this world"

(Benites 2015, 12).[13] Benites observes that although "soul" and "spirit"[14] can be synonymous in Portuguese, in the Guarani language these terms have different meanings. Therefore, the author suggests that a possible translation of *Nhe'ẽ* into Portuguese, closer to the original meaning in the Guarani language, is *spirit-name*" (Benites 2015, 12).[15]

Despite these linguistic and cosmogonic controversies, we believe that world SF has evolved inasmuch as it has recognized non-Western knowledges, even ancient pieces of knowledge and cultures. To further understand the SF cinema from the "South," it is also necessary to embrace, more receptively, the lyricism, the music, and the life-breath of other peoples, other worlds. Brazil's variety of approaches to SF gives rise to a myriad of trends and subgenres, as varied as the Tupinipunk, the Brazilian Afrofuturism, Amazofuturism, Sertãopunk, and a cannibal-carnivalesque SF manifested in literature, visual arts, graphic novels, film, and television. For all these reasons, this book ends by paying homage to life, to the joy of breathing and dreaming, in a tribute to the "good words." We hope these pages have brought you *Nhe'ẽ porã*.

# Notes

## Introduction

1. In the original:

Amor,
Estou triste porque
Sou o único brasileiro vivo
Que nunca viu um disco voador. (. . .)

Translated into English by Alfredo Suppia and Felipe de Souza Mello.

2. Lúcia Nagib suggests a more inclusive and polycentric concept of *world cinema*. Nagib reviews Andrew's atlas, and advocates the view that binarism in film criticism and theory should be scrapped. Following the thoughts raised by Ella Shohat and Robert Stam (2013), according to which old dichotomies such as "we" and the "other," "the center and the periphery," "the West and the rest," are not only mistaken but also unnecessary, Nagib says that traditional cinematography theories, based on the opposition between Hollywood and world cinema, do not cover the complexities of contemporary film production.

3. "Cinema da Retomada" was the name given to the "renaissance" of Brazilian film in the early 1990s, encompassing the Brazilian film production from 1993–94 to 1998. However, the literature still lacks consensus on this matter—this period might well stretch further into the 2000s or end earlier, in 1998, depending on the author. The Retomada was inaugurated by films such as Sérgio Rezende's *Lamarca* (1994) and Carla Camuratti's *Carlota Joaquina: Princesa do Brasil* (1995), whose box-office and critical reception were outstanding for the Brazilian standards at that time. While some authors consider Walter Salles' *Central Station* (*Central do Brasil*, 1998) the end of this film cycle, others extend the Retomada years to 2002/3, with the release of Kátia Lund and Fernando Meirelles's *City of God* or Hector Babenco's *Carandiru* (see Ortiz Ramos 1997; Souza 1998; Nagib 2002; Butcher 2005; and Marson 2009).

4. In the sense of the 1922 Brazilian modernist movement and Oswald de Andrade's "Manifesto Antropófago" (2017).

5. "nommer, définir et délimiter un genre, c'est tout d'abord poser un certain regard sur un texte. D'une certaine manière, les genres sont affaire de *point de vue*. Tel texte, selon le point de vue que l'on adopte, peut appartenir à tel ou tel genre, et tel genre, selon le point de vue que l'on adopte, peut être décrit comme tel autre genre." (Denizot 2010, 226). All translations from both Francophone and Lusophone authors into English were by me.

## Chapter 1

1. Antônio Leão da Silva Neto (2002), in his *Dictionary of Brazilian Films*, indicates 1918 as the film's release year.

2. Unfortunately, much of the Brazilian silent cinema is lost, as well as a significant portion of the national production of the first fifty years. The nitrate used in the film of the silent period, of easy combustion, added to precarious storage and transport, resulting in the loss of the vast majority of films of the time. The lack of a more ambitious preservationist mentality and management and strategy problems continued to sacrifice Brazilian titles, even those in celluloid. Only with the training of personnel and the foundation of bodies such as the Cinemateca Brasileira (São Paulo), the Cinemateca do MAM (Rio de Janeiro), and the Museums of Image and Sound (Rio, São Paulo, Campinas), has the loss of Brazilian cinematography been slowed (see Ramos and Miranda, 2004, 244). According to Carlos Roberto de Souza (2017), nearly forty-five hundred Brazilian films were produced from the late nineteenth century to the early 1930s. However, only about three hundred films, including fragments of films, can be seen today. Roughly 90 percent of that film production did not survive.

3. All the film synopses and commentaries appearing in this chapter were extracted from *Jornal do Brasil*, the biggest national newspaper in the early twentieth century in Brazil, whose microfilms are preserved and archived in the National Library (Biblioteca Nacional), in Rio de Janeiro. The commentaries were freely translated into English by this author. The film titles are also free translations made by this author.

4. Often considered a film genre, the *cantante* (loosely translated as "singing film") consisted of 1910s musical films dubbed in real time by singers behind the screens or unnoticed by the film spectators.

5. *Revista* refers to *teatro de revista*, a theatrical genre with a markedly popular taste, which played an important role in the history of the performing arts, both in Brazil and in Portugal, until the mid-twentieth century, when it reached its peak. With origins in France during the second half of the eighteenth century, the *teatro de revista* (something like "magazine theater") thus designates the kind

of theatrical show consisting of scenes with comic overtones, interspersed with musical and choreographed numbers. As in the operettas and musicals, the *revista* combines contributions from music, dance, and theater in a global performance. However, it lacks a clear narrative thread. A general theme or subject serves as a motif for the sequence of autonomous numbers, in which individual performances alternate with dance groups. This theatrical genre reached great popularity in Brazil, especially in Rio de Janeiro, due to the well-humored criticism with which it scrutinized the country's daily life.

6. The "White Table" ("Mesa Branca") is a well-known ritual in Brazilian spiritism, consisting of a meeting between mediums whose objective is to help obsessive spirits to find redemption. It is around this table covered by white cloth that the mediums gather the participants of the ceremony in order to put them in contact with their beloved ones in the afterlife.

7. For more information on the film *O Jovem Tataravô, see Cánepa* (2008) or Reis (2012), https://www.portalbrasileirodecinema.com.br/horror/filme-o-jovem-tataravo.php?indice=filmes (accessed June 3, 2024).

8. More about Kardecism and Brazilian spiritist films will be discussed in the following chapters in this book.

9. "O que impedia o desenvolvimento do cinema no Rio, para não falar no resto do território ainda mais arcaico, era a insuficiência de energia elétrica." All quotations originally in Portuguese in the body text of this book were freely translated into English by this author.

10. The foundation of the National Steel Company (Companhia Siderúrgica Nacional), CSN, on April 9, 1941, in the city of Volta Redonda, state of Rio de Janeiro, is particularly emblematic of this first wave of modernization in Brazil, under President Getúlio Vargas's dictatorship historically known as "Estado Novo" (1937–1945).

11. To know more about the Brazilian *chanchada*, see Vieira 2003.

12. "Sente-se a precariedade de tempo na feitura da película: o som é francamente ruim, primaríssimo. Isso comprova tão somente as insuportáveis dificuldades que atravancam o cinema brasileiro, a braços com a criminosa concorrência do imperialismo cinematográfico norte-americano, que domina francamente o mercado brasileiro e tudo faz para asfixiar a indústria de filmes." Source: Hemeroteca Cinemateca Brasileira, São Paulo, Brazil.

13. "É assim um filme que não acrescenta nada ao gênero, ficando em nível de comédia de objeto comercialíssimo, o que—repetimos—torna-se para o cinema nacional uma de suas únicas saídas, desde que as suas dificuldades em todos os setores da produção, distribuição e exibição persistem, não vindo em seu socorro qualquer legislação mais estimulante." Source: Hemeroteca Cinemateca Brasileira, São Paulo, Brazil.

14. A. Gomes de Prata was a pen name of Alex Viany, one of the most relevant Brazilian film critics and film historians, author of *Introduction to*

*Brazilian Cinema* (*Introdução ao Cinema Brasileiro*, 1993), as well as producer, scriptwriter, and director.

15. *Carnaval em Marte*, uma sátira à histeria dos discos voadores, é um filme que diverte." Source: Cinemateca Brasileira's Archive, São Paulo, Brazil.

16. ". . . até certo ponto, escapa aos velhos clichês, traz para a alegria do carnaval na tela coisas interessantes, ligadas à vida do nosso povo." Source: Cinemateca Brasileira's Archive, São Paulo, Brazil.

17. "É quando o repórter, ante a iminência de uma "invasão" de Marte à Terra, proclama que "em nosso mundo nem todos querem a guerra, a destruição. E o meu povo (do Brasil), envia uma mensagem de fraternidade, amizade, paz e música." Source: Cinemateca Brasileira's Archive, São Paulo, Brazil.

18. This short documentary film features, in addition to Prestes himself (leader of the BCP), the Chilean poet Pablo Neruda and the Brazilian writer Jorge Amado—two well-known Latin American Communist artists. The film has survived and can be seen today on the web at http://www.youtube.com/watch?v=GBwxg_75-sg.

19. Unreferenced newspaper film review dated July 5, 1959 (Arquivo Cinemateca Brasileira, localização: P.1959-7/35). The text goes on to state that "in Atlântida, imitation is permitted—in fact, it is the rule, since the trashy plagiarism of the classic western High Noon."

20. The *malandragem* (trickery, ruse, cheating attitude) is a characteristic artifice to every human being, but it has gained status as an anthropological concept that is particularly useful for an improved understanding of Brazilian daily life in its social dimension of contrasts and contradictions. Anthropologist Roberto DaMatta scrutinized the concept of *malandragem* along with another aspect in Brazilian social life, slightly less negative: the *jeitinho* (DaMatta 2004, 51). For a more in-depth analysis of the Brazilian *malandragem* as an anthropological concept, see DaMatta 1997.

21. Such as Mario Soffici's *The Strange Case of the Man and the Monster* (*El Extraño Caso del Hombre y la Bestia*, 1951), an adaptation of R. L. Stevenson's novella *The Strange Case of Dr. Jekyll and Mr. Hyde* (1886).

## Chapter 2

1. After the name of Alberto Santos Dumont (1873–1932), Brazilian inventor, aeronaut, and sportsman.

2. In the original: "Embora neste filme os locais sejam brasileiros, os personagens ajam como brasileiros e alguns fatos também sejam brasileiros, convém esclarecer, logo de início, que tudo não passa de mera coincidência."

3. Document from the Brazilian Film Archive in São Paulo, Brazil (Arquivo Cinemateca Brasileira), no author, 1962.

4. A very popular group of comedians in Brazilian TV and cinema throughout the late 1970s and the 80s. Sometimes also translated as "the Bunglers."

5. Excerpt from the website *Adoro Cinema Brasileiro*: http://www.adorocinemabrasileiro.com.br/filmes/quinto-poder/ quinto-poder.asp. Unfortunately, this text is not available online anymore. The quote can be retrieved, however, in Suppia 2013.

6. Quoted at http://www.adorocinemabrasileiro.com.br/filmes/quinto-poder/ quinto-poder.asp. In the original: "Época oportuna realmente, esta em que se apresenta *O Quinto Poder*, quando o espírito e os homens da nação brasileira se acham à beira do abismo esquerdista mais profundo."

7. The theme of subliminal messaging is still present in audiovisual media as a representation of how public discourse can be hijacked and corrupted. Most recently, the sixth episode in the first season of HBO's series *Watchmen* (2019) clearly features subliminal messaging as a key element in its plot—in this case, as an instrument to propagate racism.

# Chapter 3

1. The conceptual opposition adopted here ("serious" film vs. comedy film) is inspired by the distinction that Ismail Xavier (1993, 227) makes between what he calls "serious-dramatic" and "comic-parodic" ("sério-dramático" vs. "cômico-paródico") films, in his famous analysis of the "allegories of underdevelopment" in the Brazilian Cinema Novo and Cinema Marginal. This opposition, however, needs to be retrieved from the Brazilian version of Xavier's work first published in 1993, since its American version *Allegories of Underdevelopment: Aesthetics and Politics in Modern Brazilian Cinema* (1997) is slightly different in terms of both content and conceptual terminology (Xavier 1997, 17). In other words, the original dichotomy *sério-dramático* vs. *lúdico-carnavalesco* could be momentarily subsumed to an equivalent opposition: teleology (classic narrative) vs. its denial (allegory). Hence, we herein will be forced to work with both versions of Xavier's seminal work, the Brazilian edition, by Editora Brasiliense (1993), and the American version, by University of Minnesota Press (1997). All translations of Xavier's 1993 book excerpts from original Portuguese into English were made by this author.

2. The Cordel (Literatura de Cordel) is one of the most genuine Brazilian artforms, a kind of popular epic poetry introduced by the Portuguese in Brazil at the end of the eighteenth century. The genre thrived particularly in the states of Pernambuco, Alagoas, Paraíba, Pará, Rio Grande do Norte, and Ceará. For this reason, the northeastern cordel is one of the most popular in the country. Cordel's literature gained momentum in Brazil in the twentieth century, especially from the 1930s through the 1960s. Some renowned Brazilian writers were influenced by this style, such as João Cabral de Melo Neto, Ariano Suassuna, and Guimarães Rosa.

3. In the original: "Quando a gente não pode fazer nada, a gente avacalha."

4. According to Maria David Santos, from the Federal University of Espírito Santo (UFES), *Grayish Morning* was meant to be part of a trilogy. Two additional episodes were supposed to be made. However, with the first short censored, the whole project was canceled (Santos 2013, 36).

5. As explained above, there are substantial differences in terms of content between these two books by Ismail Xavier, despite sharing the same title. For instance, the thorough analysis carried out by Xavier on Walter Lima Jr.'s film *Brazil Year 2000* (*Brasil Ano 2000*, 1969) in his 1993 book *Alegorias do Subdesenvolvimento* is substantially summarized in his 1997 book *Allegories of Underdevelopment*. For these reasons we are drawing on both books to bolster our arguments.

6. It is worth noting that Walter Lima Jr.'s film has nothing to do with Joaquim Felício dos Santos's novel *Pages of Brazilian History Written in the Year 2000*, published as a booklet between 1868 and 1872 in *O Jequitinhonha*, a four-page weekly published in Diamantina, in the Brazilian state of Minas Gerais. Extremely critical of the monarchy, Felício dos Santos's story essentially revolves around Emperor D. Pedro II's time travel to Brazil in 2000, then a republic and world superpower (see Rachel Haywood Ferreira, "The First Wave: Latin American Science Fiction Its Roots Discovers," *Science Fiction Studies* 103, November 2007, 432–62).

7. Despite improvements in terms of both socioeconomic conditions in the North and Northeast administrative areas in Brazil, notably while the Workers' Party (PT) occupied the presidency, the South and especially the Southeast administrative areas of Brazil hold the highest levels of industrialization and human development. The richest states of Brazil, São Paulo and Rio de Janeiro, are also in the Southeast region.

8. Concerning the Latin-American SF literature of the period, Yolanda Molina-Gavilán et al. remind us that "in the 1970s, several mainstream authors turned to dystopian fiction to avoid censorship by the regime, disguising their critiques of its policies of fast-paced economic development in their futuristic tales. As allegorical representations of Brazil under military rule, these novels contain clear allusions to the regime's use of censorship, media control, torture, imprisonment, and disappearances, tactics of the post-1968 crackdown by military hardliners. The dystopian novels of the period are characterized by a nostalgia for the past, especially in the idealized portrayal of nature or women as repositories of authentic Brazilian identity, as seen in works such as *Fazenda Modelo* [*Model Farm*, 1974] by Chico Buarque, *Adaptação do Funcionário Ruam* [*Ruam the State Worker*, 1975] by Mauro Chaves, *O Fruto do Vosso Ventre* [*The Fruit of Thy Womb*, 1976] by Herberto Sales, *Asilo nas Torres* [*Asylum in the Towers*, 1977] by Ruth Bueno, and *Um Dia Vamos Rir Disso Tudo* [*Someday We Will Laugh about All This*, 1976] by Maria Alice Barroso. Recurrent themes include governmental

regulation of reproduction and sexual behavior, policies of modernization, the destruction of natural environments, and control of the media and the minds of citizens. In the dystopian novels *Umbra* [*Shadow*, 1977)] by Plinio Cabral and *And Still the Earth*, by Ignacio de Loyola Brandão, environmental degradation goes hand in hand with eroding personal freedoms as Brazil faces the ecological and political consequences of military rule" (2007, 382).

9. This highly allegorical aspect of *Brazil Year 2000* makes its analysis as science fiction even more complicated. As Darko Suvin asserts, "Works avowedly written within a nonrealistic mode, principally allegory (but also whimsy, satire, and lying tall tale or Münchhauseniade), constitute a category for which the question of whether they possess a novum cannot even be posed, because they do not use the new worlds, agents, or relationships as coherent albeit provisional ends, but as *immediately transitif* and *narratively nonautonomous* means for *direct* and *sustained* reference to the author's empirical world and some system of belief in it. The question whether an allegory is SF, and vice versa, is, strictly speaking, meaningless, but for classifying purposes has to be answered in the negative. This means that—except for exceptions and grey areas—most of the works of Kafka or Borges cannot be claimed for SF: though I would argue that *In the Penal Colony* and 'The Library of Babel' would be among the exceptions. But admittedly, much more work remains to be done toward the theory of modern allegory in order to render more precise the terms underlined in this note" (Suvin 1979, note 4, 65). Note that not even the experienced literary critic offers definitive answers to the controversy related to allegory and SF, or allegory *in* SF.

10. *Tropicália, tropicalismo,* or the *tropicalista movement* was a Brazilian cultural movement that emerged under the influence of the 1960s avant-garde and global pop culture, mixing traditional Brazilian culture with radical aesthetic innovations, notably in music, film, and visual arts (see Veloso 2017). According to Glauber Rocha, "Tropicalism is the acceptance, the rise of underdevelopment; therefore, there is a clear distinction between cinema before and after Tropicalism. Now we are not afraid to confront Brazilian reality, our reality, and all its meanings and depths. This acceptance is indicated by the anthropophagic relationships among characters [in Glauber's 1969 film *Antonio das Mortes*]: the professor eats Antônio, Antônio eats the cangaceiro (backland bandit), Laura eats the commissioner, the professor eats Claudia, the murderers eat the people, the professor eats the cangaceiro. The anthropophagic relation is freedom" (Rocha 1969). When asked about the films *Macunaíma* (Joaquim Pedro de Andrade, 1969) and *Brazil Year 2000*, Glauber highlights "tropicalism" in relation to the "Eisensteinian line" present in these two titles: "By putting aside the aspect of interpretation and editing, these films are quite surprising in terms of dramatic structure and staging. Concerning montage, they are very refined. But it is the concept of the show that is surprising, everything takes place inside the frame" (Rocha 2004, 202–3). "Deixando de lado o aspecto da interpretação e da montagem,

estes filmes são bastante surpreendentes do ponto de vista da estrutura dramática e da encenação. Em termos de montagem, eles são muito depurados. Mas é a concepção de espetáculo que é surpreendente, tudo se passa no interior do quadro" (Rocha 2004, 202–3).

11. Empresa Brasileira de Filmes (Embrafilme) was a Brazilian state-owned company established on September 12, 1969, for production, funding, and distribution of Brazilian films. It was created during the military dictatorship, with the decree (Decreto-Lei) n. 862 from December 12, 1969. The company was dissolved on March 16, 1990, by the Brazilian National Privatization Program.

12. An iconic city in the history of Brazilian cinema and hometown to Humberto Mauro and Pedro Comello, Cataguases gained national recognition in the 1920s, when Mauro directed four feature-length fiction films later to be historicized as the Cataguases's film cycle ("Ciclo de Cataguases"). Comello introduced Mauro to the performing arts and film culture, and they worked together in a short and two feature-length films. The duo founded the Phebo Sul America Film Co. in 1925, with the financial support of businessman Agenor Cortes de Barros. Later on, Comello and Mauro put an end to their partnership, and the latter continued to direct films in Cataguases and to win national prizes. By the end of the 1920s, Mauro moves to Rio de Janeiro, to work in Adhemar Gonzaga's studio Cinédia. With a career in the National Institute for the Educational Cinema (Instituto Nacional do Cinema Educativo, INCE), with hundreds of film directorial credits, Mauro was also consecrated by the Cinema Novo's younger generation and film historians as the Father of Brazilian cinema (see Salles Gomes 1974).

13. Still according to Ginway, "Science fiction, because of its links to science and technology, is the consummate literary vehicle for examining the perception and cultural impact of the modernization process in Brazil. [. . .] My analysis shows that a reading of Brazilian science fiction based on its use of, on the one hand, paradigms of Anglo-American science fiction, and, on the other, myths of Brazilian nationhood, provides a unique look into Brazil's modern metamorphosis" (2004, 13–14).

14. Ginway also points out that "even within the parameters of 'fantastic literature,' Brazilian literature often tends to be highly allegorical, referring specifically to a given political statement" (2004, 29).

## Chapter 4

1. "The incremental reduction of biomass in each successive phase of a food-chain" (Stableford in Seed 2007, 128).

2. Regarding the cyborg character, José de Anchieta comments in an interview given to this author, by email, on May 30, 2007: "I sought above all theatricality, and for this reason the cyborg may seem caricatural. I never wanted

to be prophetic about ecological issues, but I confess, with some pride, that I anticipated the current cyborgs in cinema." In the original: "Busquei acima de tudo uma teatralidade, e por este motivo o ciborgue pode parecer caricato. Nunca quis ser profético com relação aos assuntos ecológicos, mas confesso com uma ponta de orgulho que antecipei os ciborgues atuais." José de Anchieta, email message to author, May 30, 2007.

3. "Tupinipunk" is the term coined by writer and researcher Roberto de Sousa Causo (1996, 2015) to designate the Brazilian cyberpunk, manifested in books such as *Silicone XXI* (1985), by Alfredo Sirkis, Fausto Fawcett's *Santa Clara Poltergeist* (2020, first published in 1991), or Guilherme Kujawski's *Piritas Siderais* (1994). This neologism derives from the word Tupiniquim, relating to the Indigenous Brazilian people who belong to the Tupi nation and are also known by the names Tupinaquis, Topinaquis, or Tupinanquins. From a colonial perspective that survives to this day, the term "tupiniquim" can denote "primitive" peoples or less privileged Brazilians, as a synonym of civilizational backwardness, lack of "modernity" or "primitivism." There is some irony in Roberto Causo's term "tupinipunk," but we doubt it is actually disparaging, given the bulk of Causo's work on Brazilian SF as a literary critic, historian, and author of SF stories (see Causo 1996, 2003, and 2015).

4. José de Anchieta, email message to author, May 30, 2007.
5. José de Anchieta, email message to author, May 30, 2007.
6. José de Anchieta, email message to author, May 30, 2007.
7. André Carneiro, e-mail message to author, February 8, 2006.
8. José de Anchieta, email message to author, May 30, 2007.
9. Interview with José de Anchieta, by email, on May 30, 2007. "An aesthetics of hunger" was a film manifesto originally written in 1965 by Glauber Rocha (1997) and linked to Cinema Novo, the Brazilian modern cinematographic movement that came along in the 1960s, achieving worldwide recognition through the inspiring and nationalist endeavors of directors such as Nelson Pereira dos Santos (*Barren Lives*), Ruy Guerra (*Os Fuzis/The Guns*, 1964), and Gláuber Rocha (*Black God, White Devil*), among others.

10. "Anthropophagy" here refers to the 1922 Brazilian modernist movement, but first and foremost to Oswald de Andrade's "Cannibalist Manifesto" (originally in Portuguese: "Manifesto Antropófago"). As explained by Leslie Bary, "The Brazilian modernist poet Oswald de Andrade's 'Manifesto Antropófago' (MA) originally appeared in the first number of *Revista de Antropofagia*, directed by Alcântara Machado and Raul Bopp, in May, 1928" (Bary 1991, 35). Still, according to Bary, "The MA challenges the dualities modern/primitive, and original/derivative, which had civilization/barbarism, inform the construction of Brazilian culture since the days of the colony. In the MA, Oswald subversively appropriates the colonizer's inscription of America as a savage territory that, once civilized, would be a necessarily muddy copy of Europe. The use of the cannibal metaphor permits the Brazilian subject to

forge his specular colonial identity into an autonomous and original (as opposed to dependent, derivative) national culture. Oswald's anthropophagist—himself a cannibalization, not of Rousseau's idealized savage but of Montaigne's avowed and active cannibal—neither apes nor rejects European culture, but "devours" it, adapting its strengths and incorporating them into the native self" (Bary 1991, 35–36).

11. One of the most renowned Brazilian physicists of all time, César Lattes, was born to a family of Italian-Jewish immigrants in Curitiba, Paraná, Brazil. He graduated in mathematics and physics at the University of São Paulo in 1943. One of the young Brazilian physicists working under the supervision of European teachers like Gleb Wataghin and Giuseppe Occhialini, Lattes was considered one of the most brilliant researchers of his generation. From 1947 to 1948, Lattes started specializing in the study of cosmic rays. He registered cosmic rays using photographic plates in a weather station on top of the 5,200-meter-high Chacaltaya mountain in Bolivia. Traveling to England with his teacher Occhialini, Lattes went to work at the H. H. Wills Laboratory of the University of Bristol, directed by Cecil Powell. There, he improved on the nuclear emulsion used by Powell by adding more boron to it. In 1947, he made his great experimental discovery with Powell: the new subatomic particle known as pion (or pi meson). Lattes then wrote a paper on his discovery for *Nature*. In the same year, he was responsible for calculating the pions mass. A year later, working with Eugene H. Gardner (1913–1950) at UC Berkeley, the twenty-four-year-old Lattes detected the artificial production of pions in the lab's cyclotron by bombarding carbon atoms with alpha particles. In 1949, Lattes returned as a professor and researcher with the Federal University of Rio de Janeiro. He was one of the founders of the Brazilian Center for Physics Research (Centro Brasileiro de Pesquisas Físicas) in Rio de Janeiro, at the age of twenty-five. After another brief stay in the United States (from 1955 to 1957), he returned to Brazil and accepted a position at the Department of Physics of the University of São Paulo. In 1967, Lattes accepted a position as full professor at the new "Gleb Wataghin" Institute of Physics at the State University of Campinas (Unicamp), which he helped to found. He also became the chairman of the Department of Cosmic Rays, Chronology, High Energies and Leptons. In 1969, he and his group discovered the mass of the so-called fireballs, a phenomenon induced by naturally occurring high-energy collisions and that was detected by means of special lead-chamber nuclear emulsion plates invented by him and placed at the Chacaltaya peak of the Bolivian Andes.

12. Bahia Sci-Fi, directed by Petrus Pires and produced by Iglu Filmes. https://www.youtube.com/watch?v=Ria3OA5e1BE (accessed June 3, 2024).

13. This and more information can be found on the website of Eletronuclear—Eletrobrás Termonuclear S.A.: http://www.eletronuclear.gov.br, and the newspaper *Folha de S. Paulo*, July 1, 2007, Brasil, A10.

14. See Empresa de Pesquisa Energética, Brazilian Energy Balance, BEN Summary Report 2021, available at https://www.epe.gov.br/sites-en/publicacoes-dados-abertos/publicacoes/PublicacoesArquivos/publicacao-231/ BEN_S%C3%

ADntese_2020_EN.pdf; EIA US Energy Information Administration, "Hydropower made up 66% of Brazil's electricity generation in 2020," September 7, 2021, available at https://www.eia.gov/todayinenergy/detail.php? id=49436.

15. A Brazilian brand of car, founded in 1969, that offered national, experimental design with alternative materials (fiberglass), based on the mechanics of Volkswagen's cars (Beetle and Kombi). The Gurgel Co. had a twenty-five-year lifespan, went bankrupt, and was closed in the 1990s. However, it is still possible to see Gurgel cars on the streets of Brazil.

16. A *caboclo* (Portuguese pronunciation: [kɐˈboklu]) is a person of mixed Indigenous Brazilian and European ancestry, or, less commonly, a culturally assimilated or detribalized person of full Amerindian descent. In Brazil, a *caboclo* generally refers to this specific type of mixed race.

17. In the original: "No Rio de Janeiro, um dilúvio deixa como sobreviventes aqueles que se refugiaram no alto das montanhas. Sem comida suficiente tampouco espaço para plantações, o poder decide impedir o sacrifício de animais, exceto algumas espécies de cachorros comestíveis."

18. Anyone born in the city of Rio de Janeiro.

19. This hypothesis was addressed by Dr. Christopher J. Caes (Dept. of Germanic and Slavic Studies—Polish, University of Florida), in an insightful discussion after our lecture "Ecodystopias in Brazilian Science Fiction Film," University of Florida, January 13, 2009.

20. *Candomblé* (Portuguese pronunciation: [kɐ̃dõˈblɛ]) is an African diasporic religion that developed in Brazil during the nineteenth century. It arose through a process of syncretism between the traditional religions of West Africa and the Roman Catholic form of Christianity.

21. José de Anchieta, email message to author, May 30, 2007.

22. José de Anchieta, email message to author, May 30, 2007.

23. These and other Brazilian SF films with a focus on the environment will be further discussed in the following chapters of this book.

# Chapter 5

1. For further thoughts on the Brazilian parodies that ridiculed Brazilian cinema, see João Luiz Vieira (1995, 256–69).

2. Roberto Farias wrote and directed other films in which the famous Brazilian singer Roberto Carlos is the star: *Roberto Carlos and the Pink Diamond* (*Roberto Carlos e o diamante cor-de-rosa*, 1970) and *Roberto Carlos at 300 Km/h* (*Roberto Carlos a 300 Km/h*, 1972).

3. Before Brasília, Rio de Janeiro was the capital of Brazil and its location was also known as the District of Guanabara. When the capital moved to Brasília, the District of Guanabara was effaced and Rio (the city) restored to the condition of capital of the state of Rio de Janeiro.

4. Before this, the Beatles' films made use of similar strategy, as in *A Hard Day's Night* (1964), or *Help!* (1965).

5. Roberto Carlos and Pelé are two Brazilian celebrities popularly referred to as "kings." Whenever talking about soccer and sports, if one mentions "the King," any Brazilian implies Pelé. In the musical or showbiz milieu, Roberto Carlos is "the King." With a career that spans from 1959 up until today, Roberto Carlos has sold approximately 120 million albums.

6. Inspired by the Beatles, the term "*iêiêiê*," an onomatopoeia, was then used to refer to Brazilian rock'n'roll in the 1960s. It came from "yeah, yeah, yeah," often in the lyrics of Beatles' songs.

7. The subtitle above parodies a famous Brazilian slogan in Brazil: "The oil is ours!" ("O petróleo é nosso!"), a motto that became famous when it was pronounced by President Getúlio Vargas on the occasion of the discovery of oil reserves in Bahia. Later on, the phrase became the motto of the Petroleum Campaign, sponsored by the Center for Oil Studies and Defense and promoted by nationalists, which culminated in the creation of the national oil company, Petrobras. After becoming famous, historians discovered that the phrase had been created by Otacílio Raínho, a teacher and director of at Colégio Vasco da Gama, in Rio de Janeiro.

8. Os Trapalhões is often translated as "the Tramps" in English subtitles. Other possible English translations are "the Goofs" or "the Bunglers."

9. According to the website Memória Globo, Antonio Carlos was called "Mussum" by the famous Brazilian actor Grande Otelo (Sebastião Bernardes de Souza Prata). Mussum is the Brazilian name for a type of black, slippery eel. Mauro Gonçalves was baptized Zacarias in homage to a rooster (see http://memoriaglobo.globo.com/programas/entretenimento/humor/os-trapalhoes/ curiosidades.htm).

10. See "Lista de filmes brasileiros com mais de um milhão de espectadores," available at https://pt.wikipedia.org/wiki/Lista_de_filmes_brasileiros_com_mais_de_um_milh%C3%A3o_de_espectadores.

11. The Goofs appeared in forty-two films between 1965 and 2017, although this filmography includes films starring only Renato Aragão, like Aurélio Teixeira's *Na onda do iêiêiê* (*In the wave of iêiêiê*, 1966), starring Renato Aragão and Dedé Santana, and J. B. Tanko's *O adorável trapalhão* (*The Adorable Goof*, 1966).

12. An iconic amusement park in São Paulo in the 1980s.

13. "World exhibitions thus provide access to a phantasmagoria which a person enters in order to be distracted. Within these divertissements, to which the individual abandons himself in the framework of the entertainment industry, he remains always an element of a compact mass. This mass delights in amusement parks—with their roller coasters, their 'twisters,' their 'caterpillars'"—in an attitude that is pure reaction. It is thus led to that state of subjection which propaganda, industry as well as politics, relies on" (Benjamin 1999, 18).

14. *Terrir* is a genre created by Brazilian filmmaker Ivan Cardoso. Highly ironic and satirical, it essentially consists of an ingenious, stylistic mixture of the American B movie, science fiction, *film noir*, horror movie, and comedy.

15. To know more about the controversies revolving around the *pornochanchada* genre, as well as more in-depth analyses of this film production, see Sternheim 2005, Abreu 2006, and Abreu 2012.

16. Although *Jaws* had become better known for its efficient suspense formula than for any clearer association with SF imagery, this thriller directed by Spielberg is occasionally referred to as an SF film, or orbiting SF, since its plot concerns the motif of the confrontation between nature and humankind—a tradition that gained visibility with Merriam Cooper and Ernest Shoedsack's *King Kong* (1933), culminating in the post–World War II Japanese disaster movies. In addition, *Jaws* revisits a formula inaugurated in a famous American SF film from the 1950s: Jack Arnold's *Creature from the Black Lagoon* (1954). Thus, *Jaws* might be lined up with films like Alfred Hitchcock's *The Birds* (1963), also occasionally reclaimed as an SF film by SF scholars. *The Birds* is emblematic of the theme of an inscrutable Nature (with capital N, as if it were a sentient being) that rebels against the unscrupulous dominance of human civilization, putting in check the supposed technical or intellectual supremacy of man on the planet.

17. In the original: "O hábito que têm as plateias brasileiras de consumir filmes americanos as condiciona a achar 'ruins' os filmes brasileiros. Estabelece-se uma inferioridade essencial do filme brasileiro em relação ao ideal americano. Na paródia, esta inferioridade é assumida, ela passa a contar pontos positivos. Há aí uma aparente atitude de independência: sou independente do tubarão, já que o mostro caricato, grotesco, degradado; assumo uma atitude crítica e agressiva diante do tubarão. A paródia funciona aí como agressão ao modelo superior. Mas, contraditoriamente, nesta aparente atitude de independência, está contida uma real atitude de dependência: porque a paródia coloca o original como modelo; mesmo degradado e porque degradado pela paródia, *Tubarão* é confirmado na sua posição de modelo pelo bacalhau, já que o que se assume e se torna espetáculo é precisamente a impossibilidade de fazer o espetáculo modelar. E atitude de dependência também porque é justamente isto que os tubarões querem: que os bacalhaus sejam inferiores e degradados. Sob a capa de uma atitude irreverente, crítica e agressiva, confirma-se a opressão do opressor e a inferioridade do 'inferior'" (Bernardet 1976).

18. This information was given to this author by the Brazilian writer and SF scholar Marcello Branco, in an email sent to alfredo.luiz5@terra.com.br on September 4, 2006.

19. Francisco de Paula, e-mail message to author, February 22, 2019.

20. Francisco de Paula, e-mail message to author, February 22, 2019.

21. https://www.imdb.com/title/tt0252239/?ref_=fn_al_tt_3.

22. Interestingly, another science fictionish film resorting to handmade illustrations would reappear only in 2014: Adirley Queirós's *White Out, Black In* (*Branco sai, preto fica*), whose final sequence relies on drawings by the artist Shockito.

23. Dumovich would later create the storyboard of Hector Babenco's *At Play in the Fields of the Lord* (1991) and Walter Salles's *The Knife* (*A Grande Arte* 1991).

24. Francisco de Paula, e-mail message to author, February 22, 2019.

25. Francisco de Paula, e-mail message to author, February 22, 2019.

26. Francisco de Paula, e-mail message to author, February 22, 2019.

27. Shows like Globo's *Clip-Clip* (1984), *Videoshow* (on air from 1983 to 2019), and *Mixto-Quente* (1986), Bandeirantes's *Super Special* (1985) and *TV da Tribo* (1989), Manchete's *FMTV* (1984) and *Milk-Shake* (1988), TV Cultura's *Fábrica do som* (1983) and *Matéria-Prima* (1990), and TVE's *Som Pop* (1982) and *Cabeça Feita* (1988), among several others (Caminha 2010, 202).

28. In addition to having worked as a cameraman for Globo Repórter (1975) and for the State Company of Basic Sanitation Technology (Cetesb, where he also wrote scripts), Luiz Alberto Pereira had already directed a 35mm short film, *Dr. Alcatrão and Professor Penna's System* (*O Sistema do Dr. Alcatrão e do Professor Penna*, 1973), about a visitor to an asylum who ignores the fact that the director of the institution and his friends are in fact madmen who took power and captured the nurses. The Brazilian film critic and film scholar Paulo Emílio Salles Gomes acted in the cast (Silva Neto 2006, 888).

29. According to Luiz Alberto Pereira, "*Man in the Box* is a controversial film. There are things that I like a lot, like the Vidiot character or the family dressed in the strip of the Brazilian national soccer team. It is the type of film to be shown in a multiplex for youth to have fun, because it is a little absurd, a dark comedy that has to do with the situation in a country where everything is absurd" (Nagib 2002, 345).

30. According to the Luiz Alberto Pereira, "[*Man in the Box*] was also taken to the Riverside Film Festival, in California, and to the University of California (UCLA). A lot of people saw it. I distributed copies to several people and one of those copies must have been in the hands of people interested in my original idea. *The Truman Show* was filmed in December 1997, almost three years after *Man in the Box* was released, long enough to make the script and shoot it. I tried to sue them, but American friends dissuaded me, thinking that I could have many problems" (Nagib 2002, 345).

# Chapter 6

1. Originally: "*Réflexions sur le septième art*" (1923).

2. Brazilian Institute for Geography and Statistics (Instituto Brasileiro de Geografia e Estatística). See http://ultimosegundo.ig.com.br/brasil/2012-06-29/ibge-com-maior-rendimento-e-instrucao-espiritas-crescem-65-no-pais-em-10-anos.html or http://censo2010.ibge.gov.br/noticias-censo? view=noticia&id=3&idnoticia=2170&busca=1&t=censo-2010-numero-catolicos-cai-aumenta-evangelicos-espiritas-sem-religiao.

3. Getúlio Dornelles Vargas (1882–1954). Elected president 1930–1937, dictator 1937–1946, elected president 1951–1954, committed suicide 1954 with the words "I leave this life to enter history."

4. Chico Xavier was a famous Brazilian medium. Born Francisco de Paula Cândido (1910–2002).

5. A TV channel on air from 1960 through 1970.

6. The current largest television and communications conglomerate in Brazil. Founded 1965.

7. In Brazil, TV soap operas are classified in "timeframes" in TV programs, and this strategy was mastered by Rede Globo in its ascension as the producer of the "best" Brazilian TV soap operas, or at least the most popular. This classification impacts the budget, genre affiliation, and overall theme of the soap operas. For instance, 6 p.m. soap operas are more romantic, juvenile, narratively simplified TV shows, sometimes featuring a story set in the past. The soap operas broadcast at 7 p.m. (or around this time) are more often experimental works, aiming at broader audiences. The TV soap operas aired at prime time (8 p.m. in the past, now starting at approximately 9 p.m.) are considered to be the "big show": bigger budgets, the elite of the star system; the most experienced authors and directors are put to work in these shows. The prime time TV soap operas, notably the ones produced and broadcast by Globo, tend to be more narratively intricate, aimed at broader audiences, and featuring more "mature" themes or topics.

8. Mediumship practice developed under the auspices of one or more spiritualistic guides. It is practiced in an independent way and normally not linked to any established religion. It was largely practiced in Brazil in the first half of the twentieth century, also known as "astral session" (*sessão astral*). The white color stands for the seriousness and good intentions of the practice, frequently confused with rites such as "the glass game" (*jogo do copo*), or ouija.

9. The concept of paranormality, which has been referred to using many different terms throughout history, can be defined as something regarding human sensory and psychological phenomena that seem to violate the natural laws (Zuzne; Jones 1989, ix.). The subject was very much in vogue in the 1970s, when Cold War generated a number of scientific experiments involving individuals with supposed extrasensory powers (such as the Israeli showman Uri Geller, who claimed to be able to bend metal at distance, and traveled all over the world showing his talents). During this period, both journalism and fiction released hundreds

of reports in various media, causing great commotion and perpetuating a wide variety of stories and urban legends.

10. The telekinesis or telekinetic (gr. Τῆλε (tele) "far, from distance" and κίνησις (Kinesis) "movement"), refers to the phenomenon or ability to physically move an object with the psychic force, the power of the will or the strength of mind.

11. Possible connections of Jean Garrett with spiritism may suggest a closer look, given his contact with Francisco Cândido Xavier, as reported in the biopic of the medium, *Chico Xavier* (2010), directed by Daniel Filho.

12. Figueiredo being a veteran filmmaker who directed the aforementioned *The Medium* (*O Médium*, 1980).

13. One of the first Brazilian television stations. Operated from 1950 to 1980.

14. On July 28, 1971, Chico Xavier was in a live TV show, broadcasted to the whole country (an unusual fact in Brazilian television by that time). The *Fire Drop* show (*Pinga Fogo*), initially predicted to last one hour, was eventually extended over three hours on air, reaching the largest audience so far recorded in the history of Brazilian TV, with 75 percent of the TVs tuned in to the show. The impact on the audience led TV Tupi to repeat the invitation to the medium, for a new *Pinga Fogo* that was aired on the evening of December 21, 1971, as a New Year special event. This time the show ended up being extended for more than 4 hours. The estimated audience was twenty million Brazilians. On both occasions, Chico Xavier talked to some of the most famous journalists of the time, like Saulo Gomes, Reali Júnior, Helle Alves, Herculano Pires, Freitas Nobre, Vicente Leporace, Durval Monteiro, besides the Catholic writer João de Scantimburgo, and the spiritualistic scientist Hernani Guimarães Andrade. Themes like Spiritualism, mediumship, charity, sex, the death penalty, abortion, men's arrival on the Moon, organ transplant, artificial insemination, homosexuality and the cremation of the dead, among other subjects, were addressed (http://pt.wikipedia.org/wiki/Pinga-Fogo).

15. In the light of Tzvetan Todorov's (1975) thoughts on the fantastic narrative and its typology (the strange/uncanny, the fantastic, and the wonderful), this short film features unusual events that suggest a narrative in the fantastic key, although very likely it can also be framed within the uncanny. However, this film's script was allegedly based on statements from actual victims of the Chernobyl accident in the former Soviet Union in 1986: as explained to this author by the director himself, Flávio Soares.

16. Cordisburgo is the small town in which the renowned Brazilian writer Guimarães Rosa was born, in 1908.

17. *Joelma*'s case seems ideal for the sake of comparison: initially released as a docudrama in 1980, it was re-released in 2007 in the home video market by a distributor specialized in spiritist cinema, following a strategy of film rebranding—*mutatis mutandis*, something akin to the case of Universal Studios' monster movies, such as Jack Arnold's *Creature from the Black Lagoon* (1954), as discussed by Rick Altman (1999, 78–80).

## Chapter 7

1. *Barbosa* (1988), directed by Ana Luiza Azevedo and Jorge Furtado. https://www.youtube.com/watch?v=OjVBp0zXPcU (accessed June 9, 2024).

2. *Loop* (2002), directed by Carlos Gregório: https://www.youtube.com/watch?v=u8RLEApfc8w (accessed June 9, 2024)

3. Ceilândia is a working-class town on the periphery of Brasília. One of the "satellite-cities" ("cidades-satélites").

4. Shockito, the actor who plays the role of Sartana, actually had his leg amputated due to an accident while playing soccer. Though Schockito's story does not match his character's, it resonates with the overall violence related to the Quarentão incident and the repression of peripheral communities. The prosthetic leg Sartana uses in the film is genuine, however. It was given to him as a beta test, and it compiles data on his walking and general usage. The idea of portraying him as a "cyborg" who seeks a "hacker" to "hack" his leg came from this scenario: Shockito was a test subject of that specific model of prosthetic leg.

5. As declared by director Adirley Queirós to this author in a personal interview, the scene results from disagreements between the actor Dilmar Durães and the film crew. This "impromptu" was later incorporated during the film's editing.

6. http://lofiscifi.com/.

7. See http://lucasmafra.com/.

8. Dr. Paula Gomes originally introduced the ideas concerning the cinematic bodies in *WOBI*. This entire subtopic results from our conversations about the representation of the body in Queirós's film.

9. Palácio do Planalto is the presidential workplace.

10. The Paralympic games appears to have gained momentum among international audiences, in TV broadcast and on the internet. In Brazil, some years ago the Paralympic games were hardly big news. Now, with the international success of some Brazilian parathletes, some of them appear in advertisements and promotional events.

11. In the original: "Era 2027. O Brasil tinha mudado. A festa mais importante do país não era mais o Carnaval. Era a Festa do Amor Supremo. A redenção do corpo, o sentimento mais puro. A jura do amor eterno. A grande espera pela volta do Messias."

12. Suvin defines his *novum* as "Quantitatively, the postulated innovation can be of quite different degrees of magnitude, running from the minimum of one discrete new "invention" (gadget, technique, phenomenon, relationship) to the maximum of a setting (spatiotemporal locus), agent (main character or characters), and/or relations basically new and unknown in the author's environment" (1979, 64).

13. See Gonçalves, Alexandre. 2019. "'Divino Amor': Filme Futurista é uma Crítica à Hipocrisia do Brasil Evangélico de Bolsonaro." *The Intercept Brasil*.

July 17. https://www.intercept.com.br/2019/07/17/divino-amor-critica-evangelico-bolsonaro/ [accessed June 9, 2024]

14. See https://www.opendemocracy.net/en/democraciaabierta/rise-narco-militia-pentecostal-brazil-en/.

15. See YouTube content creators Marco Bezzi and Helder Maldonado on their channel *Ugly Heartthrobs (Galãs Feios)*: https://www.youtube.com/channel/UC2bZgihqibFD_vhaYEXQZFg.

16. Araújo refers to recent protests and street demonstrations against Sebastián Piñera's economic neoliberal government in Chile in 2020 when the people went to the streets to call for a new Constitution. The delusional Minister of Foreign Affairs also refers to the Catholic movement called "Teologia da Libertação," whose action in Brazil has been fundamental to save lives, especially during the Brazilian military dictatorship (1964–1985). It is worth noticing that Araújo's speech is publicly available at the official website of the Brazilian Ministry of Foreign Affairs: http://www.itamaraty.gov.br/pt-BR/discursos-artigos-e-entrevistas-categoria/ministro-das-relacoes-exteriores-discursos/ 21888-discurso-do-ministro-das-relacoes-exteriores-ernesto-araujo-na-formatura-da-turma-joao-cabral-de-melo-neto-2019-2020-do-instituto-rio-branco-brasilia-22-de-outubro-de-2020. It can be read as both an official document and dystopian SF.

17. The Brazilian Unified Healthcare System, a universal system, totally free of charge to the patients, was created and founded by the 1988 Brazilian Constitution, our present Constitution.

18. The case in question involved the termination of the pregnancy of a ten-year-old child who was raped by her uncle. Conservative groups acted to prevent abortion, authorized by law. Finally guaranteed by a court decision, the pregnancy termination procedure was carried out in a hospital in Recife, the capital of Pernambuco. Even so, conservative groups conducted coercion and online bullying campaigns, threatening the child (e.g., calling her a murderer because she did not proceed with the pregnancy). Despite the pandemic, protesters still went to the hospital doors on the date of the surgery to prevent the procedure. The violence directed against the 10-year-old child, a victim of rape and legally entitled to pregnancy termination, constituted crimes foreseen in the penal code, in the Child and Adolescent Statute, and crimes against human rights, with clear indications that the minister Damares Alves acted in the leak of the girl's confidential data and the incitement, if not organization, of the protests against abortion (see Jordão 2020).

19. In the original: "(. . .) le totalitarisme de demain sera religieux ou ne sera pas."

20. Official data reveal that the federal government's budget for communication and advertising flooded RecordTV (owned by the evangelical "bishop" Edir Macedo) with millions of reais in figures previously destined for the most-watched television channel, Rede Globo (Cf. Fonseca e Correia, 2020; https://

www.youtube.com/watch?v=r-XzbP2CErg). According to Fonseca and Correia (2020), "[more] than R $ 30 million—this is the amount that the Presidency's Communication Secretariat (Secom) spent on campaigns broadcast on radio and TV by religious leaders who support Jair Bolsonaro" (in the original: "[m]ais de R$ 30 milhões—esse é o valor que a Secretaria de Comunicação da Presidência (Secom) gastou em campanhas veiculadas em rádios e TVs de líderes religiosos que apoiam Jair Bolsonaro"). Edir Macedo is the founder of the Universal Church of the Kingdom of God, owner of RecordTV, one of the richest men in Brazil, and a shady international business operator. Madagascar, for example, has banned The Universal Church of the Kingdom of God from operating in its territory (Salek 2005).

21. See http://revistadecinema.com.br/2019/11/fuleiragem-fiction-e-comedia-teen-sobre-corpo-trans-no-festival-de-brasilia/

22. The *cangaceiro* is a kind of Brazilian outlaw or gunslinger, from the word *cangaço*, a social and geographic phenomenon in the Northeast Brazil in the late 19th and early 20th centuries. The hinterlands in Northeastern Brazil were known for their aridness and hard way of life, and the *cangaço* emerged as a form of "social banditry" against the government. The *cangaceiros* were gangs of nomadic bandits—men and women who roamed the hinterlands in search of money, food, and revenge, sometimes terrorizing small villages with their sudden appearance and pillages.

23. *Coronel* (pl. *coronéis*), i.e., "colonel," is an informal title used by powerful people, usually farmers and politicians, who ruled the Northeastern hinterlands in Brazil. "The colonels' politics" (*a política dos coronéis*) refers to a kind of late semi-feudal political and economic parallel regime, widespread in the 19th and 20th centuries.

24. The Manguebeat movement is a cultural movement created circa 1991 in Recife, capital of the state of Pernambuco, in Northeast Brazil. The movement largely focused on music, mixing regional rhythms of the Brazilian Northeast, such as maracatu, frevo, coco, and forró, with rock, hip hop, funk, and electronic music. Cinematic representatives of the Manguebeat movement are films like Paulo Caldas and Lírio Ferreira's *Perfumed Ball* (*Baile Perfumado*, 1996, whose soundtrack featured songs by Chico Science and Nação Zumbi, one of the leading bands in the Manguebeat music scene), and Cláudio Assis's *Mango Yellow* (*Amarelo Manga*, 2002) and *Árido Movie* (2005).

25. The *Movimento Armorial* was an artistic initiative that aimed to create erudite art from elements of the popular culture of Northeast Brazil. One of the founders and leading thinkers of the movement was the writer Ariano Suassuna.

26. For more about this controversy (Manguebeat vs. The Armorial Movement), see CHICO SCIENCE vs ARIANO SUASSUNA: BATTLE FOR PERNAMBUCO #meteoro.doc, on the YouTube channel *Meteroro Brasil*, available at https://www.youtube.com/watch?v=9tEOHb3vClQ. Accessed on February 13, 2022.

27. http://stufana.blogspot.com/

28. Quilombolas are descendants of former enslaved Blacks who escaped from plantations and lived free in autonomous communities named Quilombos, which for a long time were considered clandestine or illegal. The 1988 Constitution recognized the quilombolas as Brazilian citizens and granted legal protection to their communities.

29. "Nós estamos sob o efeito de um poderoso psicotrópico. E você vai morrer."

30. Actually, the first military president following the coup in Brazil in 1964.

## Chapter 8

1. Some examples of both feature-length and short films that illustrate this scenario include: Éder Santos's *Blue Desert* (*Deserto Azul*, 2013); Marcelo Pedroso's *Brasil S/A* (2014); Santiago Dellape's *The Time Bureau* (*A Repartição do Tempo*, 2016); Tiago Esmeraldo's *At the Edge of the Universe* (*À Margem do Universo*, 2016); Guto Parente's *The Strange Case of Ezequiel* (*O Estranho Caso de Ezequiel*, 2017); Ian SBF's *Arzok* (2017); Sérgio Andrade's *The Kawa's Black Earth* (*A Terra Negra dos Kawa*, 2018); Dhiones do Congo's *Ultraviolet* (*Ultravioleta*, 2018); Bruno Bini's *Loop* (2019); and Fernando Sanches's *The Serpent's Rock* (*A Pedra da Serpente*, 2018).

2. Thus, the preferable term today is social-environmentalism, as the environmental and social dimensions cannot be disconnected from each other.

3. As Rivera himself explains (in *Before the Making of Sleep Dealer*, a "mini-mentary" available in the DVD extras), the idea for the film dates back to 1997, when he read a 1997 article on *Wired* about telecommuting, or the impact of the internet on labor relations, and the hypothesizeds of a future in which workers could perform their professional tasks from their homes. Rivera crossed this hypothesis with the reality of immigrants labor and imagined a future wherein which foreign workers would no longer need to leave their countries. Rivera was at a loss on how to express this idea visually until he came across the documentary *Why Braceros?* (1959), found in the Prelinger Archives (available for viewing and downloading at http://www.archive.org/details/WhyBrace1959). Promoted by the US government during World War II, the Braceros program consisted in offering temporary jobs in US agriculture to Mexicans in the US crops: the Mexican workers would come to the US, work on theseasonal harvests, and then return to their home country while the US population was engaged in the war effort. *Why Cybraceros?* (https://www.youtube.com/watch?v=Xr1eqKcDZq4) parodies the Braceros program. The experimental short film was independently made, using footage from the original documentary (*Why Braceros?*) interspersed with specially recorded video footage and very simple, schematic digital animations.

Rivera made his mockumentary available on the internet and had a surprising public and critical response.

4. For an in-depth analysis of *Cold Tropics*, see Suppia and Ginway 2022.

5. This film *Gray Lives* appears to be clearly indebted to Mendonça Filho's *Cold Tropics* in terms of plot and style.

6. The movie also recalls the Tupinambás Uprising, also known as the Tupinambás Revolt, which took place on January 13, 1618, and was led by *Tuxaua* (the Cacique, or political leader) Cabelo de Velha, who gathered several Indigenous groups from Belém to fight against the Portuguese colonizers due to the exploitation of Indigenous labor and other abuses committed. This was the main rebellion among a series of uprisings that occurred in the region between 1617 and 1619. The disputes culminated with the Tupinambás's attack of the Tupinambás on the Presépio Fort, located in the city of Belém, in January 1619.

7. "Fourth Cinema" is a term originally applied to Maori cinema in New Zealand, and primarily related to Barry Barclay (see Murray 2009), one of the most important filmmakers in the history of New Zealand cinema and one of the world's leading Indigenous filmmakers. The term may be conceptually expanded to encompass the cinema made by Indigenous filmmakers around the world. *Lato sensu*, and in retrospect, the "fourth cinema" can also describe the works of Sol Worth with the Navajo people, from the mid-1960s in the US (Worth 1972), or Vincent Carelli's *Video in the Villages* (*Video nas Aldeias*, or *VNA*) project in Brazil (http://www.videonasaldeias.org.br/2009/). *VNA* is a humanitarian project that since its foundation in 1986, has supported the struggles of indigenous peoples, strengthening their identities and their territorial and cultural heritage by audiovisual resources and a film production shared with the indigenous peoples involved in the project.

8. See also João Queiróz's Instagram at https://www.instagram.com/q1r0z/

9. In the original: "A Cyberamazon foi minha primeira tentativa de inserir uma personagem próxima da minha etnia num trabalho de ficção científica, algo que sinceramente nunca tinha visto representado. Por eu ter nascido no norte do país e por ser caboclo, senti maior afinidade em trabalhar com os temas lá de minha terrinha e minha ascendência" (Queiroz qtd. Zuin 2019, available at https://lidiazuin.blogosfera.uol.com.br/2019/09/02/amazofuturismo-e-cyberagreste-por-uma-nova-ficcao-cientifica-brasileira/?cmpid=copiaecola.

10. "Cannibalist Manifesto" is how Randal Johnson translates and refers to Oswald de Andrade's original manifesto (see Johnson in King 1989, 41–59). In the original Andrade (2017): "Só a antropofagia nos une. Socialmente. Economicamente. Filosoficamente" (49), "Mas nós nunca admitimos o nascimento da lógica entre nós" (52), and "Não tivemos especulação. Mas tínhamos adivinhação. Tínhamos Política que é a ciência da distribuição. E um sistema social planetário" (56).

11. "Não viemos criticar a função da máquina, mas propor a estética do homem. Precisamos deglutir urgentemente, após o Bispo Sardinha, a pistola de

raios laser, o cientista maluco, o alienígena bonzinho, o herói invencível, a dobra espacial, o alienígena mauzinho, a mocinha com pernas perfeitas e cérebro de noz, o disco voador, que estão tão distantes da realidade brasileira quanto a mais longínqua das estrelas. A ficção científica brasileira não existe."

12. "Emulamos tecnologias sem conhecê-las. [. . .] O homem prova, todo dia, que não é merecedor da tecnologia. Queremos despertar o iconoclasta que jaz em todo peito brasileiro. Morte aos adoradores de máquinas. Um caipora verde amarelo devora hambúrgueres, destrói satélites, deglute armas e destroça tecnologias. Um índio descerá de uma estrela colorida brilhante."

13. "Mas, se algumas das atitudes deste governo tiverem semelhança com a nossa história, o problema não é da ficção, é da realidade" (2022, 76).

14. "No final das contas, *Medida Provisória* é um filme paradoxal como o Brasil. É uma história de terror, porém irá te fazer rir. Emociona, mas também desperta um debate racional intenso. É imperfeito, porém imperdível."

15. In the original: "Podemos dizer que *o racismo é uma forma sistemática de discriminação que tem a raça como fundamento, e que se manifesta por meio de praticas conscientes ou inconscientes que culminam em desvantagens ou privilégios para indivíduos, a depender do grupo racial ao qual pertençam*."

16. In the original: "O futuro será negro ou não será."

17. For more information on the success of *3%* and Netflix marketing strategies in Latin American countries see Meimaridis, Mazur, and Rios (2020).

18. Belchior, born Antonio Carlos Belchior (October 26, 1946–April 30, 2017), was one of the first MPB (música popular brasileira) musicians from the Brazilian State of Ceará (in the northeast of the country) to reach mainstream success in the early 1970s. Many critics consider his 1976 album *Hallucination* (*Alucinação*) to be the single most influential album in the history of MPB and one of the utmost essential music albums ever released in Brazil. With lyrics that criticized the Brazilian military dictatorship, the stupidity of the authoritarian State, and the crudeness of the migratory fluxes and life of Northeasterners in big cities such as São Paulo and Rio de Janeiro, Belchior became one of the most iconic Brazilian artists in the fight for democracy. His music has been remembered and retrieved over the last few years, performed by Chico César, Emicida, and Pablo Vittar, among other artists.

19. Despite evoking the Brazilian archipelago Fernando de Noronha, some scenes of the ecologically balanced Maralto were shot in Inhotim, an open-air museum in the state of Minas Gerais.

20. https://www.gambiologia.net/blog/

21. Antônio Conselheiro was a religious leader and founder of the community of Canudos, located in the state of Bahia, which he erected in October 1897 with his followers. Originally a small village that emerged during the eighteenth century on the outskirts of the Canudos Farm, on the banks of the Vaza-Barris

River, the village grew dramatically with the arrival of Antônio Conselheiro in 1893, reaching approximately 25,000 inhabitants in just a few years. Thought to be a stronghold of the monarchy to fight the republican regime, Canudos was attacked by the republican army with the heaviest Brazilian artillery of the time. Conselheiro and thousands of his followers were killed. The massacre became an epic narrative told by Euclides da Cunha in his book *Backlands: The Canudos Campaign* [*Os Sertões*] (2010). An eyewitness to the massacre, Cunha wrote his report while working for the newspaper *O Estado de S. Paulo*. The story of Canudos was adapted for screen by Sérgio Rezende in 1996 (*The War of Canudos / Guerra de Canudos*), and Antônio Conselheiro's ancient prophecy became a leitmotif in Glauber Rocha's *Black God, White Devil* and Sérgio Ricardo's soundtrack for the same film.

22. With President Lula's election in 2022, in 2023 his administration confirmed and disclosed information regarding the genocide of the Yanomami people carried out by illegal miners, farmers, and traders under the blessings of Bolsonaro's government.

23. In the original: "Só a experiência sabe! Só o infinito é!"

24. *The Pink Cloud* (*A Nuvem Rosa*, 2021), by Iuli Gerbase, is a Brazilian SF apocalyptic film in which a toxic pink mist appears in the skies and forces people to remain confined in their homes. The film allegorizes the Covid-19 pandemic in an unsettling way. What was supposed to be a short quarantine in the film becomes never-ending confinement. The main characters, a man and a woman, spend the night together after a date and awake the next morning to the appearance of a pink mist and a lockdown instituted by the authorities. The couple is then forced to cohabit for more than a year. They have a child, their relationship deteriorates, and their tolerance and sympathy are tested to the limits.

25. See Morais 2018 (https://www.politize.com.br/lgbtfobia-brasil-fatos-numeros-polemicas/), Sousa and Arcoverde 2019 (https://g1.globo.com/sp/sao-paulo/noticia/2019/05/17/brasil-registra-uma-morte-por-homofobia-a-cada-23-horas-aponta-entidade-lgbt.ghtml).

26. "C'est d'ailleurs l'une des façons d'entendre la formule de Hitchcock selon laquelle mieux vaut partir des clichés qu'y arriver : c'est quand on croit partir du neuf, du jamais dit, qu'on se retrouve souvent sans le savoir à patauger dans les stéréotypes."

27. "Le cinéma, c'est un homme qui arrive à cheval dans une ville de l'Ouest, et nous ne savons rien de lui. Il va se définir peu à peu, par ses gestes, par ses regards."

28. The title of the movie and the name of this fabulous mission evokes a verse in the Brazilian nationalanthem: . . . "eternally laid in a splendid cradle . . ." (". . . deitado eternamente em berço esplêndido . . ."). This controversial verse has

been used as an alibi for Brazil's endless condition as "the land of the future," as if the country were a "sleeping giant" cursed to eternal sleep. In Portuguese, *berço* means both cradle and crib.

29. Yet I would prefer the term "capitalocene" to best describe our present dystopian times.

30. In the original: Instituto Brasileiro do Meio-Ambiente e dos Recursos Naturais Renováveis. See https://www.gov.br/ibama/pt-br.

31. In the original: "as pessoas destroem (*sic*) o meio ambiente porque precisam comer." The speech was widely covered by the international media, as can be seen at: https://www.youtube.com/watch?v=VrXKBz8SpMM.

32. The greatest ecological disaster in Brazil's history occurred on November 5, 2015, when the Fundão tailings dam, belonging to Samarco Mineração S.A., collapsed in Mariana (state of Minas Gerais). It released around 45 million m$^3$ of tailings (about 90 million tons) in a wave almost 10 meters high, causing environmental destruction and killing 14 workers (13 outsourced and one Samarco employee) and five residents (three adults and two children) of the Bento Rodrigues subdistrict, about 5 km downstream. The destruction to the Doce River basin (Bacia do Rio Doce) in Minas Gerais and the state of Espírito Santo resulted in the loss of 10,000 jobs, disease, and damage to hundreds of local people, notably native Brazilians in preserved areas. Thousands of farmers and fishermen were left without jobs and income. About 3 years later, on January 25, 2019, Brazil experienced another catastrophic dam collapse in the city of Brumadinho, also in Minas Gerais, resulting in about 270 deaths and unmeasurable environmental damage. The mining company Vale S.A. was responsible for the dam in Brumadinho. So far, neither Vale nor Samarco have been held properly accountable for these two environmental catastrophes (see Faria 2019; Armada 2019).

33. He left office back in 2021 due to a series of scandals, including his involvement in international wood traffic investigated by the FBI.

34. As said in the cabinet meeting (See *Poder 360* 2020b, https://www.youtube.com/watch?v=VkCTwQH55Ic), publicly disclosed by the Supreme Court regarding the investigations into Bolsonaro's desire to influence the choice of the general-director for the Federal Police of Rio de Janeiro. Like the speeches of the President and other ministers, Salles's declarations echoed in the press, in articles such as that of the newspaper *El País* (May 22, 2020), headlined "Salles sees 'opportunity' with coronavirus to 'steer past' deregulation on environmental protection," and with the following fine line: "Comments by Environment Minister are a literal translation of his preservation policies, which include encouraging land grabbers, defrosters and logging companies" (Alessi 2020).

35. In the original: "A Amazônia não pode ser esquecida. Temos muitas riquezas. E gostaria muito de explorá-la junto com os Estados Unidos." See UOL 2020.

36. See https://www.youtube.com/watch?v=CPpH7FRFcY0.

37. See *Poder 360* (2020a) and the link https://www.defundbolsonaro.org/. A video published by the campaign had wide repercussions on social media and better explains the initiative: https://www.youtube.com/watch?v=Y7nMKg3TZrU.

38. Vale is the name of the mining company and in Portuguese is the word meaning valley. Doce in Portuguese means sweet and is the name of the river devastated by the Mariana dam collapse: Rio Doce. In the original poem:

"O Rio? É doce.
A Vale? Amarga.
Ai, antes fosse
Mais leve a carga. [. . .]
Quantas toneladas exportamos
De ferro?
Quantas lágrimas disfarçamos
Sem berro?"

See Souza 2019, available at https://www.unicamp.br/unicamp/ju/noticias/2019/07/16/memorias-poeticas-de-lagrima-lama-e-luta. Drummond's verse was freely translated to English by Alfredo Suppia and Felipe de Souza Mello.

# Chapter 9

1. See an interview with Márcio Napoli given to Rogério Amaral de Vasconcellos (2011) for the *Scarium* online magazine (available at: http://www.scarium.com.br/noficcao/entrevista04.html).

2. In the original: "É a questão financeira. Porque ficção científica custa caro. Cenário, roupa, efeitos especiais, etc." Interview with Paulo Bastos Martins, recorded on August 17, 2005 (mini-DV).

3. Interview with Eduardo Morettin, recorded on May 26, 2007 (mini-DV).

4. In the original: "Na verdade, o argumento de que ficção científica é caro ainda vale hoje em dia, e é, em minha opinião, uma das principais restrições ao seu crescimento em outros países que não os EUA. Embora a tecnologia tenha abrido muitas portas, o uso de efeitos especiais é, ainda, invariavelmente, caro, se quisermos manter um limite mínimo de qualidade." Carlos Canela, e-mail message to author June 5, 2007.

5. In the original: "A ficção científica está aí para quem quiser usar. Basta deixarmos a ideologia de lado e partimos para a criação pura e simples, que é

para onde tudo deve apontar no final das contas." Carlos Canela, e-mail message to author June 5, 2007.

6. "Trucage et cinéma," originally published in 1973.

7. Nowadays, for "sophisticated visual effects" please read Computer Generated Images (CGI), or digital visual effects.

8. In the original French: MRP or "mode de représentation primitif" (Burch 2007).

9. Obviously, Cuarón's *Children of Men* takes advantage of highly sophisticated visual effects, but not in terms of pure visual spectacle, and not relying on cutting-edge digital technology or software. On the contrary, much of the film's superb visual effects rely on composite or analog visual effects. It was the expertise and creativity of the film crew that ultimately guaranteed some of the most impressive SF film scenes ever made, such as the long take in the car, or the final scenes of confrontation in Bexhill.

10. In the original: "Talvez se dê em função da persistência de uma noção equivocada de que são necessários efeitos especiais grandiosos para se contar uma boa história de ficção científica. Noção equivocada típica de quem tem pouca intimidade com o gênero." Gerson Lodi-Ribeiro, e-mail message to author, March 4, 2006.

11. This film addresses the period of the Canudos War, in Northeastern Brazil, which was a conflict where the Brazilian Army fought against rebels from a religious movement headed by Antônio Conselheiro (the war lasted from 1896 to 1897). In the end, the Federal Troops murdered all the insurgents.

12. According to the Internet Movie Database ("*Solaris* (1972)." Internet Movie Database. Retrieved October 27, 2013), *Solaris*'s budget was 1,000,000 SUR (about $829,000 in 1972 USD), whereas Kubrick's *2001* cost more than US$ 10 million in the late 1960s.

13. http://www.tasteofcinema.com/.

14. This hypothesis of a "Third SF Cinema" may sound anachronic at first glance, but I would very much like to further develop it in future projects.

15. Clóvis Vieira, interview by author recorded on mini-DV, Campinas-SP, Brazil, March 7, 2006.

16. A pioneering Spanish film director, cinematographer and screenwriter, who produced many short films in France and has been compared to Méliès due to his camera tricks and optical illusions. He is considered the most internationally significant Spanish film director from the silent film era. Born in 1871, died in 1929.

17. Ferdinand Zecca (1864–1947) was a pioneering French film director, producer, actor, and screenwriter, who worked mainly for the Pathé company.

18. German film company: Universum Film AG.

19. Cultural magazine based in Madrid. Circulated between 1927 and 1932.

20. In English: *Nothing but Time*.

21. Gerson Lodi-Ribeiro, e-mail message to author, March 4, 2006.

22. Indeed, the production of Brazilian SF in a range of media is quite significant, but is still eclipsed by the equivalent production in other countries, especially the United States.

23. In Andrea Bell's original article (1999), the quotation appears on p. 441.

24. Elie Politi, interview by author recorded on mini-DV, São Paulo-SP, Brazil, December 14, 2005.

25. Ginway quotes David J. Hartwell in his edited book *The World Treasury of Science Fiction* (Boston: Little, Brown, 1989), xvi.

26. In English: *If I Were You*. A romantic comedy starring leading Globo actors Glória Pires and Tony Ramos.

27. Clóvis Vieira, interview by author, recorded on a mini-DV, Campinas-SP, Brazil, March 7, 2006.

28. Clóvis Vieira, interview by author, recorded on Mini-DV, Campinas-SP, Brazil, July 3, 2006; Elie Politi, interview by author, recorded on Mini-DV, São Paulo-SP, Brazil, December 14, 2005.

29. For more on this topic, see Vogt and Polino 2003, 119, graphs 23 and 24.

30. See "Brasil: Artigos publicados em periódicos científicos internacionais indexados no Institute for Scientific Information (ISI), 1981–2004." Source: Brazilian Ministry for Science and Technology, Brazil, http://www.mct.gov.br/index.php/content/view/9256.html.

31. http://prouniportal.mec.gov.br/.

32. http://reuni.mec.gov.br/.

33. http://cienciasemfronteiras.gov.br/web/csf/o-programa.

34. In the original: "a imaginação livre não é nacionalista."

35. A city near São Paulo, famous for its technology industries, including Embraer (aerospace) and ITA (technology university), and an important entrepreneurial and innovation hub (see https://pqtec.org.br/en/).

36. Barreira do Inferno (English: Barrier of Hell) is a rocket launch base of the Brazilian Space Agency. Established in 1965, it is located near Ponta Negra beach, close to the city of Natal, which is the capital of the state of Rio Grande do Norte, in Brazil's Northeast Region.

37. However, Argentina provides a context that makes this issue even more complex. Even though they do investigate and reaffirm the scientific, technological and creative abilities of Argentine society. The documentary *Argentina Latente* (2007), by Fernando Solanas, shows the dismantling of infrastructure in the country, serving foreign interests who preferred Brazil as the industrial hub of South America. In addition, statements by the scientific class in Solanas's film showed the total lack of a scientific and technological policy in the country, which is lagging behind in issues such as intellectual property, patents, and allocation of funding for research and development, also with regard to Brazil. This also means that, despite competitive sectors, or sectors that were once competitive, such as the aerospace industry or nuclear energy (this latter activity having been developed with fully

national technology), Argentina would appear to have industrial, scientific, and technological infrastructure below that of Brazil, taking things generally, as can be inferred from the statements made by some interviewees. On the other hand, it is well known that such an infrastructure panorama has not had a negative effect on artistic production in genres such as SF and fantasy in the literature or film industry. The Argentine film industry seems much more familiar and much more at ease when dealing with SF issues when compared to Brazil, as observed in the production that often has an allegorical quality aimed at criticizing the Argentine society in the regime of the best utopian/dystopian narratives. This affinity could have something to do with the prestige of the fantasy literature of names like Borges and Bioy-Casares—these are the plot writers of Hugo Santiago's *Invasión*. We should also mention that, during the 1980s, Argentina produced at least one feature SF film without an equivalent in Brazil, which is *Hombre Mirando al Sudeste* (1986), by Eliseo Subiela. At the same time, Argentine film production in the 1990s and 2000s continues to prove the richness of the genre in the country, in films such as *La Sonámbula* (1998) and *Adiós Querida Luna* (2004), by Fernando Spiner, *Moebius* (1996), by Gustavo Mosquera, *La Antena* (2007), by Esteban Sapir, or *Filmatron* (2007), by Pablo Pares.

38. Apparently, there are no English versions. The titles translate literally as "Captain Mendonça" and "The Immortal."

39. The moniker *anos de chumbo*—or "years of lead"—usually refers to the darkest days of the military dictatorship in Brazil, typically considered as having taken place between 1968 and 1974.

40. Ginway further observes that "even within the parameters of 'fantastic literature,' Brazilian literature often tends to be highly allegorical, referring specifically to a given political situation" (2004, 29).

# Chapter 10

1. The idea of "cordial iconoclasm" first appeared while we were supervising the PhD candidate Cauê Nunes at the University of Campinas. He was writing a dissertation on the multiple readings or manifestations of "The Legend of the Ox that Spoke" ("A Lenda do Boi Falô"), a very popular folk tale in the region of Barão Geraldo, Campinas, state of São Paulo Brazil. Nunes analyzed different interpretations and manners to tell the legend, such as the one employed according to the griots' pedagogy. He also investigated real characters cited in the legend, such as Toninho, the slaveman, and the Baron Geraldo de Rezende.

2. In the original: "Armado dessa máscara, o indivíduo consegue manter sua supremacia ante o social. E, efetivamente, a polidez implica uma presença contínua e soberana do indivíduo."

3. See also Mota (2021, 2022).

4. In the original Portuguese, Salles Gomes uses the word "occupier" instead of "colonizer." Versions of his original text have been translated into English with the word colonizer, as in the volume edited by Michael T. Martin (1997).

5. https://issuu.com/brasildistopico/docs/cata logo brasil_disto pico.

6. Named after the famous Brazilian musician/composer who died of Covid-19 in 2020, this law is intended to amplify the public endowment for the arts during the pandemic and afterward. This was created during the Bolsonaro administration by congressmen who responded to relentless campaigns set forth by artists and the media to preserve the arts.

## Final Remarks

1. The chapter title is taken from the French band M83's sixth album, *Hurry Up! We're Dreaming* (2011). M83 has clear SF influences, and the band has made some film soundtracks, such as the one for Joseph Kosinski's 2013 feature-length film *Oblivion*. As we will try to demonstrate toward the end of this chapter, "Hurry Up! We are Dreaming" means that SF has been providing us the chance to dream of alternative futures collectively, so it might be time to dive deeper into these dreams, in a hurry, to hold sway of our history and prevent any possible end of the world.

2. In Portuguese, "drama-ciência" or "dramaciência." This is an attempt to better translate SF into Portuguese, adapting the Anglophone term to our local colors. The Italian language seems to be more successful in this sense, with the term *fantascienza* (see websites like https://www.fantascienza.com/). Fantascienza is, in my opinion, an even better term than SF to name the genre. Meanwhile, in India, a vernacular variety of SF could be found in *Bangla Kalpavigyan*. To know more on Bangla Kalpavigyan and Indian SF, see Arunava Gangopadhyay's documentary *Kalpavigyan: A Speculative Journey* (2021), or the website https://www.kalpavigyan.com/.

3. We could push further into that idea of a neologism, perhaps proposing terms like "science(melo)drama" ["(melo)dramaciência"].

4. https://embaubaplay.com/catalogo/a-seita/.

5. See https://www.youtube.com/watch?v=95tOtpk4Bnw.

6. In the original: "*o sonho prepara o sonhador para o dia seguinte.*"

7. Mercerism is P. K. Dick's (1968) new technology-based religion that uses "empathy boxes" to link users simultaneously to a VR environment of collective suffering centered on a martyr-like character, Wilbur Mercer, who eternally climbs up a hill while being hit with crashing stones. The allegorical scene revisits the Myth of Sisyphus as a collectively cathartic event, regularly experienced by the followers of Mercerism as a religious rite.

8. For more on Bandeira's "Pasárgada," see Martuscelli (2012).

9. In logic, the law of excluded middle or law of excluded third (in Latin, *principium tertii exclusi* or *tertium non datur*) is the third of the three classic Laws of Thought. It states that, for any proposition, either this proposition is true, or its negation is true. The first known formulation of the law of excluded middle was Aristotle's principle of noncontradiction, first proposed in *On Interpretation*. In it, Aristotle states that out of two contradictory propositions (that is, one proposition is the negation of another), one is necessarily true, and the other is necessarily false. He also states this as a principle in Book 3 of his *Metaphysics* (1952), saying that in any case it is necessary to affirm or deny, and that it is impossible for there to be anything between the two parts of the contradiction. This principle was declared a theorem of propositional logic by Russel and Whitehead in *Principia Mathematica* (1962, reprint of 1927 edition).

10. According to Bode and Rainer, "Future Narratives" differentiate themselves from "Past Narratives" because they have "nodes." The authors explain the concept of "node" in a narrative as follows: "The fundamental idea of 'Narrating Futures' is a very simple one: as a rule, narratives have events as their minimal units. But there is a certain, hitherto undiscovered corpus of narratives that have, in addition to events, one special feature, indeed *differentia specifica*, that other narratives don't have: they have nodes. A node is a situation that allows for more than one continuation. The simplest kind of node is a bifurcation, but most nodes have more than just two continuations. If a narrative has at least one node, then we call it a 'Future Narrative' (FN), in contradistinction to narratives that have 'only' events—they are 'Past Narratives' (PN). So the definition of a FN is a purely technical one: if a narrative has a least one node, it's in—if not, it's out" (Bode and Rainer 2013, vii).

11. See "Arte como construção de futuros possíveis—com Christian Dunker e Aílton Krenak" (Itaú Cultural). March 16, 2021, https://www.youtube.com/watch?v=JSCuJtkbBNE.

12. In the original: "Nheẽ porã é 'palavra boa, bonita, linda'; é muito usada para dar conselho, para ser dirigida à pessoa que está emocionalmente abalada ou com raiva."

13. In the original: "Inclusive, para nós Guarani, só depois que a criança começa a andar é que ela tem *ã*, ou seja, *ã* é algo da terra, deste mundo."

14. Both of Latin origin, the first comes from *anima* and the second from *spiritus* (Benites 2015, 12).

15. In the original: "Talvez uma tradução possível na língua portuguesa, por exemplo, e mais próximo do significado na língua guarani, seja espírito-nome."

# References

Abertura Oficial do II FIF será OLIVER no Metro a 17. 1969. *Correio da Manhã*. March 9. https://memoria.bn.br/pdf/089842/per089842_1969_23282.pdf.

Abramovay, Ricardo. 2019. *Amazonia—por Uma Economia do Conhecimento da Natureza*. São Paulo: Elefante.

Abreu, Nuno Cesar. 2006. *Boca do Lixo: Cinema e Classes Populares*. Campinas: Ed. da Unicamp.

Abreu, Nuno Cesar. 2012. *O Olhar Pornô: a Representação do Obsceno no Cinema e no Vídeo*. 2nd ed. São Paulo: Alameda.

Alessi, Gil. 2020. Salles vê "oportunidade" com coronavírus para "passar de boiada" desregulação da proteção ao meio ambiente. *El País*. May 23. https://brasil.elpais.com/brasil/2020-05-22/salles-ve-oportunidade-com-coronavirus-para-passar-de-boiada-desregulacao-da-protecao-ao-meio-ambiente.html#:~:text=Para%20o%20ministro%20do%20Meio,..)%20de%20baciada%E2%80%9D.

Almeida, Sílvio. 2020. *Racismo Estrutural*. São Paulo: Editora Jandaíra.

Altman, Rick. 1999. *Film/Genre*. London: British Film Institute.

Alvim, Francisco. 2004. "Disseram na Câmara." In *Poemas [1968–2000]*. São Paulo/Rio de Janeiro: Cosac Naïfy/7 Letras.

Andrade, Carlos Drummond. 2015. *O Poder Ultrajovem*. São Paulo: Companhia das Letras.

Andrade, Carlos Drummond. 2015. *Multitudinous Heart: Selected Poems: A Bilingual Edition*. Farrar, Straus and Giroux.

Andrade, Mário de. 2016. *Macunaíma, O Herói sem Nenhum Caráter*. New York: Penguin.

Andrade, Oswald de. 2017. *Manifesto Antropófago e outros textos*. Penguin Classics/Companhia das Letras.

Andrade, Oswald 1991. Oswald de Andrade's "Cannibalist Manifesto." Translated by Leslie Bary. *Latin American Literary Review* 19, no. 38: 35–37. https://doi.org/10.1080/09528829908576784.

Andrew, Dudley. 2006. "An Atlas for World Cinemas." In *Remapping World Cinema: Identity, Culture, and Politics in Film*, ed. Stephanie Dennison and Song Hwee Lim, 19–29. London/New York: Wallflower Press.

Amazonense, Francisco. 1955. "Carnaval em Marte." *Notícias de Hoje*. February 9.

Appadurai, Arjun. 1996. *Modernity at Large: Cultural Dimensions of Globalization*. Minneapolis: University of Minnesota Press.

Araújo, Ernesto. 2020. *Discurso Do Ministro Das Relações Exteriores, Ernesto Araújo, Na Formatura Da Turma João Cabral de Melo Neto (2019–2020) Do Instituto Rio Branco—Brasília, 22 de Outubro de 2020*. Presented at the Formatura da Turma João Cabral de Melo Neto (2019–2020) do Instituto Rio Branco—Brasília, 22 de outubro de 2020, October 22. https://www.gov.br/mre/pt-br/centrais-de-conteudo/publicacoes/discursos-artigos-e-entrevistas/ministro-das-relacoes-exteriores/discursos-mre/ernesto-araujo/discurso-do-ministro-das-relacoes-exteriores-ernesto-araujo-na-formatura-da-turma-joao-cabral-de-melo-neto-2019-2020-do-instituto-rio-branco-brasilia-22-de-outubro-de-2020.

Aristotle. 1952. "Metaphysics." In *Great Books of the Western World*, edited by R. M. Hutchins, 499–626. Chicago: Encyclopædia Britannica.

Armada, Charles Alexandre Souza. 2019. "The Environmental Disasters of Mariana and Brumadinho and the Brazilian Social Environmental Law State." *SSRN Electronic Journal*. https://doi.org/10.2139/ssrn.3442624.

Assis, Machado de. 2015. *Obras Completas de Machado de Assis II: Coletâneas de Contos*. Rio de Janeiro: Nova Aguilar.

Assis, Wagner de. 2021. *Nosso Lar. Bastidores do Filme*. Brasília/Rio de Janeiro: FEB.

Atwood, Margaret. 1998. *The Handmaid's Tale*. New York: Knopf Doubleday.

Augusto, Sérgio. 1976. "O peixe-avestruz." *Veja*. August 18.

Avellar, José Carlos. 1976. "Macaquices." *Jornal do Brasil*, Serviço. December 31.

Bandeira, Manuel. 2021. *Libertinagem*. São Paulo: Global.

Barker, Lynn, and Robert Skotak. 1994a. "Klushantsev: Russia's wizard of *Fantastika*" (Part 1). *American Cinematographer*, v. 75, nº 63, June, 78–83.

Barker, Lynn, and Robert Skotak. 1994b. "Klushantsev: Russia's wizard of *Fantastika*" (Part 2). *American Cinematographer*, v. 75, nº 7, July, 77–82.

Barrios, José Luis. 2006. Las extraterrestres o cómo ser ficheras en clasificación A. *El futuro más acá: cine mexicano de ciencia ficción*, ed Itala Schmelz, 151–69. Mexico City: Landucci and Universidad Nacional Autónoma de México.

Bauman, Zygmunt. 1997. *Postmodernity and its Discontents*. Cambridge: Polity Press.

Bauman, Zygmunt. 2000. *Liquid Modernity*. Cambridge: Polity Press.

Bauman, Zygmunt. 2005. *Liquid Life*. Cambridge: Polity Press.

Baxter, John. 1970. *Science Fiction in the Cinema*. New York: Zwemmer Barnes.

Beaumont, Matthew. 2009. The Anamorphic Estrangements of Science Fiction. In *Red Planets Marxism and Science Fiction*, edited by China Miéville and Mark Bould, 29–46. London: Pluto Press.

Bell, Andrea. 1999. "Science Fiction in Latin America: Reawakenings." *Science Fiction Studies* 26, no. 3: 441–46.

Benites, Sandra. 2015. Nheẽ, reko porã rã: nhemboea oexakarẽ Fundamento da pessoa guarani, nosso bem-estar futuro (educação tradicional): o olhar distorcido da escola. Trabalho de Conclusão de Curso (TCC). Florianópolis: Universidade Federal de Santa Catarina. https://licenciaturaindigena.ufsc.br/files/2015/07/Sandra-Benites_TCC.pdf.

Benites, Sandra. 2020. Nheẽ para os Guarani (Nhandeva e Mbya). *Campos—Revista de Antropologia* 21, no. 1: 37–42. https://doi.org/10.5380/cra.v21i1.77443.

Berman, Marshall. 1988. *All That Is Solid Melts into Air: The Experience of Modernity*. London: Penguin Books.

Bernardet, Jean-Claude. 1975. "O novo Cinema Novo." *Opinião*, n. 119, February 14.

Bernardet, Jean-Claude. 1996. Cinema e Religião. In *O Cinema no Século*, edited by Ismail Xavier, 187–94. Rio de Janeiro: Imago.

Bernardet, Jean-Claude. 1976. "O bacalhau que vende o peixe dos tubarões." *Revista Movimento*, nº 60, August 23, 1976.

Biáfora, Ruben. 1978. "Os Trapalhões na Guerra das Estrelas." *O Estado de São Paulo*, 1978, December 17, 46. Arquivo José Inácio de Melo Souza, Cinemateca Brasileira.

Bland, Archie. 2020. "The Fall of Colston's Statue: 'It Didn't Take Long—about Four Tugs of the Ropes.'" *The Guardian*. June 19. https://www.theguardian.com/uk-news/2020/jun/08/the-fall-of-edward-colston-statue-bristol-it-didnt-even-take-long-about-four-tugs.

Bode, Christoph, and Rainer Dietrich, eds. 2013. *Future Narratives*. Amsterdam: De Gruyter.

*Billboard*. 1957. "The 'New Invisible Commercial Ad' Agency Boom." September 16. https://books.google.com.br/books?id=ZCEEAAAAMBAJ&lpg=PA1&dq=james%20vicary&hl=pt-BR&pg=PA1#v=onepage&q=james%20vicary&f=false.

Booker, M. Keith, and Anne-Marie Thomas. 2009. *The Science Fiction Handbook*. Hoboken: Wiley-Blackwell.

Borges, Jorge Luis. 2000. *The Library of Babel*. Boston: David R Godine Publisher.

Bould, Mark. 2003. "Film and Television." In *The Cambridge Companion to Science Fiction*, edited by Edward James and Farah Mendlesohn, 79–95. Cambridge: Cambridge University Press.

Bould, Mark. 2021 *The Anthropocene Unconscious: Climate Catastrophe Culture*. London: Verso.

Brandão, Ignácio de Loyola. 1981. *Não Verás País Nenhum*. São Paulo: Círculo do Livro.

Brandão, Ignácio de Loyola 2003. *O Homem que Espalhou o Deserto*. São Paulo: Global, 12a ed.

Brandão, Ignácio de Loyola. *Desta Terra Nada Vai Sobrar, A Não Ser o Vento que Sopra sobre Ela*. São Paulo: Global, 2018.

Bishop, Elizabeth, and Emanuel Brasil. 1997. *An Anthology of Twentieth-Century Brazilian Poetry*. Middletown, CT: Wesleyan University Press.
Brosnan, John. 1991. *The Primal Screen: A History of Science Fiction Film*. London/Sydney: Orbit.
Buarque de Holanda, Sérgio. 2012a. *Roots of Brazil*. Notre Dame: University of Notre Dame Press.
Buarque de Holanda, Sérgio. 2012b. *O Homem Cordial*. São Paulo: Penguin Classics/Cia. das Letras.
Buckland, Warren. 2000. *The Cognitive Semiotics of Film*. Cambridge: Cambridge University Press.
Bueno, Zuleika de Paula. 2005. Leia o livro, veja o filme, compre o disco : a produção cinematografica juvenil brasileira na década de 1980. Doctoral dissertation. Campinas: University of Campinas. https://repositorio.unicamp.br/acervo/detalhe/367540.
Bueno, Zuleika de Paula. 2016. *Leia o livro, veja o filme, compre o disco: a formação do cinema juvenil brasileiro*. Maringá: EDUEM.
Bui, Camille. 2019. "Village Global." *Cahiers du Cinéma*, 758, September, 8–9.
Bui, Camille, and Joachim Lepastier. 2019. "Écouter le présent: Entretien avec Kleber Mendonça Filho et Juliano Dornelles." *Cahiers du Cinéma*, 758, September, 10–14.
Bürch, Noel. 1987. *El tragaluz del infinito*. Madrid: Cátedra.
Bürch, Noel. 2007. *La Lucarne de l'infini. Naissance du langage cinématographique*. Paris: L'Harmattan.
Butcher, Pedro. 2005. *O Cinema Brasileiro Hoje*. São Paulo: Publifolha.
Cadogan, León. 1959. Ayvu Rapyta. Textos míticos de los Mbyá-Guaraní del Guairá. Doctoral dissertation. Universidade de São Paulo, São Paulo, São Paulo, Brasil.
Caetano, M. R. 2019. "Fuleiragem fiction" e comédia teen sobre corpo trans, no Festival de Brasília. *Revista de Cinema*. November 26, 2019. https://revistadecinema.com.br/2019/11/fuleiragem-fiction-e-comedia-teen-sobre-corpo-trans-no-festival-de-brasilia/.
Calazans, Flávio. 1992. *Propaganda Subliminar Multimidia*. São Paulo: Summus.
Caminha, Marina. 2010. A teledramaturgia juvenil brasileira. In *História da televisão no Brasil: do início aos dias de hoje*, edited by A. P. Ribeiro, I. Sacramento, and M. Roxo, 197–215. São Paulo: Contexto.
Câmpera, Francisco. 2019. "Vale, exemplo mundial de incompetência e descaso." *El País*. January 29. https://brasil.elpais.com/brasil/2019/01/27/opinion/1548547908_087976.html.
Cândido, Antonio. 2000. *Literatura e Sociedade*. São Paulo: PubliFolha.
Cánepa, Laura. 2005. "O Jovem Tataravô." *Revista Carcasse*. October 1. http://www.carcasse.com/revista/anfiguri/o_jovem_tataravo/index.php.
Cánepa, Laura. 2008. *Medo de quê?: uma historia do horror nos filmes brasileiro*. PhD diss., Unicamp, Campinas, São Paulo, Brasil.

Cánepa, Laura. 2012. "Tecnologias da comunicação, horror e ficção-científica: o caso de três filmes brasileiros." *Revista Contemporânea Comunicação e Cultura* (10)1. January-April 2012. https://periodicos.ufba.br/index.php/contemporaneaposcom/article/view/5674/4354.

Cánepa, Laura, and Alfredo Suppia. 2017. "O filme espírita brasileiro: entre dois mundos." *ALCEU* 17, no. 34, 81–97. http://revistaalceu-acervo.com.puc-rio.br/media/alceu34_pp81-97.pdf.

Canudo, Ricciotto. "Reflections on the Seventh Art." 1988 (1923). In *French Film Theory and Criticism*, edited by Richard Abel, 291–302. Princeton, NJ: Princeton University Press.

Carneiro, André. 1966. *O Homem que Adivinhava*. São Paulo: EdArt.

Carneiro, André. 1967. *Introdução ao estudo da science fiction*. São Paulo: Imprensa do Estado.

Carneiro, André. 1980. *Piscina Livre*. São Paulo: Moderna.

Carneiro, André. 1991. *Amorquia*. São Paulo: Aleph.

Causo, Roberto de Sousa. 1996. "Tupinipunk—Cyberpunk Brasileiro." *Papêra Uirandê Especial 1: O Retorno*. August 1996.

Causo, Roberto de Sousa. 2003. *Ficção Científica, Fantasia e Horror no Brasil*. Editora UFMG.

Causo, Roberto de Sousa. 2007. *Os Melhores Contos Brasileiros de Ficção Científica*. São Paulo: Devir.

Causo, Roberto de Sousa. 2015. "O Estado da Arte: Ficção Científica Tupinipunk." *Papêra Uirandê Especial 1: Tupinipunk no Século XXI*. October 2015.

Causo, Roberto de Sousa. 2020. *Brasa 2000 e mais ficção científica*. São Paulo: Patuá.

Cesário, Lia Bahia. 2010. Majors e Globo Filmes: uma parceria de sucesso no cinema nacional. In *Estudos de Cinema Socine X*, ed. Mariarosaria Fabris et al., 135–49. São Paulo: Socine. https://www.socine.org/wp-content/uploads/2015/11/X_ESTUDOS_SOCINE_b.pdf.

Chu, Seo-Young. 2010. *Do Metaphors Dream of Literal Sleep? A Science-Fictional Theory of Representation*. Cambridge MA: Harvard University Press.

Clareson, Thomas D. 1971. *SF: The Other Side of Realism*. Madison: Popular Press 1.

Clark, Andy. 2003. *Natural-Born Cyborgs: Minds, Technology, and the Future of Human Intelligence*. Oxford/New York: Oxford University Press.

Clastres, Pierre. 1990. *A Fala Sagrada: mitos e cantos sagrados dos índios Guarani*. Campinas: Papirus.

Cordoba, Antonio. 2017. Astral Cities, New Selves: Utopian Subjectivities in *Nosso Lar* and *Branco Sai, Preto Fica*. In *Space and Subjectivity in Contemporary Brazilian Cinema*, edited by Antônio Márcio da Silva and Mariana Cunha, 133–47. New York: Palgrave Macmillan.

Correia, Mariama, and Bruno Fonseca. 2020. *Governo gastou mais de R$ 30 milhões em rádios e TVs de pastores que apoiam Bolsonaro. Brasil de Fato*.

June 19. https://www.brasildefato.com.br/2020/06/16/governo-gastou-r-30-milhoes-em-radios-e-tvs-de-pastores-que-apoiam-bolsonaro.

Cuarterolo, Andrea. 2007. "Distopías vernáculas. El cine de ciencia-ficción en la Argentina." In *Cines al margen. Nuevos modos de representación en el cine argentino contemporáneo*, eds. María José Moore and Paula Wolkowicz, 81–107. Buenos Aires: Libraria.

Cunha, Fausto. 1976. Ficção Científica no Brasil: um planeta quase desabitado. In L. David Allen, *No Mundo da Ficção Científica*, 5–20. São Paulo: Summus.

Cunha, Euclides da. 2010. *Backlands: The Canudos Campaign*. London: Penguin Classics.

DaMatta, Roberto. 1997. *Carnavais, Malandros e Herois: Para Uma Sociologia do Dilema Brasileiro*. Rio de Janeiro: Rocco.

DaMatta, Roberto. 2004. *O Que É O Brasil?*. Rio de Janeiro: Rocco.

Del Priore, Mary. 2014. *Do Outro Lado—A História do Sobrenatural e do Espiritismo*. São Paulo: Planeta.

Delgado, Miguel Ángel Fernández. 2001. *Visiones Perifericas*. Buenos Aires: Lumen.

Denford et al. 2017. A comprehensive review of reviews of school-based interventions to improve sexual-health. *Health Psychology Review* 11, no. 1: 33–52. https://doi.org/10.1080/17437199.2016.1240625.

Denizot, Nathalie. 2010. Genres littéraires et genres textuels dans la discipline français. *Pratiques*, 145–46, 211–30. https://doi.org/10.4000/pratiques.1562.

Dennison, Stephanie, and Song Hwee Lim. 2006. *Remapping World Cinema: Identity, Culture, and Politics in Film*. London: Wallflower Press.

Dery, Mike. 1994. Black to the Future: Interviews with Samuel R. Delany, Greg Tate, and Tricia Rose. In *Flame Wars: The Discourse of Cyberculture*. ed. Mark Dery, 179–222. Durham, NC: Duke University Press Books.

Dias Jr., Jocimar. 2020. Bacurau as Science-Fiction Revenge Fantasy. *Film Quarterly* 74, no 2: 84–86. https:// doi.org/10.1525/fq.2020.74.2.84.

Dick, Phillip K. 1968. *Do Androids Dream of Electric Sheep?* New York: Doubleday.

Duarte, Lílian Cristina Burlamaqui. 2003. *Política Externa E Meio Ambiente*. Rio de Janeiro: JZE.

Dufour, Éric. 2011. *Le cinéma de science-fiction: Histoire et philosophie*. Paris: Armand Colin.

Dutra, Mari. 2020. Amazofuturismo imagina um futuro indígena e cyberpunk. *Hypeness*. March 11. https://www.hypeness.com.br/2020/03/amazofuturismo-imagina-um-futuro-indigena-e-cyberpunk/.

Eco, Umberto. 1989. *Sobre os Espelhos e Outros Ensaios*. Rio de Janeiro: Nova Fronteira.

Escobar, Herton. 2020. *Blog*. Jornal da USP. August 12. https://jornal.usp.br/ciencias/desmatamento-da-amazonia-dispara-de-novo-em-2020/.

Essenfelder, Renato. 2006. Talentos migram para TV, diz McKee. *Folha de S. Paulo—Ilustrada*. December 12. https://www1.folha.uol.com.br/fsp/ilustrad/fq1212200607.htm.

Fanon, Frantz. 1986. *Black Skin, White Masks*. London: Pluto Press.
Fanon, Frantz. 2005. *The Wretched of the Earth*. New York: Grove Press.
Faria, Mário Parreiras de. 2019. Mariana and Brumadinho: Repercussion of Mining Disasters on Environmental Health. *Revista Brasileira de Medicina do Trabalho* 17. https://www.rbmt.org.br/details/403/pt-BR/mariana-e-brumadinho.
Fávero, Bruno. 2020. Como a ciência contradiz os planos de Damares para estimular a abstinência sexual entre jovens. *Aos Fatos*. April 7. https://www.aosfatos.org/noticias/como-ciencia-contradiz-os-planos-de-Damares-para-estimular-abstinencia-sexual-entre-jovens/.
Fawcett, Fausto. 2020. *Santa Clara Poltergeist*. Curitiba: Arte e Letra.
Fernandes, P. C. C. 2008. As Origens do Espiritismo no Brasil: Razão, Cultura e Experiência no Início de uma Experiência. Master thesis. Brasília: Universidade de Brasília. https://www.scielo.br/j/se/a/rwYBqfTsQ3dXssB6mBwpqNs/.
Fernandes, Florestan. 2017. *Significado do Protesto Negro*. São Paulo: Expessão Popular/Perseu Abramo.
Ferreira, Jairo. 1986. *Cinema de Invenção*. São Paulo: Editora Max Limonad/Embrafilme.
Ferreira, Jairo. 2007. Otoniel, o pedestre. *Cinema de Invenção—Textos de Jairo Ferreira*. May 13. http://cinema-de-invencao.blogspot.com/2007/05/otoniel-o-pedestre.html.
Fisher, Mark. 2009. *Capitalist Realism: Is There No Alternative?* Winchester, UK: Zero Books.
Foucault, Michel. 1997. "*Il Faut Défendre la Sociéte*": *Cours au Collège de France, 1975–1976*. Paris: Seuil.
Fowler, Alastair. 2002. *Kinds of Literature—An Introduction to the Theory of Genres and Modes*. Oxford: Oxford University Press.
Freitas, Jânio de. 2004. "O golpe inequívoco via telex." *Folha de S. Paulo*. March 31. https://www1.folha.uol.com.br/fsp/brasil/fc3103200421.htm.
Frow, John. 2014. *Genre*. 2nd ed. London: Routledge.
Gama, Zilda. *Na Sombra e na Luz*. Brasília: Federação Espírita Brasileira, 2007.
Garcia, Estevão. 2006. "A partir de agora vamos falar em espanhol"—Sobre a mostra sci-fi mexicano do Festival do Rio. *Contracampo Revista de Cinema*. December 1. http://www.contracampo.com.br/84/artscifimexico.htm.
Gates, Marya. 2022. "Medusa." *RogerEbert.com*. July 29. https://www.rogerebert.com/reviews/medusa-movie-review-2022#:~:text=%E2%80%9CMedusa%E2%80%9D%20follows%20two%20lifelong%20friends,awash%20in%20purple%2Dpink%20neon.
Gaycken, Oliver. 2015. *Devices of Curiosity: Early Cinema and Popular Science*. Oxford: Oxford University Press.
Genelli, Lyn D., and Tom D. Genelli. 2013. *Death at the Movies: Hollywood's Guide to the Hereafter*. Wheaton, IL: Quest Books.
Genette, Gérad. 1992. *Palimpsestes: la littérature au second degré*. Paris: Éd. du Seuil.

Ghazala, Reed. 2005. *Circuit-Bending: Build Your Own Alien Instruments.* 1st ed. Hoboken, NJ: Wiley.

Ginway, Mary E. 2004. *Brazilian Science Fiction: Cultural Myths and Nationhood in the Land of the Future.* Lewisburg, PA: Bucknell University Press.

Ginway Mary E., and Alfredo Suppia. 2012. Science Fiction and Metafiction in the Cinematic Works of Brazilian Director Jorge Furtado. In *Latin American Science Fiction*, ed. Mary E. Ginway and J. Andrew Brown. Palgrave Macmillan, New York. https://doi.org/10.1057/9781137312778_11.

Ginway, Mary E. 2021. Subverted Dichotomies and Permeable Borders in Semente Exterminadora. In *YWY, Searching for a Character Between Future Worlds: Gender, Ecology, Science Fiction*, ed. Pedro Neves Marques, 90–98. London: Sternberg Press.

Gonçalves, Alexandre. 2019. "'Divino amor': filme futurista é uma crítica à hipocrisia do Brasil evangélico de Bolsonaro." *Intercept Brasil.* July 18. https://www.intercept.com.br/2019/07/17/divino-amor-critica-evangelico-bolsonaro/.

Grant, Barry Keith. 1999. Sensuous Elaboration: Reason and the Visible in Science Fiction Film. In *Alien Zone II: The Spaces of Science Fiction Cinema*, ed. Annette Kuhn, 16–30. London and New York: Verso.

Giddens, Anthony. 1984. *The Constitution of Society: Outline of the Theory of Structuration.* Berkeley: University of California Press.

Guimarães Rosa, João. 2001. *Primeiras Estórias.* 15th ed. Rio de Janeiro: Nova Fronteira.

Gunning, Tom. 1990. "The Cinema of Attraction: Early Cinema, Its Spectator and the Avant-Garde." In *Early Cinema: Space, Frame, Narrative*, ed. Thomas Elsaesser and Adam Barker, 63–69. London: British Film Institute.

Gutfreind, Cristiane, Helena Stigger, and Luiza Carmona. 2011. A experiência através da repetição: a Ditadura Militar no cinema brasileiro. *Revista Contracampo* 22:147. https://periodicos.uff.br/contracampo/article/view/17215.

Hardy, Phil. 1995. *The Overlook Film Encyclopedia: Science Fiction.* New York: Overlook Press.

Hartwell, David. 1989. *The World Treasury of Science Fiction.* 1st ed. Boston: Little Brown & Co.

Haywood Ferreira, Rachel. 2007. "The First Wave: Latin American Science Fiction Its Roots Discovers," *Science Fiction Studies* no. 103: 432–62.

Haywood Ferreira, Rachel. 2011. *The Emergence of Latin American Science Fiction.* Middletown, CT: Wesleyan University Press.

Hinz, Kristina, Doriam Borges, Aline Coutinho, and Thiago Cury Andries. 2021. The rise of Brazil's neo-Pentecostal narco-militia. *OpenDemocracy.* May 6. https://www.opendemocracy.net/en/democraciaabierta/rise-narco-militia-pentecostal-brazil-en/.

Holcombe, Madeline. 2020. John C. Calhoun: Charleston Removes a Statue of Slavery Defender and Former Vice President. *CNN.* June 25. https://edition.cnn.com/2020/06/24/us/charleston-statue-removal-calhoun-trnd/index.html

Holmberg, Eduardo Ladislao. 2019. *Viaje maravilloso del señor Nic-Nac: Fantasía espiritista*. 1st ed. La Casa de las Palabras.
Hutchison, David. 1987. *Film Magic: The Art and Science of Special Effects*. Hoboken, NJ: Prentice Hall Direct.
IBGE. 2012. Número de católicos cai e aumenta o de evangélicos, espíritas e sem religião. *IBGE Censo 2010*. June 29. https://agenciadenoticias.ibge.gov.br/agencia-sala-de-imprensa/2013-agencia-de-noticias/releases/14244-asi-censo-2010-numero-de-catolicos-cai-e-aumenta-o-de-evangelicos-espiritas-e-sem-religiao#:~:text=Em%202010%2C%20chegaram%20a%2022,64%2C6%25%20em%202010.
The Incredible Hulk. n.d. *InfanTv*. http://infantv.com.br/infantv/?p=8022.
Jodorowsky, Alejandro. 2004. *Psicomagia*. Madrid: Siruela.
Johnson, Randall. 1989. Tupy or not Tupy: Cannibalism and Nationalism in Contemporary Brazilian Literature and Culture. In *On Modern Latin American Fiction*, ed. John King, 41–59. New York: Hill and Wang.
Johnson, Randall, and Robert Stam, eds. 1995. *Brazilian Cinema*. New York: Columbia.
Jordão, Pedro. 2020. "Atos contrários e em defesa do aborto de menina de 10 anos atraem deputados e vereadores no Recife." *Estadão*. August 17. https://www.estadao.com.br/brasil/atos-contrarios-e-em-defesa-do-aborto-de-menina-de-10-anos-atraem-deputados-e-vereadores-no-recife/.
Jornal da Record. "Ministro Paulo Guedes participa de debates sobre meio ambiente no Fórum Econômico Mundial." YouTube video, 1:39. January 21, 2020. https://www.youtube.com/watch?v=VrXKBz8SpMM.
José, Ângela. 2007. "Cinema marginal, a estética do grotesco e a globalização da miséria." *Alceu* 8, no. 15 (July–December): 155–63.
Kardec, Allan. 1998 (1857). *Le Livres des Esprits*. Union Spirite Française et Francophone. https://www.cesakparis.fr/wp-content/uploads/2010/02/allan-kardec-esprits.pdf.
Kardec, Allan. 1863. *Le Livre des Mediums*. 6th ed. Paris: Didier et Cie. http://www.oconsolador.com.br/linkfixo/bibliotecavirtual/frances/le-livre-des-mediums.pdf.
Karremans, Johann, Wolfgang Stroebe, and Jasper Claus. 2006. "Beyond Vicary's Fantasies: The Impact of Subliminal Priming and Brand Choice. *Journal of Experimental Social Psychology* 42, no. 6: 792–98. https://doi.org/10.1016/j.jesp.2005.12.002.
Kincaid, Paul. Winter 2003. "On the Origins of Genre." *Extrapolation* 44, 409–19.
Kopenawa, Davi, and Bruce Albert. 2013. *The Falling Sky: Words of a Yanomami Shaman*. Cambridge, Mass: Belknap Press: An Imprint of Harvard University Press.
Kracauer, Sigfried. 2019 *From Caligari to Hitler: A Psychological History of the German Film*. Princeton, NJ: Princeton University Press.

Krenak, Aílton. 2020. *Ideas to Postpone the End of the World*. Toronto: House of Anansi Press.

Kujawski, Guilherme. 1994. *Piritas Siderais*. Rio de Janeiro: Francisco Alves.

Le Monde and AFP. 2020. "Une déforestation inquiétante en Amazonie brésilienne depuis le début de l'année." *Le Monde.fr*. May 9. https://www.lemonde.fr/planete/article/2020/05/09/une-deforestation-record-en-amazonie-bresilienne-depuis-le-debut-de-l-annee_6039133_3244.html.

Leme, Caroline Gomes. 2012. "Podemos Falar Sobre Isso Agora?—A Ditadura Sob As Lentes Do Cinema Brasileiro dos Anos 1980." *Revista Eletrônica Literatura e Autoritarismo*—Dossiê, Maio de 2012, 272–97. https://periodicos.ufsm.br/LA/article/view/75238.

Leme, Caroline Gomes. 2016. *Ditadura em imagem e som*. São Paulo: Editora Unesp.

Lévi-Strauss, Claude. 1986. *O Olhar Distanciado*. Lisboa: Edições 70.

Lewgoy, Bernardo. 2000. *Os espíritas e as letras:* um estudo antropológico sobre cultura escrita e oralidade no espiritismo kardecista. Doctoral dissertation. Universidade de São Paulo, São Paulo, São Paulo, Brasil. https://lume.ufrgs.br/handle/10183/16244.

Lewgoy, Bernardo. 2004. O livro religioso no Brasil recente. *Ciencias Sociales y Religión/Ciências Sociais e Religião* 6, no. 6: 51–69. https://doi.org/10.22456/1982-2650.2266.

Lim, Dennis. 2009. "'Sin Nombre' and 'Sleep Dealer' Address Immigration, Between Politics and Thrills." *New York Times*, March 13. https://www.nytimes.com/2009/03/15/movies/15denn.html.

Lispector, Clarice. 1988. *The Passion According to GH*. Minneapolis: University of Minnesota Press.

Lista de filmes brasileiros com mais de um milhão de espectadores. 2021. In *Wikipedia*. May 9. https://pt.wikipedia.org/wiki/Lista_de_filmes_brasileiros_com_mais_de_um_milh%C3%A3o_de_espectadores.

Lyra, Bernadette, and Gelson Santana. 2006. *Cinema de bordas*. São Paulo: A Lápis.

Rivera, Lysa. 2012. Future Histories and Cyborg Labor: Reading Borderlands Science Fiction after NAFTA. *Science Fiction Studies* 39, no. 3, 415. https://doi.org/10.5621/sciefictstud.39.3.0415.

Macedo, Valéria. 2017. Misturar e circular em modulações guarani. Uma etiologia das (in)disposições. *Mana* 23, no. 3: 511–43. https://doi.org/10.1590/1678-49442017v23n3p511.

Maior, Marcel Souto. 2003. *As Vidas De Chico Xavier*. São Paulo: Leya.

Marson, Melina Izar. 2009. *Cinema e políticas de estado da Embrafilme à Ancine*. São Paulo: Escrituras.

Martuscelli, Tania. 2012. Pasárgada as Dreamland in the Portuguese-speaking World. *Portuguese Studies* 28, no. 1: 50. https://doi.org/10.5699/portstudies.28.1.0050.

Marx, Karl. 2006 (1952). *The Eighteenth Brumaire of Louis Bonaparte*. Project Gutenberg. http://www.gutenberg.org/ebooks/1346.

Mbembe, Achille. 2003. "Necropolitics." *Public Culture* 15, no. 1 (Winter): 11–40.
McClean, Shilo. 2007. *Digital Storytelling: The Narrative Power of Visual Effects in Film*. Cambridge, MA: MIT Press.
McKee, Robert. 1997. *Story: Substance, Structure, Style and the Principles of Screenwriting*. 1st ed. New York: ReganBooks.
Meadows, Dennis, et al. 1972. *The Limits to Growth; A Report for the Club of Rome's Project on the Predicament of Mankind*. New York: Universe Books.
Meimaridis, M., Daniela Mazur, and Daniel Rios. 2020. "A Empreitada Global da Netflix: uma análise das estratégias da empresa em mercados periféricos." *Revista GEMInIS*, 11, no. 1: 4–30. https://www.revistageminis.ufscar.br/index.php/geminis/article/view/492.
Melià, Bartolomeu. 2010. *Pasado, presente y futuro de la lengua guaraní*. Paraguay: Ediciones Montoya.
Melo Souza, José Inacio de. 1993. "A morte e as mortes do cinema brasileiro—E outras histórias de arrepiar." *Revista USP*, no. 19: 51–57. https://doi.org/10.11606/issn.2316-9036.v0i19p51-57.
Mendes, Wallace G., and Cosme M. F. P. da Silva. 2020. "Homicide of Lesbians, Gays, Bisexuals, Travestis, Transexuals, and Transgender people (LGBT) in Brazil: a Spatial Analysis." *Ciência & Saúde Coletiva* 25, no. 5:1709–22. http://doi.org/ 10.1590/1413-81232020255.33672019.
Merten, Luiz Carlos. 2013. "Brasil é o tema em 'Uma História de Amor e Fúria.'" *O Estado de S. Paulo*, "Caderno 2," D6. April 5.
Meteoro. 2019. "Chico Science vs. Ariano Suassuna: Battle for Pernambuco." YouTube video, 13:17. January 5. https://www.youtube.com/watch?v=9tEOHb3vClQ.
Metz, Christian. 1977. "Trucage" and the Film. Translated by Françoise Meltzer. *Critical Inquiry* 3, no. 4: 657–75. https://doi.org/10.1086/447911.
Miranda, Luiz Felipe. 1990. *Dicionário de Cineastas Brasileiros*. São Paulo: Art Editora.
Mitchell, David T., and Sharon L. Snyder. 2008. "Representation and Its Discontents: The Uneasy Home of Disability in Literature and Film." In *Multi-Cultural Film: An Anthology*, edited by M. Martínes, J. Lowe, and Eugene Crook, 203–22. Boston: Pearson.
Molina-Gavilán, Yolanda, Andrea Bell, Miguel Ángel Fernández-Delgado, M. Elizabeth Ginway, Luis Pestarini, and Juan Carlos Toledano Redondo. 2007. "Chronology of Latin American Science Fiction, 1775–2005." *Science Fiction Studies* 34, no. 3: 369–431.
Monteiro, Lea, Luís Oliveira, Cecília Lobo, and Alfredo Suppia, eds. 2021. *Antropokaos: Mostra de Ficção Científica Brasileira*. Belo Horizonte: MG: Maria Cecília Silva Lobo Lima. https://www.academia.edu/73266023/Antropokaos_Mostra_de_Fic%C3%A7%C3%A3o_Cient%C3%ADfica_Brasileira.
Morais, Pâmela. 2018. "LGBTfobia no Brasil: fatos, números e polêmicas." October 5. https://www.politize.com.br/lgbtfobia-brasil-fatos-numeros-polemicas/.

Moser, Sandra. 2014. Quando Os Trapalhões eram os reis do cinema. *Gazeta do Povo*. August 9. https://www.gazetadopovo.com.br/caderno-g/quando-os-trapalhoes-eram-os-reis-do-cinema-ebw6ow1z75q9cdsi1pr96g47i/.

Mota, Camilla Veras. 2021. "Por que Brasil e EUA ficaram tão diferentes? Curso na Universidade de Chicago tenta explicar." *BBC News Brasil*. December 5. https://www.bbc.com/portuguese/geral-59499807.

Mota, Camilla Veras. 2022. "Por que Brasil e EUA ficaram tão diferentes? Curso na Universidade de Chicago tenta explicar." January 14. https://www.bbc.com/portuguese/geral-60004557.

Murray, Stuart. 2009. *Images of Dignity: Barry Barclay and Fourth Ciy nema*. Wellington: HUIA Publishers.

Nascimento, Abdias, ed. 1966. *Teatro Experimental do Negro: Testemunhos*. Rio de Janeiro: GRD.

Nagib, Lúcia, ed. 2002. *O Cinema da Retomada*. São Paulo: Editora 34.

Nagib, Lúcia, ed. 2003. *The New Brazilian Cinema*. London and New York: I.B. Tauris.

Nagib, Lúcia. 2006. "Toward a Positive Definition of World Cinema." In *Remapping World Cinema—Identity, Culture and Politics in Film*, ed. Song Hwee Lim and Stephanie Dennison, 30–37. London and New York: Wallflower.

Nama, Adilifu. 2015. *Race on the QT: Blackness and the Films of Quentin Tarantino*. Austin: University of Texas Press.

Napolitano, Marcos, and Eduardo V. Morettin, eds. 2018. *O cinema e as ditaduras militares*. São Paulo: Editora Intermeios.

Neves, Paulo. 1977. "O Trapalhão no Planalto dos Macacos." *Cinema em Close-up*, ano II, nº 13. São Paulo: Lamana.

Nicholls, Peter. 1984. *Fantastic Cinema: An Illustrated Survey*. London: Ebury Press.

Noronha, Jurandyr. 1997. *Pioneiros do Cinema Brasileiro: 1896 a 1936*. São Paulo: EMC Melhoramentos [CD-ROM].

Noronha, Jurandyr. 2008. *Dicionário de Cinema Brasileiro: De 1896 a 1936 Do Nascimento ao Sonoro*. São Paulo: EMC Edições.

Novaes, Claudio C., and Mírian. S. C. Reis. 2011. Olney São Paulo Breves Aspectos da Pesquisa Sobre o Percurso do Cineasta. *A Cor Das Letras* 11, no. 1: 127–42. https://doi.org/10.13102/cl.v11i1.1502.

Novaes, Claudio. C. 2011. *Aspectos Críticos da Literatura e do Cinema na Obra de Olney São Paulo*. Salvador: Quarteto.

((o))eco. O que é a Amazônia Legal. 2021. https://oeco.org.br/dicionario-%20 ambiental/28783-o-que-e-a-amazonia-legal/.

Odin, Roger. 1983. Mise en phase, déphasage et performativité. *Communications* 38, no. 1: 213–38. https://doi.org/10.3406/comm.1983.1574.

Oricchio, Luiz Z. 2006. "*O 5o Poder*, ou 'Rouba, mas Faz.'" *Estadão Cultura*, blogs Luiz Zanin: Cinema, cultura e afins. November 30. https://www.estadao.com.br/cultura/luiz-zanin/o-quinto-poder/.

Ortiz Ramos, José Mário. 1997. Cinema Brasileiro: Depois do Vendaval. *Revista USP* 0, no. 32: 102–7. https://doi.org/10.11606/issn.2316-9036.v0i32p102-107.

Ortiz Ramos, José Mário. 2004. *Cinema, Televisão e Publicidade: cultura popular de massa no Brasil nos anos 1970–1980*. Annablume.
Paiva, Vitor. 2019. "Ilustrador brasileiro cria o cybergreste, mistura de Lampião com Blade Runner." *Hypeness*. May 21. https://www.hypeness.com.br/2019/05/ilustrador-brasileiro-cria-o-cybergreste-mistura-de-lampiao-com-blade-runner/.
Paz, Mariano. 2008. "South of the Future: An Overview of Latin American Science Fiction Cinema." *Science Fiction Film & Television* 1, no. 1: 81–103. https://doi.org/10.3828/sfftv.1.1.7.
Pesquisa Fapesp. 2021. "Intensidade de P&D na estrutura produtiva dos países," 11. https://revistapesquisa.fapesp.br/intensidade-de-pd-na-estrutura-produtiva-dos-paises/.
Pissolato, Elizabeth. 2007. *A duração da pessoa : mobilidade, parentesco e xamanismo mbya (guarani)*. São Paulo: UNESP/ISA/NuTI.
Poder 360. 2020a. "Campanha 'Defund Bolsonaro' culpa presidente por destruição da Amazônia." YouTube video. 1:27. September 2. https://www.youtube.com/watch?v=Y7nMKg3TZrU.
Poder 360. 2020b. "Reunião ministerial de 22 de abril de 2020, na qual Bolsonaro teria indicado interferência na PF." YouTube video. 1:55:20. May 22. https://www.youtube.com/watch?v=VkCTwQH55Ic.
Portal do José. 2020. "Delírios no Poder!" YouTube video, 17:50. October, 22, 2020. https://www.youtube.com/watch?v=15dfcXwnX0w.
Santos, Ruy. 2009 (1945). "Comício: São Paulo a Luís Carlos Prestes." YouTube video. 9:16. March 19. https://www.youtube.com/watch?v=GBwxg_75-sg.
Ramos, Alberto Guerreiro. 1957. *Introdução crítica à sociologia brasileira*. Rio de Janeiro: Editorial Andes Ltda.
Ramos, Fernão P., and Luiz Felipe Miranda. 2004. *Enciclopédia do Cinema Brasileiro*. 2nd ed. São Paulo: Senac.
Ramos, Lázaro. 2022. *Medida Provisória: Diário do Diretor*. Rio de Janeiro: Cobogó.
Rampell, Ed. 2021. "The Ministry of Return: A Futuristic "Final Solution" to the "Race Problem." *Hollywood Progressive*. February 18. https://hollywoodprogressive.com/film/executive-order.
Rangel, Natália. 2010. Blockbuster de outro mundo. *ISTOÉ*. August 27. https://istoe.com.br/98236_BLOCKBUSTER+DE+OUTRO+MUNDO/.
Regina, Ivan C. 1988. *Manifesto Antropofágico da Ficção Científica Brasileira*. fcbrasileira.wordpress.com—Ficção científica brasileira: 60 anos em manifestos. https://fcbrasileira.wordpress.com/inicial/manifesto-antropofagico-da-ficcao-cientifica-%20brasileira-1988/.
Reis, Lúcio. 2012. "O Jovem Tataravô." Portal Brasileiro de Cinema/Horror no Cinema Brasileiro. São Paulo: Heco. https://www.portalbrasileirodecinema.com.br/horror/filme-o-jovem-tataravo.php?indice=filmes.
Ribeiro, Darcy. 2000. *The Brazilian People: The Formation and Meaning of Brazil*. 1st ed. Gainesville: University Press of Florida.

Ribeiro, Djamila. 2019. *Pequeno Manual Antirracista*. São Paulo: Cia. das Letras.
Ribeiro, Pedro Henrique. 2024. "Biônicos adapta estética cyberpunk para drama familiar brasileiro." *Omelete*. June 3. https://www.omelete.com.br/filmes/criticas/bionicos-netflix-filme-nacional.
Rickman, Gregg. 2004. *The Science Fiction Film Reader*. 1st ed. Lanham, MD: Limelight.
Rieder, John. 2008. *Colonialism and the Emergence of Science Fiction*. Middletown, CT: Wesleyan University Press.
Rieder, John. 2010. "On Defining SF, or Not: Genre Theory, SF, and History." *Science Fiction Studies* 37, no. 2, 191–209. https://warwick.ac.uk/fac/arts/english/currentstudents/undergraduate/modules/en361fantastika/bibliography/1.1reider_j._2010-on_defining_sf_or_not.pdf.
Rieder, John. 2011. "Race and Revenge Fantasies in *Avatar*, *District 9* and *Inglourious Basterds*. *Science Fiction Film & Television* 4, no. 1: 41–56. https://doi.org/10.3828/sfftv.2011.3.
Rieder, John. 2017. *Science Fiction and the Mass Cultural Genre System*. Middletown, CT: Wesleyan University Press.
Roberts, Adam. 2000. *Science Fiction*. London: Routledge.
Rocha, Glauber. 1969. "Tropicalism, Anthropophagy, Myth, Ideogram"—Tropicália. *Tropicalia: A Project of Ana de Oliveira*. http://tropicalia.com.br/en/eubioticamente-atraidos/verbo-tropicalista/tropicalismo-antropofagia-mito.
Rocha, Glauber. 1997. "An Esthetic of Hunger" (Randal Johnson and Burnes Hollyman, Trad.). In *New Latin American Cinema, Theory, Practices and Transcontinental Articulations*, ed. Michael T. Martin, 59–61. Detroit: Wayne State University Press.
Rocha, Glauber. 2004. *Revolução do Cinema Novo*. São Paulo: Cosac Naify.
Rodrigues, João Carlos. 2004. "Os Monstros de Babaloo." In *Cinema Marginal Brasileiro e suas Fronteiras*, ed. Eugênio Puppo, 66–67. São Paulo: Heco. https://docs.wixstatic.com/ugd/eb2c1e_99e22f99ff26452babd4d8321deb329a.pdf?index=true.
Roque, Daniel Salomão. 2018. "Os primórdios da propaganda subliminar no Brasil." *Vice*. July 18. https://www.vice.com/pt/article/a3a4jp/os-primordios-da-propaganda-subliminar-no-brasil.
Sá, Alan de. 2019. "Estão inventando o Nordeste. De novo—Explico melhor escrevendo." *Medium*. September 4. https://medium.com/alan-de-s%C3%A1/est%C3%A3o-inventando-o-nordeste-de-novo-808943b6a759.
Sá, Alan de, G. G. Diniz, and Alec Silva. 2020. *Sertãopunk: Histórias de um Nordeste do Amanhã*. 2nd ed. Self-published.Alan de Sá, G. G. Diniz, and Alec Silva. [e-book]
Sadlier, Darlene J. 2008. *Brazil Imagined: 1500 to the Present*. Austin: University of Texas Press.

Salek, Silvia. 2005. "Madagáscar proíbe Igreja Universal e expulsa pastores." *Folha de S. Paulo.* February 4. https://www1.folha.uol.com.br/folha/bbc/ult272u39367.shtml.
Salles Gomes, Paulo Emílio, Carlos Augusto Calil, and Maria Teresa Machado. 1986. *Paulo Emilio, um intelectual na linha de frente.* São Paulo: Brasiliense.
Salles Gomes, Paulo Emílio. 1974. *Humberto Mauro, Cataguases, Cinearte.* 1st ed. São Paulo: Perspectiva.
Salles Gomes, Paulo Emílio. 1981. *Crítica de cinema no Suplemento Literário—Volume 1.* Rio de Janeiro: Paz e Terra.
Salles Gomes, Paulo Emílio. 1996. *Cinema: Trajetória no Subdesenvolvimento.* Rio de Janeiro: Paz e Terra.
Salles Gomes, Paulo Emílio. 1997. Cinema: A Trajectory within Underdevelopment. In *New Latin American Cinema Vol. Two Studies of National Cinemas*, edited by Michael T. Martin, 263–71. Detroit: Wayne State University Press.
Santana, Gelson, ed. 2008. *Cinema de Bordas 2.* São Paulo: A Lápis.
Santana, Gelson, ed. 2012. *Cinema de Bordas 3.* São Paulo: A Lápis.
Santos, Maria David. 2013. Olney São Paulo: Maldição e Esplendor em *Manhã Cinzenta*. Master thesis. Universidade Estadual de Feira de Santana, Feira de Santana, Bahia, Brasil. https://docplayer.com.br/54815906-Olney-sao-paulo-maldicao-e-esplendor-em-manha-cinzenta.html.
Sanz, José, ed. 1969. *FC Simpósio/SF Symposium.* Rio de Janeiro: Instituto Nacional do Cinema.
Schmelz, Ítala, ed. 2006. *El Futuro Más Acá: Cine Mexicano de Ciencia-Ficción.* Ciudad de Mexico: Consejo Nacional para la Cultura y las Artes—Instituto Nacional de Bellas Artes/UNAM/Landucci.
Schroder, André. 2014. O médico, o fotógrafo e a romancista. *Dossiê Superinteressante: Chico Xavier*, 11–15. São Paulo: Editora Abril.
Schwarz, Roberto. 1992. *Misplaced Ideas: Essays on Brazilian Culture.* London: Verso.
Schweitzer, Ariel. September 2019. "Le cinéma brésilien à l'ère Bolsonaro." *Cahiers du Cinéma*, no. 759: 80–84. https://www.cahiersducinema.com/boutique/produit/septembre-2019-n758/.
Shaw, Lisa, and Stephanie Dennison. 2004. *Popular Cinema in Brazil, 1930–2001.* Manchester: Manchester University Press.
Shaw, Lisa, and Stephanie Dennison. 2007. *Brazilian National Cinema.* London: Routledge.
Shelley, Mary. 2003. *Frankenstein.* London: Penguin Classics.
Shohat, Ella, and Robert Stam. 2013. *Unthinking Eurocentrism: Multiculturalism and the Media.* 2nd ed. London: Routledge.
Silva Neto, Antônio Leão da. 2002. *Dicionário de Filmes Brasileiros.* Author's edition.
Silva Neto, Antônio Leão da. 2006. *Dicionário de Filmes Brasileiros: Curta-metragem.* Author's edition.

Simis, Anita. 2015. *Estado e Cinema no Brasil.* São Paulo: Ed. Unesp.
Sirkis, Alfredo. 1985. *Silicone XXI.* São Paulo: Círculo do Livro.
Skorupa, Francisco Alberto. 2002. *Viagem às Letras do Futuro—Extratos de bordo da ficção científica brasileira: 1947-1975.* Curitiba: Aos Quatro Ventos.
Smith, Kirk H., and Martha Rogers. 1994. Effectiveness of Subliminal Messages in Television Commercials: Two Experiments. *Journal of Applied Psychology* 79, no. 6: 866-74. https://doi.org/10.1037/0021-9010.79.6.866.
Subero, Gustavo. 2016. *Gender and Sexuality in Latin American Horror Cinema: Embodiments of Evil.* 1st ed. London: Palgrave Macmillan.
Solanas, Fernando, and Octavio Getino. 1997. "Toward a Third Cinema: Notes and Experiences for the Development of a Cinema of Liberation in the Third World." In *New Latin American Cinema, vol. 1, Theory, Practices and Transcontinental Articulations*, edited by Michael T. Martin, 33-58. Detroit: Wayne State University Press.
Sontag, Susan. 1990. *Against Interpretation and Other Essays.* London: Picador.
Sousa, Viviane, and Léo Arcoverde. 2019. "Brasil registra uma morte por homofobia a cada 23 horas, aponta entidade LGBT." *G1.* May 18. https://g1.globo.com/sp/sao-paulo/noticia/2019/05/17/brasil-registra-uma-morte-por-homofobia-a-cada-23-horas-aponta-entidade-lgbt.ghtml.
Souza, Carlos Roberto de. 2007. Os Pioneiros do Cinema Brasileiro: Raízes do Cinema Brasileiro. *ALCEU*—v.8—n.15 (July-December): 20-37. http://revistaalceu-acervo.com.puc-rio.br/media/Alceu_n15_Souza.pdf.
Souza, Andressa Menezes de. 2019. "Memórias poéticas de lágrima, lama e luta." *Jornal da Unicamp.* July 16. https://www.unicamp.br/unicamp/ju/noticias/2019/07/16/memorias-poeticas-de-lagrima-lama-e-luta.
Staal, Jonas. 2014. *Nosso Lar Brasilia—Spiritism, Modernism, Architecture.* Prinsenbeek: Jap Sam Books.
Stableford, Brian. 1993. "Proto Science Fiction." In *The Encyclopedia of Science Fiction*, edited by John Clute and Peter Nicholls, 965-67. New York: St. Martin's Press.
Stableford, Brian. 2007. Science Fiction and Ecology. In *A Companion to Science Fiction*, ed. David Seed, 127-41. Malden, MA: Blackwell.
Stam, Robert, and Randall Johnson. 1979. "Beyond Cinema Novo." *Jump Cut*, no. 21 (November): 13-18. https://www.ejumpcut.org/archive/onlinessays/JC21folder/BrazilStamJohnson.html.
Sternheim, Alfredo. 1978. "Nova comédia com Renato Aragão." *Folha da Tarde Ilustrada*, São Paulo, December 20, 26 (Hemeroteca Cinemateca Brasileira).
Sternheim, Alfredo. 2005. *Cinema da Boca do Lixo—Dicionário de Diretores.* São Paulo: Imprensa Oficial/Fundação Padre Anchieta.
Stoll, Sandra. J. 2004. *Espiritismo à brasileira.* São Paulo: Edusp/Orion.
Strauven, Wanda, ed. 2006. *The Cinema of Attractions Reloaded.* Amsterdam: Amsterdam University Press.

Suppia, Alfredo. 2007. "Limite de Alerta! Ficção Científica em Atmosfera Rarefeita: Uma Introdução ao Estudo da FC no Cinema Brasileiro e em Algumas Cinematografias off-Hollywood." PhD diss., Universidade Estadual de Campinas, Campinas, São Paulo, Brasil. https://repositorio.unicamp.br/acervo/detalhe/415315.

Suppia, Alfredo. 2008. "Science Fiction in the Brazilian Cinema: A Brief Overview." *Film International* 6, no. 2: 6–13. https://doi.org/10.1386/fiin.6.2.6.

Suppia, Alfredo. 2013. *Atmosfera Rarefeita. A Ficção Científica no Cinema Brasileiro*. São Paulo: Devir.

Suppia, Alfredo. 2014. "The Quest for Latin American Science Fiction & Fantasy Film." *Frames Cinema Journal*. December. https://framescinemajournal.com/article/the-quest-for-latin-american-science-fiction-fantasy-film/.

Suppia, Alfredo. 2020. "On the Present and Future of Brazilian Film Studies: Some Preliminary Notes." *Romance Quarterly* 67, no. 1: 36–51. http://doi-org/10.1080/08831157.2020.1698890.

Suppia, Alfredo, and Paula Gomes. 2015. Por um cinema infiltrado: entrevista com Adirley Queirós e Maurílio Martins a propósito de *Branco Sai, Preto Fica*. *DOC Online—Revista Digital de Cinema Documentário*, 28. https://doi.org/10.20287/doc.d18.

Suppia, Alfredo, and Mary E. Ginway. 2022. Kléber Mendonça Filho, *Recife Frio* (2009)/ Visualizing Disparity in Brazil. In *Uneven Futures: Strategies for Community Survival from Speculative Fiction*, edited by Ida Yoshinaga, Sean Guynes, and Gerry Canavan, 127–33. Cambridge, MA: MIT Press.

Suvin, Darko. 1972. "On the Poetics of the Science Fiction Genre." *College English* 34, no. 3: 372. https://doi.org/10.2307/375141.

Suvin, Darko. 1979. *Metamorphoses of Science Fiction: On the Poetics and History of a Literary Genre*. New Haven, CT: Yale University Press.

Swinburn, Boyd A., et al. 2019. "The Global Syndemic of Obesity, Undernutrition, and Climate Change: The Lancet Commission report. *The Lancet* 393, no. 10173: 791–846. DOI:https://doi.org/10.1016/S0140-6736(18)32822-8. https://www.thelancet.com/journals/lancet/article/PIIS0140-6736(18)32822-8/fulltext

Telford, William. 2000. "Religion, the Bible and Theology in Recent Films (1993–2004)." *Epworth Review* 27, no. 4: 31–40.

Telford, William. 2005. "Religion, the Bible and Theology in Recent Films (1993–2004)." In *Cinéma Divinité: Religion, Theology, and the Bible in Film*, edited by E. Christianson, P. Francis, and W. Telford. London: SCM.

Telotte, J. P. 2001. *Science Fiction Film*. 1st ed. Cambridge: Cambridge University Press.

Terto, A. 2017. A primeira série brasileira da Netflix, "3%" virou um baita sucesso nos EUA. *Huffpost Brasil*. https://www.reddit.com/r/brasil/comments/60ukh1/primeira_s%C3%A9rie_brasileira_da_netflix_3_virou_um/.

Todorov, Tzvetan. 1975. *The Fantastic: A Structural Approach to a Literary Genre.* Ithaca, NY: Cornell University Press.

Underhill, Kristen, Paul Montgomery, and Don Operario. 2007. "Sexual Abstinence only Programmes to Prevent HIV Infection in High Income Countries: Systematic Review. *BMJ* 335, no. 7613: 248. https://doi.org/10.1136/bmj.39245.446586.be.

UOL. 2020. "Davos: Bolsonaro diz a Al Gore que 'gostaria muito' de ter EUA como parceiro na Amazônia." YouTube video, 2:10. August 24. https://www.youtube.com/watch?v=CPpH7FRFcY0.

Vadico, Luiz. 2011. *Revista Fronteiras—Estudos Midiáticos,* 13, no. 1: 32–40, January/April. https://doi.org/10.4013/fem.2011.131.04.

Vadico, Luiz A. 2015. *O campo do filme religioso: Cinema, religião e sociedade.* Jundiaí: Paco Editorial.

Valenti, Peter L. 1978. The "Film Blanc": Suggestions for a Variety of Fantasy, 19404-5. *Journal of Popular Film* 6, no. 4: 294–304. https://doi.org/10.1080/00472719.1978.9943446.

Van Jafa. 1955. "Carnaval em Marte." *A Noite* [Rio de Janeiro]. February 17. São Paulo: Arquivo Cinemateca Brasileira.

Vasconcellos, R. A. 2011. Entrevista com Márcio Napoli para a revista Scarium online. *Revista Scarium* online. https://www.scarium.com.br/noficcao/entrevista04.html.

Veloso, Caetano. 2017. *Verdade tropical.* 3rd ed. São Paulo: Companhia das Letras.

Ventura, Zuenir. 2013. "Fora de ordem e de lugar." *Repórter Nordeste.* March 13. https://reporternordeste.com.br/fora-de-ordem-e-de-lugar/.

Viany, Alex. 1993. *Introdução ao Cinema Brasileiro.* Rio de Janeiro: Revan.

Vint, Sherryl, and Mark Bould. 2009. There is no such thing as science fiction. In *Reading Science Fiction*, eds. James Gunn, Marleen S. Barr, and Matthew Candelaria, 43–51. New York: Palgrave Macmillan.

Vieira, João Luiz. 1995. From *High Noon* to *Jaws*: Carnival and Parody in Brazilian Cinema. In *Brazilian Cinema—expanded edition*, eds., Randall Johnson and Robert Stam, 256–69. New York: Columbia University Press.

Vieira, João Luiz. 2004. "Chanchada." In *Enciclopédia do Cinema Brasileiro*, edited by Fernão Ramos and Luiz Felipe Miranda, 152–54. 2nd ed. São Paulo: Senac.

Vinicius, Bruno. 2020. "Conheça 'Inabitável,' curta pernambucano selecionado para o Festival de Gramado." *Folha PE.* August 13. https://www.folhape.com.br/cultura/conheca-inabitavel-%20curta-pernambucano-selecionado-para-o-festival/150633/.

Vianna, Katiúscia. 2021. "Medida Provisória: A voz negra não pode ser calada." *Adoro Cinema.* https://www.adorocinema.com/filmes/filme-273189/criticas-adorocinema/.

Vogt, Carlos, and Carmelo Polino. 2003. *Percepção Pública da Ciência.* 1st ed. Editora da Unicamp/Fapesp.

Vokey, J. R., and J. D. Read. 1985. "Subliminal Messages: Between the Devil and the Media." *American Psychologist* 40, no. 11: 1231–39. http:/doi.org/10.1037//0003-066x.40.11.1231.
Whitehead, Alfred North, and Bertrand Russell. [1927] 1962. *Principia Mathematica*. 2nd ed. Cambridge: Cambridge University Press.
Wolfe, Gary. K. 1979. *The Known and The Unknown: The Iconography of Science Fiction*. Kent, OH: Kent State University Press.
Worth, Sol, and John Adair. 1972. *Through Navajo Eyes: An Exploration In Film Communication and Anthropology*. 1st ed. Bloomington: Indiana University Press.
Wright, Melanie J. 2006. *Religion and Film: An Introduction*. London: I.B. Tauris.
Xavier, Francisco Cândido. 1976. *Somos Seis*. São Bernardo do Campo: GEEM.
Xavier, Chico. 2014. *Brasil, coração do mundo pátria do evangelho*. 34th ed. FEB Editora.
Xavier, Ismail. 1993. *Alegorias do Subdesenvolvimento: Cinema Novo, Tropicalismo, Cinema Marginal*. São Paulo: Brasiliense.
Xavier, Ismail. 1997. *Allegories Of Underdevelopment: Aesthetics and Politics in Modern Brazilian Cinema*. 1st ed. Minneapolis: University of Minnesota Press.
Zola, Irving. K. 2003. *Missing Pieces: A Chronicle Of Living With A Disability* (Reprint ed.). Philadelphia, PA: Temple University Press.
Zuboff, Shoshana. 2019. *The Age of Surveillance Capitalism: The Fight for a Human Future at the New Frontier of Power*. New York: PublicAffairs.
Zuin, Lidia. 2019. "Amazofuturismo e Cyberagreste: por uma nova ficção científica brasileira." *Lidia Zuin*. September 2. https://lidiazuin.blogosfera.uol.com.br/2019/09/02/amazofuturismo-e-cyberagreste-por-uma-nova-ficcao-cientifica-brasileira/.
Zweig, Stefan. 1942. *Brazil: A Land of the Future*. New York: Viking.
Zweig, Stefan. 2013. *Brasil, um país do futuro*. Porto Alegre, RS: L&PM Editores.

# Interviews

## Interviews recorded on video

Martins, Paulo Bastos. 2005. Interview by author. Campinas, SP. August 17. [mini-DV].
Vieira, Clóvis. 2006. Interview by author. Campinas, SP. March 7. [mini-DV].
Morettin, Eduardo V. 2007. Interview by author. São Paulo, SP, May 26. [mini-DV].

## Interviews by e-mail

André Carneiro, February 8, 2006, e-mail message to author. [alfredo.luiz5@terra.com.br].
Carlos Canela, June 5, 2007, e-mail message to author. [alfredo.luiz5@terra.com.br]
Gerson Lodi-Ribeiro, March 4, 2006, e-mail message to author. [alfredo.luiz5@terra.com.br].
José de Anchieta, May 30, 2007, May 30, e-mail message to author. [alfredo.luiz5@terra.com.br]
Marcello Branco, September 4, 2006, e-mail message to author. [alfredo.luiz5@terra.com.br]

# Index

#DefundBolsonaro, 237

1964 coup d'état, the, 8, 39, 41, 42, 45, 46, 64, 316
*1984* (1948), 35, 71, 159, 170, 181, 210
1988 Brazilian Constitution, the, 72, 171, 314, 316, 318
*2001: A Space Odyssey* (1968), 57, 254, 255
2016 coup, the, 146, 147, 159, 173, 217, 265
*2030* (2019), 183, 184
*3%* (2016–2020), 147, 153, 163, 206, 212, 217, 218, 219, 220, 245, 257, 275, 318, 343
*5th Power, The* (*O Quinto Poder*, 1962), 8, 28, 34, 35, 37–43, 46, 61, 76, 178, 184, 254
*606*, aka *606 Against the Pale Spirochete* (*606 Contra o Espiroqueta Pálido*, 1910), 15
*93o Tunnel* (*Túnel 93o*, 1972), 64, 65, 70, 79, 80

*A$suntina das Amérikas* (1976), 221
*Abbott and Costello Go to Mars* (1953), 21
*Abbott and Costello Meet Frankenstein* (1948), 34
Abertura (Opening) period, 60

*Abjetas 288* (2020), 177, 221
*Above our Heads* (*Sobre Nossas Cabeças*, 2020), 227, 228, 245
Abramovay, Ricardo, 68, 235, 236
Abreu, Gilda de, 125
Abreu, Silvio de, 124
Ackerman, Forrest J., 57
*Acquaria* (2003), 244, 254
*Adiós Querida Luna* (2004), 324
Adriano Stuart, 9, 86, 92, 94, 97, 99, 100, 102, 103
*Adventures of Paulo Bruscky, The* (2010), 282
*Aelita, Queen of Mars* (1924), 22, 95, 255, 270
Aesthetics of Hunger, An (1997) ("Uma Estética da Fome," aka "Estétyka da Fome," originally published in 1965), 70, 179, 305
Africa in Motion Festival, 202
African-Brazilian, 96, 137, 139, 207, 211, 213, 214, 279; Afro-descendants, 202, 203; African-Brazilian religion, 82, 279
Afrobunker, 208
Afrofuturism, 7, 18, 197, 201, 202, 204, 215–217, 231, 296; Afrofuturist, 158, 194, 201–203, 205, 216, 245; Afrofuturistic, 133, 204

# Index

*Afronauts* (2014), 216
*Age of Surveillance Capitalism, The* (2019), 182
Agence France-Presse (AFP), 36
Agenda, 21, 77
Agrippino, José, 59
Aguilera, Pedro, 147, 217, 245
AI (Artificial Intelligence), 61, 211, 183, 230
AI-5 (Institutional Act No. 5/Ato Institucional n. 5), 46, 60, 70
AIDS, 169
Aïnouz, Karim, 146, 233, 234, 238
*Akumulator 1* (1994), 110
Álamo Studios, 106
Albergaria, Helena, 136
Albert, Bruce, 224
Aldir Blanc Law (Lei Aldir Blanc), 282
Aldiss, Brian W., 57
*Algorithm* (*Algoritmo*, 2020), 180–184, 211, 245
*Alien, the 8th Passenger* (1979), 97, 126
*Alive in Joburg* (2005), 189
*Allegories of Underdevelopment* (*Alegorias do Subdesenvolvimento*): 52, 55, 56, 301
allegory, 43, 47, 51, 53, 55, 58, 60, 61, 149, 150, 174, 189, 205–207, 217, 272, 301, 303; allegorical, 51, 53, 56, 81, 193, 205, 207, 221, 302–304, 324, 325;
Allen, Woody, 109
*Alley of the Missing Ones, 113, The* (*Alameda da Saudade, 113*, 1951), 125
Almeida, Neville de, 104
Almeida, Rodrigo, 282
Almeida, Sílvio, 211, 228
*Alphaville* (1965), 191
Alqueres, Marcus, 187, 244
Altman, Rick, 3, 4, 142, 312

Álvarez, Fede, 147, 244
Amado, Jorge, 300
Amante da Heresia (aka Léo Pimentel Souto), 224
Amazofuturism, 187, 194, 195, 199, 200, 296; Amazofuturist, 245
Amazon, the, 5, 64; Amazon Basin, 68; Legal Amazon (Amazônia Legal), 68
*Ambassadors, The* (1533), 4
Amenábar, Alejandro, 128, 253
*American Astronaut, The* (2001), 253
American blockbusters, 86, 100
American culture, 23, 280
American SF television, 86
Amerindians, 201, 290
Amnesty Law (Lei da Anistia), 60
Amorim, Dora, 282
*Amorquia* (1991), 50
amphitextuality (amphitextualité), 11, 12
*An Adventure at 40* (*Uma Aventura aos 40*, 1947), 18, 19, 25
*An American Werewolf in London* (1981), 87
*An Inconvenient Truth* (2006), 70
anamorphic estrangement, 4
Anchieta, José de, 64–65, 67–70, 83, 236, 272, 304, 305, 307
*Anchieta, José from Brazil* (*Anchieta, José do Brasil*, 1977), 141
Ancine (National Cinema Agency/ Agência Nacional de Cinema), 92, 209
*And Life Goes On* (*E a Vida Continua*), 124
*And Still the Earth* (*Não Verás País Nenhum*, 1981), 71, 79, 159, 303
*And The Life Goes On . . .* (*E a Vida Continua . . .* , 2011), 130
and then the backlands will turn into seacoast and the seacoast into

backlands ("O sertão vai virar mar e o mar vai virar sertão"), 223
Anderson, Karen, 56, 57
Anderson, Michael, 170
Anderson, Poul, 57
Andrade, Carlos Drummond de, 1, 239, 292
Andrade, Floro Freitas, 50
Andrade, Joaquim Pedro de, 6
Andrade, Jonathas de, 282
Andrade, Lucas, 282
Andrade, Oswald de, 196, 305, 317, 327
Andrade, Sérgio, 199, 245
André Luiz, 123, 124, 132
Andress, Ursula, 57
Andrew, Dudley, 2
Andries, Thiago Cury, 164
Anglo-Saxon SF, 80
Angra 1 (first Brazilian nuclear power plant), 72; atomic bomb, 72, 75
Angra dos Reis, 71, 74, 75
animation(s), 29, 83, 105, 193, 194, 217, 222, 223, 225, 230, 254, 316
Annecy Film Festival, 194
*Announcer: The Man of the Storms, The* (*O Anunciador: O Homem das Tormentas*, 1970), 58–59
*Another Earth* (2011), 253
*Antena, La* (2007), 324
anthropocene, 201, 231, 234, 285; anthropocene unconscious, 231, 234
anthropophagic, 7, 8, 303 (*See also* carnivalesque)
anthropophagy (antropofagia), 70, 196, 305
*Anthropophagy Review* (*Revista de Antropofagia*), 196, 305
anti-imperialist, 40
anti-SF, 54
anticommunist, 40

*Antiviral* (2012), 253
Antônio Conselheiro, 112, 319, 322
*Antonio das Mortes* (*O Dragão da Maldade contra o Santo Guerreiro*, 1969), 180, 303
Antônio, André, 286
Antônio, Ângelo, 131
Antropokaos: Brazilian Science Fiction Exhibition (Antropokaos: Mostra de Ficção Científica Brasileira, 2019 and 2021), 282–283
Anunciação, Aldri, 207
apartheid, 189, 205, 214, 234
Apertus (Open-Source Cinema), 136
Appadurai, Arjun: 11, 280
*Aquarius* (2016), 173, 177
Aquino, Thomas, 178
*Araby* (*Arábia*, 2017), 147
Aragão, Renato, 91–94, 96–99, 308
Araújo, Ernesto, 165–167, 314
Araújo, Taís, 208
*Area Q* (*Área Q*, 2012), 135, 175
Aristotle, 326
Arkush, Allan, 87
*Armação Ilimitada* (1985), 100
*Armadillo Blood* (*Sangue de Tatu*, 1986), 64, 74–76, 79, 80
Armorial Movement (Movimento Armorial), 177, 315
Arnold, Jack, 64, 309, 312
Aronofsky, Darren, 251, 253
Arruda, Henrique, 177, 225, 227, 231, 245
Artaxo, Paulo, 235
Arthuso, Raul Lemos, 191, 245
*Arzok* (2017), 316
*As Weird as It Seems* (*Por Incrível que Pareça*, 1986), 106, 108, 112
Assis, Wagner de, 130, 132–135, 161
*At the Edge of the Universe* (*À Margem do Universo*, 2017), 215, 216, 316

Atlântida Cinematográfica, 20, 22–24, 28, 86
*Atlantis Ocean* (*Oceano Atlantis*, 1993), 77–79, 193, 245
Audiovisual Law (Lei do Audiovisual n. 8.685, July 20, 1993), 79
authoritarianism, 8, 46, 48, 54, 61, 83, 121, 185, 209, 217, 234, 236
Autran, Paulo, 129
*Avatar* (2009), 175, 224
Avellar, José Carlos, 50, 94
Ayala, Walmir, 50
Azevedo, Alinor, 20–22
Azevedo, Ana Luiza, 148, 313

B movies, 32, 34, 89, 108, 254
Babenco, Hector, 188, 297, 310
*Back to the Future* film series, 113; *Back to the Future—Part II* (1989), 113
*Backlands: The Canudos Campaign* [*Os Sertões*] (2010), 319
*Backyard* (*Quintal*, 2015), 202, 283
*Bacurau* (2019), 42, 147, 173–175, 177–180, 201, 202, 218, 275, 295
BAFICI, 283
*Bahia Sci-Fi* (2015), 71, 306
Ballard, J. G., 57
Bandeira, Manuel, 292
Baratier, Jacques, 57
bárbaro tecnizado (technofied barbarian), 196
*Barbosa* (1988), 113, 148–150, 153, 191, 244, 251, 313
Barbosa, Moacir, 148
Barclay, Barry, 317
Bardot, Brigitte, 23
*Barravento* (1962), 27, 140, 141
Barreira do Inferno, 267, 323
*Barren Lives* (*Vidas Secas*, 1963), 27
Barreto, Bruno, 105
Barro, Máximo, 125

Barros, Adhemar de, 37
Barros, Luiz de (aka Lulu de Barros), 16, 22, 124
Bass, Saul, 23
Bastos, Orimar, 131
*basurapunk*, 217
Batmanglij, Zal, 140, 253
*Battle of Canudos, The* (*Guerra de Canudos*, 1996), 252, 319
Baxter, John, 277, 280
Báya, Anderson Kary, 199
BBC, 36
*Beast Man or The Adventures of Captain Richard, The* (*El Hombre Bestia, o Las Aventuras del Capitan Richard*, 1934), 25
*Beasts of the Southern Wild* (2012), 253
Beaumont, Matthew, 4
Belchior, Antonio Carlos, 219, 318
Beliaev, Alexander, 108
*Believe, I Have a Spirit on Me* (*Acredite, Um Espírito Baixou em Mim*, 2007), 129
Belo Horizonte, 30, 283
Benayoun, Robert, 57
Benites, Sandra, 295–296
Bente, Mário, 195
Beresford, J. D., 63
Berlin Film Festival, 53
Berman, Marshall, 268
Bernardet, Jean-Claude, 94, 102, 103, 140, 141, 153, 309
Bertoni, Marcos, 64, 74–76
Besson, Luc, 256
Bester, Alfred, 56, 57
*Beyond the Black Rainbow* (2010), 253
*Bezerra de Menezes—The Diary of a Spirit* (*Bezerra de Menezes: O Diário de um Espírito*, 2008), 130, 135, 142
Big Stick politics, 23

Bini, Bruno, 316
*Bionic* (*Biônicos*, 2024), 160–161
Biosphere Conference in Paris 1968, 67
Bioy-Casares, Adolfo, 42, 324
*Birds, The* (1963), 309
*Biutiful* (2010), 116
Bixby, Bill, 100
*Black God, White Devil* (*Deus e o Diabo na Terra do Sol*, 1964), 6, 27, 305, 319
Black Seminoles, 199
*Blackout* (2020), 203
*Blade Runner* (1982), 66, 80, 195
Blashfield, Edwin, 277–278
Bloch, Robert, 57
Blomkamp, Neil, 175, 189
*Blue Desert* (*Deserto Azul*, 2013), 316
*Blues Brothers, The* (1980), 86
Boca do Lixo (Cinema da Boca do Lixo), 125
*Boldest Experiment of the Century, The* (*A Mais Arrojada Experiência do Século*), 38
Boliveira, Fabrício, 202
Bolognesi, Luiz, 83, 188, 192–194, 245
Bolsonaro, Flávio, 192
Bolsonaro, Jair, 159, 163–165, 170–171, 192, 204, 209, 217, 235, 237, 261, 313, 315, 320; Bolsonaro's administration or the Bolsonaro administration, 147, 173, 184, 185, 200, 210, 218, 234–237, 319, 325; Bolsonarism, 175
*Bomb, The* ("A Bomba"), 292
Bond films, 39, 86, 89; Bond series, 89
Bonet, Pep, 216
Bonitzer, Pascal, 227
Bopp, Raul, 305
Borges, Doriam, 164
Borges, Jorge Luis, 42, 288
*Born in Flames* (1983), 210

Botelho, Chico, 66
Bould, Mark, 231, 234, 252, 294
Bracero program, 189, 316
Bradbury, Ray, 56
Braga, Rômulo, 191
*Brain that Wouldn't Die, The* (1962), 108
Branagh, Kenneth, 128
*Branch, A* (*Um Ramo*, 2007), 135
Brandão, Ignácio de Loyola, 71, 79, 146, 159, 303
*Brasil S/A* (2014), 234, 316
Brasilia Film Festival (Festival de Cinema de Brasília), 42, 78, 176, 281, 283
Brasília, 5, 31, 42, 78, 99, 132, 135, 151, 154, 155, 158, 159, 165, 176, 183, 205, 241, 283, 307, 313
*Brasyl* (2007), 5
*Brave New World* (1932), 36, 37, 71, 159, 210
*Brave New World Revisited* (1959), 36, 37
*Brazil Year 2000* (*Brasil Ano 2000*), 51–56, 58, 81, 196, 302, 303
*Brazil, Heart of the World, Homeland of the Gospel* (*Brasil, Coração do Mundo, Pátria do Evangelho*, 2014, originally published in 1938), 118, 120–123
*Brazil, The Movie* (1985), 5, 241
Brazil: Love it or leave it! ("Brasil: Ame-o ou deixe-o"), 8, 82
Brazilian "manifest destiny," 122
Brazilian Advertising Association (ABP—Associação Brasileira de Propaganda), 36
Brazilian Afrofuturism, 201–202, 216–217, 296
Brazilian Carnival, 22, 204, 208
Brazilian Economic Miracle (Milagre Econômico Brasileiro), 52, 101

Brazilian Popular Music (MPB—Música Popular Brasileira), 70, 291–292, 318
Brazilian Spiritist Federation (FEB—Federação Espírita Brasileira), 123;
Brazilian Transcendental Film Festival, the (Festival Brasileiro de Cinema Transcendental), 283
*Breakfast Club, The* (1985), 87
Brichta, Vladimir, 129
BRICS, 145, 267
*Bride of Frankenstein* (1935), 223
Bridges, James, 75
Brito, Gilberto, 226
Brooks, Mel, 96, 97
Brosnan, John, 104, 253
*Brothers Karamazov, The*, 23
Brumadinho, 235, 239, 320
Brundtland, Gro Harlem, 74; Brundtland Report, the, 74
Brunner, John, 57
Buckland, Warren, 249
Bueno, Zuleika, 87
Bui, Camille, 174, 175, 177, 178, 179
Bujalski, Andrew, 253
Buñuel, Luís, 255
Burch, Noël, 248, 322
*Burial of Gods, The* (*O Enterro dos Deuses*, 2020), 225
Buriti Filmes, 193
Burle, José Carlos, 20
*Bus 174* (*Ônibus 174*, 2002), 188

caboclo, 76, 79, 80, 307, 317
Cabral, Plínio, 79, 303
*Cachoeira* (2010), 199
Cadogan, León, 295
Caen, Michel, 57
Caetano, Joel, 136, 137, 228, 229, 231, 245
Caeté, 197

*Cahiers du Cinéma*, 174
Cahill, Mike, 253
Caixa Cultural, 282
Cajado Filho, José, 22
Calatrava, Santiago, 133
Calhoun, John C., 280
Camargo, Claudinê Perina, 64, 65, 236
Cambridge Analytica, 182
Cameron, James, 175, 229
Cammel, Donald, 126
Campillo, Robin, 116
Campinas, 65, 69, 113, 298, 306, 322
Campolina, Clarissa, 223, 225, 231, 294
Campos, Antonio, 13
Campos, Humberto de, 118, 122, 123
Camurati, Carla, 105
Candeias, Ozualdo, 104, 221
Candelaria, Matthew, 294
Cândido, Antonio, 152
Candomblé, 82, 119, 164, 307
Canela, Carlos, 233, 246, 262, 321
Cánepa, Laura, 299
cangaço, 315; cangaceiro, 176, 303, 315;
Cannes, 27, 174, 194, 283; Cannes Film Festival, 51, 136
cannibal-carnivalesque SF, 296
cannibalism, 196 (*See also* anthropophagy, anthropophagic);
Cannibalist Manifesto (*See also* "Manifesto Antropófago"), 196, 305, 317; cannibalistic, 160, 221; Cannibalist Manifesto for the Brazilian SF ("Manifesto Antropofágico da Ficção Científica Brasileira," 1988), 196
*cantante*, 15, 298
Cantinflas, 25
Canudo, Ricciotto, 115, 116
Canudos War (Canudos, Guerra de), 252, 319, 322
Capanna, Pablo, 271, 272

Cape Canaveral, 29; "Cape Carnival," 29; Cape Kennedy, 89
Čapek, Karel, 159
capitalist realism, 290
Capitalocene, 198, 233, 238, 285, 320
Capra, Frank, 129
Captain Mendonça ("O Capitão Mendonça," 1870), 271
*Carandiru* (2003), 188, 297
Carboni, Bruno, 282
Cardoso, Pedro, 129
Carelli, Vincent, 317
*carioca*, 78
Carmo, Ana do, 202
Carneiro, André, 50, 57, 69, 292, 305
*Carnival on Mars* (*Carnaval em Marte*, 1954), 20–22
Carnival, 5, 20, 87, 125, 161, 208; carnivalesque, 7, 20, 23, 30, 46, 87, 221, 296
Carpenter, John, 172, 192
Carr, Terry, 290
Carrasco, Walcyr, 124
*Carrie* (1976), 112
Carrière, Jean-Claude, 227
Carruth, Shane, 253
Cartagena Festival, 283
*Cartuchos de Super-Nintendo em Anéis de Saturno* (2018), 202
Carvalho, Eduardo, 212
Carvalho, Enock, 177, 221, 222
Carvalho, Marcos, 212
Casagrande, Rebeca, 137
*Cassiopéia* (1996), 254
Castelo Branco, 185
Castro, Ewerton de, 127
Cataguases, 58, 304
Catholic, 65, 111, 126, 130, 139, 153, 196, 206, 207, 307, 312, 314; Catholicism, 207
Causo, Roberto de Sousa, 2, 34, 67, 152, 176, 199, 262, 270, 271, 305

Cavalcanti, Alberto, 20, 255
Cavalcanti, Ana Flávia, 202
CBS, 100
Ceará, 130, 135, 175, 176, 185, 220, 301, 318
Ceicine, 150
Ceilândia, 150, 151, 152, 154, 158, 313
Celestino, Vicente, 125
censorship, 6, 46, 49, 51, 53, 64, 83, 209, 302
*Central Station* (*Central do Brasil*, 1998), 188, 297
*Cesium 137: Goiânia's Nightmare* (*Césio 137: O Pesadelo de Goiânia*, 1990), 73; cesium-137, 73, 74
CGI, 142, 188, 226, 233, 251, 322
Chagas, Dolabela, 48
*chanchada(s)*, 6, 8, 9, 18–20, 22–25, 28–29, 33–34, 41, 70, 85–88, 90–91, 100–103, 113, 257, 299, 309
Chang, Ha-Joon, 67
Chapada dos Veadeiros National Park, 215
Chapman, Leigh, 57
*Chat with the Afterlife, A* (*Bate-Papo com o Além*, 1982), 123
*Chatô, the King of Brazil* (*Chatô, O Rei do Brasil*, 2015), 252
*Cheese Mites, The* (1903), 255
*Chef's Duel* (*Duello de Cozinheiros*, 1908), 14
Chernobyl, 74, 312
*Chico* (2016), 212, 216–217, 245
Chico César, 218
Chico Science, 177
*Chico Xavier* (2010), 130
*Children of Men* (2006), 252, 322
Chilson, Louis, 75
chimeric, 3–5, 12, 277; chimerical, 11, 294
*China Syndrome, The* (1979), 75

Chomón, Segundo de, 13, 255
Christianity, 119, 123, 207, 307; Christian, 117, 119, 139, 141, 163–166, 171, 225; Jesus Christ, 139, 232; Christian theocracy, 163
*Christmas on Mars* (2008), 253
Christophobia, 165
chronotope(s), 152, 286
Chu, Seo-Young, 291–293
Ciambroni, Ronaldo, 129
Ciberpajé (Cybershaman), 224, 225
Ciclo de Cataguases, 304
Cinecittà, 35
Cinédia, 124, 304
Cinefantasy, 183, 282
Cinema Marginal, 6, 48, 49, 55, 59, 192, 221, 301
Cinema Novo, 6, 23, 27, 28, 41, 47, 49, 51, 53, 55, 56, 58, 59, 70, 81, 141, 147, 301, 304, 305
cinema of attractions, 248, 254, 256
cinéma-vérité, 49, 50
Cinemateca Brasileira (São Paulo), 298
Cinemateca do MAM (Rio de Janeiro), 50, 298
Cines, 35
circuit-bend(ing) (circuit bending), 71, 153–155, 159, 203, 221
Cisjordan, 214
*Citizen Kane* (1941), 28
*City of God* (*Cidade de Deus*, 2002), 6, 188, 297
civil-military coup, 46; civil-military government, 173
Clair, René, 39
Clara Chroma, 220
Clarke, Arthur C., 57, 138
Clastres, Pierre, 295
climate catastrophe, 188; climate change, 188, 189, 203, 231, 232, 233, 235, 238, 285

*Clockwork Orange, A* (1971), 66, 173, 252
*Close Encounters of the Third Kind* (1977), 227
Club of Rome, The, 67
*Code 46* (2003), 252
*Coded Bias* (2020), 211
*Codfish* (*Bacalhau* or *Bacs*, 1976), 9, 102, 103
Coffin Joe (Zé do Caixão) (*See also* José Mojica Marins), 99
cognitive estrangement, 4, 154, 155, 162, 293, 294
*Cold Tropics* (*Recife Frio*, 2009), 83, 188–192, 194, 203, 236, 245, 282, 317
Cold War, 8, 22, 23, 32, 33, 42, 46, 282, 311
Colen, Bárbara, 177
Collor, Fernando, 76
colonial(ist), 6, 87, 175, 202, 212, 216, 270, 271, 305, 306; neo-colonial(ist), 271
Colston, Edward, 280
*Comet, The* (*O Cometa*, 1910), 15
*Cometa Itabirano*, 239
comico-phantastico, 14; comic-fantastic, 13, 14
Common National Curriculum Base (BNCC—Base Nacional de Currículos Comuns), 168
Communist Party, 69, 83, 125
*Computer Chess* (2013), 253
Conan Doyle, Arthur, 5, 64
Conde, Eduardo, 97
Congo, Dhiones do, 316
Coni Campos, Fernando, 50
Conselheiro, Antônio, 112, 223, 319, 322
Conspiração Filmes, 113
Constantine, Eddie, 191
Contagem, 282, 283

Cooper, Merian, 39
Cordero, Sebastián, 253
cordial iconoclasm, 278–280, 324
cordial man ("homem cordial"), 278–279, 295
Cordoba, Antonio, 133–134, 157–158
Córes, Jessica, 160
Corman, Roger, 57
coronavirus disease (Covid-19), 7; Covid-19 (pandemic), 7, 159, 168, 209, 217, 231, 233, 237, 238, 261, 285, 291, 295, 319, 325
corpo fechado ("closed body" or "unbreakable"), 76
Corsac, Francis, 56
Cosmatos, Panos, 253
*Cosmonauts, The* (*Os Cosmonautas*, 1962), 8, 23, 27–29, 31–34, 46
Costa e Silva, 46
Costa, Júlia da, 221
Costa, Matheus, 131
Costa, Petra, 173, 192
Coutinho, Aline, 164
Coutinho, Eduardo, 46
Coyne, Wayne, 253
creative incapacity for copying ("incompetência criativa em copiar"), 29, 276
*Creature from the Black Lagoon* (1954), 309, 312
Crevenna, Alfredo B., 25
Cria_Ciber Research Group (Grupo de Pesquisa Cria_Ciber), 224
Crichton, Michael, 195
Cronenberg, Brandon, 253
Cronenberg, David, 112
Csicsery-Ronay, István, 274
Cuarón, Alfonso, 252, 322
Cuban missile crisis, 33, 46
*Cuddly and the Lost Spaceship* (*Fofão e a Espaçonave Perdida*, 1989), 86
Cunha, Clery, 127

Cunha, Euclides da, 319
Cunha, Fausto, 3, 5, 103, 243, 257, 267
Cunha, Wilson, 57
Cyberagreste, 176, 194, 317
Cyberpunk, 67, 78, 160, 163, 176, 195, 199, 203, 217, 219, 305
cyborg(s), 66, 160, 196, 220, 304, 305, 313, 331, 336

Dadá, Severino, 175
Damiani, Damiano, 174
*Dancin' Days* (1978–1979), 95
Dante, Joe, 87
*Daughters of the Fire, The* (*As Filhas do Fogo*, 1978), 125, 127
Davos (*See also* World Economic Forum), 234, 237
*Day the Earth Stood Still, The* (1951), 31, 33, 138
daydreaming, 293
De Middel, Cristina, 216
De Palma, Brian, 112
*Dead Again* (1991), 128
*Deadline According to Chico Xavier* (*Data Limite Segundo Chico Xavier*, 2014), 137
Dedé (*See also* Manfried Santana), 91–94, 97, 308
DeepDream neural network, 225
*Defeating the Past* (*Vencendo o Passado*, 2008), 123
deforestation, 7, 9, 68, 74, 83, 231, 234–237
Del Priore, Mary, 118, 119
del Toro, Guillermo, 128, 244
Delany, Samuel R., 202
Delgado, Miguel M., 25
Dellape, Santiago, 316
DeMille, Cecil B., 18, 140
*Demon Seed* (1977), 126
Dennison, Stephanie, 6, 19, 20, 23, 28

dependency theory, 87
Dery, Mark, 202
Descartes, Marat, 136, 200
*Destination Moon* (1950), 270
*Devil Spine, The* (*Espiñazo del Diablo*, 2001), 128
*Devil, The* (*O Diabo*, 1908), 13
Dias Gomes, Alfredo, 27
Dias Jr., Jocimar, 174
Dias, André, 131
Dias, Arlete, 204
Dias, Mary, 204
Dias, Wall, 204
Dick, Philip K., 290
Didi (*See also* Renato Aragão), 91–92, 94–95, 98
Diegues, Carlos, 104, 105
Dines, Alberto, 241
disability, 156–158; disability studies, 156
*District 9* (2009), 175, 189
*Divine Love* (*Divino Amor*, 2019), 161–173, 245, 275, 295
*Do Androids Dream of Electric Sheep?* (1968), 290
Doce River Basin (Bacia do Rio Doce), 320
docudrama, 128, 185, 312
documentary, 15, 22, 29, 30, 31, 38, 39, 41, 70, 71, 74, 75, 78, 89, 91, 96, 127, 128, 148, 150, 154, 155, 173, 180, 182, 188, 189, 197, 198, 200, 202, 211, 231, 233, 248, 251, 255, 300, 316, 323, 325
*Dog Factory* (1904), 14
Doo, John, 125
*Doomed* (*Encosto*, 2013), 135
DOPS (Department of Political and Social Order), 41
Dória, Gumercindo da Rocha, 257
Dória, João, 171
Dornelles, Juliano, 42

Dostoyevsky, Fiodor, 23
dream of literal sleep, 293
dreams, 287; dreaming, 287
Dreyer, Carl Theodor, 140
*Dry Ground Burning* (*Mato Seco em Chamas*, 2022), 180
Duarte, Anselmo, 27
Dubret, Michel, 130
Dufour, Éric, 170, 171, 181, 182, 183
Dumovich, Otto, 106
Dunbar, David Lincoln, 32
Duncan, Francis Martin, 255
Duplass, Mark, 253
Durães, Dilmar, 150
Dutra, Marco, 135
Duval, Liana, 128
Dystopia(n), 7, 8, 40, 47, 49, 53, 60, 61, 104, 106, 145, 146, 155, 159, 161, 165–168, 170, 172, 174, 176, 179, 180, 182–185, 194, 203–205, 207, 210–211, 213, 216–217, 219, 221, 229, 231, 233–234, 236, 238, 272, 282, 295, 302–303, 314, 320, 324
Dystopian Brazil Film Exhibition, the (Mostra Brasil Distópico, 2017), 282

early cinema, 248; early film, 248;
*Earthbound* (1920), 115
Eastwood, Clint, 174
Eco, Umberto, 93
ecocriticism, 201; eco-sci-fi movies, 63; eco-social-criticism, 231
ecodystopia(n), 8, 63, 65, 74, 77, 79, 80–84, 190, 191, 192, 194, 200, 218, 219, 233–234, 236, 238
ecology, 63, 67, 273; ecological, 9, 63–64, 69, 70, 74, 77, 79, 82, 176, 198, 215, 218–219, 223–224, 231, 234–235, 239, 303, 305, 320
ecumenical, 139, 140, 199, 202

*Edge of Democracy, The* (*Democracia em Vertigem*, 2019), 173
Edison, Thomas, 14
Edwards, Gareth, 253
Ehrlich, Paul, 15, 63
Elbakyan, Alexandra, 183
*Electoral Matchstick, The* (*O Fósforo Eleitoral* or *O Caso do Rio*, 1909), 14
Eliachar, Leon, 32
*Elite Squad* (*Tropa de Elite*, 2007), 188
*Elite Squad 2* (*Tropa de Elite 2*, 2010), 188
*Elixir of Youth, The* (*Elixir da Juventude* or *Elixir da Juventude Carioca*, 1908), 14
Elizabeth Moss, 165
Ellison, Harlan, 57
Eltonian pyramid, 63
Embrafilme (Brazilian Film Company/ Empresa Brasileira de Filmes), 56, 70, 76, 86, 92, 106, 243, 245, 304
Emmanuel, 120, 131
Empresa F. Serrador & Cia., 15
Emshwhiller, Carol, 56
Emshwhiller, Ed, 56
End of the World, The ("O Fim do Mundo"), 292
Enlightenment, 117, 134
Enoch, Alfred, 207
*Equilibrium* (2002), 170
Erasmo Carlos, 90
Esmeraldo, Tiago, 215
Estação da Luz, 130, 283
Estado Novo (New State) dictatorship, 121
Esteves, Adriana, 213
esthetics of science, 285
estrangement and cognition, 4
estrangement, 4, 132, 142, 154, 155, 162, 293, 294
*ET—The Extraterrestrial* (1982), 104
*Éternau* (2006), 282

Eurocentrism, 243, 280
*Europa Report* (2013), 253
EVA (Economic Value Added), 265
evangelical, 162–165, 167, 169, 172, 207, 279, 314
Excelsior (TV), 124
Executive Order (*Medida Provisória*, 2020), 207–214
*Expanse, The* (2015–), 215
Experimental Psychology (*Psicologia Experimental*), 38
Exterminator Seed (*Semente Exterminadora*, 2017), 197–198, 245
extrapolative science, 32
extreme-right, 70, 173; extreme right, 84, 145–147, 165, 180, 183, 295

Fagundes, Antônio, 147
fake news, 7, 43, 183
fake SF movie, 105
Falabella, Miguel, 129
Falcão, Gustavo, 129
Falcão, João, 129
*Falling Sky: Words of a Yanomami Shaman, The* (2013), 224
Fanon, Frantz, 211
*fantascienza*, 325
Fantasporto, 282
*Fantástico* (TV show), 106
*Fantômas*, 40
Farias, Matheus, 177, 221, 222
Farias, Roberto, 61
Farkas, Pedro, 78
Farmer, Philip José, 57
fascism, 145, 147, 161, 171, 174, 178, 182, 225; fascist, 43, 163, 173, 218, 293
Fávero, Bruno, 168
Fawcett, Fausto, 305
Federation of Rio de Janeiro's Film Clubs (Federação Carioca de Cineclubistas), 50

Fenelon, Moacir, 20
Fernandes Júnior, José, 166
Fernando de Noronha (archipelago), 78
Ferraz, Carlos Eduardo, 226
Ferreira, Dan, 228
Ferrez, Julio, 15
Ferrigno, Lou, 100
*Ferris Bueller's Day Off* (1986), 87
Fers, Luiz (Luiz Carlos Ferreira da Silva), 224
Feuillade, Louis, 40, 255
FID Marseille, 283
Fidalgo, Sabrina, 202
*Fifth Element, The* (1997), 256
Fight of the Jedi Cangaceiro, The ("A Luta do Cangaceiro Jedi" 2020), 176
Figueiredo, Paulo, 127
Filho, Daniel, 92
Filho, Glauber, 130
Film & Transcendence Festival (Festival Cinema & Transcendência), 283
*film blanc*, 116–117
*film noir*, 78, 116, 309; technoir, 78, 163
*Filmatron* (2007), 324
Filmes de Plástico, 283
*Fire Drop* (*Pinga-Fogo*) (TV show), 131, 312
Fisher, David, 290
Fisher, Mark, 172
Flammarion, Camille, 17, 115, 116, 134
*Flash Happy Society* (2009), 282
*Flatliners* (1990), 128
Fleischer, Richard, 80
Flores, Marina, 136
*Flying Man, The* (2013), 187, 244
Fonseca, Sóstenes, 226
Fontes, Guilherme, 252
Foreign Legion, 184

Foresti, Thiago, 180
*Forum, The* (2020), 237
Fósforo-Cerillos, 16
Foucault, Michel, 213–214
Fourth Cinema, 194
Franco, Edgar, 224
Franco, Marielle, 192
Franco, Wilton, 91
*Frankenstein* (1818) (novel), 223, 250
*Frankenstein* (1931) (film), 223, 250
Fred 04, 177
*Free Swimming Pool* (*Piscina Livre*, 1980), 50
Freire, Jussara, 127
Freire, Mozart, 245, 282
Freixo, Marcelo, 192
Freud, Sigmund, 287
Fukasaku, Kinji, 95
*fuleiragem* fiction, 176; *fuleira* SF, 176
Furtado, Jorge, 113, 148, 150, 153, 191, 244, 251, 313
futurism, 135, 163, 242; retro-futurism, 135
*Futuristic Disillusions* (*Le Couple Témoin*, 1977), 181

Gabz, 160
Gagarin, Yuri, 30
Gagliasso, Bruno, 160
Gaia hypothesis, 63
Galãs Feios, 166
Galvão, Maria Rita, 13
Gama, Zilda, 123
gambiarra, 221
Gambiologia, 221
Garcia, Clóvis, 57
Garcia, Estevão, 96
Garrett, Jean, 126, 135, 312
*Garrincha, Joy of the People* (*Garrincha, Alegria do Povo*), 41
Gasca, Luis, 57
Gasparetto, Luiz Antonio, 124

Gasparetto, Zíbia, 123
*Gattaca* (1997), 252
Gaycken, Oliver, 255
Gaza, 214
GDP, 235
Genette, Gérard, 12
Gerbasi, Iuli, 226, 231, 319
Getino, Octavio, 179, 254
Ghazala, Reed, 155
*Ghost* (1990), 128
Giddens, Anthony, 212
Gilliam, Terry, 5, 241
Ginway, Mary Elizabeth "Libby," 1, 2, 10, 54, 60, 61, 67, 79, 80, 146, 196, 197, 198, 258, 259, 270, 271, 272, 304, 317, 323, 324
Girão, Luís Eduardo, 135
*Given Word, The* (*O Pagador de Promessas*, 1962), 27
Glass, Philip, 133
Glazer, Jonathan, 202
Globo Filmes, 113
GMO (Genetic Modified Organism), 197
Godard, Jean-Luc, 191, 225
Goethe-Institut, 282
Golias, Ronald, 29, 30
Gomes, Antônio Carlos Bernardes (*See also* Mussum), 91
Gomes, Custódio, 103
Gomes, Halder, 130
Gomes, Thiago, 227
Gomide, Geórgia, 127
Gonçalves, Alexandre, 162
Gonçalves, Dercy, 78
Gonçalves, Mauro Faccio (*See also* Zacarias), 91
Gondry, Michel, 253
Gonzaga, Adhemar, 304
González, Rogélio A., 96
*Good Manners, The* (*As Boas Maneiras*, 2017), 180
*Goof Acrobats, The* (*Os Saltimbancos Trapalhões*, 1981), 98
*Goofs at the Ape's Plateau, The* (*Os Trapalhões no Planalto dos Macacos*, 1976), 86
*Goofs in the War of the Planets, The* (*Os Trapalhões na Guerra dos Planetas*, 1978) (See also *TGWP*), 9, 86, 94, 96
Goofs, The (*Os Trapalhões*), 34
Gore, Al, 70, 237
*Gospel According to Saint Matthew, The* (*Il Vangelo Secondo Matteo*, 1964), 140
Goulart, Beth, 128
Goulart, João, 41
Gowariker, Ashutosh, 140
Gramado Film Festival, 75, 127, 200, 281
Grande Otelo (*See also* Sebastião Bernardes de Souza Prata), 29, 30
Grant, Barry Keith, 250
*Gray Lives* (*Vidas Cinzas*, 2020), 192, 317
*Grayish Morning* (*Manhã Cinzenta*, 1969), 49–51, 58, 181, 272, 302
*Great Discovery by Dr. Right, A* (*Uma Grande Descoberta do Dr. Right*), 15
Greatest Train in the World, The ("O Maior Trem do Mundo"), 292
*Green Vinyl* (*Vinil Verde*, 2004), 245
Green, Joseph, 108
Greenpeace, 63
Greenwald, Glenn, 192
Gregório, Carlos, 113, 148, 149, 224, 313
*Gremlins* (1984), 87
Griffith, D. W., 116
*Gringo* (*Quién sabe?*, 1967), 174
Guajajara, Zahy, 195, 197
Guarani, 193, 295, 296, 326, 329, 331
Guedes, Paulo, 234, 235

Guedes, Thelma, 124
Guerreiro Ramos, Alberto, 211, 213
Guest, Val, 57
Guggenheim, Davis, 70
*Guide for the Post-Truth, A* (*Manual da Pós-Verdade*, 2022), 183
Guimarães Rosa, João, 58, 195, 301, 312
Gullane, 193
Gunn, James, 294
Gunning, Tom, 248, 254
Gurgel, 75, 307

Haeckel, Ernst, 63
*Handmaid's Tale, The* (2017), 165, 173, 210
Haraway, Donna, 196
*Hard Labour* (*Trabalhar Cansa*, 2011), 136
Hardy, Phil, 45, 53, 56
Hardy, Robin, 140
Harrison, Harry, 57
Harryhausen, Ray, 254
Hartwell, David G., 259
*Heart and Souls* (1993), 128
Heinlein, Robert A., 57
Henrique, Maurício Garcez, 131
*Her* (2013), 253
Herbert Richers, 23
Hevey, David, 157
*Hidden Tiger, The* (*A Vizinhança do Tigre*, 2016), 180
*High Noon* (1952), 18–19, 87, 300
*High Plains Drifter* (1973), 174
*High Spirits* (*Alto Astral*, soap opera, 2014–2015), 124
Hill, Walter, 103
Hinz, Kristina, 164, 334
*Hiperselva* (2014), 282
Hitchcock, Alfred, 39, 40, 227, 309, 319

*Hitler 3rd World* (*Hitler 3o Mundo*, 1968), 59
Hitler, Adolf, 121, 230
HIV, 168, 291
Holanda, Sérgio Buarque de, 218, 278–279, 295
Holbein, Hans, 4
*Hollywood Progressive*, 210
Hollywood, 9, 17, 23, 28, 32, 98, 102, 128, 129, 132, 210, 230, 243, 244, 245, 250, 253, 254, 256, 281, 294, 297
Holmberg, Eduardo Ladislao, 16
*How Tasty was my Frenchman* (*Como Era Gostoso o meu Francês*, 1971), 82
Hoyt, Harry, 5, 64
*Huffpost Brasil*, 217
Hughes, John, 87
Hulu, 165
*Hunger for Love* (*Fome de Amor*, 1968), 82
*Hunger Game, The* (2012–2015), 174, 220
Hunter, T. Hayes, 115
Hutchison, David, 249
Huxley, Aldous, 36, 37, 71, 159, 210
hybrid war, 172
hyperreal ideas, 280

IBAMA (Brazilian Institute of Environment and Renewable Natural Resources/Instituto Brasileiro do Meio Ambiente e dos Recursos Naturais Renováveis), 234, 236, 237
IBGE (Brazilian Institute of Geography and Statistics/Instituto Brasileiro de Geografia e Estatística), 119, 311

*Ideas to Postpone the End of the World*, 201
iêiêiê, 90 (*See also* Jovem Guarda), 90, 92, 308
*If I Were You* (*Se Eu Fosse Você*), 113, 129, 323; trilogy *If I Were You* (2006, 2009, and 2013), 113
Ignez, Helena, 48
II International Film Festival (II Festival Internacional do Filme), 56
imaginary science, 32
Imagination of Disaster, The (1965), 138
Immortal, The ("O Imortal," 1882), 271, 324
impeachment, 146, 173, 204
imperialism, 22, 23, 41, 48, 60, 75, 122, 269, 270, 299
*In August* (*En Agosto*, 2009), 193
*In the Country of the Dreams* (*No Paiz dos Sonhos*), 15
Iñárritu, Alejandro González, 116
INC (National Institute of Cinema/Instituto Nacional do Cinema), 56
*Inception* (2010), 290
*Incredible Goof Monster, The* (*O Incrível Monstro Trapalhão*, 1981) (See also *TIGM*), 86, 97, 101
Incredible Hulk, The, 99, 100, 108
Indie Lisboa, 283
Indie Memphis Film Festival, 209
Indigenous Futurism(s), 7, 197, 198, 201, 225
*(In)Finitum*, 224, 225
*Inglourious Basterds* (2009), 174
INPA (National Institute for Research in the Amazon/Instituto Nacional de Pesquisas da Amazônia), 236
INPE (National Institute for Space Research/Instituto Nacional de Pesquisas Espaciais), 237

*Inquest of Pilot Pirx* (*Test Pilota Pirxa*, 1979), 195
Intercept, The, 162
International Transcendental Film Festival (*Festival de Cinema Transcendental de Brasília*), 135
*Intolerance* (1916), 116
Introduction to the Study of *"Science Fiction"* (*Introdução ao Estudo da "Science Fiction,"* 1967), 57–58
*Invaders from Mars* (1953), 22
*Invasión* (1969), 42, 178, 184, 324
*Invention of Dr. Right, The* (*O Invento do Dr. Right*), 15
IPCC (Intergovernmental Panel on Climate Change), 69, 235
*Isle of Flowers* (*Ilha das Flores*, 1989), 191
*It Glues Everything . . . Even Iron!* (*Colla Tudo, Mesmo . . . Ferro!*), 14–15
It Lacks a Flying Saucer ("Falta um Disco") (poem), 292
*It's a Wonderful Life* (1946), 129
Itamaracá, Lia de, 177
Itamaraty, 36
Ivan Cardoso, 86, 101, 309
Izzo, Alcino, 67

J. Walter Thompson (advertising agency), 35
Jahn, Gustavo, 282
*Janaína Overdrive* (2016), 245, 282
*Jaws* (1975), 9
Jetty, The (*La Jetée*, 1962), 152, 251, 253
Jodorowsky, Alejandro, 283
Joelma Building, 127
*Joelma, 23rd Floor* (*Joelma, 23o Andar*, 1980), 127
Johnson, Kenneth, 100

Johnson, Randal, 76
Jonathas' Forest (*A Floresta de Jonathas*, 2012), 199
Jones, Duncan, 253
Jonze, Spike, 253
*Jornal da USP*, 237
Jovem Guarda (See also *iêiêiê*), 90–92
Jungmann, Ruy, 57

K., Wimmer, 170
Kafkaesque, 173
kakistocracy, 163
Kalik, Susan, 227
Kantayya, Shalini, 211
Kardec, Allan, 17, 115, 117, 118, 119, 128, 134
Kardecism (*See also* Spiritism), 9, 117, 118, 119, 125, 134, 135, 299
*Kawa's Black Earth, The* (*A Terra Negra dos Kawa*), 198–199, 245, 316
Keaton, Michael, 128
Kedassere, Severiano, 199
*Keeping the Faith* (2000), 140
Khouri, Walter Hugo, 9, 103, 104, 125, 127, 254
Kier, Udo, 175
Kincaid, Paul, 277
*King Kong* (1933), 39
King, Basil, 115
King, Geoff, 254
Kinski, Klaus, 174
Kiss Before the Sleep, The ("O Beijo Antes do Sono," 1984) (short story), 103
*Kiss me Deadly*, 23
kitsch, 257
Klein, William, 181
Knight, Damon, 57
Kopenawa, Davi, 224
Krakauer, Sigfried, 146

Krenak, Aílton, 200, 201, 223–225, 237–238, 275–276, 280, 286–290, 294–295, 326
Kubitsheck, Juscelino, 71
Kubrick, Stanley, 57, 66, 173, 252, 270, 322
Kucinski, Bernardo, 146
Kujawski, Guilherme, 305
Kurt, Carlos (aka Carlos Kumstat), 93
Kyoto Protocol, 77

*La Gaceta Literária*, 255
Labanca, Giuseppe, 14
Labanca, Leal & Co., 14
Labatti, Marcus, 205
Lacerda, Flávia, 207
*Lagaan* (2001), 140
Lamont, Charles, 20–21
Lampião and Maria Bonita, 176
land of the future, 5, 8, 119–123, 145, 234, 241–242, 320
Landis, John, 86
Lang, Fritz, 39
Langoni, Flávio, 244
*Last Romantics of the World, The* (*Os Últimos Românticos do Mundo*, 2020), 177, 225–226
*Last Temptation of Christ, The* (1988), 140
Lattes, César, 70
Laughorror (*See also* "Terrir"), 101
lawfare, 217
*Le Monde*, 236
*Le Scorpion Languedocien* (1913), 255
Leal, Antônio, 14
Legião Urbana, 113
Leib, Monica, 57
Leite, Maria, 222
Leoneé, Rossandra, 203
Lepastier, Joachim, 175
Lessa, Helena, 282

Lessa, Pedro, 282
Lévi-Strauss, Claude, 266, 267
Lewgoy, Bernardo, 117, 119
Lewis, Jerry, 99, 100
LGBT, 222, 337; LGBTQIA+, 222, 226, 245
Library of Babel, The ("La Biblioteca de Babel"), 288
Lima Jr., Walter, 51–56, 58, 81, 196, 272, 302
Lima, Mariana, 200
Lima, Naloana, 136
Lima, Victor, 8, 27–28, 31, 34, 46
*Limits to Growth, The*, 67
Lins, Lucinha, 98
Lira Itabirana (1984) (poem), 239, 292
Lispector, Clarice, 285
*Literature and Society* (*Literatura e Sociedade*, 2000), 152
*Lives of Chico Xavier, The* (*As Vidas de Chico Xavier*, 2003), 130
Lizzie Borden, 210
lo-fi sci-fi, 153, 154, 161, 185, 198, 217, 226, 228, 253, 285
Locarno Film Festival, 283
Lodi-Ribeiro, Gerson, 252, 257, 262, 322
Logan, Joshua, 35
*Logan's Run* (1976), 170
*Loop* (2002), 113, 148, 149, 244, 313
*Loop* (2019), 316
Los Angeles Brazilian Film Festival, 283
*Lost World, The* (1912) (film), 5, 64
*Lost World, The* (1912) (novel), 5
*Love Insect, The* (*O Inseto do Amor*, 1980), 101
Lovelock, James, 63
Lozano, Rafael, 218
Lucas, George, 9, 71, 85, 95, 96, 100, 191, 210, 250, 251

Lucas, Luiz Felipe, 197
*lucha libre*, 25
Luciano, Thiago, 184
*lúdico-carnavalesco*, 301
Lufti, Dib, 78
Lumière Brothers, 14
lumpenproletariat, 163
*Luna* (1965), 255
*Lunatique* (2016), 187, 244
Lund, Kátia, 6, 188, 297
Lussier, Patrick, 128
Lyna Lurex, 220
Lyra, Bernadette, 88

Ma-Hôre (1960) (short story), 135
Macedo, Valéria, 295
Macedo, Watson, 20–22
Machado de Assis, 271
Machado, Samir Machado de, 146
Machine of the World, The ("A Máquina do Mundo") (poem), 292
*Machine, The* (*A Máquina*, 2006), 129
Maciel, Luís Carlos, 46
*Macunaíma* (1969), 6, 56, 303
MAD (magazine), 102
*Mad Max* (1979), 66, 80, 125, 180
Madersbacher, Fred, 57
magic(al) realism (realism mágico), 108, 112, 137
*Magical World of the Goofs, The* (*O Mundo Mágico dos Trapalhões*, 1981), 96
Maia, Mateus, 226
*malandragem*, 23, 33, 300
Malheiros, Álvaro, 57
*Man Facing Southeast* (*Hombre Mirando al Sudeste*, 1986), 253
*Man from the Future, The* (*O Homem do Futuro*, 2011), 25, 112–113, 244
*Man in the Box* (*O Efeito Ilha*, 1984), 108–112, 310

*Man Who Bought the World, The* (*O Homem que Comprou o Mundo*, 1968), 46–47, 49
*Man Who Hated Flies, The* (1929), 63
Man Who Spread the Desert, The ("O Homem que Espalhou o Deserto," 2003 [originally published in 1979]) (short story), 79
*Man with the Golden Arm, The* (1955), 23
*Mané Socó's Spaceship* (*A Nave de Mané Socó*, 2019), 175
Manga, Carlos, 19, 22, 24, 27, 33, 87, 92
Manguebeat, 177
Manifesto Antropófago (*See also* Cannibalist Manifesto), 196, 298, 305
Mansur, Fauzi, 101
Mara, Deyse, 185
Maranhão, 200; Lençóis Maranhenses, 200
Margaret Atwood, 165
Mariana, 223, 235, 239, 320, 321
Maristella (film studio), 28
Marker, Chris, 152, 251, 253
Marouço, André, 130
Marques, Pedro Neves, 195
Marquim do Tropa, 150
*Mars* (2010), 253
Martello, Nilson D., 32
Martinelli, Leonardo, 192, 231–232
Martins, Paulo Bastos, 58–59, 246, 272
Martins, Renata, 202
Martins, Walter, 57
*Marvelous Journey of Mr. Nic-Nac to the Planet Mars, The* (*Viaje maravilloso del Señor Nic-Nac en el que se refieren las prodijiosas aventuras de este señor y se dan á conocer las instituciones, costumbres y preocupaciones de um mundo desconocido: Fantasia espiritista*, 2006 [1875]), 16, 17
Marx, Karl, 42; Marxism, 274; Marxist, 166;
Mascaro, Gabriel, 148, 161–162, 164–167, 173, 207, 245, 275, 282, 295
*Master Blaster—Hans Lucas's Adventure in Nebula 2907N* (*Master Blaster—Uma Aventura de Hans Lucas na Nebulosa 2907N*, 2013), 191
*Maternal Heart* (*Coração Materno*, 1951), 125
Mato Grosso do Sul, 198
*Matrix, The* (1999), 81, 191, 203
*Mauá: The Emperor and the King* (*Mauá—O Imperador e o Rei*, 1999), 252
Mauro, Humberto, 58
Mbembe, Achille, 169, 214, 280
McAbee, Cory, 253
McCarthyism, 51
McClean, Shilo, 249–250
McDonald, Ian, 5
McKee, Robert, 256
*Mechanical Butcher, The* (*La Charcuterie Méchanique*, 1895), 14
Medeiros, Fabio, 137
mediascapes, 3, 5, 11–12, 81
*Medium: The Truth about Reincarnation, The* (*O Médium: A Verdade sobre a Reencarnação*, 1980), 127
*Medusa* (2022), 172–173
Meirelles, Elena, 185
Meirelles, Fernando, 6, 188, 297
*Melancholia* (2011), 253
Melià, Bartolomeu, 295
Méliès, Georges, 13, 248, 249, 250, 254, 255, 322

Mello, Selton, 193
Melo Neto, João Cabral de, 292
Melo Souza, José Inacio de, 76
melodrama, 2, 40, 128, 135, 141, 251, 286
Menaker, Leonid, 108
Mendonça Filho, Kléber, 42, 83, 146–148, 173, 175, 177, 179, 188–191, 201, 203, 212, 245, 275, 282, 286, 295, 317
Menezes, Adolfo Bezerra, 123, 130
Menezes, Levy, 32
Menzies, William Cameron, 22, 39
Mercerism, 290
Mercury Theater, 38, 48, 175
Mesquita, Danilo, 228
*Message from Space* (1978), 95
Mestre Touro (aka Antônio Oliveira Bemvindo), 100
*Metamorphoses of Science Fiction* (1979), 4
*Meteorango Kid—Herói Intergalático* (1969), 59, 221
Meteoro Brasil (YouTube channel), 177
Metz, Christian, 247
Mexico in the Year 1970 ("México en el año 1970"), 16
MGM, 165
Miaqui, Tadao, 217
military dictatorship, 45, 49–50, 60–61, 74–75, 81–82, 101, 113, 193–194, 204–205, 272, 282, 304, 314, 324
militias, 184, 192–193, 207
Miller, George, 66, 80, 180
*mise-en-abyme* (abyss effect), 110
*mise-en-phase*, 249
misplaced idea(s), 3, 10, 31, 268
*Miss Ferrovia 1999* (1982), 48
Mitchell, David T., 156
mockumentary, 188, 192, 317

*Moebius* (1996), 253
Mojica Marins, José (*See also* Coffin Joe or Zé do Caixão), 99, 101
Molo, Uberto, 106, 108
*Monsters* (2010), 253
*Monsters of Babaloo, The* (*Os Monstros de Babaloo*), 59–60
Monteiro, Jerônymo, 33, 57
Monteiro, Lea, 282
*Moon* (2009), 253
Moore, Demi, 129
Moraes, Alinne, 129
Moraes, Flávia, 244
*More Sex, the Better, The* (*O Etesão: Quanto mais Sexo Melhor*, 1986), 103
Moreno, Jorge, 129
Morettin, Eduardo, 246
Moskowitz, Sam, 57
Mosquera, Gustavo, 253
*Most Dangerous Game, The* (1932), 174
*Mother* (*Madre*), 195
*Mothers of Chico Xavier, The* (*As Mães de Chico Xavier*, 2011), 130
Moura, Luís Fernando, 282
Moura, Matheus, 205–206, 231, 245
Moura, Wagner, 112–113, 192
Mourão, Hamilton, 242
Mourão, Renata, 177, 221
MR-8 organization, 50
Mucci, Gabriel Kalim, 187, 244
*Mummy's Secret, The* (*O Segredo da Múmia*, 1982), 86, 101
*Murder in Copacabana* (*Assassinato em Copacabana*), 27
Museums of Image and Sound, the (Rio, São Paulo, Campinas), 298
musical comedy, 6, 8, 19, 78
Mussum (*See also* Antônio Carlos Bernardes Gomes), 91–94, 97, 308
*My Son the Fanatic* (1997), 140

*Na onda do iê-iê-iê* (*On the Wave of Iêiêiê*, 1966), 92
Nagib, Lúcia, 2, 6, 106, 109, 297–298, 310
Nama, Adilifu, 174
Namíbia, No! ("Namíbia, Não!"), 207, 209
Napoli, Márcio, 244, 321
narco-militia, 164; narco-Pentecostalism, 164
NASA, 29, 89
Nascimento, Abdias do, 211
Nathalie Denizot, 11–12, 298
National Bank of Minas Gerais (Banco Nacional de Minas Gerais), 38
National Commission for Nuclear Energy (CNEN—Comissão Nacional de Energia Nuclear), 71–72
National Laboratory of Synchrotron Light (LNLS—Laboratório Nacional de Luz Síncrotron), 113
National Steel Company (CSN—Companhia Siderúrgica Nacional), 299
*Nave de los Monstruos, La* (1959), 96
necrolumpenkakistocracy, 163
*Necropolis's Symphony* (*Sinfonia da Necrópole*, 2014), 136
necropolitics, 159, 169, 214
*Negrum3* (2018), 202
*Neighboring Sounds* (*O Som ao Redor*, 2013), 147, 173, 177
*Neither Samson nor Delilah* (*Nem Sansão nem Dalila*, 1954), 19, 87
neo-Pentecostal(ism), 162–165, 172, 207; "neo-Pentec," 163; "neon-pentec," 163–164
neoliberalism, 7, 114, 134, 171–172, 188, 236; neoliberal capitalism, 147, 191; neoliberal transhumanism, 133

Neruda, Pablo, 300
Netflix, 147, 160, 212, 217, 245, 318
Neves, Tancredo, 75
*New Criterion, The*, 166
*New Order, The* (*A Nova Ordem*, 2019), 146
*New Terra, The* (*A Nova Terra*, 2012), 50
*New World, The* (*Il Nuovo Mondo*), 225
*News from a Personal War* (*Notícias de uma Guerra Particular*, 1999), 188
*nheẽ* (See also spirit-name), 295; *nheẽ porã*, 295
Nicácio, Glenda, 204
Niccol, Andrew, 252
Nicholls, Peter, 32, 247–248
Nichols, Jeff, 253
Nicolelis, Miguel, 160
Niemeyer, Oscar, 132
nodal situation, 293
Nogueira, Carlos Eduardo, 282
Nolan, Christopher, 290
*Non-semsical School* (*Escola Sem Sentido*, 2019), 183
non-Western, 280
Norton, Edward, 140
*Nosso Lar, Brasília: Spiritism—Modernism—Architecture* (2014), 132
nostalgia, 80
*Nothing But Time* (*Rien que les Heures*, 1926), 255
*novum*, 4, 161, 248, 303
*Nuclear Shelter* (*Abrigo Nuclear*, 1981), 64, 70–73, 79–80, 163, 272
Nunes, Cauê, 324
Nunes, José Divino, 131
*Nutty Professor, The* (1963), 99, 100

Oberhausen Film Festival, 51

Odin, Roger, 249
Ogum's Amulet (O Amuleto de Ogum, 1974), 140
Oliveira, André Luiz, 59, 221
Oliveira, André Novais, 202, 283
Oliveira, Luís, 282
Oliveira, Vaneza, 218
Oliver (1968), 56
Once There Was Brasília (Era uma vez Brasília, 2017), 159, 180, 234
Onyx-Havaí Filmes, 102
Open your Eyes (Abre los Ojos, 1997), 253
Ordem do Dia, A (1982), 48
Orlok Sombra, 220
Orlowski, Jeff, 182
Ortiz Ramos, José Mário, 76, 88–93, 96, 100, 297
Ortiz, Carlos, 125
Ortiz, Daniel, 124
Orwell, George, 35, 71, 159, 181, 210; Orwellian, 185
Os Trapalhões (See also The Goofs), 92
Other Side of the Protocol, The (O Outro Lado do Protocolo, 1985), 50
Others, The (2001), 128
Our Common Future, 74
Our Home (Nosso Lar, 1944) (novel), 123–124
Our Home (Nosso Lar, 2010) (film), 130, 132–135, 141, 158, 161
Overlook Film Encyclopedia, The—Science Fiction (1995), 53, 56

Pacífico (2010), 282
Padilha, José, 188
Paes, Dira, 162
Pages from the History of Brazil Written in the Year 2000 (Páginas da História do Brasil Escripta no Anno de 2000, 1957 [1868–72]), 16–17, 312

Paiva, Lívia de, 185
pajé, 76
Pajemancer, The, ("O Pajemancer") (short story), 195
Pal, George, 56
Palestine, 214; Palestinian, 214
Panic Attack (Ataque de Pánico, 2009), 187, 244
Paramount Pictures, 113
paranormal phenomena, 125; telekinesis, 125; poltergeist phenomena, 125
Parente, Guto, 282
Pares, Pablo, 324
Paris Qui Dort (1923), 39
parody 5, 7–8, 18, 20, 23, 33, 46, 54, 58, 86–91, 94–97, 102, 181, 191, 254
Pasárgada, 292
Pasolini, Pier Paolo, 140
Passion of Joan of Arc, The (La Passion de Jeanne d'Arc, 1928), 140
Passô, Grace, 202–203, 212, 245, 293–294
pastiche, 9, 20, 42, 94, 96, 102–103
Paths in Search of a Time (Not Yet Cataloged) (Caminhos em busca de um tempo (ainda não catalogado), 2001), 233
Patterson, Andrew, 228
Paula, Francisco de, 9, 77–78, 104–107, 113, 193, 245, 309, 310
Paulino, Diego, 202
Paulo Thiago, 105
Pavel Klushantsev, 255
Pedestrian, The (O Pedestre), 56
Pedregal, Carlos, 35, 37–42, 254
Pedroso, Marcelo, 234, 316
Pêra, Sandra, 129
Pereira, Luiz Alberto (aka Gal), 108–111, 245, 310
Pereira, Marco Antônio, 136

Pereira, Otoniel Santos, 56
Pereira, Silvero, 175
Perfect Marriage, The ("O Casamento Perfeito," 1966) (short story), 50
Pernambuco, 175
*Persephone Mission* (*Missão Perséfone*, 2020), 233
*Personal Vivator* (2014), 202–203, 212, 245
Pesaro Film Festival, 51
*Pesquisa Fapesp*, 265–266
Philip K. Dick, 10, 290
Photo-Cinematographia Co., 14
*Pi* (1998), 251, 253
Pichel, Irving, 174, 270
*Picnic* (1955), 35
*Pictures of Ghosts* (*Retratos Fantasmas*, 2023), 286
Pieralisi, Alberto, 8, 10, 28, 35, 38–40, 46, 61, 76, 178, 184, 254
Piestrak, Marek, 195
Pietro, Rogério, 195
Pimenta, Joana, 180
Pimentel, Joel, 130
*Pink Cloud, The* (*A Nuvem Rosa*, 2021), 226, 231, 319
Pirate Bay, 183
Pires, Petrus, 71
Pires, Roberto, 64, 70–73, 163, 257, 252
*Piritas Siderais* (1994), 305
Pissolato, Elizabeth, 295
Pitanga, Camila, 193
*Planet of the Apes, The* (1968), 85, 93–94, 97
*Planeta Bur* (1961), 255
Plano Piloto, 152, 155
Plato, 291
*Pleasure of Killing Bugs, The* (*O Prazer de Matar Insetos*, 2020), 231
PMR (Primitive Mode of Representation), 248
*Poder 360*, 320–321

Pohl, Frederik, 57
Polino, Carmelo, 259–265, 269, 323
Politi, Elie, 258, 262
Polo, Jorge, 282
popular science, 40; popular science film, 255
population bomb, 63
pornochanchada(s), 87–88, 101–103, 257
Post-human Tantra, 225
postapocalyptic, 65, 70, 81–82, 163, 187, 193, 219, 221, 286; postapocalyptic-tropicalist, 163
Poyart, Afonso, 160
Pozati, Juliano, 137
Prasad, Udayan, 140
Prata, A. Gomes de, 299
pre-Columbian, 201
Preminger, Otto, 23
Prestes, Luiz Carlos, 22, 300
Pretto, Davi, 282
*Primer* (2004), 253
principle of the excluded third, the (*principium tertii exclusi* or *tertium non datur*), 292, 326
probabilistic oracle ("oráculo probabilístico"), 288–289
Professor Baskarán, 37–38
*Professor Dowell's Head* (1925) (novel), 108
*Professor Dowell's Testament* (1984) (film), 108
Project Apolo (1968), 56
*Projeto Pulex* (1991), 217
Protazanov, Yakov, 21, 95, 255
Protestantism, 207
proto-SF (early SF), 13–17, 95, 202
*Psychomagic: A Healing Art* (*Psicomagia: A Arte da Cura* 2019), 283
*Punishment Park* (1971), 49
*Punks, Sons of the Night* (*Punk's, Os Filhos da Noite*, 1983), 103

*Purple Dictatorship* (*Ditadura Roxa*, 2020), 205

queer sci-fi, 10, 187, 226, 228, 245; queer SF, 220, 228; queer-fi, 226
Queirós, Adirley, 10, 133, 146–148, 150–152, 154, 156–159, 173, 180, 185, 201, 204, 207, 234, 275, 295, 310, 313, 343
Queiróz, João, 194
Queiroz, Rachel de, 135
*quilombo(s)*, 179, 208; neoquilombo, 208; quilombola(s), 200, 316
*Quintal* (2015), 202, 283

Rabelo, Wilson, 179
Rachel Haywood Ferreira, 2, 16–17, 271–272, 302
racial utopia, 121–122
Rádio Globo, 37
Radiohead, 113
Rady, José, 103
*Rally: São Paulo to Luiz Carlos Prestes* (*Comício: São Paulo a Luiz Carlos Prestes*, 1945), 22
Ramos, Eurides, 27
Ramos, Lázaro, 207
Ramos, Maria, 173
Ramos, Paulo de Sousa, 50
Ramos, Tony, 131
Rampell, Ed, 210
rarefied dialectics, 276
*Rascals in the Fourth Dimension* (*Malandros na Quarta Dimensão*, 1954), 22
RCAR (See also *Roberto Carlos in Adventure Rhythm*), 88–90, 105–106
reactionary modernization, 34, 55
real SF, 20; realism, 136–137, 141, 156–157, 275, 285, 290, 295; realism-naturalism, 10
*realismo maravilhoso* (See also magic realism), 108

realist-naturalist style, 248
Recife, 162, 173, 177, 188–189, 190, 203, 286, 314, 315
RecordTV (See also TV Record), 91–92, 314–315
*Red Forest* (*Floresta Vermelha*, 2013), 135
*Red Light Bandit, The* (*O Bandido da Luz Vermelha*), 47–49, 55, 221
*Red Spectre, The* (*Le Spectre Rouge*, 1907), 13
Rede Globo (See also TV Globo), 86, 91, 96, 101, 124, 311, 314
*Redeemer* (*Redentor*, 2004), 128
Redemocratization, 45, 74, 83, 104, 236
Reed, Carol, 56
Reflections on the Seventh Art ("Réflexions sur le septième art," 1923), 115–116, 310
Regina, Ivan Carlos, 196
Reichenbach, Carlos, 101, 126
Reis, Leon, 202
Reis, Lúcio, 299
Renha, Lia, 132
*Republic* (*República*, 2020), 202–204, 212, 245, 293
Rescala, Tim, 108
Resnais, Alain, 152
Retomada (Cinema da Retomada), 6–7, 79, 242, 297
retro-futuristic, 134, 135; retro-futuristic ideology, 134, 135; retro-futuristic landscape, 134, 135
*Revelations of the Subconscious* (*Revelações do Subconsciente*) (radio show), 37
*Revenants, Les* (2004), 116
Rezende, Sérgio, 252, 297, 319
Ribeiro, Clarissa, 282
Ribeiro, Darcy, 10, 273
Ribeiro, Djamila, 242
Ribeiro, Ivani, 124

Ribeiro, Laísa, 176
Ribeiro, Luís Severiano, 20
Ribeiro, Sidarta, 283, 287, 290
Rickman, Gregg, 254–255
Rieder, John, 3–4, 12, 175, 276–277
Rilla, Wolf, 57
*Rio 2096: A Story of Love and Fury* (*Uma História de Amor e Fúria*, 2013), 83, 188, 192–194, 236
Rio Branco Institute (Instituto Rio Branco), 165
Rio de Janeiro, 5, 14–15, 17–20, 36, 38–39, 50, 56, 71, 77, 82, 89, 148, 162, 164, 193–193, 197, 202, 207, 232, 246, 275, 279, 298–299, 302, 304, 306–308, 318, 320
Rio Film Festival, 96, 210, 281
Rio-92 (aka ECO-92), 77
Riocine, 109
Rivail, Hippolyte Léon Denizard, 17, 115
Rivera, Alex, 153, 189, 193, 252–253, 294
Rizzi, Anderson di, 184
*Ro.Go.Pa.G.* (1963), 225
*Road to the Stars* (*Doroga k zvezdam*, 1957), 255
*Roberto Carlos in Adventure Rhythm* (*Roberto Carlos em Ritmo de Aventura*, 1968) (See also RCAR), 61, 88
Roberto Carlos, 88–90, 92, 101, 307–308
Roberts, Adam, 247, 251, 269–270, 281
*Robocop* (1987), 161, 230
robot, 49, 61, 292
Rocha, Felipe, 200
Rocha, Glauber, 6, 27, 53, 70, 88, 140–141, 179–180, 303, 305, 319
*Rock 'n' Roll High School* (1979), 87

Rodrigues, Meibe, 205
*Rodson (Rodson ou Onde o Sol não tem Dó)*, 220–221
Rojas, Juliana, 135–136, 180
*romans scientifiques*, 134
*Roots of Brazil, The* (*Raízes do Brasil*), 278
Rosa, Ary, 204
Rose, Tricia, 202
Rosemberg, Luiz, 221
Ross, Gary, 174
Rotterdam Festival, 283
Rouanet Law (Lei Rouanet n. 8.313, December 23, 1991), 79
Rousseff, Dilma, 145–147, 159, 173, 185, 217, 235, 265
Rubro, Fernando, 218
*RUR* (1921), 159

Sá, Alan de, 176
Sadlier, Darlene, 6, 68, 145
Sadoul, Jacques, 57
*Safety not Guaranteed* (2012), 253
Salgado, Levy, 103
Salles Gomes, Paulo Emílio, 17–18, 29, 58–59, 87–88, 246, 255, 276, 281, 304, 310, 325
Salles, João Moreira, 188
Salles, Ricardo, 237
Salles, Walter, 188
Salú, Lila, 185
Salvagepunk, 133
Samarco (mining company), 223, 235, 320
Sampaio, Silveira, 18–19, 123
*Samson and Delilah* (1949), 18
Sanches, Fernando, 316
Sanginitto, Gérson, 135, 175
*Santa Clara Poltergeist* (1991), 305
Santana, Dedé (See also Manfried Santana), 93
Santana, Gelson, 88

Santana, Manfried (*See also* Dedé Santana), 91
Santiago, Hugo, 42, 178, 184, 324
Santo (Mexican wrestler), 25
*Santo vs. the Martian Invasion* (*El Santo contra la Invasión de los Marcianos*, 1967), 25
Santos Dumont, Alberto, 300; "Santos Dumont effect," 29
Santos, Éder, 316
Santos, Joaquim Felício dos, 16, 302
Santos, Maria David, 302
Santos, Nelson Pereira dos, 27, 81–82, 140–141, 163, 176, 305
Santos, Osmar, 111–112
Santos, Ruy, 22
Santucci, Dulce, 127
Sanz, José, 56–58
São José dos Campos, 267
São Paulo International Film Festival, 109
São Paulo, 5, 17, 22, 28, 30, 33, 41, 58–59, 61, 67–69, 87, 89, 102, 109, 113, 125, 127, 160, 162, 171, 183–184, 246, 257, 272, 281, 293, 298–300, 302, 306, 308, 318–319, 323–324, 327–333, 336–345, 347
São Paulo, Olney, 49–51, 58, 61, 181, 272
Sapir, Esteban, 324
Sara, Kay, 199
Saraceni, Paulo César, 141
Sardinha (Bishop Sardinha), 196, 317
Sarney, José, 65, 74–75
Sarno, Geraldo, 141
Sassi, Guido Wilmar, 32
Sax, Geoffrey, 128
SBF, Ian, 316
*Scalding Sands* (*Areias Escaldantes*, 1985), 9, 78, 86, 104–107, 113
scarcely-inhabited planet ("um planeta quase desabitado"), 3, 5–6

Schaffner, Franklin J., 85, 93–94, 97, 100
Schlöndorff, Volker, 165
Schoedsack, Ernest B., 39, 174
Schüfftan process, 254
Schumacher, Joel, 128
Schwarz, Roberto, 10, 268
Schweitzer, Ariel, 173
science drama (dramaciência), 286, 325
Science Fiction (poem), 292
Science Fiction from the South, 253; SF from the South, 294
Science fiction in Brazil: an almost uninhabited planet ("Ficção científica no Brasil: um planeta quase desabitado"), 243
*Science of Sleep* (2006), 253
scientific culture, 243, 258–260, 262–263, 266; scientific cinema, 255
Scorsese, Martin, 140
Scott, Ridley, 66, 80, 97, 126, 161, 195
scrapper punk, 199
Sebastião Bernardes de Souza Prata (*See also* Grande Otelo), 308
*Second Man, The* (*O Segundo Homem*, 2022), 184–185
*Sect, The* (*A Seita*, 2015), 286
*Sem Asas* (2019), 202
sense of wonder, 113, 154
Sentinel, The (1951) (short story), 138
*sério-dramático*, 301
Serling, Rod, 228
*Serpent's Rock, The* (*A Pedra da Serpente*, 2018), 316
Serra, Antonio, 14
Sertãopunk, 175–177, 220–221, 296
*Sertãopunk: Stories from a Northeast of Tomorrow* (*Sertãopunk: Histórias de um Nordeste do Amanhã*, 2020), 177
*sertões* (hinterlands), 176

Seu Jorge, 208
*Seven Eves, The* (*As Sete Evas*), 27
*Seven Vampires, The* (*As Sete Vampiras*, 1986), 86, 101
sexually transmitted diseases (STDs), 167
SF Symposium (FC Simpósio), 56–58
SF, fantasy and horror (SF&F&H), 2, 7
Sganzerla, Rogério, 47–49, 52, 55, 176, 221
Shaw, Lisa, 6, 19–20, 23, 28
Shelley, Mary, 223, 250
Shockito, 151, 310, 313
Shohat, Ella, 280, 297
Shyamalan, M. Night, 128
silent cinema, 298; silent film, 13, 322
*Silent Running* (1979), 81
*Silicone XXI* (1985), 305
Silva Neto, Antônio Leão da, 41, 53, 69, 78, 125, 298, 310
Silva, Alec, 176
Silva, Domingos Carvalho da, 32
Silveira, Anita Rocha da, 172
*Simon, the One-Eyed* (*Simão, o Caolho*, 1952), 20
Sirkis, Alfredo, 305
*Sixth Sense, The* (1999), 128
Skorupa, Francisco Alberto, 266–269
Sky Light Cinema, 106
slavery, 36, 101, 121–122, 145, 147, 173, 190, 201, 203, 208, 210, 214, 217, 234, 273–274
*Sleep Dealer* (2008), 153, 189, 193, 252, 316
*Sleepwalker, The* (*La Sonámbula: Recuerdos del Futuro*, 1998), 184, 324
Smith, Percy, 255
Snyder, Sharon L., 156–158
Snyder, Zack, 133
soap opera(s), 95, 109; TV soap operas, 25, 113, 118, 124, 311

Soares, Diogo (aka Caos Nechrofagos Soturnums), 225
Soares, Flávio, 135
Soares, Jofre, 108
*Social Dilemma, The* (2020), 182
social-environmentalist cinema, 192
Soffici, Mario, 300
Solanas, Fernando, 179, 254, 323
*Solaris* (1972), 252, 255, 322
*Solon* (2016), 223, 225, 231, 294
*Somewhere in Time* (1980), 128
*Somnium*, 197
Sons of Metal and the Caatinga ("Filhos do Metal e da Caatinga") (short story), 176
Sontag, Susan, 138
*Sooty Skies* (*Céus de Fuligem*, 2005), 244
Soprani, C. Z., 25
Sorogoyen, Rodrigo, 195
Sorrah, Renata, 213
*Sound of My Voice, The* (2011), 140, 253
South by Southwest Film Festival, 209
Souto Maior, Marcel, 130
Souto, Marcial, 57
Souza, Carlos Roberto de, 298
Souza, Flávio de, 129
Souza, Luciana, 222
Souza, Márcio, 48
*Soylent Green* (1975), 80, 171
*Space Invasion (2019)*, 183, 200, 245
*Spaceballs* (1987), 96–97
Special Bureau for the Environment (SEMA—Secretaria Especial do Meio Ambiente), 74
speculative fiction, 2, 4, 13, 45, 150, 202, 295
Spielberg, Steven, 9, 85, 93, 102, 104, 176, 227, 250, 254, 309
Spiner, Fernando, 184, 324
spirit-name (See also *nheẽ*), 296

Spiritism (*See also* Kardecism), 9, 117, 115, 117–119, 123–125, 129–130, 132, 134, 136, 138, 141, 299, 312; spiritist films, 9, 115, 141–143, 283, 299
*Spirits' Film, The* (*O Filme dos Espíritos*, 2010), 130
*Splendid Cradle Mission* (*Missão Berço Esplêndido*, 2021), 228–230, 245
*Sputnik Man, The* (*O Homem do Sputnik*, 1959), 22–24, 33
Staal, Jonas, 132
Stableford, Brian, 13, 63, 79, 304
*Stalker* (1979), 252
Stam, Robert, 6, 76, 280, 297
Star Plus, 184
*Star Wars* (1977), 9, 85, 95–97, 100, 254
*Stay With Me Tonight* (*Fica Comigo Esta Noite*, 2006), 129
Stevenson, Robert Louis, 85, 97, 99, 300
Stoll, Sandra, 118, 123
*Stop 88: Alert Limit* (*Parada 88: O Limite de Alerta*, 1978), 64–70, 79–80, 83, 160, 236, 272
stop-motion animation, 222, 230
*Strange Case of Dr. Jekyll and Mr. Hyde, The* (1886), 99, 300
*Strange Case of Ezequiel, The* (*O Estranho Caso de Ezequiel*, 2017), 316
*Strange Case of the Man and the Monster, The* (*El Extraño Caso del Hombre y la Bestia*, 1951), 300
*Strange Love Story, A* (*Uma Estranha História de Amor*, 1979), 125
*Strangers, The* (*Os Estranhos*, 1969) (soap opera), 124
*Strength of the Senses, The* (*A Força dos Sentidos*, 1979), 125

structural racism, 207, 211–214, 228; *Structural Racism* (2020), 211
Stuart Hall, 280
*Stufana* (2010), 177
Suassuna, Ariano, 177
Subiela, Eliseo, 253, 324
subliminal technology, 35, 37, 42; subliminal messaging, 35–36, 39, 42, 301
SUDAM (Superintendência do Desenvolvimento da Amazônia), 68
Sumaré, 184
Sundance Film Festival, 221
Sunjo, Petra, 215–216
Super-8, 65, 71, 74, 233
*Superwiseman, The* (*El Supersabio*, 1948), 25
Supreme Court, 171, 207
Suruwahá, 215; Suruwahá people (aka Zuruahãs), 215
Suvin, Darko, 4, 155, 161, 248, 293, 303, 313
Švankmajer, Jan, 223
Svěrák, Jan, 110
Swaggart, Jimmy, 112
Swayze, Patrick, 129
Szulkin, Piotr, 103
Szwark, Jeannot, 128

tachistoscope, 35
*Take Shelter* (2011), 253
Tanko, J. B., 86, 93–93, 100, 308
Tarantino, Quentin, 174
*Tarik's Puzzle* (*O Quebra-Cabeças de Tarik*, 2015), 222
Tarkovsky, Andrei, 103, 252, 255
*Taste of Cinema*, 253
Tate, Greg, 202
*teatro de revista*, 29, 298
techno spy film, 39
techno-feudalism, 8
teenpic, 87

Teixeira, Aurélio, 92
Telford, William, 138–139
Telotte, J. P., 248
Temer, Michel, 235, 265
*Ten Commandments, The* (1956), 140
Tendler, Silvio, 96
*Tenth Victim, The* (*La Decima Vittima*, 1965), 57
*Terminal Game* (*Jogo Terminal*, 1988), 50
*Terminator*, 229–230
terraforming, 63
Terrir (See also "Laughorror"), 101, 309
*Test Tube Woman, The* (*A Mulher de Proveta*, 1984), 103
TGWP (See also *Goofs in the War of the Planets, The*), 94–97
*The Adventures of Paulo Bruscky, The*, (*As Aventuras de Paulo Bruscky*, 2010), 282
*The New York Times*, 236
*Thelma and Louise* (1991), 161
*Theory on a Strange Planet* (*Teoria sobre um Planeta Estranho*, 2018), 136–137
*There Will Be Nothing Left from this Earth but the Wind that Blows Over It* (*Desta Terra nada vai sobrar anão ser o vento que sopra sobre ela*), 146
*They Live!* (1988), 192
Third Cinema, 254; Third SF Cinema, 253–254, 322; Third World, 48, 146, 259, 272, 280
*Three Stooges in Orbit, The* (1962), 34
*Thrill* (*Excitação*, 1976), 125–126, 135
*THX 1138* (1971), 71, 170, 181, 210
TIGM (See also *Incredible Goof Monster, The*), 97–99, 106
*Time Bureau, The* (*A Repartição do Tempo*, 2016), 316

*Time Machine, The* (1960), 56
*Time Was Endless* (*Antes o Tempo Não Acabava*, 2016), 199
*Timecrimes* (*Los Cronocrímenes*, 2007), 253
*Tired Death* (*Der Müde Tod*, 1921), 116
*To Kill or to Run* (*Matar ou Correr*, 1954), 19
*Tocaia no Asfalto* (1962), 70
Todorov, Tzvetan, 222, 228, 312
Toland, Gregg, 28
Torres, Cláudio, 25, 112–113, 128, 244
totalitarian, 170–171, 181–182, 209; totalitarianism, 36, 50, 170–172, 182; *totalitarianismization*, 182
*Totem* (1963), 56
Toward a Third Cinema ("Hacia un Tercer Cine," 1969/1997), 179
*Transfiguration* (*Transfiguração*), 15
transgender, 221–222
*Tremor Iê* (2019), 184–185
Trevisan, João Silvério, 101
Trevorrow, Colin, 253
*Trial, The* (*O Processo*, 2018), 173
Tribunal de Contas da União (TCU), 209
Trigueiro, Ingrid, 175
Trindade, Paulo, 205
*Trip, The* (*A Viagem*, 1975) (TV soap opera), 124; *Trip, The* (*A Viagem*, remake, 1994), 124
tropical fascism, 147
*Tropicália*, 60, 303; *tropicalismo*, 303
trucage, 247, 332
*Truman Show* (1998), 110, 181
Trumbull, Douglas, 81, 254
Trump, Donald, 165, 171, 200, 261
Tullgren, Terence, 83
Tupi, or not Tupi, that is the question, 196
Tupinambá(s), 193, 194, 317

*Tupiniland* (*Tupinilândia*, 2018), 146
Tupiniquim, 221, 305; Tupiniquins, 193
TV Globo, 95, 101, 129, 226
TV Record (*See also* Record TV), 28
TV Rio, 28
TV Tupi, 38, 131, 312
*Twilight Zone, The*, 228
*Twin Souls* (*Alma Gêmea*, soap opera, 2005–2006), 124

Uchôa, Affonso, 147, 180
UFO, 48–49, 175–176, 228
Ulmer, Edgar G., 39
*Ultraviolet* (*Ultravioleta*, 2018), 316
Umbanda, 119, 140, 164, 293
*Umbra* (1977), 79, 303
*Uncle Bonmee, Who Can Remember His Past Lives* (*Loong Boonmee Raleuk Chat*, 2010), 116;
*Under the Skin* (2013), 202
Underwood, Ron, 128
UNEP (United Nations Environment Program), 74
Unified Healthcare System (SUS—Sistema Único de Saúde), 168–169, 314
United Nations World Conference on the Environment, The (aka the Stockholm Conference, 1972), 68, 74
Federal University of Goiás (UFG—Universidade Federal de Goiás), 224
University of Chicago, 280
*Unliveable* (*Inabitável*, 2020), 177, 221–222
*Unsocial Ones, The* (*Os Insociáveis*, 1972–74) (TV show), 91
*Until the End of the World* (*Bis ans Ende der Welt*, 1991), 82
*Upstream Color* (2013), 253

Uranga, Arturo, 78, 105–106
Urban, Charles, 255
Urbano, Julio, 183–184
US Federal Communications Commission, 36
Utopia, 122, 166, 220, 293; Utopian, 5, 22, 31, 78, 122, 132, 134, 179, 196, 215, 217, 271, 274, 289, 324

Vadico, Luiz, 138–139
Vale do Rio Doce (mining company), 235
Valente, Rodolfo, 218
Valenti, Peter, 116
*Vampires, Les*, 40
Van Vogt, A. E., 57
*vaporpunk*, 226
Vargas, Getúlio, 21, 121, 299, 308, 311
*Vast of Night, The* (2019), 228
Ventura, Zuenir, 214
Vera Cruz Studios (Cia. Cinematográfica Vera Cruz), 35
Vereza, Carlos, 130
Verhoeven, Paul, 161, 230
vernacular SF, 11, 274
Vernant, Jean-Pierre, 182
*Very Crazy Asylum, A* (*Azyllo Muito Louco*, 1970), 82
Very White Man, A ("Moço Muito Branco, Um") (short story), 58
Vetter, Marcus, 237
Viana, Geraldo, 105
Viana, Zelito, 46, 105
Vianna, Katiúscia, 210
Viany, Alex, 53, 90, 299
Vicary, James M., 35–38
Vidal, Thaís, 282
video games, 86, 258, 281, 290–291
Video in the Villages Project, the (VNA—Video nas Aldeias), 317
Video Spirit Collection, 128
*Videodrome* (1984), 112

Vieira, Clóvis, 254, 258–259, 262, 322–323
Vieira, João Luiz, 9, 19, 28, 87, 307
Vigalondo, Nacho, 253
Viña del Mar International Film Festival, 51
Vint, Sherryl, 294
*Viramundo* (1965), 141
Visconti, Elyseu, 59–60
visual effects, 54, 93–95, 104, 133, 142, 154, 187, 222, 224, 244–246, 248, 250–251, 281, 322; special effects, 9, 103, 243, 245–257, 269, 281, 293
Vogt, Carlos, 10, 57, 259–265, 268, 323
Volta Grande, 58
*Voltei!* (2020), 204
von Trier, Lars, 253
*Voracious Love* (*Amor Voraz*, 1984), 9, 103–104, 254
Vorlíček, Václav, 5

Wachowski, Andy and Larry (aka the Wachowski Bros., and now the Wachowski Sisters), 81, 191, 203
*Waiting Room* (*Quarto de Espera*, 2009), 282
Wanderléa, 90
*War of the Worlds* (radio show), 38, 48
*War of the Worlds, The* (1898) (novel), 48, 175, 269
*Warriors, The* (1979), 103
wasteland, 65–65, 136, 220, 223
*Watchmen* (2009) (film), 133
*Watchmen* (2019) (HBO series), 301
Watkins, Peter, 49, 181, 210
*We* (1924), 71, 159
*We Are Six* (*Éramos Seis*), 127
Weerasethakul, Apichatpong, 116
Weir, Peter, 110, 181

*Weird Science* (1985), 87
Welles, Orson, 28, 38–39, 48, 175
Wells, H. G., 17, 48, 175, 269, 291
Wenders, Wim, 82
*Westworld* (1973), 195
*Westworld* (2016–) (HBO series), 196
Whale, James, 223, 250
*What Lies Beneath* (2000), 126
*When I Was Alive* (*Quando Eu Era Vivo*, 2014), 136
*White Noise* (2005), 128
*White Noise—The Light* (2007), 128
*White Out, Black In* (*Branco Sai, Preto Fica*, 2014) (See also *WOBI*), 10, 133, 147, 150–151, 173, 201, 208, 275, 295, 310
*White Table* (*Mesa Branca*), 16, 124, 299
*Who is Beta?* (*Quem é Beta?*, or *Pas de Violence entre Nous*, 1972), 81–82, 163
*Who Wants to Kill Jessie?* (*Kdo chce zabít Jesii?*, 1966), 5
*Why Cybraceros?* (1997), 189, 316
*Wicker Man, The* (1973), 140
Wiedergrün, Vitor, 176
Wilhelm, Kate, 56–57
Winterbottom, Michael, 252
*Wired*, 316
Wise, Robert, 31, 33, 104, 138, 200
*Withdrawal to a Rough Heart* (*A Retirada para um Coração Bruto*, 2017), 137
*WOBI* (See also *White Out, Black In/Branco Sai, Preto Fica*, 2014), 150–160, 202, 204, 234, 313
*Woman at the End of the World, The* (*A Mulher No Fim do Mundo*, 2019), 202
*Wonderful Eggs* (*Ovos Maravilhosos*), 15
Workers' Party (PT), 10, 203, 261, 265

World Cup, 109, 148, 160
World Economic Forum (*See also* Davos), 234, 237
World War II, 121, 242, 309, 316
Wright, Melanie J., 138–140

*X-Files, The*, 228
*X-Manas* (2017), 282
Xavier, Francisco Cândido (aka Chico Xavier), 118–120, 123, 127, 130–132, 137–138, 311
Xavier, Cleyton, 220
Xavier, Ismail, 48, 52–55, 301, 302
Xavier, Nelson, 131
XIX International Week of Mannheim, 51

Yanomami(s), 224, 275, 319
Yapario, Ermelinda, 199
*Young Great-Grandfather, The* (*O Jovem Tataravô*, 1936), 16, 124
YouTube, 91, 167, 188

*YWY, The Android* (*YWY, A Andróide*, 2017), 195, 196, 197

Zacarias (*See also* Gonçalves, Mauro Faccio), 91, 92, 97, 308
Zamyatin, Yevgeny, 71, 159
Zani, Mariana, 228, 231
Zapata Western, 174–175
Zecca, Ferdinand, 13, 255, 322
Zeitlin, Behn, 253
Zemeckis, Robert, 113, 126
*Zézero* (1974), 221
*Zigurate* (2009), 282
Zinnemann, Fred, 18
Ziraldo, 29
Zola, Irving, 157
zombie, 82
Zuboff, Shoshana, 182
Zucker, Jerry, 128–129
Zulawski, Andrej, 103
Zweig, Stefan, 5, 119–123, 145, 241–242

www.ingramcontent.com/pod-product-compliance
Ingram Content Group UK Ltd.
Pitfield, Milton Keynes, MK11 3LW, UK
UKHW041921140426
5217IPUK00014B/260